TECHNOLOGY
AND THE FUTURE

Ninth Edition

www.wadsworth.com

wadsworth.com is the World Wide Web site for Wadsworth and is your direct source to dozens of online resources.

At *wadsworth.com* you can find out about supplements, demonstration software, and student resources. You can also send email to many of our authors and preview new publications and exciting new technologies.

wadsworth.com
Changing the way the world learns®

TECHNOLOGY
AND THE FUTURE

Ninth Edition

Albert H. Teich

Editor

American Association
for the Advancement of Science

THOMSON
™
WADSWORTH

Australia • Canada • Mexico • Singapore • Spain
United Kingdom • United States

Publisher: Clark Baxter

Acquisitions Editor: David Tatom

Editorial Assistant: Dianna Long

Technology Project Manager: Mindy Newfarmer

Marketing Manager: Janise Fry

Marketing Assistant: Mary Ho

Advertising Project Manager: Stacey Purviance

Project Manager, Editorial Production: Ray Crawford

Print/Media Buyer: Judy Inouye

Permissions Editor: Joohee Lee

Production Service: Stratford Publishing Services

Copy Editor: Colleen Clifford

Cover Designer: Jeanette Barber

Cover Image: © Simon Osborne/Digital Vision

Cover Printer: Webcom Limited

Compositor: Stratford Publishing Services

Printer: Webcom Limited

Printed in Canada
1 2 3 4 5 6 7 06 05 04 03 02

For more information about our products, contact us at:
Thomson Learning Academic Resource Center
1-800-423-0563
For permission to use material from this text,
contact us by: **Phone:** 1-800-730-2214
Fax: 1-800-730-2215
Web: http://www.thomsonrights.com

Library of Congress Control Number: 2002108085

ISBN 0-534-60426-9

Wadsworth/Thomson Learning
10 Davis Drive
Belmont, CA 94002-3098
USA

Asia
Thomson Learning
5 Shenton Way #01-01
UIC Building
Singapore 068808

Australia
Nelson Thomson Learning
102 Dodds Street
South Melbourne, Victoria 3205
Australia

Canada
Nelson Thomson Learning
1120 Birchmount Road
Toronto, Ontario M1K 5G4
Canada

Europe/Middle East/Africa
Thomson Learning
High Holborn House
50/51 Bedford Row
London WC1R 4LR
United Kingdom

Latin America
Thomson Learning
Seneca, 53
Colonia Polanco
11560 Mexico D.F.
Mexico

Spain
Paraninfo Thomson Learning
Calle/Magallanes, 25
28015 Madrid, Spain

To my wife, Jill; my daughter, Samantha;
and my sons Mitch, Ken, and their families

Contents

Topical Contents

EMPLOYMENT AND WORK

FUTURES STUDIES

TECHNOLOGY AND SOCIAL PROBLEMS

About the Editor

Albert H. Teich has served as Director of Science and Policy Programs at the American Association for the Advancement of Science (AAAS) since 1990. In this position, he is responsible for the association's activities in science and technology policy and serves as its chief spokesperson on science policy issues.

AAAS, founded in 1848, is the world's largest federation of scientific and engineering societies, as well as a professional organization with over 135,000 members and the publisher of *Science* magazine. The Directorate for Science and Policy Programs, which includes activities in ethics, law, science and religion, human rights, and science policy, has a staff of forty and a yearly budget of over $8 million.

Dr. Teich received a B.S. degree in physics and a Ph.D. in political science, both from the Massachusetts Institute of Technology. Prior to joining the AAAS staff in 1980, he held positions at George Washington University, the State University of New York, and Syracuse University.

Dr. Teich is quoted frequently in the press and has made many appearances on radio and television. He is well known as a speaker on science and technology policy and is the author of numerous articles, reports, and book chapters. He is a Fellow of AAAS and a member of the editorial advisory boards to the journals *Science Communication; Science, Technology, and Human Values;* and *Prometheus,* as well as a consultant to government agencies, national laboratories, industrial firms, and international organizations. He is founding codirector of a new Center for Innovation Policy Research and Education for Central and Eastern Europe, based in Budapest, Hungary. He chaired the advisory committee to the National Science Foundation's Division of Science Resources Studies from 1987 through 1990 and is currently chair of the advisory board of the School of Public Policy at Georgia Tech, a member of the executive committee of the Board of Governors of the U.S.–Israel Binational Science Foundation, and a member of the advisory board of Columbia University's Center for Science, Policy and Outcomes, as well as the Loka Institute. His home page may be found at <http://www.alteich.com>.

Preface

A great deal has changed since the eighth edition of *Technology and the Future* appeared in late 1999. The stock market bubble, based largely on technology stocks, the hype surrounding the commercial potential of the Internet, and the "dot.coms" has burst. As a result, early in 2001 the economies of the United States and other industrialized nations, together with those of much of the developing world, began drifting into recession. Then, on September 11, 2001, the horrendous terrorist strikes that killed over 3,000 people, destroyed New York's World Trade Center, and severely damaged the Pentagon, shook the confidence of governments, industry leaders, financiers, and virtually everyone else who had become accustomed to relative stability and continuing technology-based economic growth in much of the world. For a short while, the world seemed to stop and catch its breath as rescue workers dug frantically (and mostly fruitlessly) through the rubble, searching for anyone who might have survived.

Things have more or less returned to normal as I write this in the spring of 2002. But 2002's normal is different from that of 2001. The economic exuberance of the late 1990s and 2000 is gone. The stock market is down; unemployment is up; and, in the United States, the federal government's enormous budget surplus, which appeared unexpectedly at the end of the 1990s, has gone up in smoke, and the government, once again, is deeply in the red. (All this may have changed for the better by the time you read this — or it may not.)

The effects of the terrorist attacks went deeper than these economic impacts, which are, hopefully, transient. The shocking ease with which a small number of committed individuals created so much havoc highlighted the fragility and vulnerability of today's complex technology-based society. People began to look at skyscrapers, power plants, monuments, water supply systems, and even the Internet not just as symbols of modernity, wealth, and technological prowess but also as potential terrorist targets. The attacks also abruptly shifted the balance in public attitudes between the desire for personal privacy and for security. As New York Senator Charles E. Schumer observed nearly three months after the attacks, "Sept. 11 has forced all but the most doctrinaire on the right and the left to be open to a recalibration of the balance between security and liberty."[1] In fact, according to a *New York Times*/CBS News poll taken in late September, nearly four-fifths of Americans expressed a willingness to "give up some of their personal freedoms in order to make the country safe from terrorist attacks."

As the voices of privacy and civil liberties advocates have become more muted, governments in the United States and elsewhere have begun to expand their use

---

[1] Laurie Goodstein, "Jewish Groups Endorse Tough Security Laws," *The New York Times* (January 3, 2002), p. A-12.

of eavesdropping, biometrics (e.g., computerized facial identification), and electronic surveillance technologies. Research priorities have shifted, too. The U.S. National Institutes of Health, beneficiary of large budget increases in recent years directed at fighting cancer, AIDS, Alzheimer's, and other diseases, as well as conducting basic research in such areas as genetics, neuroscience, and cell biology, received another big financial boost in President Bush's proposed budget for fiscal year 2003 (released in February 2002). But this time, instead of fighting diseases, half of the $3.9 billion increase would be devoted to research aimed at countering bioterrorism. What effect the shift in priorities — not just in NIH but throughout the government and industry as well — might ultimately have on the pace of technological innovation and, thus, on economic growth in the United States and the rest of the world, is an open question at this point.

One other victim of the shifting *zeitgeist* is likely to be the highly optimistic view of the future that has been so prominent in recent years in the media as well as in popular writings (such as those of Nicholas Negroponte, whose book, *Being Digital*, was excerpted in the eighth edition of *Technology and the Future* but dropped from this one). "Was That the Future We Just Passed By?" asked John Leland in a *New York Times* commentary in late 2001.[2] Leland notes that much of the futurist hype of the 1990s was ahistorical. By this he means that rather than looking at social trends and how they might interact with new technologies, the gurus of this high-tech future simply extrapolated their visions of technological progress without reckoning how these technologies might fit into social patterns and themselves be shaped by society. An example he cites is the e-book, a clever technology that was developed "to meet a consumer need that did not exist." So far, at least, it has failed to lure very many people away from the old-fashioned ink and paper variety (although it may yet find a niche in libraries).

In a sense, it is surprising that we allowed ourselves to be seduced by this simplistic approach to technology and its role in society. Perhaps it was the excitement of all the new technological innovations that cascaded into our lives during the past few years. In any case, the tools for a more dispassionate way of thinking about the possibilities and the pitfalls of technology exist, and it is the purpose of this book to equip both those people who are creating or will create that technology, and the rest of us who will have to live with it, with some of these tools.

Our understanding of technology's relationship to society and our attitudes toward technology have changed substantially over the years. I first conceived of *Technology and the Future*[3] in an era when many Americans looked upon technology with fear rather than excitement. In the atmosphere of social turmoil that gripped the United States in the late 1960s and early 1970s, a large segment of society (at least in the academic world, of which I was part) saw technology either as a force that was careening out of control or a tool of oppression by which those in positions of power maintained their hold over the rest of the populace.

---

[2] Sunday, December 9, 2001, Week in Review section, p. 5.

[3] Instructors who have used this book over the years may recall that it was originally called *Technology and Man's Future*, a title that was retained through the first three editions but that seems almost impossibly inappropriate today.

Technologists, who had been lionized for their accomplishments during World War II and the early postwar years, were put on the defensive, and discussions of technology often degenerated into sterile "pro" and "con" debates. I was teaching a course called "The Future of Technological Society" at Syracuse University during the early 1970s, and I found these pro and con arguments tiresome and unproductive. I developed this book in the hope that it might contribute to reasoned discussion of the relations between technology and society. I wanted to give students an opportunity to examine the subtleties in these relations and the tools with which to examine the thoughts of some of the most significant writers on the subject and to form their own opinions. That was thirty years ago.

Today, although the problems created by human uses of technology are very much with us, technology itself is no longer demonized as it was in the early 1970s. Indeed, technologies are increasingly woven into the fabric of our everyday lives. Moreover, 9/11 notwithstanding, concerns about the negative impacts of technology, are, with a few exceptions (such as genetically modified foods), taking a backseat to a broad-based desire to share in technology's benefits.

The possibilities for technological change are being created by the huge engine of research, development, and innovation that involves governments, universities, and private sector firms and organizations in an increasingly globalized network of knowledge generation. However, whether these possibilities will be exploited and, if so, who will gain and who will lose depends on the structures of human society. The sometimes startling rate of technological change may also cause us to overlook the fundamental stability of human nature. There is a tension here that revolves around the need for societies to employ the tools of technology to promote change, not for the sake of change itself, but as a means of advancing civilization according to moral and ethical principles that cannot come from science and technology alone.

This ninth edition of *Technology and the Future* is a significant update and revision of the previous edition. The organization of the book has not changed, however, and the first couple of sections remain largely the same. In Part I, "Thinking about Technology," the authors raise the big questions: Is technology good, bad, or neutral? Is it synonymous with progress? How does it influence society? The most important change in this section is the addition of a superb article by Robert Pool taken from his book, *Beyond Technology*, replacing a piece by Thomas Hughes. Pool's analysis of the mutual impacts of technology and society mirrors my own perspective and puts this important concept in easily understandable terms. Otherwise in Part I, the best elements of previous editions are retained and serve to introduce readers to the process of thinking about technology.

The dated, but still very relevant, debate over the role of technology in society between the late Emmanuel Mesthene and John McDermott, a feature of the book since the first edition, comprises Part II, entitled, "Debating Technology: 1960s Style." Both the substance and the rhetoric of the Mesthene–McDermott debate contrast with Part VII, "Debating Technology: 21st Century Style," in which Bill Joy, a computer scientist responsible for several major software innovations, presents his rather scary vision of a future in which nanotechnology, genetics, and robotics converge and threaten the existence of humanity.

Paired with Joy is an article by two other leading technologists that debunks his vision.

Part III brings together seven authors who challenge the technological status quo in different ways. Their essays discuss alternatives to contemporary mainstream technology or view mainstream technology from unorthodox perspectives. Included are Langdon Winner's provocative chapter, "Do Artifacts Have Politics?" as well as an article by Timothy Jenkins, which adds an African American perspective to the mix. New to this edition is a piece by Muslim scholar and commentator Ziauddin Sardar, in which he critiques the increasingly dominant western views of the future and exhorts the nonwestern world to think of a future in its own terms.

The three sections that follow explore some of the ethical, social, and human dimensions of technology. Reflecting a heightened sensitivity to the fragility of our technological society in the aftermath of 9/11, Part IV presents two articles on what the authors of one, Amory and Hunter Lovins, call the "brittleness" of the complex, centralized systems we have created. The Lovinses' article, written in the fall of 2001, draws on their prescient earlier work on energy systems. It is followed by a 1996 article by Australian scholar and social activist Brian Martin that dissects the issue of technological vulnerability in a systematic fashion.

Parts V and VI focus on technological areas that are certain to play key roles in our future — genetics and information technology. In the bioethics section are discussions of the exquisitely difficult dilemmas posed by our growing knowledge of molecular genetics and biotechnology — discussion of the prospects for human cloning; differing perspectives on the controversial issue of stem cell research, including President George W. Bush's August 2001 address to the nation on that subject; and an examination of the possibilities for choosing traits in our offspring. Under the heading of information technology are articles on why those who created the IT revolution failed to anticipate its extent or its impact; a broad-based survey of the ethical issues raised by computers and information technology; discussions of the impact of computers on the organization and character of work, as well as on warfare (the latter, by Gene Rochlin, new to this edition); and a new, highly topical article by Lawrence Lessig, who fears that the promise of the Internet is being wasted as outmoded ideas based on old technology choke off the innovative potential of this revolutionary new technology.

Finally, following the debate over Bill Joy's ideas in Part VII, described above, Seth Shostak's short story, "In Touch at Last," provides some entertaining and thought-provoking speculation on perhaps the ultimate scientific/technological achievement — discovery of extraterrestrial intelligence.

As in previous editions, my selections are a mixed bag. Not all students or all instructors will find all twenty-nine readings to their liking. Most readers will probably love some and hate others, find some fascinating, others tedious. The individual essays do not represent my own views, and I do not necessarily endorse their perspectives. As a whole, however, the book reflects what I hope is a balanced view of the important issues in the field of technology and society, a view that I hope will be useful to others who are interested in these topics.

Technology and the Future has been a part of my life throughout most of my professional career. It is gratifying to have watched the growing interest in the study of science, technology, and society in American colleges and universities over the past three decades and to feel that the book may have made a modest contribution to this important intellectual development.

Throughout the life of this book, I have benefited from the interest, suggestions, and helpful feedback from the book's users. This feedback increased significantly with the establishment, in 1996, of the *Technology and the Future* Web site, which became *Al Teich's Technology and the Future Toolkit* in 1999. Through the Web site and the e-mail traffic it generates, I have had the opportunity to correspond with many instructors and students, as well as with others who share an interest in this subject area. I am indebted to them all for the ideas that they shared with me, some of which they may recognize in this volume.

My thanks go also to the staff of Wadsworth Publishing, which in 2001 acquired the political science list of Bedford/St. Martin's, including the previous edition of this book. It was St. Martin's Press's College Division, forerunner of Bedford/St. Martin's, whose editors had the foresight to publish the first edition of this book in 1972 and who, through a generation of staff changes, mergers, acquisitions, and restructurings, remained helpful, interested, and unfailingly supportive. I have been fortunate in having a series of editors over the years with whom it has always been a pleasure to work.

Finally, a very special note of appreciation goes to my family, to whom I have dedicated this edition: my wife, Jill; my daughter, Samantha; and my grown sons, Mitch and Ken, their wives Gretchen and Sara, and my grandson Calvin Avery Teich; for the meaning they have given to my life and for the strength I draw from our relationships.

In the hope that readers continue to find this book useful and that there will be future editions, I once again invite readers — both faculty and students — to contact me with comments and suggestions. I can be reached most readily by e-mail either directly, at <ateich@aaas.org>, or through the links on my Web site, which can be found at <http://www.alteich.com>. The Web site also contains a variety of supplementary resources related to the book, including links to more information about the authors of the various articles, tables of contents of earlier editions, the full text of several hard-to-find articles from earlier editions, my personal home page, and more.

Albert H. Teich

PART I
THINKING ABOUT TECHNOLOGY

Technology is more than just machines. It is a pervasive, complex system whose cultural, social, political, and intellectual elements are manifest in virtually every aspect of our lives. Small wonder, then, that it has attracted the attention of such a large and diverse group of writers and commentators. A small sampling of the range of writings on the social dimensions of technology is contained in this first section of *Technology and the Future*. All of the writers represented here are attempting to understand — from one perspective or another — these social dimensions of technology. Little else ties them together. Their points of view are vastly different. Their common goal is not so much to prescribe particular courses of action as it is to explore the conceptual, metaphysical issues underlying technology–society interactions.

In the opening selection, historian Leo Marx explores the development of the American notion of progress and looks at its connections with technological advance. Next, Robert Pool, former senior writer at *Science* and news editor at *Nature*, explains in lucid terms the ways in which technology and society shape one another. Pool's essay is drawn from a book that began as a straightforward treatment of the commercial nuclear industry. Instead of the simple story he expected to find, Pool discovered "a complex, often convoluted tale of how the technology had been shaped by a host of nontechnical factors in addition to the expected technical ones." His approach transcends both the notions of technological determinism (which sees technology as an autonomous force that produces social change) and social constructivism (which views technology as purely a product of social and cultural influences) in favor of a more subtle explanation of the relations between technology and society.

Following Pool, in an essay dating from the mid-1960s that captures some of the heights of post–World War II technological optimism, physicist Alvin Weinberg suggests that we can find shortcuts to the solution of social problems by transforming them into technological ones — since technological problems are much easier to solve. This selection, though out of sync with much current thinking, has become a classic for the perspective it represents and for introducing the concept of the "technological fix," which continues to be the subject of debate and discussion.

Wendell Berry, farmer, author, and poet, meanwhile rejects not only the technological fix, but even such ubiquitous elements of our technological society as the personal computer, explaining why he does his writing instead by daylight, on a manual typewriter. Finally, Samuel Florman, a practicing engineer as well as a humanist, proposes an alternative approach — a "tragic view" that recognizes the role of technology in human life, including its limits.

The reader looking for unequivocal answers to the problems posed by technology will not find them here. On the whole, the readings in this section, like those in the remainder of the book, raise many more questions than they answer.

1. Does Improved Technology Mean Progress?

LEO MARX

The concepts of technology and progress have been firmly linked in the minds of most Americans for the past 150 years. Only in the past three decades, however, has the question that Leo Marx asks in his essay, "Does Improved Technology Mean Progress?" begun to receive serious attention in our culture. This question is the perfect starting point for Technology and the Future. *Deceptive in its simplicity, it underlies most of what follows in this book.*

Leo Marx is Senior Lecturer and William R. Kenan Professor of American Cultural History Emeritus in the Program in Science, Technology, and Society at MIT. He is the author of The Machine in the Garden: Technology and the Pastoral Ideal in America *(1964) and is coeditor, with Merritt Roe Smith, of* Does Technology Drive History? *(Cambridge, MA: MIT Press, 1995). He holds a Ph.D. in history of American civilization from Harvard and has taught at that institution and at the University of Minnesota and Amherst College. He has twice been a Guggenheim Fellow and was a Rockefeller Humanities Fellow in 1983–1984. Marx was born in New York City in 1919.*

In this reading (first published in Technology Review *in 1987), he examines how the concept of progress has itself evolved since the early days of the Republic and what that evolution means for understanding the technological choices that confront us today. Improved technology could mean progress, Marx concludes, "But only if we are willing and able to answer the next question: Progress toward what?"*

Does improved technology mean progress? If some variant of this question had been addressed to a reliable sample of Americans at any time since the early nineteenth century, the answer of a majority almost certainly would have been an unequivocal "yes." The idea that technological improvements are a primary basis for — and an accurate gauge of — progress has long been a fundamental belief in the United States. In the last half-century, however, that belief has lost some of its credibility. A growing minority of Americans has adopted a skeptical, even negative, view of technological innovation as an index of social Progress.

The extent of this change in American attitudes was brought home to me when I spent October 1984 in China. At that time, the announced goal of the People's Republic was to carry out (in the popular slogan) "Four Modernizations" — agriculture, science and technology, industry, and the military. What particularly struck our group of Americans was the seemingly unbounded, largely

From *Technology Review* (January, 1987), p. 33–41. © 1987 *Technology Review.* Reprinted with permission.

uncritical ardor with which the Chinese were conducting their love affair with Western-style modernization — individualistic, entrepreneurial, or "capitalist," as well as scientific and technological. Like early nineteenth-century visitors to the United States, we were witnessing a society in a veritable transport of improvement: long pent-up, innovative energies were being released, everyone seemed to be in motion, everything was eligible for change. It was assumed that any such change almost certainly would be for the better.

Most of the Chinese we came to know best — teachers and students of American studies — explicitly associated the kind of progress represented by the four modernizations with the United States. This respect for American wealth and power was flattering but disconcerting, for we often found ourselves reminding the Chinese of serious shortcomings, even some terrible dangers, inherent in the Western mode of industrial development. Like the Americans whom European travelers met 150 years ago, many of the Chinese seemed to be extravagantly, almost blindly, credulous and optimistic.

Our reaction revealed, among other things, a change in our own culture and, in some cases, in our own personal attitudes. We came face-to-face with the gulf that separates the outlook of many contemporary Americans from the old national faith in the advance of technology as the basis of social progress.

The standard explanation for this change includes that familiar litany of death and destruction that distinguishes the recent history of the West: two barbaric world wars, the Nazi holocaust, the Stalinist terror, and the nuclear arms race. It is striking to note how many of the fearful events of our time involve the destructive use or misuse, the unforeseen consequences, or the disastrous malfunction of modern technologies: Hiroshima and the nuclear threat, the damage inflicted upon the environment by advanced industrial societies, and spectacular accidents like Three Mile Island.

Conspicuous disasters have helped to undermine the public's faith in progress, but there also has been a longer-term change in our thinking. It is less obvious, less dramatic, and less tangible than the record of catastrophe that distinguishes our twentieth-century history, but I believe it is more fundamental. Our very conception — our chief criterion — of progress has undergone a subtle but decisive change since the founding of the Republic, and that change is at once a cause and a reflection of our current disenchantment with technology. To chart this change in attitude, we need to go back at least as far as the first Industrial Revolution.

THE ENLIGHTENMENT BELIEF IN PROGRESS

The development of radically improved machinery (based on mechanized motive power) used in the new factory system of the late eighteenth century coincided with the formulation and diffusion of the modern Enlightenment idea of history as a record of progress. This conception became the fulcrum of the dominant American worldview. It assumes that history, or at least modern history, is driven by the steady, cumulative, and inevitable expansion of human knowledge of and power over nature. The new scientific knowledge and technological power were expected to make possible a comprehensive improvement in all the conditions of life — social, political, moral, and intellectual, as well as material.

The modern idea of progress, as developed by its radical French, English, and American adherents, emerged in an era of political revolution. It was a revolutionary doctrine, bonded to the radical struggle for freedom from feudal forms of domination. To ardent republicans like the French philosopher Condorcet, the English chemist Priestley, and Benjamin Franklin, a necessary criterion of progress was the achievement of political and social liberation. They regarded the new sciences and technologies not as ends in themselves, but as instruments for carrying out a comprehensive transformation of society. The new knowledge and power would provide the basis for alternatives to the deeply entrenched authoritarian, hierarchical institutions of *l'ancien régime:* monarchical, aristocratic, and ecclesiastical. Thus, in 1813 Thomas Jefferson wrote to John Adams describing the combined effect of the new science and the American Revolution on the minds of Europeans:

> Science had liberated the ideas of those who read and reflect, and the American example had kindled feelings of right in the people. An insurrection has consequently begun, of science, talents, and courage, against rank and birth, which have fallen into contempt. . . . Science is progressive.

Admittedly, the idea of history as endless progress did encourage extravagantly optimistic expectations, and in its most extreme form it fostered some wildly improbable dreams of the "perfectability of Man" and of humanity's absolute mastery of nature. Yet, the political beliefs of the radical republicans of the eighteenth century, such as the principle of making the authority of government dependent upon the consent of the governed, often had the effect of limiting those aspirations to omnipotence.

The constraining effect of such ultimate, long-term political goals makes itself felt, for example, in Jefferson's initial reaction to the prospect of introducing the new manufacturing system to America. "Let our work-shops remain in Europe," he wrote in 1785.

Although a committed believer in the benefits of science and technology, Jefferson rejected the idea of developing an American factory system on the ground that the emergence of an urban proletariat, which he then regarded as an inescapable consequence of the European factory system, would be too high a price to pay for any potential improvement in the American material standard of living. He regarded the existence of manufacturing cities and an industrial working class as incompatible with republican government and the happiness of the people. He argued that it was preferable, even if more costly in strictly economic terms, to ship raw materials to Europe and import manufactured goods. "The loss by the transportation of commodities across the Atlantic will be made up in happiness and permanence of government." In weighing political, moral, and aesthetic costs against economic benefits, he anticipated the viewpoint of the environmentalists and others of our time for whom the test of a technological innovation is its effect on the overall quality of life.

Another instance of the constraining effect of republican political ideals is Benjamin Franklin's refusal to exploit his inventions for private profit. Thus, Franklin's reaction when the governor of Pennsylvania urged him to accept a patent for his successful design of the "Franklin stove":

> Governor Thomas was so pleased with the construction of this stove as described in . . . [the pamphlet] that . . . he offered to give me a patent for the sole vending of them for a term of years; but I declined it from a principle which has ever weighed with me on such occasions, namely; viz., *that as we enjoy great advantages from the inventions of others, we should be glad of an opportunity to serve others by any invention of ours, and this we should do freely and generously* [emphasis in original].

What makes the example of Franklin particularly interesting is the fact that he later came to be regarded as the archetypal self-made American and the embodiment of the Protestant work ethic. When Max Weber sought out of all the world the exemplar of that mentality for his seminal study, *The Protestant Ethic and the Spirit of Capitalism*, whom did he choose but our own Ben? But Franklin's was a principled and limited self-interest. In his *Autobiography*, he told the story of his rise in the world not to exemplify a merely personal success, but rather to illustrate the achievements of a "rising people." He belonged to that heroic revolutionary phase in the history of the bourgeoisie when that class saw itself as the vanguard of humanity and its principles as universal. He thought of his inventions as designed not for his private benefit but for the benefit of all.

THE TECHNOCRATIC CONCEPT OF PROGRESS

With the further development of industrial capitalism, a quite different conception of technological progress gradually came to the fore in the United States. Americans celebrated the advance of science and technology with increasing fervor, but they began to detach the idea from the goal of social and political liberation. Many regarded the eventual attainment of that goal as having been assured by the victorious American Revolution and the founding of the Republic.

The difference between this later view of progress and that of Jefferson's and Franklin's generation can be heard in the rhetoric of Daniel Webster. He and Edward Everett were perhaps the leading public communicators of this new version of the progressive ideology. When Webster decided to become a senator from Massachusetts instead of New Hampshire, the change was widely interpreted to mean that he had become the quasi-official spokesman for the new industrial manufacturing interests. Thus Webster, who was generally considered the nation's foremost orator, was an obvious choice as the speaker at the dedication of new railroads. Here is a characteristic peroration of one such performance in 1847:

> It is an extraordinary era in which we live. It is altogether new. The world has seen nothing like it before. I will not pretend, no one can pretend, to discern the end; but everybody knows that the age is remarkable for scientific research

into the heavens, the earth, and what is beneath the earth; and perhaps more remarkable still for the application of this scientific research to the pursuits of life. . . . We see the ocean navigated and the solid land traversed by steam power, and intelligence communicated by electricity. Truly this is almost a miraculous era. What is before us no one can say, what is upon us no one can hardly realize. The progress of the age has almost outstripped human belief; the future is known only to Omniscience.

By the 1840s, as Webster's rhetoric suggests, the idea of progress was already being dissociated from the Enlightenment vision of political liberation. He invests the railroad with a quasi-religious inevitability that lends force to the characterization of his language as the rhetoric of the technological sublime. Elsewhere in the speech, to be sure, Webster makes the obligatory bow to the democratic influence of technological change, but it is clear that he is casting the new machine power as the prime exemplar of the overall progress of the age, quite apart from its political significance. Speaking for the business and industrial elite, Webster and Everett thus depict technological innovation as a sufficient cause, in itself, for the fact that history assumes the character of continuous, cumulative progress.

At the same time, discarding the radical political ideals of the Enlightenment allowed the idea of technological progress to blend with other grandiose national aspirations. Webster's version of the "rhetoric of the technological sublime" is of a piece with the soaring imperial ambitions embodied in the slogan "Manifest Destiny," and by such tacit military figurations of American development as the popular notion of the "conquest of nature" (including Native Americans) by the increasingly technologized forces of advancing European–American "civilization." These future-oriented themes easily harmonized with the belief in the coming of the millennium that characterized evangelical Protestantism, the most popular American religion at the time. Webster indicates as much when, at the end of his tribute to the new railroad, he glibly brings in "Omniscience" as the ultimate locus of the meaning of progress.

The difference between the earlier Enlightenment conception of progress and that exemplified by Webster is largely attributable to the difference between the groups they represented. Franklin, Jefferson, and the heroic generation of founding revolutionists constituted a distinct, rather unusual social class in that for a short time the same men possessed authority and power in most of its important forms: economic, social, political, and intellectual. The industrial capitalists for whom Daniel Webster spoke were men of a very different stripe. They derived their status from a different kind of wealth and power, and their conception of progress, like their economic and social aspirations, was correspondingly different. The new technology and the immense profits it generated belonged to them, and since they had every reason to assume that they would retain their property and power, they had a vested interest in technological innovation. It is not surprising, under the circumstances, that as industrialization proceeded these men became true believers in technological improvement as the primary basis for — and virtually tantamount to — universal progress.

This dissociation of technological and material advancement from the larger political vision of progress was an intermediate stage in the eventual impoverishment of that radical eighteenth-century worldview. This subtle change prepared the way for the emergence, later in the century, of a thoroughly technocratic idea of progress. It was "technocratic" in that it valued improvements in power, efficiency, and rationality as ends in themselves. Among those who bore witness to the widespread diffusion of this concept at the turn of the century were Henry Adams and Thorstein Veblen, who were critical of it, and Andrew Carnegie, Thomas Edison, and Frederick Winslow Taylor and his followers, who lent expression to it. Taylor's theory of scientific management embodies the quintessence of the technocratic mentality, "the idea," as historian Hugh Aitken describes it, "that human activity could be measured, analyzed, and controlled by techniques analogous to those that had proved so successful when applied to physical objects."

The technocratic idea of progress is a belief in the sufficiency of scientific and technological innovation as the basis for general progress. It says that if we can ensure the advance of science-based technologies, the rest will take care of itself. (The "rest" refers to nothing less than a corresponding degree of improvement in the social, political, and cultural conditions of life.) Turning the Jeffersonian ideal on its head, this view makes instrumental values fundamental to social progress and relegates what formerly were considered primary, goal-setting values (justice, freedom, harmony, beauty, or self-fulfillment) to a secondary status.

In this century, the technocratic view of progress was enshrined in Fordism and an obsessive interest in economies of scale, standardization of process and product, and control of the workplace. This shift to mass production was accompanied by the more or less official commitment of the U.S. government to the growth of the nation's wealth, productivity, and global power and to the most rapid possible rate of technological innovation as the essential criterion of social progress.

But the old republican vision of progress — the vision of advancing knowledge empowering humankind to establish a less hierarchical, more just, and peaceful society — did not disappear. If it no longer inspired Webster and his associates, it lived on in the minds of many farmers, artisans, factory workers, shopkeepers, and small-business owners, as well as in the beliefs of the professionals, artists, intellectuals, and other members of the lower-middle and middle classes. During the late nineteenth century, a number of disaffected intellectuals sought new forms for the old progressive faith. They translated it into such political idioms as utopian socialism, the single-tax movement, the populist revolt, Progressivism in cities, and Marxism and its native variants.

THE ROOTS OF OUR ADVERSARY CULTURE

Let me turn to a set of these late-eighteenth-century ideas that was to become the basis for a powerful critique of the culture of advanced industrial society. Usually described as the viewpoint of the "counter-Enlightenment" or the "romantic reaction," these ideas have formed the basis for a surprisingly long-lived adversarial culture.

According to conventional wisdom, this critical view originated in the intellectual backlash from the triumph of the natural sciences we associate with the great discoveries of Galileo, Kepler, Harvey, and Newton. Put differently, this tendency was a reaction against the extravagant claims of the universal, not to say exclusive, truth of "the Mechanical Philosophy." That term derived from the ubiquity of the machine metaphor in the work of Newton and other natural scientists ("celestial mechanics") and many of their philosophic allies, notably Descartes, all of whom tended to conceive of nature itself as a "great engine" and its subordinate parts (including the human body) as lesser machines.

By the late eighteenth century, a powerful set of critical, antimechanistic ideas was being developed by Kant, Fichte, and other German idealists and by great English poets like Coleridge and Wordsworth. But in their time the image of the machine also was being invested with greater tangibility and social import. The Industrial Revolution was gaining momentum, and as power machinery was more widely diffused in Great Britain, Western Europe, and North America, the machine acquired much greater resonance: It came to represent both the new technologies based on mechanized motive power and the mechanistic mindset of scientific rationalism. Thus, the Scottish philosopher and historian Thomas Carlyle, who had been deeply influenced by the new German philosophy, announced in his seminal 1829 essay, "Signs of the Times," that the right name for the dawning era was the "Age of Machinery." It was to be the Age of Machinery, he warned, in every "inward" and "outward" sense of the word, meaning that it would be dominated by mechanical (utilitarian) thinking as well as by actual machines.

In his criticism of this new era, Carlyle took the view that neither kind of "machinery" was inherently dangerous. In his opinion, indeed, they represented potential progress as long as neither was allowed to become the exclusive or predominant mode in its respective realm.

In the United States, a small, gifted, if disaffected minority of writers, artists, and intellectuals adopted this ideology. Their version of Carlyle's critical viewpoint was labeled "romantic" in reference to its European strains, or "transcendentalist" in its native use. In the work of writers like Emerson and Thoreau, Hawthorne and Melville, we encounter critical responses to the onset of industrialism that cannot be written off as mere nostalgia or primitivism. These writers did not hold up an idealized wilderness, a pre-industrial Eden, as preferable to the world they saw in the making. Nor did they dismiss the worth of material improvement as such. But they did regard the dominant view, often represented (as in Webster's speech) by the appearance of the new machine power in the American landscape, as dangerously shallow, materialistic, and one sided. Fear of "mechanism," in the several senses of that word — especially the domination of the individual by impersonal systems — colored all of their thought. In their work, the image of the machine-in-the-landscape, far from being an occasion for exultation, often seems to arouse anxiety, dislocation, and foreboding. Henry Thoreau's detailed, carefully composed account of the intrusion of the railroad into the Concord woods is a good example; it bears out his delineation of the new inventions as "improved means to unimproved ends."

This critical view of the relationship between technological means and social ends did not merely appear in random images, phrases, and narrative episodes. Indeed, the whole of Walden may be read as a sustained attack on a culture that had allowed itself to become confused about the relationship of ends and means. Thoreau's countrymen are depicted as becoming "the tools of their tools." Much the same argument underlies Hawthorne's satire, "The Celestial Railroad," a modern replay of Pilgrim's Progress in which the hero, Christian, realizes too late that his comfortable railroad journey to salvation is taking him to hell, not heaven. Melville incorporates a similar insight into his characterization of Captain Ahab, who is the embodiment of the Faustian aspiration toward domination and total control given credence by the sudden emergence of exciting new technological capacities. Ahab exults in his power over the crew, and he explicitly identifies it with the power exhibited by the new railroad spanning the North American continent. In reflective moments, however, he also acknowledges the self-destructive nature of his own behavior: "Now in his heart, Ahab had some glimpse of this, namely, all my means are sane, my motive and my object mad."

Of course, there was nothing new about the moral posture adopted by these American writers. Indeed, their attitude toward the exuberant national celebration of the railroad and other inventions is no doubt traceable to traditional moral and religious objections to such an exaggeration of human powers. In this view, the worshipful attitude of Americans toward these new instruments of power had to be recognized for what it was: idolatry like that attacked by Old Testament prophets in a disguised, new-fashioned form. This moral critique of the debased, technocratic version of the progressive worldview has slowly gained adherents since the mid-nineteenth century, and by now it is one of the chief ideological supports of an adversary culture in the United States.

The ideas of writers like Hawthorne, Melville, and Thoreau were usually dismissed as excessively idealistic, nostalgic, or sentimental and hence impractical and unreliable. They were particularly vulnerable to that charge at a time when the rapid improvement in the material conditions of American life lent a compelling power to the idea that the meaning of history is universal progress. Only in the late twentieth century, with the growth of skepticism about scientific and technological progress, and with the emergence of a vigorous adversary culture in the 1960s, has the standpoint of that earlier eccentric minority been accorded a certain intellectual respect. To be sure, it is still chiefly the viewpoint of a relatively small minority, but there have been times, like the Vietnam upheaval of the 1960s, when that minority has won the temporary support of, or formed a tacit coalition with, a remarkably large number of other disaffected Americans. Much the same antitechnocratic viewpoint has made itself felt in various dissident movements and intellectual tendencies since the 1960s: the antinuclear movements (against both nuclear power and nuclear weaponry), some branches of the environmental and feminist movements, the "small is beautiful" and "stable-state" economic theories, as well as the quest for "soft energy paths" and "alternative (or appropriate) technologies."

TECHNOCRATIC VERSUS SOCIAL PROGRESS

Perhaps this historical summary will help explain the ambivalence toward the ideal of progress expressed by many Americans nowadays. Compared with prevailing attitudes in the United States in the 1840s, when the American situation was more like that of China today, the current mood in this country would have to be described as mildly disillusioned.

To appreciate the reasons for that disillusionment, let me repeat the distinction between the two views of progress on which this analysis rests. The initial Enlightenment belief in progress perceived science and technology to be in the service of liberation from political oppression. Over time, that conception was transformed, or partly supplanted, by the now familiar view that innovations in science-based technologies are in themselves a sufficient and reliable basis for progress. The distinction, then, turns on the apparent loss of interest in, or unwillingness to name, the social ends for which the scientific and technological instruments of power are to be used. What we seem to have instead of a guiding political goal is a minimalist definition of civic obligation.

The distinction between two versions of the belief in progress helps sort out reactions to the many troubling issues raised by the diffusion of high technology. When, for example, the introduction of some new labor-saving technology is proposed, it is useful to ask what the purpose of this new technology is. Only by questioning the assumption that innovation represents progress can we begin to judge its worth. The aim may well be to reduce labor costs, yet in our society the personal costs to the displaced workers are likely to be ignored.

The same essential defect of the technocratic mindset also becomes evident when the president of the United States calls upon those who devise nuclear weapons to provide an elaborate new system of weaponry, the Strategic Defense Initiative, as the only reliable means of avoiding nuclear war. Not only does he invite us to put all our hope in a "technological fix," but he rejects the ordinary but indispensable method of international negotiation and compromise.[1] Here again, technology is thought to obviate the need for political ideas and practices.

One final word. I perhaps need to clarify the claim that it is the modern, technocratic worldview of Webster's intellectual heirs, not the Enlightenment view descended from the Jeffersonians, that encourages the more dangerous contemporary fantasies of domination and total control. The political and social aspirations of the generation of Benjamin Franklin and Thomas Jefferson *provided tacit limits to, as well as ends for, the progressive vision of the future.* But the technocratic version so popular today entails a belief in the worth of scientific and technological innovations as ends in themselves.

All of which is to say that we urgently need a set of political, social, and cultural goals comparable to those formulated at the beginning of the Industrial Era if we are to accurately assess the worth of new technologies. Only such goals can provide the criteria required to make rational and humane choices among alternative technologies and, more important, among alternative long-term policies.

Does improved technology mean progress? Yes, it certainly could mean just that. But only if we are willing and able to answer the next question: Progress toward what? What is it that we want our new technologies to accomplish? What do we want beyond such immediate, limited goals as achieving efficiencies, decreasing financial costs, and eliminating the troubling human element from our workplaces? In the absence of answers to these questions, technological improvements may very well turn out to be incompatible with genuine, that is to say social, progress.

NOTE

1. See Alvin M. Weinberg, "Can Technology Replace Social Engineering?" (Chapter 3), for a discussion of the concept of the "technological fix." — ED.

2. How Society Shapes Technology

ROBERT POOL

Why do we all use VHS cassette recorders instead of Betamax, when most experts (and many nonexperts) agree that Betamax is a better technology? The two formats came on the market around the same time. They are incompatible, however, so consumers had to choose one or the other. When VHS gained a small lead, perhaps because of better marketing, perhaps because it uses six-hour cassettes instead of Betamax's five, or perhaps for other reasons, video rental stores began to stock more VHS tapes. This led people to buy more VHS machines and started a self-reinforcing cycle that, in a few years, made Betamax as obsolete as eight-track audio players.

This kind of interplay between the developers of technology and the society that uses that technology is characteristic of the way in which technology and society interact. It's not technological determinism and it's not just social construction, it's a combination of the two. Robert Pool examines this fascinating interplay in depth in his book, Beyond Engineering: How Society Shapes Technology, *from which the following selection is taken. "Modern technology," he writes, "is like a Great Dane in a small apartment. It may be friendly, but you still want to make sure there's nothing breakable within reach." Pool, a freelance writer who has written for* Science *and* Discover *and was news editor at* Nature, *is the author of* Fat: Fighting the Obesity Epidemic (2001) *and* Eve's Rib: The Biological Roots of Sex Differences (1994).

Any modern technology is the product of a complex interplay between its designers and the larger society in which it develops.

Consider the automobile. In the early part of this century, gas-powered cars shared the roads with those powered by boilers and steam engines, such as the Stanley Steamer.[1] Eventually, internal combustion captured the market and the old steamers disappeared. Why? The usual assumption is that the two contenders went head to head and the best technology won. Not at all.

Although the internal combustion engine did have some advantages in performance and convenience, steam-powered cars had their own pluses: They had no transmission or shifting of gears, they were simpler to build, and they were smoother and quieter to operate. Experts then and now have called it a draw — The "better" technology was mostly a matter of opinion. Instead, the steamers were killed off by several factors that had little or nothing to do with their engineering merits. For one, the Stanley brothers, builders of the best steam-powered cars of the time, had little interest in mass production. They were content to sell a few cars at high prices to aficionados who could appreciate their superiority. Meanwhile, Henry Ford and other Detroit automakers were flooding the country with inexpensive gas-powered cars. Even so, the steamers might well have survived as high-end specialty cars were it not for a series of unlucky breaks. At one point, for example, an outbreak of hoof-and-mouth disease caused public horse troughs to be drained, removing a major source of water for refilling the cars' boilers. It took the Stanley brothers three years to develop a closed-cycle steam engine that didn't need constant refilling, but by then World War I had begun, bringing strict government limits on the number of cars that businesses could build for the consumer market. The Stanley company never recovered, and it folded a few years later. The remnants of the steam automobile industry died during the Depression, when the market for high-priced cars all but disappeared.

Nonengineering factors play a role in the development of all technologies, even the simplest. In *The Pencil*, Henry Petroski tells how pencil designers in the late 1800s, in order to get around a growing shortage of red cedar, devised a pencil with a paper wrapping in place of the normal wood.[2] It "worked well technically and showed great promise," Petroski writes, "but the product failed for unanticipated psychological reasons." The public, accustomed to sharpening pencils with a knife, wanted something that could be whittled. The paper pencil never caught on.

Today, particularly for such sophisticated creations as computers, genetic engineering, or nuclear power, nontechnical factors have come to exert an influence that is unprecedented in the history of technology. Invention is no longer, as Ralph Waldo Emerson's aphorism had it, simply a matter of "Build a better mousetrap and the world will beat a path to your door." The world is already at your door, and it has a few things to say about that mousetrap.

The reasons for this are several, some grounded in the changing nature of technology itself and others arising from transformations in society. A hundred years ago, people in western nations generally saw technological development as a good thing.[3] It brought prosperity and health; it represented "progress." But the past century has seen a dramatic change in western society, with a resulting shift in people's attitudes toward technology.[4] As countries have become more prosperous and secure, their citizens have become less concerned about increasing their material well-being and more concerned with such aesthetic considerations as maintaining a clean environment. This makes them less likely to accept new technologies uncritically. At the same time, citizens of western democracies have become more politically savvy and more active in challenging the system with lawsuits, special interest groups, campaigns to change public opinion, and other weapons. The result is that the public now exerts a much greater influence on the development of technologies — particularly those seen as risky or otherwise undesirable — than was true one hundred, or even fifty, years ago.

Meanwhile, the developers of technology have also been changing. A century ago, most innovation was done by individuals or small groups. Today, technological development tends to take place inside large, hierarchical organizations. This is particularly true for complex, large-scale technologies, since they demand large investments and extensive, coordinated development efforts. But large organizations inject into the development process a host of considerations that have little or nothing to do with engineering. Any institution has its own goals and concerns, its own set of capabilities and weaknesses, and its own biases about the best ways to do things. Inevitably, the scientists and engineers inside an institution are influenced — often quite unconsciously — by its culture.

A closely related factor is the institutionalization of science and engineering. With their professional societies, conferences, journals, and other means of communion, scientists and engineers have formed themselves into relatively close-knit — though large — groups that have uniform standards of practice and hold similar ideas. Today, opinions and decisions about a technology tend to reflect a group's thinking more than any given individual's.

The existence of large organizations and the institutionalization of the professions allow a technology to build up a tremendous amount of momentum in a relatively short time.[5] Once the choice has been made to go a certain way, even if the reasons are not particularly good ones, the institutional machinery gears up and shoves everybody in the same direction. It can be tough to resist.

But the most important changes have come in the nature of technology itself. In the twentieth century, the power of our machines and devices has grown dramatically — along with their unanticipated consequences. When DDT was introduced, it seemed an unalloyed good: a cheap, effective way to kill insect pests and improve crop yields. It took years to understand that the pesticide made its way up the food chain to weaken the shells of birds' eggs and wreak other unintended havoc. Similarly, chlorofluorocarbons, or CFCs, were widely used for decades — as refrigerants, as blowing agents in making foams, and as cleaners for computer chips — before anyone realized they were damaging the ozone layer.

Even normally benign technologies can take on different complexions when multiplied to meet the needs of a world with five billion people. Burning natural gas is an economical, safe, and clean way to heat homes and generate electricity. Its only major waste material is carbon dioxide, the same gas that humans exhale with each breath. But carbon dioxide, in the quantities now being produced worldwide by burning fossil fuels (coal and oil as well as natural gas), is exaggerating the greenhouse effect in the earth's atmosphere and threatening major changes in the global climate.

Modern technology is like a Great Dane in a small apartment. It may be friendly, but you still want to make sure there's nothing breakable within reach. So to protect the china and crystal, government bodies, special interest groups, businesses, and even individuals are demanding an increasing say in how technologies are developed and applied.

Besides its power, modern technology has a second feature — more subtle, but equally important — that makes it qualitatively different from earlier technologies: its complexity. The plow, the cotton gin, even the lightbulb — these are simple devices. No matter how much they are changed and improved, it is still easy to understand their functions and capabilities. But for better or worse, technology has reached the point where no individual can understand completely how, say, a petrochemical plant works, and no team of experts can anticipate every possible outcome once a technology is put to work. Such complexity fundamentally changes our relationship with technology.

Consider the accident that destroyed the space shuttle *Challenger*.[6] Although the cause was eventually established as the failure of O-rings at low temperatures, which allowed the escape of hot gases and led to an explosion of a fuel tank, the real culprit was the complexity of the system. Space-shuttle engineers had been concerned about how the O-rings would behave in below-freezing weather, and some even recommended the launch be postponed to a warmer day, but no one could predict with any certainty what might happen. There were too many variables, too many ways in which the components of the system could interact. Management decided to proceed with the launch despite the engineers' disquiet, and it was only months later that experts pieced together the chain of events that led to the explosion.

Complexity creates uncertainty, limiting what can be known or reasonably surmised about a technology ahead of time. Although the shuttle engineers had vague fears, they simply did not — could not — know enough about the system to foresee the looming disaster. And in such cases, when there is not a clear technical answer, people fall back on subjective, often unconscious reasoning — biases and gut feelings, organizational goals, political considerations, the profit motive. In the case of the *Challenger*, NASA was feeling pressure to keep its shuttles going into space on a regular basis, and no one in the organization wanted to postpone a launch unless it was absolutely necessary. In this case, it was, but no one knew.

For all these reasons, modern technology is not simply the rational product of scientists and engineers that it is often advertised to be. Look closely at any technology today, from aircraft to the Internet, and you'll find that it truly makes sense only when seen as part of the society in which it grew up.

The insight is not a particularly new one. Thoughtful engineers have discussed it for some time. As early as the 1960s, Alvin Weinberg, the longtime director of Oak Ridge National Laboratory, was writing on the relationship between technology and society, particularly in regard to nuclear power.[7] There have been others. But until recently no one had studied the influence of society on technology in any consistent, comprehensive way. Philosophically inclined engineers like Weinberg did not have the time, the temperament, or the training to make careful studies. They reported what they saw and mused about the larger implications, but nothing more. And social scientists, when they noticed technology at all, viewed it primarily in terms of how it shapes society. Sociologists, economists, and others have long seen technology as the driving force behind much of history — a theory usually referred to as "technological determinism"[8] — and they have happily investigated such things as how the invention of the printing press triggered the Reformation, how the development of the compass ushered in the Age of Exploration and the discovery of the New World, and how the cotton gin created the conditions that led to the Civil War.[9] But few of these scientists turned the question around and asked how society shapes technology.

In just the past decade or two, however, that has begun to change. Indeed, it has now become almost fashionable for economists, political scientists, and sociologists to bring their analytical tools to bear on various technologies, from nuclear power and commercial aviation to medical instruments, computers, even bicycles.[10] Part of the reason for this is, I suspect, the increasing importance of technology to our world, and another part is the realization by social scientists that science and technology are just as amenable to social analysis as politics or religion. Whatever the reason, the result has been to put technology in a whole new light. Scholars now talk about the push and pull between technology and society, rather than just the push of technology on society. Engineers have been brought down from the mountain to take their place as one — still very important — cog in the system by which technology is delivered to the world.

Unfortunately, very little of this has filtered down. It remains mostly specialists talking to other specialists in books and journals that few outside their fields ever see. [The book from which this chapter is taken] aims to changes that. From its original design as a study of how engineers are creating a new generation of nuclear power, it has metamorphosed into a more general — and more ambitious — look at how nontechnical forces shape modern technologies. In it I collect and synthesize work from a wide variety of disciplines: history, economics, political science, sociology, risk analysis, management science, psychology. At various points, the book touches on personal computers, genetic engineering, jet aircraft, space flight, automobiles, chemical plants, even steam engines and typewriters. Such a book obviously cannot be comprehensive. Instead, my goal is to introduce a different way to think about technology and to show how many things make much more sense when technology is viewed in this way.

* * *

Lurking just beneath the surface . . . is one of the most intriguing and frustrating questions of our time, although it seldom gets much attention outside universities and other scholarly places: How do we know what we know? Or, to put it differently, What is the nature of human knowledge? This may sound like the sort of abstract question that only a philosopher could love, but its answer has practical — and important — ramifications for how we deal with science and technology.

There are two schools of thought on the nature of human knowledge, and they have little common ground. One has its roots in the physical sciences and goes by such names as positivism or objectivism or rationalism. Positivism accepts as knowledge only those things that have been verified by the scientific method of hypothesis formation and testing. It is, of course, impossible to verify anything absolutely — no matter how many times the sun comes up right on schedule, there is no guarantee it won't be a couple of hours late tomorrow — but positivists are generally content with verifying something beyond a reasonable doubt. Karl Popper, the influential philosopher of science, put a slightly different spin on it: Scientific statements, he said, are those that can be put to the test and potentially proven wrong, or falsified. It's not possible to prove a hypothesis is true, but if the hypothesis is tested extensively and never proven false, then one accepts it as provisionally true. If it later turns out to be false in certain situations, it can be modified or replaced. By this method, one hopes to get better and better approximations to the world's underlying physical reality. Absolute knowledge is not attainable. This provisional knowledge is the best we can do.

The strength of positivism — its insistence on verification — is also its weakness, for there is much that people think of as "knowledge" that cannot be verified in the same way that theories in physics or biology can. "The United States is a capitalist country" is a statement most would accept as true, but how does one prove it? Or how about, "Santa Claus wears a red suit and rides in a sleigh pulled by eight reindeer"? This is clearly knowledge of a sort — everyone in our culture older than two or three "knows" it — and though it may not be in the same intellectual league as, say, the general theory of relativity, it's much more important to most people than anything Einstein came up with. Yet the positivist approach has no place for such folderol.

For many years, social scientists, impressed with the success of the physical sciences, modeled their methods along the same positivist lines. They made observations, formed hypotheses, and tested their theories, attempting to make their research as objective as possible. Many social scientists still do, but in the past few decades an influential new school of thought has appeared, one that offers a different take on human knowledge. This approach, often referred to as "social construction"[11] or "interpretation," is designed explicitly to deal with social reality — the web of relationships, institutions, and shared beliefs and meanings that exist in a group of people — instead of physical reality. It sees knowledge not as something gleaned from an underlying physical reality but as the collective product of a society. Social constructionists speak not of objective facts but only of interpretations of the world, and they set out to explain how those interpretations arise. They make no attempt to judge the truth or falsity of socially constructed knowledge. Indeed, they deny that it even makes sense to ask whether such knowledge is true or false.

Thus, positivism and social construction offer diametrically opposed views of knowledge. Positivists see knowledge as arising from nature, social constructionists see it as a product of the human mind. Positivists speak of proof, social constructionists of interpretation. Positivists assume knowledge to be objective, social constructionists believe it to be subjective. In general, positivists have been willing to defer to the social constructionists in the case of social knowledge. After all, information about Santa Claus or the importance of capitalism is not really what a positivist has in mind when he speaks about "knowledge." But the social constructionists have been unwilling to return the favor and so have triggered a sharp, if so far bloodless, battle.

All human knowledge is social knowledge, the social constructionists say, even science.[12] After all, scientific knowledge is created by groups of people — the scientific community and its various subsets — and so it inevitably has a collective character. There is no such thing as a scientific truth believed by one person and disbelieved by the rest of the scientific community; an idea becomes a truth only when a vast majority of scientists accept it without question. But if this is so, the argument goes, then science is best understood as socially constructed rather than derived in some objective way from nature.

The earliest and best-known example of this approach to science is Thomas Kuhn's *The Structure of Scientific Revolutions*.[13] In it, Kuhn depicts most science as taking place inside a "paradigm" — a set of beliefs and expectations that guide the research, defining which questions are important and designating the proper ways to go about answering them. Scientific revolutions — such as the shift from the Ptolemaic to the Copernican view of the universe — occur when a paradigm breaks down and the scientific community collectively settles on a new paradigm in which to work. Kuhn argued that because such a paradigm shift is a change of the rules by which science is done, there can be no objective reasons for making the shift or for deciding on one paradigm over another. The choice is a subjective one. Ironically, much of the positivist scientific community has accepted the general idea of paradigms without understanding the deeper implications of Kuhn's work. It's not unusual to hear a scientist speak of "working within a paradigm" even though that scientist would be appalled by Kuhn's claim that scientific paradigms have no objective basis.

Today, many social scientists agree with Kuhn that the positivist claims for science were a myth. For example, in 1987 the sociologists Trevor Pinch and Wiebe Bijker wrote:

> [T]here is widespread agreement that scientific knowledge can be, and indeed has been, shown to be thoroughly socially constructed. . . . The treatment of scientific knowledge as a social construction implies that there is nothing epistemologically special about the nature of scientific knowledge: It is merely one in a whole series of knowledge cultures (including for instance, the knowledge systems pertaining to "primitive" tribes). Of course, the successes and failures of certain knowledge cultures still need to be explained, but this is to be seen as a sociological task, not an epistemological one.[14]

Such comments anger many scientists. Physicists especially dispute the conclusions of the social constructionists.[15] Yes, they admit, of course the creation of scientific knowledge is a joint effort, but nonetheless it *is* epistemologically special. Quantum mechanics, for instance, provides predictions that are consistently accurate to a dozen or more decimal places. This is no accident, they insist, but instead reflects the fact that science is uncovering and explaining some objective reality.

On the whole, the physicists get the better of this particular argument. Social construction theory is useful in explaining social knowledge and belief, but it does little to explain why physicists accept general relativity or quantum mechanics as accurate portrayals of physical reality. Social constructionists like Pinch and Bijker ignore a key difference between science and other knowledge cultures: science's insistence that its statements be falsifiable.[16] As long as science restricts itself in this way and continues testing its theories and discarding those that disagree with experiments, it is indeed epistemologically special. This and nothing else explains why science has been so much more successful than other knowledge cultures. Science may not be as objective as the positivists would like to believe, but the positivist approach comes closer than any other to capturing the essence of science.

This all may seem to be a tempest in an academic teapot, a question of interest to no one besides philosophers and the handful of scientists with an interest in epistemology, but it underlies many of the debates on scientific issues that affect the public. Consider the controversy in the mid-1980s over the use of recombinant bovine growth hormone in dairy cattle. Although the scientific community pronounced it safe, opponents of its use suggested that the researchers were influenced more by the sources of funding for their research and by their own inherent biases than by evidence.[17] This argument depended implicitly upon the assumption that the scientific opinions were not objective but rather were socially constructed. In general, if science is accepted as objective, people will give a great deal of weight to the conclusions of the scientific community and to the professional opinions of individual scientists. But if science is seen as a social construct, vulnerable to biases and fashion, people will question or even dismiss its conclusions.

Which brings us back to our original subject. At its heart, [the book from which this chapter was taken is] about technological knowledge: What is it? and, How is it formed? Traditionally, engineers have seen their work in positivist terms. Like scientists, they take it for granted that their work is objective, and they believe that to understand a technology, all one needs are the technical details. They see a strict dichotomy between the pure logic of their machines and the subjectivity and the irrationality of the world in which they must operate. On the other hand, a growing school of social scientists sees technology as socially constructed. Its objectivity, they say, is a myth created and propagated by engineers who believe their own press. As with science, this is no mere academic debate. Our attitudes toward technology hinge, in large part, on what we believe about the nature of the knowledge underlying it.

To understand technological knowledge, this book argues, it is necessary to marry the positivist and the social constructionist perspectives. Technology combines the physical world with the social, the objective with the subjective, the machine with the man. If one imagines a spectrum with scientific knowledge on one end and social knowledge on the other, technological knowledge lies somewhere in the middle. It is falsifiable to a certain extent, but not nearly to the same degree as science. Conversely, much of technological knowledge is socially constructed, but there are limits — no matter what a group of people thinks or does, an airplane design that can't fly won't fly. In short, the physical world restricts technology. Some things work better than others, some don't work at all, and this leads to a certain amount of objectivity in technological knowledge. But, unlike scientists, engineers are working with a world of their own creation, and the act of creation cannot be understood in positivist terms.

Ultimately, any understanding of technological knowledge must recognize the composite nature of that knowledge. Our technological creations carry with them the traces of both the engineer and the larger society.

NOTES

1. Charles McLaughlin, "The Stanley Steamer: A Study in Unsuccessful Innovation," *Explorations in Entrepreneurial History* 7 (October 1954), pp. 37–47.
2. Henry Petroski, *The Pencil* (New York: Alfred A. Knopf, 1989), p. 207.

3. Merritt Roe Smith, "Technological Determinism in American Culture," in Merritt Roe Smith and Leo Marx, (eds.), *Does Technology Drive History?* (Cambridge, MA: MIT Press, 1994), pp. 1–35.

4. Ronald Inglehart, *The Silent Revolution: Changing Values and Policy Styles Among Western Publics* (Princeton, NJ: Princeton University Press, 1977), p. 3.

5. Hughes, "Technological History and Technical Problems," p. 141.

6. Maureen Hogan Casamayou, *Bureaucracy in Crisis: Three Mile Island, the Shuttle Challenger and Risk Assessment* (Boulder, CO: Westview, 1993), pp. 57–85.

7. Alvin M. Weinberg, *Nuclear Reactions: Science and Trans-Science* (New York: American Institute of Physics, 1992). See also Alvin M. Weinberg, *The First Nuclear Era: The Life and Times of a Technological Fixer* (New York: American Institute of Physics, 1994).

8. For a critical review of technological determinism, see Merritt Roe Smith and Leo Marx, eds., *Does Technology Drive History?* (Cambridge, MA: MIT Press, 1994).

9. Leo Marx and Merritt Rowe Smith, introduction to Marx and Smith, *Does Technology Drive History?* p. x.

10. There have been a number of books published recently that analyze technology from a social science perspective. They include Wiebe E. Bijker, Thomas P. Hughes, and Trevor Pinch, eds., *The Social Construction of Technological Systems: New Directions in the Sociology and History of Technology* (Cambridge, MA: MIT Press, 1987); Marcel C. LaFollette and Jeffrey K. Stine, eds., *Technology and Choice: Readings from Technology and Culture* (Chicago: University of Chicago Press, 1991); Meinolf Dierkes and Ute Hoffmann, eds., *New Technology at the Outset: Social Forces in the Shaping of Technological Innovations* (Boulder, CO: Westview, 1992); Wiebe Bijker and John Law, eds., *Shaping Technology/Building Society: Studies in Sociotechnical Change* (Cambridge, MA: MIT Press, 1992); Wiebe E. Bijker, *Of Bicycles, Bakelites, and Bulbs: Toward a Theory of Sociotechnical Change* (Cambridge, MA: MIT Press, 1995). See also various issues of *Technology and Culture; Technology in Society; Science, Technology & Human Values;* and *Technology Review.*

11. The seminal work here is Peter L. Berger and Thomas Luckmann, *The Social Construction of Reality: A Treatise in the Sociology of Knowledge* (New York: Doubleday, 1966).

12. A good summary of the social constructionist approach to scientific knowledge can be found in Trevor J. Pinch and Wiebe E. Bijker, "The Social Construction of Facts and Artifacts: Or How the Sociology of Science and the Sociology of Technology Might Benefit Each Other," in Bijker, Hughes, and Pinch, *The Social Construction of Technological Systems,* pp. 17–50.

13. Thomas S. Kuhn, *The Structure of Scientific Revolutions* (Chicago: University of Chicago Press, 1962).

14. Pinch and Bijker, "The Social Construction of Facts and Artifacts," pp. 18–19.

15. David Mermin, a very thoughtful physicist at Cornell University, offers a careful refutation of the social construction of physics in a two-part article: "What's Wrong with the Sustaining Myth?" *Physics Today* 49 (March 1996), pp. 11, 13; and "The Golemization of Relativity," *Physics Today* 49 (April 1996), pp. 11, 13.

    In spring 1996, the dispute between physicists and social constructionists took an amusing turn — amusing, at least, for the physicists — when Alan Sokal published an article entitled "Transgressing the Boundaries: Toward a Transformative Hermeneutics of Quantum Gravity" in *Social Text,* a "postmodernist" journal devoted to social constructionist analyses. Sokal, a physicist at New York University, later revealed that it was all a hoax. He had cobbled together bad science, even worse logic, and a bunch of catchphrases from postmodernist theorizing and had somehow convinced the editors of *Social Text* that the nonsensical article was a contribution worthy of publication. The editors were understandably not amused but neither were they contrite. They did not seem to see it as a weakness on their part — or even less, on the part of the entire postmodernist movement — that they could not tell the difference between an obvious hoax and what passes for serious work in their field. The original article appeared in *Social Text* 46/47 (Spring/Summer 1996), pp. 217–252. Sokal revealed the hoax in "A Physicist Experiments with Cultural Studies," *Lingua Franca* (May/June 1996), pp. 62–64.

16. This argument is modified from one offered by Thelma Lavine, Clarence J. Robinson Professor of Philosophy at George Mason University in Fairfax, Virginia.

17. W. P. Norton, "Just Say Moo," *The Progressive* (November 1989), pp. 26–29. See also Gina Kolata, "When the Geneticists' Fingers Get in the Food," *New York Times* (February 20, 1994), sec. 4, p. 14.

3. Can Technology Replace Social Engineering?

ALVIN M. WEINBERG

Since Alvin Weinberg's essay "Can Technology Replace Social Engineering?" was first published in the mid-1960s, it has become a classic in the literature of technology and society. Indeed, the term Technological Fix, *introduced here, has become part of the lexicon of the field. Weinberg, one of the pioneers of large-scale atomic energy R&D and an inveterate technological optimist, argues that technology is capable of finding shortcuts (technological fixes) to the solution of social problems. For example, faced with a shortage of fresh water, he suggests, society can try either social engineering — altering life-styles and the ways people use water — or a technological fix, such as the provision of additional fresh water through nuclear-powered desalting of sea water. The reader should keep in mind that this article dates from 1966. Although aspects are anachronistic and out of tune with contemporary views of technology, society, and politics, the questions it raises are as relevant today as they were more than thirty years ago.*

Alvin M. Weinberg is a physicist who joined the World War II Manhattan Project early in his career. He went to Oak Ridge National Laboratory in 1945 and served as its director from 1955 through 1973. He currently holds the title of Distinguished Fellow at Oak Ridge Associated Universities. Weinberg was a member of the President's Science Advisory Committee in 1960–1962 and is the recipient of many awards, including the President's Medal of Science and the Enrico Fermi Award. He was born in Chicago in 1915 and holds A.B., A.M., and Ph.D. degrees from the University of Chicago.

During World War II, and immediately afterward, our federal government mobilized its scientific and technical resources, such as the Oak Ridge National Laboratory, around great technological problems. Nuclear reactors, nuclear weapons, radar, and space are some of the miraculous new technologies that have been created by this mobilization of federal effort. In the past few years, there has been a major change in focus of much of our federal research. Instead of being preoccupied with technology, our government is now mobilizing around problems that are largely social. We are beginning to ask what can we do about world population, about the deterioration of our environment, about our educational system, our decaying cities, race relations, poverty. Recent administrations have dedicated the power of a scientifically oriented federal apparatus to finding solutions for these complex social problems.

Social problems are much more complex than are technological problems. It is much harder to identify a social problem than a technological problem: How do

From *University of Chicago Magazine*, 59 (October 1966): p. 6–10. Reprinted by permission of the author.

we know when our cities need renewing, or when our population is too big, or when our modes of transportation have broken down? The problems are, in a way, harder to identify just because their solutions are never clear-cut: How do we know when our cities are renewed, or our air clean enough, or our transportation convenient enough? By contrast, the availability of a crisp and beautiful technological solution often helps focus on the problem to which the new technology is the solution. I doubt that we would have been nearly as concerned with an eventual shortage of energy as we now are if we had not had a neat solution — nuclear energy — available to eliminate the shortage.

There is a more basic sense in which social problems are much more difficult than are technological problems. A social problem exists because many people behave, individually, in a socially unacceptable way. To solve a social problem one must induce social change — One must persuade many people to behave differently than they have behaved in the past. One must persuade many people to have fewer babies, or to drive more carefully, or to refrain from disliking blacks. By contrast, resolution of a technological problem involves many fewer individual decisions. Once President Roosevelt decided to go after atomic energy, it was by comparison a relatively simple task to mobilize the Manhattan Project.

The resolution of social problems by the traditional methods — by motivating or forcing people to behave more rationally — is a frustrating business. People don't behave rationally; it is a long, hard business to persuade individuals to forgo immediate personal gain or pleasure (as seen by the individual) in favor of longer term social gain. And, indeed, the aim of social engineering is to invent the social devices — usually legal, but also moral and educational and organizational — that will change each person's motivation and redirect his activities along ways that are more acceptable to the society.

The technologist is appalled by the difficulties faced by the social engineer; to engineer even a small social change by inducing individuals to behave differently is always hard, even when the change is rather neutral or even beneficial. For example, some rice eaters in India are reported to prefer starvation to eating wheat that we send to them. How much harder it is to change motivations where the individual is insecure and feels threatened if she acts differently, as illustrated by the poor white's reluctance to accept the black as an equal. By contrast, technological engineering is simple: The rocket, the reactor, and the desalination plants are devices that are expensive to develop, to be sure, but their feasibility is relatively easy to assess and their success relatively easy to achieve once one understands the scientific principles that underlie them. It is, therefore, tempting to raise the following question: In view of the simplicity of technological engineering, and the complexity of social engineering, to what extent can social problems be circumvented by reducing them to technological problems? Can we identify "Quick Technological Fixes" for profound and almost infinitely complicated social problems, "fixes" that are within the grasp of modern technology and which would either eliminate the original social problem without requiring a change in the individual's social attitudes, or would so alter the problem as to make its resolution more feasible? To paraphrase Ralph Nader, to what extent can technological remedies be found for social problems without first having to remove the causes of the problem? It is in this sense that I ask, "Can technology replace social engineering?"

THE MAJOR TECHNOLOGICAL FIXES OF THE PAST

To better explain what I have in mind, I shall describe how two of our most profound social problems — poverty and war — have in some limited degree been solved by the "Technological Fix," rather than by the methods of social engineering. Let me begin with poverty.

The traditional Marxian view of poverty regarded our economic ills as being primarily a question of maldistribution of goods. The Marxist recipe for elimination of poverty, therefore, was to eliminate profit, in the erroneous belief that it was the loss of this relatively small increment from the worker's paycheck that kept him poverty stricken. The Marxist dogma is typical of the approach of the social engineer: One tries to convince or coerce many people to forgo their short-term profits in what is presumed to be the long-term interest of the society as a whole.

The Marxian view seems archaic in this age of mass production and automation not only to us, but apparently to many Eastern bloc economists. For the brilliant advances in the technology of energy, of mass production, and of automation have created the affluent society. Technology has expanded our productive capacity so greatly that even though our distribution is still inefficient, and unfair by Marxian precepts, there is more than enough to go around. Technology has provided a "fix" — greatly expanded production of goods — which enables our capitalistic society to achieve many of the aims of the Marxist social engineer without going through the social revolution Marx viewed as inevitable. Technology has converted the seemingly intractable social problem of widespread poverty into a relatively tractable one.

My second example is war. The traditional Christian position views war as primarily a moral issue: If people become good, and model themselves after the Prince of Peace, they will live in peace. This doctrine is so deeply ingrained in the spirit of all civilized people that I suppose it is a blasphemy to point out that it has never worked very well — that people have not been good and that they are not paragons of virtue or even of reasonableness.

Though I realize it is terribly presumptuous to claim, I believe that Edward Teller may have supplied the nearest thing to a Quick Technological Fix to the problem of war. The hydrogen bomb greatly increases the provocation that would precipitate large-scale war — and not because people's motivations have been changed, not because people have become more tolerant and understanding, but rather because the appeal to the primitive instinct of self-preservation has been intensified far beyond anything we could have imagined before the H-bomb was invented. To point out these things today [in 1966], with the United States involved in a shooting war, may sound hollow and unconvincing, yet the desperate and partial peace we have now is much better than a full-fledged exchange of thermonuclear weapons. One cannot deny that the Soviet leaders now recognize the force of H-bombs and that this has surely contributed to the less militant attitude of the USSR. One can only hope that the Chinese leadership, as it acquires familiarity with H-bombs, will also become less militant. If I were to be asked who has given the world a more effective means of achieving peace, our great religious leaders who urge people to love their neighbors and, thus, avoid fights, or our weapons technologists who simply present people with no rational alternative to peace, I would vote for the weapons technologists. That the peace we get is at best terribly fragile, I cannot deny, yet, as I shall explain, I think technology can help stabilize our imperfect and precarious peace.

THE TECHNOLOGICAL FIXES OF THE FUTURE

Are there other Technological Fixes on the horizon, other technologies that can reduce immensely complicated social questions to a matter of "engineering"? Are there new technologies that offer society ways of circumventing social problems and at the same time do not require individuals to renounce short-term advantage for long-term gain?

Probably the most important new Technological Fix is the intrauterine device for birth control. Before the IUD was invented, birth control demanded very strong motivation of countless individuals. Even with the Pill, the individual's motivation had to be sustained day in and day out; should it flag even temporarily, the strong motivation of the previous month might go for naught. But the IUD, being a one-shot method, greatly reduces the individual motivation required to induce a social change. To be sure, the mother must be sufficiently motivated to accept the IUD in the first place, but, as experience in India already seems to show, it is much easier to persuade the Indian mother to accept the IUD once than it is to persuade her to take a pill every day. The IUD does not completely replace social engineering by technology, and, indeed, in some Spanish American cultures where the husband's manliness is measured by the number of children he has, the IUD attacks only part of the problem. Yet, in many other situations, as in India, the IUD so reduces the social component of the problem as to make an impossibly difficult social problem much less hopeless.

Let me turn now to problems that from the beginning have had both technical and social components — broadly, those concerned with conservation of our resources: our environment, our water, and our raw materials for production of the means of subsistence. The social issue here arises because many people by their individual acts cause shortages and, thus, create economic, and ultimately social, imbalance. For example, people use water wastefully, or they insist on moving to California because of its climate, and so we have water shortages, or too many people drive cars in Los Angeles with its curious meteorology, and so Los Angeles suffocates from smog.

The water resources problem is a particularly good example of a complicated problem with strong social and technological connotations. Our management of water resources in the past has been based largely on the ancient Roman device, the aqueduct: Every water shortage was to be relieved by stealing water from someone else who at the moment didn't need the water or was too poor or too weak to prevent the steal. Southern California would steal from Northern California, New York City from upstate New York, the farmer who could afford a cloud-seeder from the farmer who could not afford a cloud-seeder. The social engineer insists that such shortsighted expedients have gotten us into serious trouble; we have no water resources policy, we waste water disgracefully, and, perhaps, in denying the ethic of thriftiness in using water we have generally undermined our moral fiber. The social engineer, therefore, views such technological shenanigans as being shortsighted, if not downright immoral. Instead, he says, we should persuade or force people to use less water or to stay in the cold Middle West where water is plentiful instead of migrating to California where water is scarce.

The water technologist, on the other hand, views the social engineer's approach as rather impractical. To persuade people to use less water, to get along with expensive water, is difficult, time-consuming, and uncertain in the extreme. Moreover, say the technologists, what right does the water resources expert have to insist that people use water less wastefully? Green lawns and clean cars and swimming pools are part of the good life, American style . . . and what right do we have to deny this luxury if there is some alternative to cutting down the water we use?

Here we have a sharp confrontation of the two ways of dealing with a complex social issue: the social engineering way, which asks people to behave more "reasonably," and the technologists' way, which tries to avoid changing people's habits or motivation. Even though I am a technologist, I have sympathy for the social engineer. I think we must use our water as efficiently as possible, that we ought to improve people's attitudes toward the use of water, and that everything that can be done to rationalize our water policy will be welcome. Yet, as a technologist, I believe I see ways of providing more water more cheaply than the social engineers may concede is possible.

I refer to the possibility of nuclear desalination. The social engineer dismisses the technologist's simpleminded idea of solving a water shortage by transporting more water primarily because, in so doing, the water user steals water from someone else — possibly foreclosing the possibility of ultimately utilizing land now only sparsely settled. But surely water drawn from the sea deprives no one of his share of water. The whole issue is then a technological one: Can fresh water be drawn from the sea cheaply enough to have a major impact on our chronically water-short areas, like Southern California, Arizona, and the eastern seaboard?

I believe the answer is yes, though much hard technical work remains to be done. A large program to develop cheap methods of nuclear desalting has been undertaken by the United States, and I have little doubt that within the next ten to twenty years we shall see huge dual-purpose desalting plants springing up on many parched seacoasts of the world.* At first, these plants will produce water at municipal prices. But, I believe, on the basis of research now in progress at ORNL [Oak Ridge National Laboratory] and elsewhere, water from the sea at a cost

---

*Here, as elsewhere, the reader should bear in mind that the essay dates from the mid-1960s. — ED.

acceptable for agriculture — less than ten cents per 1,000 gallons — is eventually in the cards. In short, for areas close to the seacoasts, technology can provide water without requiring a great and difficult-to-accomplish change in people's attitudes toward the utilization of water.

The Technological Fix for water is based on the availability of extremely cheap energy from very large nuclear reactors. What other social consequences can one foresee flowing from really cheap energy eventually available to every country, regardless of its endowment of conventional resources? Though we now see only vaguely the outlines of the possibilities, it does seem likely that from very cheap nuclear energy we shall get hydrogen by electrolysis of water, and, thence, the all-important ammonia fertilizer necessary to help feed the hungry of the world; we shall reduce metals without requiring cooking coal; we shall even power automobiles with electricity, via fuel cells or storage batteries, thus reducing our world's dependence on crude oil, as well as eliminating our air pollution insofar as it is caused by automobile exhaust or by the burning of fossil fuels. In short, the widespread availability of very cheap energy everywhere in the world ought to lead to an energy autarky in every country of the world and eventually to an autarky in the many staples of life that should flow from really cheap energy.

WILL TECHNOLOGY REPLACE SOCIAL ENGINEERING?

I hope these examples suggest how social problems can be circumvented or at least reduced to less formidable proportions by the application of the Technological Fix. The examples I have given do not strike me as being fanciful, nor are they at all exhaustive. I have not touched, for example, upon the extent to which really cheap computers and improved technology of communication can help improve elementary teaching without having first to improve our elementary teachers. Nor have I mentioned Ralph Nader's brilliant observation that a safer car, and even its development and adoption by the auto company, is a quicker and probably surer way to reduce traffic deaths than is a campaign to teach people to drive more carefully. Nor have I invoked some really fanciful Technological Fixes — like providing air conditioners and free electricity to operate them for every black family in Watts on the assumption (suggested by Huntington) that race rioting is correlated with hot, humid weather, or the ultimate Technological Fix, Aldous Huxley's soma pills that eliminate human unhappiness without improving human relations in the usual sense.

My examples illustrate both the strength and the weakness of the Technological Fix for social problems. The Technological Fix accepts man's intrinsic shortcomings and circumvents them or capitalizes on them for socially useful ends. The Fix is, therefore, eminently practical and, in the short term, relatively effective. One does not wait around trying to change people's minds: If people want more water, one gets them more water rather than requiring them to reduce their use of water; If people insist on driving autos while they are drunk, one provides safer autos that prevent injuries even after a severe accident.

But the technological solutions to social problems tend to be incomplete and metastable, to replace one social problem with another. Perhaps the best example of this instability is the peace imposed upon us by the H-bomb. Evidently the pax hydrogenica is metastable in two senses: in the short term, because the aggressor still enjoys such an advantage, the long term, because the discrepancy and have-not nations must eventually be resolved if we are to have permanent peace. Yet, for these particular shortcomings, technology has something to offer. To the imbalance between offense and defense, technology says let us devise passive defense that redresses the balance. A world with H-bombs and adequate civil defense is less likely to lapse into thermonuclear war than a world with H-bombs alone, at least if one concedes that the danger of the thermonuclear war mainly lies in the acts of irresponsible leaders. Anything that deters the irresponsible leader is a force for peace: A technologically sound civil defense therefore would help stabilize the balance of terror.

To the discrepancy between haves and have-nots, technology offers the nuclear energy revolution, with its possibility of autarky for haves and have-nots alike. How this might work to stabilize our metastable thermonuclear peace is suggested by the possible politic effect of the recently proposed Israeli desalting plant. The Arab states I should think would be much less set upon destroying the Jordan River Project if the Israelis had a desalination plant in reserve that would nullify the effect of such actions. In this connection, I think countries like ours can contribute very much. Our country will soon have to decide whether to continue to spend 5.5×10^9 per year for space exploration after our lunar landing. Is it too outrageous to suggest that some of this money be devoted to building huge nuclear desalting complexes in the arid ocean rims of the troubled world? If the plants are powered with breeder reactors, the out-of-pocket costs, once the plants are built, should be low enough to make large-scale agriculture feasible in these areas. I estimate that for 4×10^9 per year we could build enough desalting capacity to feed more than ten million new mouths per year (provided we use agricultural methods that husband water), and we would, thereby, help stabilize the metastable, bomb-imposed balance of terror.

Yet, I am afraid we technologists shall not satisfy our social engineers, who tell us that our Technological Fixes do not get to the heart of the problem; they are at best temporary expedients; they create new problems as they solve old ones; to put a Technological Fix into effect requires a positive social action. Eventually, social engineering, like the Supreme Court decision on desegregation, must be invoked to solve social problems. And, of course, our social engineers are right. Technology will never replace social engineering. But technology has provided and will continue to provide to the social engineer broader options, to make intractable social problems less intractable; perhaps, most of all, technology will buy time — that precious commodity that converts violent social revolution into acceptable social evolution.

Our country now recognizes and is mobilizing around the great social problems that corrupt and disfigure our human existence. It is natural that in this mobilization we should look first to the social engineer. But, unfortunately, the apparatus most readily available to the government, like the great federal laboratories, is technologically oriented, not socially oriented. I believe we have a great opportunity here; for, as I hope I have persuaded you, many of our seemingly social problems do admit of partial technological solutions. Our already deployed technological apparatus can contribute to the resolution of social questions. I plead, therefore, first for our government to deploy its laboratories, its hardware contractors, and its engineering universities around social problems. And I plead, secondly, for understanding and cooperation between technologist and social engineer. Even with all the help he can get from the technologist, the social engineer's problems are never really solved. It is only by cooperation between technologist and social engineer that we can hope to achieve what is the aim of all technologists and social engineers — a better society and, thereby, a better life, for all of us who are part of society.

4. Why I Am Not Going to Buy a Computer

WENDELL BERRY

Wendell Berry may be the antithesis of the "technological fixer" Alvin Weinberg describes in the preceding chapter. His short essay — concise and spare — explains why he prefers a thirty-year-old manual typewriter to a personal computer or even an electric typewriter. The essay, originally published in New England Review *and* Bread Loaf Quarterly, *was reprinted in* Harper's *and is followed by several letters to the editor that* Harper's *received, together with Berry's response. It is a simple, elegant indictment of centralization, bigness, and consumption-driven technological society that some will resonate with and others will utterly reject.*

A writer and farmer, Wendell Berry lives in Port Royal, Kentucky, and is a former member of the English faculty at the University of Kentucky. "Why I Am Not Going to Buy a Computer" is included in a book of his essays entitled, What Are People For? *Berry's other writings include several novels and collections of short stories, poems, and essays.*

Like almost everybody else, I am hooked to the energy corporations which I do not admire. I hope to become less hooked to them. In my work, I try to be as little hooked to them as possible. As a farmer, I do almost all of my work with horses. As a writer, I work with a pencil or a pen and a piece of paper.

My wife types my work on a Royal standard typewriter bought new in 1956 and as good now as it was then. As she types, she sees things that are wrong and marks them with small checks in the margins. She is my best critic because she is the one most familiar with my habitual errors and weaknesses. She also understands, sometimes better than I do, what ought to be said. We have, I think, a literary cottage industry that works well and pleasantly. I do not see anything wrong with it.

A number of people, by now, have told me that I could greatly improve things by buying a computer. My answer is that I am not going to do it. I have several reasons, and they are good ones.

The first is the one I mentioned at the beginning. I would hate to think that my work as a writer could not be done without a direct dependence on strip-mined coal. How could I write conscientiously against the rape of nature if I were, in the act of writing, implicated in the rape? For the same reason, it matters to me that my writing is done in the daytime, without electric light.

I do not admire the computer manufacturers a great deal more than I admire the energy industries. I have seen their advertisements, attempting to seduce struggling or failing farmers into the belief that they can solve their problems by buying yet another piece of expensive equipment. I am familiar with their propaganda campaigns that have put computers into public schools in need of books. That computers are expected to become as common as TV sets in "the future" does not impress me or matter to me. I do not own a TV set. I do not see that computers are bringing us one step nearer to anything that does matter to me: peace, economic justice, ecological health, political honesty, family and community stability, good work.

What would a computer cost me? More money, for one thing, than I can afford, and more than I wish to pay to people whom I do not admire. But the cost would not be just monetary. It is well understood that technological innovation always requires the discarding of the "old model" — the "old model" in this case being not just our old Royal standard, but my wife, my critic, my closest reader, my fellow worker. Thus (and I think this is typical of present-day technological innovation), what would be superseded would be not only something, but somebody. In order to be technologically up to date as a writer, I would have to sacrifice an association that I am dependent upon and that I treasure.

My final and perhaps my best reason for not owning a computer is that I do not wish to fool myself. I disbelieve, and therefore strongly resent, the assertion that I or anybody else could write better or more easily with a computer than with a pencil. I do not see why I should not be as scientific about this as the next fellow: When somebody has used a computer to write work that is demonstrably better than Dante's, and when this better is demonstrably attributable to the use of a computer, then I will speak of computers with a more respectful tone of voice, though I still will not buy one.

To make myself as plain as I can, I should give my standards for technological innovation in my own work. They are as follows:

1. The new tool should be cheaper than the one it replaces.
2. It should be at least as small in scale as the one it replaces.
3. It should do work that is clearly and demonstrably better than the one it replaces.
4. It should use less energy than the one it replaces.
5. If possible, it should use some form of solar energy, such as that of the body.
6. It should be repairable by a person of ordinary intelligence, provided that he or she has the necessary tools.
7. It should be purchasable and repairable as near to home as possible.
8. It should come from a small, privately owned shop or store that will take it back for maintenance and repair.
9. It should not replace or disrupt anything good that already exists, and this includes family and community relationships.

1987

After the foregoing essay, first published in the *New England Review* and *Bread Loaf Quarterly*, was reprinted in *Harper's*, the *Harper's* editors published the following letters in response and permitted me a reply.

W. B.

LETTERS

Wendell Berry provides writers enslaved by the computer with a handy alternative: Wife — a low-tech, energy-saving device. Drop a pile of handwritten notes on Wife and you get back a finished manuscript, edited while it was typed. What computer can do that? Wife meets all of Berry's uncompromising standards for technological innovation: She's cheap, repairable near home, and good for the family structure. Best of all, Wife is politically correct because she breaks a writer's "direct dependence on strip-mined coal."

History teaches us that Wife can also be used to beat rugs and wash clothes by hand, thus eliminating the need for the vacuum cleaner and washing machine, two more nasty machines that threaten the act of writing.

Gordon Inkeles
Miranda, Calif.

I have no quarrel with Berry because he prefers to write with pencil and paper; that is his choice. But he implies that I and others are somehow impure because we choose to write on a computer. I do not admire the energy corporations, either. Their shortcoming is not that they produce electricity but how they go about it. They are poorly managed because they are blind to long-term consequences. To solve this problem, wouldn't it make more sense to correct the precise error they are making rather than simply ignore their product? I would be happy to join Berry in a protest against strip mining, but I intend to keep plugging this computer into the wall with a clear conscience.

James Rhoads
Battle Creek, Mich.

I enjoyed reading Berry's declaration of intent never to buy a personal computer in the same way that I enjoy reading about the belief systems of unfamiliar tribal cultures. I tried to imagine a tool that would meet Berry's criteria for superiority to his old manual typewriter. The clear winner is the quill pen. It is cheaper, smaller, more energy efficient, human powered, easily repaired, and nondisruptive of existing relationships.

Berry also requires that this tool must be "clearly and demonstrably better" than the one it replaces. But surely we all recognize by now that "better" is in the mind of the beholder. To the quill-pen aficionado, the benefits obtained from elegant calligraphy might well outweigh all others.

I have no particular desire to see Berry use a word processor; if he doesn't like computers, that's fine with me. However, I do object to his portrayal of this reluctance as a moral virtue. Many of us have found that computers can be an invaluable tool in the fight to protect our environment. In addition to helping me write, my personal computer gives me access to up-to-the-minute reports on the workings of the EPA and the nuclear industry. I participate in electronic bulletin boards on which environmental activists discuss strategy and warn each other about urgent legislative issues. Perhaps Berry feels that the Sierra Club should eschew modern printing technology, which is highly wasteful of energy, in favor of having its members hand-copy the club's magazines and other mailings each month?

Nathaniel S. Borenstein
Pittsburgh, Pa.

The value of a computer to a writer is that it is a tool not for generating ideas but for typing and editing words. It is cheaper than a secretary (or a wife!) and arguably more fuel efficient. And it enables spouses who are not inclined to provide free labor more time to concentrate on their own work.

We should support alternatives both to coal-generated electricity and to IBM-style technocracy. But I am reluctant to entertain alternatives that presuppose the traditional subservience of one class to another. Let the PCs come and the wives and servants go seek more meaningful work.

Toby Koosman
Knoxville, Tenn.

Berry asks how he could write conscientiously against the rape of nature if in the act of writing on a computer he was implicated in the rape. I find it ironic that a writer who sees the underlying connectedness of things would allow his diatribe against computers to be published in a magazine that carries ads for the National Rural Electric Cooperative Association, Marlboro, Phillips Petroleum, McDonnell Douglas, and yes, even Smith Corona. If Berry rests comfortably at night, he must be using sleeping pills.

Bradley C. Johnson
Grand Forks, N.D.

WENDELL BERRY REPLIES

The foregoing letters surprised me with the intensity of the feelings they expressed. According to the writers' testimony, there is nothing wrong with their computers; they are utterly satisfied with them and all that they stand for. My correspondents are certain that I am wrong and that I am, moreover, on the losing side, a side already relegated to the dustbin of history. And yet they grow huffy and condescending over my tiny dissent. What are they so anxious about?

I can only conclude that I have scratched the skin of a technological fundamentalism that, like other fundamentalisms, wishes to monopolize a whole society and, therefore, cannot tolerate the smallest difference of opinion. At the slightest hint of a threat to their complacency, they repeat, like a chorus of toads, the notes sounded by their leaders in industry. The past was gloomy, drudgery ridden, servile, meaningless, and slow. The present, thanks only to purchasable products, is meaningful, bright, lively, centralized, and fast. The future, thanks only to more purchasable products, is going to be even better. Thus, consumers become salesmen, and the world is made safer for corporations.

I am also surprised by the meanness with which two of these writers refer to my wife. In order to imply that I am a tyrant, they suggest by both direct statement and innuendo that she is subservient, characterless, and stupid — a mere "device" easily forced to provide meaningless "free labor." I understand that it is impossible to make an adequate public defense of one's private life, and so I will only point out that there are a number of kinder possibilities that my critics have disdained to imagine: that my wife may do this work because she wants to and likes to, that she may find some use and some meaning in it, that she may not work for nothing. These gentlemen obviously think themselves feminists of the most correct and principled sort, and yet they do not hesitate to stereotype and insult, on the basis of one fact, a woman they do not know. They are audacious and irresponsible gossips.

In his letter, Bradley C. Johnson rushes past the possibility of sense in what I said in my essay by implying that I am or ought to be a fanatic. That I am a person of this century and implicated in many practices that I regret is fully acknowledged at the beginning of my essay. I did not say that I proposed to end forthwith all my involvement in harmful technology, for I do not know how to do that. I said merely that I want to limit such involvement and to a certain extent I do know how to do that. If some technology does damage to the world — as two of [these] letters seem to agree that it does — then why is it not reasonable, and indeed moral, to try to limit one's use of that technology? Of course, I think that I am right to do this.

I would not think so, obviously, if I agreed with Nathaniel S. Borenstein that "'better' is in the mind of the beholder." But if he truly believes this, I do not see why he bothers with his personal computer's "up-to-the-minute reports on the workings of the EPA and the nuclear industry" or why he wishes to be warned about "urgent legislative issues." According to his system, the "better" in a bureaucratic, industrial, or legislative mind is as good as the "better" in his. His mind apparently is being subverted by an objective standard of some sort, and he had better look out.

Borenstein does not say what he does after his computer has drummed him awake. I assume from his letter that he must send donations to conservation organizations and letters to officials. Like James Rhoads, at any rate, he has a clear conscience. But this is what is wrong with the conservation movement. It has a clear conscience. The guilty are always other people, and the wrong is always somewhere else; that is why Borenstein finds his "electronic bulletin board" so handy. To the conservation movement, it is only production that causes environmental degradation; the consumption that supports the production is rarely acknowledged to be at fault. The ideal of the run-of-the-mill conservationist is to impose restraints upon production without limiting consumption or burdening the consciences of consumers.

But virtually all of our consumption now is extravagant, and virtually all of it consumes the world. It is not beside the point that most electrical power comes from strip-mined coal. The history of the exploitation of the Appalachian coal fields is long, and it is available to readers. I do not see how anyone can read it and plug in any appliance with a clear conscience. If Rhoads can do so, that does not mean that his conscience is clear; it means that his conscience is not working.

To the extent that we consume, in our present circumstances, we are guilty. To the extent that we guilty consumers are conservationists, we are absurd. But what can we do? Must we go on writing letters to politicians and donating to conservation organizations until the majority of our fellow citizens agree with us? Or can we do something directly to solve our share of the problem?

I am a conservationist. I believe wholeheartedly in putting pressure on the politicians and in maintaining the conservation organizations. But I wrote my little essay partly in distrust of centralization. I don't think that the government and the conservation organizations alone will ever make us a conserving society. Why do I need a centralized computer system to alert me to environmental crises? That I live every hour of every day in an environmental crisis I know from all my senses. Why then is not my first duty to reduce, so far as I can, my own consumption?

Finally, it seems to me that none of my correspondents recognizes the innovativeness of my essay. If the use of a computer is a new idea, then a newer idea is not to use one.

5.   Technology and the Tragic View

SAMUEL C. FLORMAN

In Part II, which follows this chapter, two writers of an earlier generation engage in a famous debate that, in many ways, epitomizes the bitter divisions between the advocates and critics of technology in the late 1960s and early 1970s. Though no longer tied to the domestic conflict over U.S. participation in the Vietnam War or to the social revolution that was then raging in the United States, these pro- and anti-technology divisions still exist today. However, to treat a subject as complex as the relations of technology and society in such simplistic, for-or-against terms is ultimately less than satisfying. Samuel Florman's insighful essay, "Technology and the Tragic View," taken from his book, Blaming Technology, *suggests another approach. Florman draws on the classical Greek concept of tragedy to develop a new perspective on technology. In the tragic view of life, says Florman,*

> [it] is man's destiny to die, to be defeated by the forces of the universe. But in challenging his destiny, in being brave, determined, ambitious, resourceful, the tragic hero shows to what heights a human being can soar. This is an inspiration to the rest of us. After witnessing a tragedy we feel good, because the magnificence of the human spirit has been demonstrated.

The tragic view accepts responsibility but does not seek to cast blame. It challenges us to do, with caution, what needs to be done, and to consider at the same time the consequences of not acting. Florman's view is ultimately an affirmation of the value of technology in human life, tempered by a recognition of its limits in sustaining human happiness. It is a uniquely constructive approach to thinking about technology and society and a fitting note on which to close the first section of this book. Samuel C. Florman, author of The Existential Pleasures of Engineering, *is a practicing engineer and chairman of Kreisler Borg Florman Construction Company in Scarsdale, New York. His more than 100 articles dealing with the relationship of technology to general culture have appeared in professional journals and popular magazines. His new book,* The Aftermath: A Novel of Survival *(St. Martin's Press, 2001), is an adventure story set on Earth after a cataclysmic collision with a comet. Florman, born in New York City in 1925, is a fellow of the American Society of Civil Engineers and a member of the New York Academy of Sciences. He holds a bachelor's degree and a civil engineer's degree from Dartmouth College and an M.A. in English literature from Columbia University.*

The blaming of technology starts with the making of myths — most importantly, the myth of the technological imperative and the myth of the technocratic elite.

From *Blaming Technology: The Irrational Search for Scapegoats* by Samuel C. Florman. Copyright © 1981 by Samuel C. Florman. Reprinted with permission from Bedford/St. Martin's.

In spite of the injunctions of common sense, and contrary to the evidence at hand, the myths flourish.

False premises are followed by confused deductions — a maligning of the scientific view, the assertion that small is beautiful, the mistake about job enrichment, an excessive zeal for government regulation, the hostility of feminists toward engineering, and the wishful thinking of the Club of Rome. These, in turn, are followed by distracted rejoinders from the technological community, culminating in the bizarre exaltation of engineering ethics.

In all of this it is difficult to determine how much is simple misunderstanding and how much is willful evasion of the truth, a refusal to face up to the harsh realities that underlie life, not only in a technological age, but in every age since the beginning of civilization.

Out of the confusion has come a dialogue of sorts, shaped around views that are deemed "pro" technology or "anti," "optimistic" or "pessimistic." I believe that we should be thinking in different terms altogether.

House & Garden magazine, in celebration of the American Bicentennial, devoted its July 1976 issue to the topic "American Know-How." The editors invited me to contribute an article, and, enticed by the opportunity to address a new audience, plus the offer of a handsome fee, I accepted. We agreed that the title of my piece would be "Technology and the Human Adventure," and I thereupon embarked on a strange adventure of my own.

I thought that it would be appropriate to begin my Bicentennial-inspired essay with a discussion of technology in the time of the Founding Fathers, so I went to the library and immersed myself in the works of Benjamin Franklin, surely the most famous technologist of America's early days. Remembering stories from my childhood about Ben Franklin the clever tinkerer, I expected to find a pleasant recounting of inventions and successful experiments, a cheering tale of technological triumphs. I found such a tale, to be sure, but along with it I found a record of calamities caused by the technological advances of his day.

In several letters and essays, Franklin expressed concern about fire, an ever-threatening scourge in Colonial times. Efficient sawmills made it possible to build frame houses, more versatile and economical than log cabins — but less fire resistant. Advances in transport made it possible for people to crowd these frame houses together in cities. Cleverly conceived fireplaces, stoves, lamps, and warming pans made life more comfortable, but contributed to the likelihood of catastrophic fires in which many lives were lost.

To deal with this problem, Franklin recommended architectural modifications to make houses more fireproof. He proposed the licensing and supervision of chimney sweeps and the establishment of volunteer fire companies, well supplied and trained in the science of firefighting. As is well known, he invented the lightning rod. In other words, he proposed technological ways of coping with the unpleasant consequences of technology. He applied Yankee ingenuity to solve problems arising out of Yankee ingenuity.

In Franklin's writings I found other examples of technological advances that brought with them unanticipated problems. Lead poisoning was a peril. Contaminated rum was discovered coming from distilleries where lead parts had been substituted for wood in the distilling apparatus. Drinking water collected from lead-coated roofs was also making people seriously ill.

The advancing techniques of medical science were often a mixed blessing, as they are today. Early methods of vaccination for smallpox, for example, entailed the danger of the vaccinated person dying from the artificially induced disease. (In a particularly poignant article, Franklin was at pains to point out that his four-year-old son's death from smallpox was attributable to the boy's not having been vaccinated and did not result, as rumor had it, from the vaccination itself.)

After a while, I put aside the writings of Franklin and turned my attention to American know-how in the nineteenth century. I became engrossed in the story of the early days of steamboat transport. This important step forward in American technology was far from being the unsullied triumph that it appears to be in our popular histories.

Manufacturers of the earliest high-pressure steam engines often used materials of inferior quality. They were slow to recognize the weakening of boiler shells caused by rivet holes and the danger of using wrought-iron shells together with cast iron heads that had a different coefficient of expansion. Safety valve openings were often not properly proportioned, and gauges had a tendency to malfunction. Even well-designed equipment quickly became defective through the effects of corrosion and sediment. On top of it all, competition for prestige led to racing between boats, and, during a race, the usual practice was to tie down the safety valve so that excessive steam pressure would not be relieved.

From 1825 to 1830, 42 recorded explosions killed upward of 270 persons. When, in 1830, an explosion aboard the *Helen McGregor* near Memphis killed more than fifty passengers, public outrage forced the federal government to take action. Funds were granted to the Franklin Institute of Philadelphia to purchase apparatus needed to conduct experiments on steam boilers. This was a notable event: the first technological research grant made by the federal government.

The institute made a comprehensive report in 1838, but it was not until fourteen years later that a workable bill was passed by Congress providing at least minimal safeguards for the citizenry. Today, we may wonder why the process took so long, but at the time Congress was still uncertain about its right, under the interstate commerce provision of the Constitution, to control the activities of individual entrepreneurs.

When I turned from steamboats to railroads I found another long-forgotten story of catastrophe. Not only were there problems with the trains themselves, but the roadbeds, and particularly the bridges, made even the shortest train journey a hazardous adventure. In the late 1860s, more than twenty-five American bridges were collapsing each year, with appalling loss of life. In 1873, the American Society of Civil Engineers set up a special commission to address the problem, and eventually the safety of our bridges came to be taken for granted.

The more I researched the history of American know-how, the more I perceived that practically every technological advance had unexpected and unwanted side effects. Along with each triumph of mechanical genius came an inevitable portion of death and destruction. Instead of becoming discouraged, however, our forebears seemed to be resolute in confronting the adverse consequences of their own inventiveness. I was impressed by this pattern of progress/setback/renewed creative effort. It seemed to have a special message for our day, and I made it the theme of my essay for *House & Garden.*

No matter how many articles one has published, and no matter how much one likes the article most recently submitted, waiting to hear from an editor is an anxious experience. In this case, as it turned out, I had reason to be apprehensive. I soon heard from one of the editors who, although she tried to be encouraging, was obviously distressed. "We liked the part about tenacity and ingenuity," she said, "but, oh dear, all those disasters — They are so depressing."

I need not go into the details of what follows: the rewriting, the telephone conferences, the rewriting — the gradual elimination of accidents and casualty statistics and a subtle change in emphasis. I retreated, with some honor intact I like to believe, until the article was deemed to be suitably upbeat.

I should have known that the Bicentennial issue of *House & Garden* was not the forum in which to consider the dark complexities of technological change. My piece was to appear side by side with such articles as, "A House That Has Everything," "Live Longer, Look Younger," and "Everything's Coming Up Roses" (devoted to a review of Gloria Vanderbilt's latest designs).

In the United States today, magazines like *House & Garden* speak for those, and to those, who are optimistic about technology. Through technology we get better dishwashers, permanent-press blouses, and rust-proof lawn furniture. "Better living through chemistry," the old Du Pont commercial used to say. Not only is *House & Garden* optimistic, that is, hopeful, about technology, it is cheerfully optimistic. There is no room in its pages for failure, or even for struggle, and in this view it speaks for many Americans, perhaps a majority. This is the lesson I learned — or I should say, relearned — in the Bicentennial year.

Much has been written about the shallow optimism of the United States: about life viewed as a Horatio Alger success story or as a romantic movie with a happy ending. This optimism is less widespread than it used to be, particularly as it relates to technology. Talk of nuclear warfare and a poisoned environment tends to dampen one's enthusiasm. Yet, optimistic materialism remains a powerful force in American life. The poll-takers tell us that people believe technology is, on balance, beneficial. And we all know a lot of people who, even at this troublesome moment in history, define happiness in terms of their ability to accumulate new gadgets. The business community, anxious to sell merchandise, spares no expense in promoting a gleeful consumerism.

Side by side with what I have come to think of as *House & Garden* optimism, there is a mood that we might call *New York Review of Books* pessimism. Our intellectual journals are full of gloomy tracts that depict a society debased by technology. Our health is being ruined, according to this view, our landscape despoiled, and our social institutions laid waste. We are forced to do demeaning work and consume unwanted products. We are being dehumanized. This is happening because a technological demon has escaped from human control or, in a slightly different version, because evil technocrats are leading us astray.

It is clear that in recent years the resoluteness exhibited by Benjamin Franklin, and other Americans of similarly robust character, has been largely displaced by a foolish optimism on the one hand and an abject pessimism on the other. These two opposing outlooks are actually manifestations of the same defect in the American character. One is the obverse, the "flip side," of the other. Both reflect a flaw that I can best describe as immaturity.

A young child is optimistic, naively assuming that his needs can always be satisfied and that his parents have it within their power to "make things right." A child frustrated becomes petulant. With the onset of puberty a morose sense of disillusionment is apt to take hold. Sulky pessimism is something we associate with the teenager.

It is not surprising that many inhabitants of the United States, a rich nation with seemingly boundless frontiers, should have evinced a childish optimism and declared their faith in technology, endowing it with the reassuring power of a parent — also regarding it with the love of a child for a favorite toy. It then follows that technological setbacks would be greeted by some with the naive assumption that all would turn out for the best and by others with peevish declarations of despair. Intellectuals have been in the forefront of this childish display, but every segment of society has been caught up in it. Technologists themselves have not been immune. In the speeches of nineteenth-century engineers, we find bombastic promises that make us blush. Today, the profession is torn between a blustering optimism and a confused guilt.

The past fifty years have seen many hopes dashed, but we can see in retrospect that they were unrealistic hopes. We simply cannot make use of coal without killing miners and polluting the air. Neither can we manufacture solar panels without worker fatalities and environmental degradation. (We assume that it will be less than with coal, but we are not sure.) We cannot build highways or canals or airports without despoiling the landscape. Not only have we learned that environmental dangers are inherent in every technological advance, but we find that we are fated to be dissatisfied with much of what we produce because our tastes keep changing. The sparkling, humming, paved metropolises of science fiction — even if they could be realized — are not, after all, the home to which humankind aspires. It seems that many people find such an environment "alienating." There can never be a technologically based utopia because we discover belatedly that we cannot agree on what form that utopia might take.

To express our disillusionment, we have invented a new word: "trade-off." It is an ugly word, totally without grace, but it signifies, I believe, the beginning of maturity for American society.

It is important to remember that our disappointments have not been limited to technology. (This is a fact that the antitechnologists usually choose to ignore.) Wonderful dreams attended the birth of the New Deal, and later the founding of the United Nations, yet we have since awakened to face unyielding economic and political difficulties. Socialism has been discredited, as was *laissez-faire* capitalism before it. We have been bitterly disappointed by the labor movement, the educational establishment, efforts at crime prevention, the ministrations of psychiatry, and, most recently, by the abortive experiments of the so-called counterculture. We have come face to face with limits that we had presumed to hope might not exist.

Those of us who have lived through the past fifty years have passed personally from youthful presumptuousness to mature skepticism at the very moment that American society has been going through the same transition. We have to be careful not to define the popular mood in terms of our personal sentiments, but I do not think I am doing that when I observe the multiple disenchantments of our time. We also have to be careful not to deprecate youthful enthusiasm, which is a force for good, along with immaturity, which is tolerable only in the young.

It can be argued that there was for a while good reason to hold out hope for utopia, since modern science and technology appeared to be completely new factors in human existence. But now that they have been given a fair trial, we perceive their inherent limitations. The human condition is the human condition still.

To persist in saying that we are optimistic or pessimistic about technology is to acknowledge that we will not grow up.

I suggest that an appropriate response to our new wisdom is neither optimism nor pessimism, but rather the espousal of an attitude that has traditionally been associated with men and women of noble character — the tragic view of life.

As a student in high school, and later in college, I found it difficult to comprehend what my teachers told me about comedy and tragedy. Comedy, they said, expresses despair. When there is no hope, we make jokes. We depict people as puny, ridiculous creatures. We laugh to keep from crying.

Tragedy, on the other hand, is uplifting. It depicts heroes wrestling with fate. It is man's destiny to die, to be defeated by the forces of the universe. But in challenging his destiny, in being brave, determined, ambitious, resourceful, the tragic hero shows to what heights a human being can soar. This is an inspiration to the rest of us. After witnessing a tragedy, we feel good, because the magnificence of the human spirit has been demonstrated. Tragic drama is an affirmation of the value of life.

Students pay lip service to this theory and give the expected answers in examinations. But sometimes the idea seems to fly in the face of reason. How can we say we feel better after Oedipus puts out his eyes, or Othello kills his beloved wife and commits suicide, than we do after laughing heartily over a bedroom farce?

Yet, this concept, which is so hard to grasp in the classroom, where students are young and the environment is serene, rings true in the world where mature people wrestle with burdensome problems.

I do not intend to preach a message of stoicism. The tragic view is not to be confused with world-weary resignation. As Moses Hadas, a great classical scholar of a generation ago, wrote about the Greek tragedians, "Their gloom is not fatalistic pessimism but an adult confrontation of reality, and their emphasis is not on the grimness of life but on the capacity of great figures to adequate themselves to it."[1]

It is not an accident that tragic drama flourished in societies that were dynamic: Periclean Athens, Elizabethan England, and the France of Louis XIV. For tragedy speaks of ambition, effort, and unquenchable spirit. Technological creativity is one manifestation of this spirit, and it is only a dyspeptic antihumanist who can feel otherwise. Even the Greeks, who for a while placed technologists low on the social scale, recognized the glory of creative engineering. Prometheus is one of the quintessential tragic heroes. In viewing technology through a tragic prism, we are at once exalted by its accomplishments and sobered by its limitations. We thus ally ourselves with the spirit of great ages past.

The fate of Prometheus, as well as that of most tragic heroes, is associated with the concept of hubris, "overweening pride." Yet pride, which in drama invariably leads to a fall, is not considered sinful by the great tragedians. It is an essential element of humanity's greatness. It is what inspires heroes to confront the universe, to challenge the status quo. Prometheus defied Zeus and brought technological knowledge to the human race. Prometheus was a revolutionary. So were Gutenberg, Watt, Edison, and Ford. Technology is revolutionary. Therefore, hostility toward technology is antirevolutionary, which is to say it is reactionary. This charge is currently being leveled against environmentalists and other enemies of technology. Since antitechnologists are traditionally "liberal" in their attitudes, the idea that they are reactionary confronts us with a paradox.

The tragic view does not shrink from paradox; it teaches us to live with ambiguity. It is at once revolutionary and cautionary. Hubris, as revealed in tragic drama, is an essential element of creativity; it is also a tragic flaw that contributes to the failure of human enterprise. Without effort, however, and daring, we are nothing. Walter Kerr has spoken of "tragedy's commitment to freedom, to the unflinching exploration of the possible." "At the heart of tragedy," he writes, "feeding it energy, stands godlike man passionately desiring a state of affairs more perfect than any that now exists."[2]

This description of the tragic hero well serves, in my opinion, as a definition of the questing technologist.

An aspect of the tragic view that particularly appeals to me is its reluctance to place blame. Those people who hold pessimistic views about technology are forever reproaching others, if not individual engineers, then the "technocratic establishment," the "megastate," "the pentagon of power," or some equally amorphous entity. Everywhere they look they see evil intent.

There is evil in the world, of course, but most of our disappointments with technology come when decent people are trying to act constructively. "The essentially tragic fact," says Hegel, "is not so much the war of good with evil as the war of good with good."

Pesticides serve to keep millions of poor people from starving. To use pesticides is good; to oppose them when they create havoc in the food chain is also good. To drill for oil and to transport it across the oceans is good, since petroleum provides lifesaving chemicals and heat for homes. To prevent oil spills is also good. Nuclear energy is good, as is the attempt to eliminate radioactivity. To seek safety is a worthy goal, but in a world of limited resources, the pursuit of economy is also worthy. We are constantly accusing each other of villainy when we should be consulting together on how best to solve our common problems.

Although the tragic view shuns blame, it does not shirk responsibility. "The fault, dear Brutus, is not in our stars, but in ourselves. . . ." We are accountable for what we do or, more often, for what we neglect to do. The most shameful feature of the antitechnological creed is that it so often fails to consider the consequences of not taking action. The lives lost or wasted that might have been saved by exploiting our resources are the responsibility of those who counsel inaction. The tragic view is consistent with good citizenship. It advocates making the most of our opportunities; it challenges us to do the work that needs doing.

Life, it may be said, is not a play. Yet we are constantly talking about roles — role-playing, role models, and so forth. It is a primordial urge to want to play one's part. The outlook I advocate sees value in many different people playing many different parts. A vital society, like a meaningful drama, feeds on diversity. Each participant contributes to the body social: scientist, engineer, farmer, craftsman, laborer, politician, jurist, teacher, artist, merchant, entertainer. . . . The pro-growth industrialist and the environmentalist are both needed, and, in a strange way, they need each other.

Out of conflict comes resolution; out of variety comes health. This is the lesson of the natural world. It is the moral of ecological balance; it is also the moral of great drama. We cannot but admire Caesar, Brutus, and Antony all together. So should we applaud the guardians of our wilderness, even as we applaud the creators of dams and paper mills. I am a builder, but I feel for those who are afraid of building, and I admire those who want to endow all building with grace.

George Steiner, in *The Death of Tragedy* (1961), claimed that the tragic spirit was rendered impotent by Christianity's promise of salvation. But I do not think that most people today are thinking in terms of salvation. They are thinking of doing the best they can in a world that promises neither damnation nor transcendent victories, but instead confronts us with both perils and opportunities for achievement. In such a world, the tragic spirit is very much alive. Neither optimism nor pessimism is a worthy alternative to this noble spirit.

We use words to communicate, but sometimes they are not as precise as we pretend, and then we confuse ourselves and each other. "Optimism," "pessimism," "tragic view" — These are mere sounds or scratches on paper. The way we feel is not adequately defined by such sounds or scratches. René Dubos used to write a column for *The American Scholar* that he called "The Despairing Optimist." I seem to recall that he once gave his reasons for not calling it "The Hopeful Pessimist," although I cannot remember what they were. What really counts, I suppose, is not what we say, or even what we feel, but what we want to do.

By saying that I espouse the tragic view of technology I mean to ally myself with those who, aware of the dangers and without foolish illusions about what can be accomplished, still want to move on, actively seeking to realize our constantly changing vision of a more satisfactory society. I mean to oppose those who would evade harsh truths by intoning platitudes. I particularly mean to challenge those who enjoy the benefits of technology but refuse to accept responsibility for its consequences.

Earlier in this essay I mentioned the problems I encountered in preparing an article for *House & Garden*, and I would like to close by quoting the last few lines from that much-rewritten opus. The prose is somewhat florid, but please remember that it was written in celebration of the American Bicentennial:

For all our apprehensions, we have no choice but to press ahead. We must do so, first, in the name of compassion. By turning our backs on technological change, we would be expressing our satisfaction with current world levels of hunger, disease, and privation. Further, we must press ahead in the name of human adventure. Without experimentation and change our existence would be a dull business. We simply cannot stop while there are masses to feed and diseases to conquer, seas to explore and heavens to survey.

The editors of *Home & Garden* thought I was being optimistic. I knew that I was being tragic, but I did not argue the point.

NOTES

1. Moses Hadas, *A History of Greek Literature* (New York: Columbia University Press, 1950), p. 75.
2. Walter Kerr, *Tragedy and Comedy* (New York: Simon & Schuster, 1967), p. 107.

PART II
DEBATING TECHNOLOGY: 1960S STYLE

Chapter 6, Emmanuel Mesthene's essay, "The Role of Technology in Society," and the piece that follows it, "Technology: The Opiate of the Intellectuals" by John McDermott (Chapter 7), constitute a classic debate about the role of technology in society. The articles date from the late 1960s, when the war in Vietnam was in full swing and intellectual and political life in the United States was torn by bitter conflicts between the "establishment" and the "New Left."

The two articles are included here, as they have been in every edition of *Technology and the Future* since 1972, as a means of illustrating in sharp relief the different perspectives on technology of the powerful and powerless. Mesthene, a Harvard professor and former RAND Corporation analyst, funded by a large grant from IBM, is comfortable with technology. He and his colleagues feel that technology is something that they can control and use. It is a neutral tool which can be employed for purposes that are good as well as those that are evil and which often has both positive and negative effects on society.

McDermott, on the other hand, sees technology from the lower rungs of society's ladder. A professor of labor studies writing in the then-radical left *New York Review of Books,* his viewpoint is that of the factory worker struggling to make ends meet rather than the highly paid industry executive. He is the foot soldier slogging through the jungles of Vietnam in a war whose purpose he doesn't understand, rather than the systems analyst comfortably ensconced in the Pentagon or in RAND's Santa Monica headquarters. Technology, seen from McDermott's side of the fence, is hardly a neutral tool; it is the means by which those in power maintain their control of society while perpetuating social injustice.

Some of the illustrations the authors use in these two essays — which were instantly recognizable and conjured up clear images to readers of their day — may be unfamiliar to today's college students. But the issues they raise and the differing perspectives on technology of the rulers and the ruled are as important today as they were three decades ago.

6.   The Role of Technology in Society

EMMANUEL G. MESTHENE

Emmanuel Mesthene's essay, "The Role of Technology in Society," originated as the overview section of the fourth annual report of the Harvard Program on Technology and Society, an interdisciplinary program of academic studies funded by a $5 million grant from IBM. Mesthene was the program's director, and this essay was his general statement of what the program had learned, during its first four years, about the implications of technological change for society.

According to Mesthene, technology appears to induce social change in two ways: by creating new opportunities and by generating new problems for individuals and for societies. "It has both positive and negative effects, and it usually has the two at the same time and in virtue of each other." By enlarging the realm of goal choice, or by altering the relative costs associated with different values, technology can induce value change. In all areas, technology is seen to have two faces, one positive and one negative.

Emmanuel G. Mesthene directed the Harvard Program on Technology and Society from 1964 through 1974, following eleven years with the Rand Corporation. He joined Rutgers University in 1974, serving as dean of Livingston College for several years, then as distinguished professor of philosophy and professor of management. Mesthene died in 1990. Among his books are Technological Change: Its Impact on Man and Society *(1970) and* How Language Makes Us Know *(1964).*

SOCIAL CHANGE

Three Unhelpful Views about Technology

While a good deal of research is aimed at discerning the particular effects of technological change on industry, government, or education, systematic inquiry devoted to seeing these effects together and to assessing their implications for contemporary society as a whole is relatively recent and does not enjoy the strong methodology and richness of theory and data that mark more established fields of scholarship. It therefore often has to contend with facile or one-dimensional views about what technology means for society. Three such views, which are prevalent at the present time, may be mildly caricatured somewhat as follows.

The first holds that technology is an unalloyed blessing for man and society. Technology is seen as the motor of all progress, as holding the solution to most of our social problems, as helping to liberate the individual from the clutches of a

From *Technology and Culture* 10:4 (1969), p. 489–536, © Society for the History of Technology. Reprinted with permission of The Johns Hopkins University Press.

complex and highly organized society, and as the source of permanent prosperity; in short, as the promise of utopia in our time. This view has its modern origins in the social philosophies of such nineteenth-century thinkers as Saint Simon, Karl Marx, and Auguste Comte. It tends to be held by many scientists and engineers, by many military leaders and aerospace industrialists, by people who believe that man is fully in command of his tools and his destiny, and by many of the devotees of modern techniques of "scientific management."

A second view holds that technology is an unmitigated curse. Technology is said to rob people of their jobs, their privacy, their participation in democratic government, and even, in the end, their dignity as human beings. It is seen as autonomous and uncontrollable, as fostering materialistic values and as destructive of religion, as bringing about a technocratic society and bureaucratic state in which the individual is increasingly submerged, and as threatening, ultimately, to poison nature and blow up the world. This view is akin to historical "back-to-nature" attitudes toward the world and is propounded mainly by artists, literary commentators, popular social critics, and existentialist philosophers. It is becoming increasingly attractive to many of our youth, and it tends to be held, understandably enough, by segments of the population that have suffered dislocation as a result of technological change.

The third view is of a different sort. It argues that technology as such is not worthy of special notice, because it has been well recognized as a factor in social change at least since the Industrial Revolution, because it is unlikely that the social effects of computers will be nearly so traumatic as the introduction of the factory system in eighteenth-century England, because research has shown that technology has done little to accelerate the rate of economic productivity since the 1880s, because there has been no significant change in recent decades in the time periods between invention and widespread adoption of new technology, and because improved communications and higher levels of education make people much more adaptable than heretofore to new ideas and to new social reforms required by technology.

While this view is supported by a good deal of empirical evidence, however, it tends to ignore a number of social, cultural, psychological, and political effects of technological change that are less easy to identify with precision. It thus reflects the difficulty of coming to grips with a new or broadened subject matter by means of concepts and intellectual categories designed to deal with older and different subject matters. This view tends to be held by historians, for whom continuity is an indispensable methodological assumption, and by many economists, who find that their instruments measure some things quite well while those of the other social sciences do not yet measure much of anything.

Stripped of caricature, each of these views contains a measure of truth and reflects a real aspect of the relationship of technology and society. Yet they are oversimplifications that do not contribute much to understanding. One can find empirical evidence to support each of them without gaining much knowledge about the actual mechanism by which technology leads to social change or significant insight into its implications for the future. All three remain too uncritical or too partial to guide inquiry. Research and analysis lead to more differentiated conclusions and reveal more subtle relationships.

* * *

How Technological Change Impinges on Society

It is clearly possible to sketch a more adequate hypothesis about the interaction of technology and society than the partial views outlined [here]. Technological change would appear to induce or "motor" social change in two principal ways. New technology creates new opportunities for men and societies, and it also generates new problems for them. It has both positive and negative effects, and it usually has the two at the same time and in virtue of each other. Thus, industrial technology strengthens the economy, as our measures of growth and productivity show. . . . However, it also induces changes in the relative importance of individual supplying sectors in the economy as new techniques of production alter the amounts and kinds of materials, parts and components, energy, and service inputs used by each industry to produce its output. It thus tends to bring about dislocations of businesses and people as a result of changes in industrial patterns and in the structure of occupations.

The close relationship between technological and social change itself helps to explain why any given technological development is likely to have both positive and negative effects. The usual sequence is that (1) technological advance creates a new opportunity to achieve some desired goal; (2) this requires (except in trivial cases) alterations in social organization if advantage is to be taken of the new opportunity; (3) which means that the functions of existing social structures will be interfered with; (4) with the result that other goals, which were served by the older structures, are now only inadequately achieved.

As the Meyer–Kain[1] study has shown, for example, improved transportation technology and increased ownership of private automobiles have increased the mobility of businesses and individuals. This has led to altered patterns of industrial and residential location, so that older unified cities are being increasingly transformed into larger metropolitan complexes. The new opportunities for mobility are largely denied to the poor and black populations of the core cities, however, partly for economic reasons, and partly as a result of restrictions on choice of residence by blacks, thus leading to persistent black unemployment despite a generally high level of economic activity. Cities are thus increasingly unable to perform their traditional functions of providing employment opportunities for all segments of their populations and an integrated social environment that can temper ethnic and racial differences. The new urban complexes are neither fully viable economic units nor effective political organizations able to upgrade and integrate their core populations into new economic and social structures. The resulting instability is further aggravated by modern mass communications technology, which heightens the expectations of the poor and the fears of the well-to-do and adds frustration and bitterness to the urban crisis. . . .

In all such cases, technology creates a new opportunity and a new problem at the same time. That is why isolating the opportunity or the problem and construing it as the whole answer is ultimately obstructive of, rather than helpful to, understanding.

How Society Reacts to Technological Change

The heightened prominence of technology in our society makes the interrelated tasks of profiting from its opportunities and containing its dangers a major intellectual and political challenge of our time.

Failure of society to respond to the opportunities created by new technology means that much actual or potential technology lies fallow, that is, is not used at all or is not used to its full capacity. This can mean that potentially solvable problems are left unsolved and potentially achievable goals unachieved, because we waste our technological resources or use them inefficiently. A society has at least as much stake in the efficient utilization of technology as in that of its natural or human resources.

There are often good reasons, of course, for not developing or utilizing a particular technology. The mere fact that it can be developed is not sufficient reason for doing so. . . .

But there are also cases where technology lies fallow because existing social structures are inadequate to exploit the opportunities it offers. . . . Community institutions wither for want of interest and participation by residents. City agencies are unable to marshal the skills and take the systematic approach needed to deal with new and intensified problems of education, crime control, and public welfare. Business corporations, finally, which are organized around the expectation of private profit, are insufficiently motivated to bring new technology and management know-how to bear on urban projects where the benefits will be largely social. All these factors combine to dilute what may otherwise be a genuine desire to apply our best knowledge and adequate resources to the resolution of urban tensions and the eradication of poverty in the nation. . . .

Containing the Negative Effects of Technology

The kinds and magnitude of the negative effects of technology are no more independent of the institutional structures and cultural attitudes of society than is realization of the new opportunities that technology offers. In our society, there are individuals or individual firms always on the lookout for new technological opportunities, and large corporations hire scientists and engineers to invent such opportunities. In deciding whether to develop a new technology, individual entrepreneurs engage in calculations of expected benefits and expected costs to themselves and proceed if the former are likely to exceed the latter. Their calculations do not take adequate account of the probable benefits and costs of the new developments to others than themselves or to society generally. These latter are what economists call external benefits and costs.

The external benefits potential in new technology will thus not be realized by the individual developer and will rather accrue to society as a result of deliberate social action, as has been argued above. Similarly with the external costs. In minimizing only expected costs to himself, the individual decision-maker helps to contain only some of the potentially negative effects of the new technology. The external costs and therefore the negative effects on society at large are not of principal concern to him and, in our society, are not expected to be.

Most of the consequences of technology that are causing concern at the present time — pollution of the environment, potential damage to the ecology of the planet, occupational and social dislocations, threats to the privacy and political significance of the individual, social and psychological malaise — are negative externalities of this kind. They are with us in large measure because it has not been anybody's explicit business to foresee and anticipate them. They have fallen between the stools of innumerable individual decisions to develop individual technologies for individual purposes without explicit attention to what all these decisions add up to for society as a whole and for people as human beings. This freedom of individual decision making is a value that we have cherished and that is built into the institutional fabric of our society. The negative effects of technology that we deplore are a measure of what this traditional freedom is beginning to cost us. They are traceable, less to some mystical autonomy presumed to lie in technology, and much more to the autonomy that our economic and political institutions grant to individual decision making. . . .

Measures to control and mitigate the negative effects of technology, however, often appear to threaten freedoms that our traditions still take for granted as inalienable rights of men and good societies, however much they may have been tempered in practice by the social pressures of modern times; the freedom of the market, the freedom of private enterprise, the freedom of the scientist to follow truth wherever it may lead, and the freedom of the individual to pursue his fortune and decide his fate. There is thus set up a tension between the need to control technology and our wish to preserve our values, which leads some people to conclude that technology is inherently inimical to human values. The political effect of this tension takes the form of inability to adjust our decision-making structures to the realities of technology so as to take maximum advantage of the opportunities it offers and so that we can act to contain its potential ill effects before they become so pervasive and urgent as to seem uncontrollable.

To understand why such tensions are so prominent a social consequence of technological change, it becomes necessary to look explicitly at the effects of technology on social and individual values.

VALUES

* * *

Technology as a Cause of Value Change

Technology has a direct impact on values by virtue of its capacity for creating new opportunities. By making possible what was not possible before, it offers individuals and society new options to choose from. For example, space technology makes it possible for the first time to go to the moon or to communicate by satellite and thereby adds those two new options to the spectrum of choices available to society. By adding new options in this way, technology can lead to changes in values in the same way that the appearance of new dishes on the heretofore standard menu of one's favorite restaurant can lead to changes in one's tastes and choices of food. Specifically, technology can lead to value change either (1) by bringing some previously unattainable goal within the realm of choice or (2) by making some values easier to implement than heretofore, that is, by changing the costs associated with realizing them. . . .

One example related to the effect of technological change on values is implicit in our concept of democracy. The ideal we associate with the old New England town meeting is that each citizen should have a direct voice in political decisions. Since this has not been possible, we have elected representatives to serve our interests and vote our opinions. Sophisticated computer technology, however, now makes possible rapid and efficient collection and analysis of voter opinion and could eventually provide for "instant voting" by the whole electorate on any issue presented to it via television a few hours before. It thus raises the possibility of instituting a system of direct democracy and gives rise to tensions between those who would be violently opposed to such a prospect and those who are already advocating some system of participatory democracy.

This new technological possibility challenges us to clarify what we mean by democracy. Do we construe it as the will of an undifferentiated majority, as the resultant of transient coalitions of different interest groups representing different value commitments, as the considered judgment of the people's elected representatives, or as by and large the kind of government we actually have in the United States, minus the flaws in it that we would like to correct? By bringing us face to face with such questions, technology has the effect of calling society's bluff and thereby preparing the ground for changes in its values.

In the case where technological change alters the relative costs of implementing different values, it impinges on inherent contradictions in our value system. To pursue the same example, modern technology can enhance the values we associate with democracy. But it can also enhance another American value — that of "secular rationality," as sociologists call it — by facilitating the use of scientific and technical expertise in the process of political decision making. This can in turn further reduce citizen participation in the democratic process. Technology thus has the effect of facing us with contradictions in our value system and of calling for deliberate attention to their resolution.

* * *

ECONOMIC AND POLITICAL ORGANIZATION

The Enlarged Scope of Public Decision Making

When technology brings about social changes (as described in the first section of this essay) that impinge on our existing system of values (in ways reviewed in the second section), it poses for society a number of problems that are ultimately political in nature. The term "political" is used here in the broadest sense: It encompasses all of the decision-making structures and procedures that have to do with the allocation and distribution of wealth and power in society. The political organization of society thus includes not only the formal apparatus of the state but also industrial organizations and other private institutions that play a role in the decision-making process. It is particularly important to attend to the organization of the entire body politic when technological change leads to a blurring of once-clear distinctions between the public and private sectors of society and to changes in the roles of its principal institutions.

It was suggested above that the political requirements of our modern technological society call for a relatively greater public commitment on the part of individuals than in previous times. The reason for this, stated most generally, is that technological change has the effect of enhancing the importance of public decision making in society, because technology is continually creating new possibilities for social action as well as new problems that have to be dealt with.

A society that undertakes to foster technology on a large scale, in fact, commits itself to social complexity and to facing and dealing with new problems as a normal feature of political life. Not much is yet known with any precision about the political imperatives inherent in technological change, but one may nevertheless speculate about the reasons why an increasingly technological society seems to be characterized by enlargement of the scope of public decision making.

For one thing, the development and application of technology seems to require large-scale, and hence increasingly complex, social concentrations, whether these be large cities, large corporations, big universities, or big government. In instances where technological advance appears to facilitate reduction of such first-order concentrations, it tends to instead enlarge the relevant system of social organization, that is, to lead to increased centralization. Thus, the physical dispersion made possible by transportation and communications technologies, as Meyer and Kain have shown, enlarges the urban complex that must be governed as a unit.

A second characteristic of advanced technology is that its effects cover large distances, in both the geographical and social senses of the term. Both its positive and negative features are more extensive. Horse-powered transportation technology was limited in its speed and capacity, but its nuisance value was also limited, in most cases to the owner and to the occupant of the next farm. The supersonic transport can carry hundreds across long distances in minutes, but its noise and vibration damage must also be suffered willy-nilly by everyone within the limits of a swath 3,000 miles long and several miles wide.

The concatenation of increased density (or enlarged system) and extended technological "distance" means that technological applications have increasingly wider ramifications and that increasingly large concentrations of people and organizations become dependent on technological systems. . . . The result is not only that more and more decisions must be social decisions taken in public ways, as already noted, but that, once made, decisions are likely to have a shorter useful life than heretofore. That is partly because technology is continually altering the spectrum of choices and problems that society faces, and partly because any decision taken is likely to generate a need to take ten more.

These speculations about the effects of technology on public decision making raise the problem of restructuring our decision-making mechanisms — including the system of market incentives — so that the increasing number and importance of social issues that confront us can be resolved equitably and effectively.

* * *

The Promise and Problems of Scientific Decision Making

There are two further consequences of the expanding role of public decision making. The first is that the latest information-handling devices and techniques tend to be utilized in the decision-making process. This is so (1) because public policy can be effective only to the degree that it is based on reliable knowledge about the actual state of the society, and thus requires a strong capability to collect, aggregate, and analyze detailed data about economic activities, social patterns, popular attitudes, and political trends, and (2) because it is recognized increasingly that decisions taken in one area impinge on and have consequences for other policy areas often thought of as unrelated, so that it becomes necessary to base decisions on a model of society that sees it as a system and that it is capable of signaling as many as possible of the probable consequences of a contemplated action.

As Professor Alan F. Westin points out, reactions to the prospect of more decision making based on computerized data banks and scientific management techniques run the gamut of optimism to pessimism mentioned in the opening of this essay. Negative reactions take the form of rising political demands for greater popular participation in decision making, for more equality among different segments of the population, and for greater regard for the dignity of individuals. The increasing dependence of decision making on scientific and technological devices and techniques is seen as posing a threat to these goals, and pressures are generated in opposition to further "rationalization" of decision-making processes. These pressures have the paradoxical effect, however, not of deflecting the supporters of technological decision making from their course, but of spurring them on to renewed effort to save the society before it explodes under planlessness and inadequate administration

The paradox goes further and helps to explain much of the social discontent that we are witnessing at the present time. The greater complexity and the more extensive ramifications that technology brings about in society tend to make social processes increasingly circuitous and indirect. The effects of actions are widespread and difficult to keep track of, so that experts and sophisticated techniques are increasingly needed to detect and analyze social events and to formulate policies adequate to the complexity of social issues. The "logic" of modern decision making thus appears to require greater and greater dependence on the collection and analysis of data and on the use of technological devices and scientific techniques. Indeed, many observers would agree that there is an "increasing relegation of questions which used to be matters of political debate to professional cadres of technicians and experts which function almost independently of the democratic political process."[2] In recent times, that process has been most noticeable, perhaps, in the areas of economic policy and national security affairs.

This "logic" of modern decision making, however, runs counter to that element of traditional democratic theory that places high value on direct participation in the political processes and generates the kind of discontent referred to above. If it turns out on more careful examination that direct participation is becoming less relevant to a society in which the connections between causes and effects are long and often hidden — which is an increasingly "indirect" society, in other words — elaboration of a new democratic ethos and of new democratic processes more adequate to the realities of modern society will emerge as perhaps the major intellectual and political challenge of our time.

The Need for Institutional Innovation

The challenge is, indeed, already upon us, for the second consequence of the enlarged scope of public decision making is the need to develop new institutional forms and new mechanisms to replace established ones that can no longer deal effectively with the new kinds of problems with which we are increasingly faced. Much of the political ferment of the present time — over the problems of technology assessment, the introduction of statistical data banks, the extension to domestic problems of techniques of analysis developed for the military services, and the modification of the institutions of local government — is evidence of the need for new institutions. . . .

CONCLUSION

As we review what we are learning about the relationship of technological and social change, a number of conclusions begin to emerge. We find, on the one hand, that the creation of new physical possibilities and social options by technology tends toward, and appears to require the emergence of, new values, new forms of economic activity, and new political organizations. On the other hand, technological change also poses problems of social and psychological displacement.

The two phenomena are not unconnected, nor is the tension between them new: Man's technical prowess always seems to run ahead of his ability to deal with and profit from it. In America, especially, we are becoming adept at extracting the new techniques, the physical power, and the economic productivity that are inherent in our knowledge and its associated technologies. Yet we have not fully accepted the fact that our progress in the technical realm does not leave our institutions, values, and political processes unaffected. Individuals will be fully integrated into society only when we can extract from our knowledge not only its technological potential but also its implications for a system of values and a social, economic, and political organization appropriate to a society in which technology is so prevalent. . . .

NOTES

1. Unless otherwise noted, studies referred to in this article are described in the *Fourth Annual Report (1967–68) of the Harvard University Program on Technology and Society.*
2. Harvey Brooks, "Scientific Concepts and Cultural Changes," in G. Holton, ed., *Science and Culture* (Boston: Houghton Mifflin, 1965), p. 71.

7. Technology: The Opiate
of the Intellectuals

JOHN MCDERMOTT

Several months after the report containing Emmanuel Mesthene's article was pub-
lished by Harvard, a sharply critical review–essay by John McDermott appeared in
The New York Review of Books. *McDermott's piece, which follows here, is not*
a point-by-point analysis or rebuttal of the Mesthene work. Rather, it is McDer-
mott's attempt to critique the entire point of view that he sees as epitomized by Mes-
thene — "not of a new but of a newly aggressive right-wing ideology in this
country." McDermott focuses on a notion he calls laissez innover, *which holds*
that technology is a self-correcting system. Mesthene, he claims, finds this principle
acceptable because he defines technology abstractly. McDermott himself, however,
rejects laissez innover *because he claims to see specific characteristics in contem-*
porary technology that contradict the abstraction.

Concentrating on the application of technology to the war in Vietnam, McDer-
mott examines its nature and concludes that "technology, in its concrete, empirical
meaning, refers fundamentally to systems of rationalized control over large groups
of men, events, and machines by small groups of technically skilled men operating
through organized hierarchy." Using this definition, he proceeds to discuss the social
effect of modern technology in America, concluding that the ideology of laissez
innover *is attractive to those in power since they are in a position to reap technol-*
ogy's benefits while avoiding its costs.

John McDermott has served on the faculty of the State University of New York
at Old Westbury in the Department of Labor Studies.

I

. . . If religion was formerly the opiate of the masses, then surely technology is the
opiate of the educated public today, or at least of its favorite authors. No other
single subject is so universally invested with high hopes for the improvement of
mankind generally and of Americans in particular. . . .

These hopes for mankind's, or technology's, future, however, are not unalloyed. Technology's defenders, being otherwise reasonable men, are also aware
that the world population explosion and the nuclear missile race are also the fruit
of the enormous advances made in technology during the past half-century or so.
But here, too, a cursory reading of their literature would reveal widespread
though qualified optimism that these scourges, too, will fall before technology's

might. Thus, population (and genetic) control and permanent peace are sometimes added to the already imposing roster of technology's promises. What are we
to make of such extravagant optimism?

[In early 1968], Harvard University's Program on Technology and Society . . .
issued its Fourth Annual Report to the accompaniment of full front-page coverage in *The New York Times* (January 18). Within the brief (fewer than 100) pages
of that report, and most clearly in the concluding essay by the Program's director,
Emmanuel G. Mesthene, one can discern some of the important threads of belief
that bind together much current writing on the social implications of technology.
Mesthene's essay is worth extended analysis, because these beliefs are of interest
in themselves and, of greater importance, because they form the basis not of a
new but of a newly aggressive right-wing ideology in this country, an ideology
whose growing importance was accurately measured by the magnitude of the
Times's news report.

. . . Mesthene believes there are two distinct problems in technology's relation
to society, a positive one of taking full advantage of the opportunity it offers and
the negative one of avoiding unfortunate consequences that flow from the
exploitation of those opportunities. Positive opportunities may be missed because
the costs of technological development outweigh likely benefits (e.g., Herman
Kahn's "Doomsday Machine"). Mesthene seems convinced, however, that a
more important case is that in which

> . . . technology lies fallow because existing social structures are inadequate to
> exploit the opportunities it offers. This is revealed clearly in the examination of
> institutional failure in the ghetto carried on by [the Program]. . . .

His diagnosis of these problems is generous in the extreme:

> All these factors combine to dilute what may be otherwise a genuine desire to
> apply our best knowledge and adequate resources to the resolution of urban
> tensions and the eradication of poverty in the nation.

Moreover, because government and the media ". . . are not yet equipped for the
massive task of public education that is needed . . .," if we are to exploit technology more fully, many technological opportunities are lost because of the lack of
public support. This, too, is a problem primarily of "institutional innovation."

Mesthene believes that institutional innovation is no less important in com-
bating the negative effects of technology. Individuals or individual firms that
decide to develop new technologies normally do not take "adequate account" of
their likely social benefits or costs. His critique is anticapitalist in spirit, but lacks
bite, for he goes on to add that

> . . . [most of the negative] consequences of technology that are causing con-
> cern at the present time — pollution of the environment, potential damage to
> the ecology of the planet, occupational and social dislocations, threats to the
> privacy and political significance of the individual, social and psychological
> malaise — are *negative externalities of this kind.* They are with us in large mea-
> sure because it has not been anybody's explicit business to foresee and antici-
> pate them. [Italics added.]

Mesthene's abstract analysis and its equally abstract diagnosis in favor of "institutional innovation" place him in a curious and, for us, instructive position. If existing social structures are inadequate to exploit technology's full potential, or if, on the other hand, so-called negative externalities assail us because it is nobody's business to foresee and anticipate them, doesn't this say that we should apply technology to this problem, too? That is, we ought to apply and organize the appropriate *organizational* knowledge for the practical purpose of solving the problems of institutional inadequacy and "negative externalities." Hence, in principle, Mesthene is in the position of arguing that the cure for technology's problems, whether positive or negative, is still more technology. This is the first theme of the technological school of writers and its ultimate First Principle.

Technology, in their view, is a self-correcting system. Temporary oversight or "negative externalities" will and should be corrected by technological means. Attempts to restrict the free play of technological innovation are, in the nature of the case, self-defeating. Technological innovation exhibits a distinct tendency to work for the general welfare in the long run. *Laissez innover!*

I have so far deliberately refrained from going into any greater detail than does Mesthene on the empirical character of contemporary technology, for it is important to bring out the force of the principle of *laissez innover* in its full generality. Many writers on technology appear to deny in their definition of the subject — organized knowledge for practical purposes — that contemporary technology exhibits distinct trends, which can be identified or projected. Others, like Mesthene, appear to accept these trends, but then blunt the conclusion by attributing to technology so much flexibility and "scientific" purity that it becomes an abstraction infinitely malleable in behalf of good, pacific, just, and egalitarian purposes. Thus, the analogy to the *laissez-faire* principle of another time is quite justified. Just as the market or the free play of competition provided in theory the optimum long-run solution for virtually every aspect of virtually every social and economic problem, so too does the free play of technology, according to its writers. Only if technology or innovation (or some other synonym) is allowed the freest possible reign, they believe, will the maximum social good be realized.

What reasons do they give to believe that the principle of *laissez innover* will normally function for the benefit of humankind rather than, say, merely for the belief of the immediate practitioners of technology, their managerial cronies, and for the profits accruing to their corporations? As Mesthene and other writers of his school are aware, this is a very real problem, for they all believe that the normal tendency of technology is, and ought to be, the increasing concentration of decision-making power in the hands of larger and larger scientific-technical bureaucracies. *In principle*, their solution is relatively simple, though not often explicitly stated.[1]

Their argument goes as follows: The men and women who are elevated by technology into commanding positions within various decision-making bureaucracies exhibit no generalized drive for power such as characterized by, say, the landed gentry of preindustrial Europe or the capitalist entrepreneur of the last century. For their social and institutional position and its supporting culture as well are defined solely by the fact that these men are problem-solvers. (Organized knowledge for practical purposes again.) That is, they gain advantage and reward only to the extent that they can bring specific technical knowledge to bear on the solution of specific technical problems. Any more general drive for power would undercut the bases of their usefulness and legitimacy.

Moreover, their specific training and professional commitment to solving technical problems creates a bias against ideologies in general, which inhibits any attempts to formulate a justifying ideology for the group. Consequently, they do not constitute a class and have no general interests antagonistic to those of their problem-beset clients. We may refer to all of this as the disinterested character of the scientific-technical decision-maker, or, more briefly and cynically, as the principle of the Altruistic Bureaucrat. . . .

This combination of guileless optimism with scientific tough-mindedness might seem to be no more than an eccentric delusion were the American technology it supports not moving in directions that are strongly antidemocratic. To show why this is so, we must examine more closely Mesthene's seemingly innocuous distinction between technology's positive opportunities and its "negative externalities." In order to do this, I will make use of an example drawn from the very frontier of American technology: the war in Vietnam.

II

* * *

Advanced technological systems such as those employed in the bombardment of South Vietnam make use not only of extremely complex and expensive equipment but, quite as important, of large numbers of relatively scarce and expensive-to-train technicians. They have immense capital costs: a thousand aircraft of a very advanced type; literally hundreds of thousands of spare parts; enormous stocks of rockets, bombs, shells, and bullets; in addition to tens of thousands of technical specialists — pilots, bombardiers, navigators, radar operators, computer programmers, accountants, engineers, electronic and mechanical technicians, to name only a few. In short, they are "capital intensive."

Moreover, the coordination of this immense mass of esoteric equipment and its operators in the most effective possible way depends upon an extremely highly developed technique both in the employment of each piece of equipment by a specific team of operators and in the management of the program itself. Of course, all large organizations standardize their operating procedures, but it is peculiar to advanced technological systems that their operating procedures embody a very high degree of information drawn from the physical sciences, while their managerial procedures are equally dependent on information drawn from the social sciences. We may describe this situation by saying that advanced technological systems are both "technique intensive" and "management intensive."

It should be clear, moreover, even to the most casual observer, that such intensive use of capital, technique, and management spills over into almost every area touched by the technological system in question. An attack program delivering

330,000 tons of munitions more or less selectively to several thousand different targets monthly would be an anomaly if forced to rely on sporadic intelligence data, erratic maintenance systems, or a fluctuating and unpredictable supply of heavy bombs, rockets, jet fuel, and napalm tanks. Thus, it is precisely because the bombing program requires an intensive use of capital, technique, and management that the same properties are normally transferred to the intelligence, maintenance, supply, coordination, and training systems that support it. Accordingly, each of these supporting systems is subject to sharp pressures to improve and rationalize the performance of its machines and men, the reliability of its techniques, and the efficiency and sensitivity of the management controls under which it operates. Within integrated technical systems, higher levels of technology drive out lower, and the normal tendency is to integrate systems.

From this perverse Gresham's Law of Technology follow some of the main social and organizational characteristics of contemporary technological systems: the radical increase in the scale and complexity of operations that they demand and encourage; the rapid and widespread diffusion of technology to new areas; the great diversity of activities that can be directed by central management; an increase in the ambition of management's goals; and, as a corollary, especially to the last, growing resistance to the influence of so-called negative externalities.

Complex technological systems are extraordinarily resistant to intervention by persons or problems operating outside or below their managing groups, and this is so regardless of the "politics" of a given situation. Technology creates its own politics. The point of such advanced systems is to minimize the incidence of personal or social behavior that is erratic or otherwise not easily classified, of tools and equipment with poor performance, of improvisory techniques, and of unresponsiveness to central management. . . .

To define technology so abstractly that it obscures these observable characteristics of contemporary technology — as Mesthene and his school have done — makes no sense. It makes even less sense to claim some magical malleability for something as undefined as "institutional innovation." Technology, in its concrete, empirical meaning, refers fundamentally to systems of rationalized control over large groups of men, events, and machines by small groups of technically skilled men operating through organizational hierarchy. The latent "opportunities" provided by that control and its ability to filter out discordant "negative externalities" are, of course, best illustrated by extreme cases. Hence, the most instructive and accurate example should be of a technology able to suppress the humanity of its rank-and-file and to commit genocide as a by-product of its rationality. The Vietnam bombing program fits technology to a "T."

* * *

IV

Among the conventional explanations for the rise and spread of the democratic ethos in Europe and North America in the seventeenth, eighteenth, and nineteenth centuries, the destruction of the gap in political culture between the mass of the population and that of the ruling classes is extremely important. . . .

Similarly, it is often argued that with the expansion and improvement of road and postal systems, the spread of new tools and techniques, the growth in the number and variety of merchants, the consequent invigoration of town life, and other numerous and familiar related developments, the social experience of larger numbers of people became richer, more varied, and similar in fact to those of the ruling class. . . .

The same period also witnessed a growth in the organized means of popular expression. . . .

This description by no means does justice to the richness and variety of the historical process underlying the rise and spread of what has come to be called the democratic ethos. But it does, I hope, isolate some of the important structural elements and, moreover, it enables us to illuminate some important ways in which the new technology, celebrated by Mesthene and his associates for its potential contributions to democracy, contributes instead to the erosion of that same democratic ethos. For if, in an earlier time, the gap between the political cultures of the higher and lower orders of society was being widely attacked and closed, this no longer appears to be the case. On the contrary, I am persuaded that the direction has been reversed and that we now observe evidence of a growing separation between ruling- and lower-class culture in America, a separation that is particularly enhanced by the rapid growth of technology and the spreading influence of its *laissez innover* ideologues.

Certainly, there has been a decline in popular literacy, that is to say, in those aspects of literacy that bear on an understanding of the political and social character of the new technology. Not one person in a hundred is even aware of, much less understands, the nature of technologically highly advanced systems such as are used in the Vietnam bombing program. . . .

Secondly, the social organization of this new technology, by systematically denying to the general population experiences that are analogous to those of its higher management, contributes very heavily to the growth of social irrationality in our society. For example, modern technological organization defines the roles and values of its members, not vice versa. An engineer or a sociologist is one who does all those things but only those things called for by the "table of organization" and the "job description" used by his employer. Professionals who seek self-realization through creative and autonomous behavior without regard to the defined goals, needs, and channels of their respective departments have no more place in a large corporation or government agency than squeamish soldiers in the army. . . .

However, those at the top of technology's most advanced organizations hardly suffer the same experience. For reasons that are clearly related to the principle of the Altruistic Bureaucracy, the psychology of an individual's fulfillment through work has been incorporated into management ideology. As the pages of *Fortune, Time,* or *Business Week* . . . serve to show, the higher levels of business and government are staffed by men and women who spend killing hours looking after the economic welfare and national security of the rest of us. The rewards of this life are said to be very few: The love of money would be demeaning and, anyway, taxes are said to take most of it; its sacrifices are many, for failure brings economic depression to the masses or gains for communism as well as disgrace to the erring managers. Even the essential high-mindedness or altruism of our managers earns no reward, for the public is distracted, fickle, and, on occasion, vengeful. . . . Hence, for these "real revolutionaries of our time," as Walt Rostow has called them, self-fulfillment through work and discipline is the only reward. The managerial process is seen as an expression of the vital personalities of our leaders and the right to it an inalienable right of the national elite.

In addition to all this, their lonely and unrewarding eminence in the face of crushing responsibility, etc., tends to create an air of mystification around technology's managers. . . .

It seems fundamental to the social organization of modern technology that the quality of the social experience of the lower orders of society declines as the level of technology grows no less than does their literacy. And, of course, this process feeds on itself, for with the consequent decline in the real effectiveness and usefulness of local and other forms of organization open to easy and direct popular influence, their vitality declines still further, and the cycle is repeated.

The normal life of men and women in the lower and, I think, middle levels of American society now seems cut off from those experiences in which near social means and distant social ends are balanced and rebalanced, adjusted and readjusted. But it is from such widespread experience with effective balancing and adjusting that social rationality derives. To the degree that it is lacking, social irrationality becomes the norm, and social paranoia a recurring phenomenon. . . .

Mesthene himself recognizes that such "negative externalities" are on the increase. His list includes ". . . pollution of the environment, potential damage to the ecology of the planet, occupational and social dislocations, threats to the privacy and political significance of the individual, social and psychological malaise. . . ." Minor matters all, however, when compared to the marvelous opportunities *laissez innover* holds out to us: more GNP, continued free-world leadership, supersonic transports, urban renewal on a regional basis, institutional innovation, and the millennial promises of his school.

This brings us finally to the ideologies and doctrines of technology and their relation to what I have argued is a growing gap in political culture between the lower and upper classes in American society. Even more fundamentally than the principles of *laissez innover* and the altruistic bureaucrat, technology in its very definition as the organization of knowledge for practical purposes assumes that the primary and really creative role in the social processes consequent on technological change is reserved for a scientific and technical elite, the elite that presumably discovers and organizes that knowledge. But if the scientific and technical elite and their indispensable managerial cronies are the really creative (and hardworking and altruistic) elements in American society, what is this but to say that the common mass of people are essentially drags on the social weal? This is precisely the implication which is drawn by the *laissez innover* school. Consider the following quotations from an article that appeared in *The New Republic* in December 1967, written by Zbigniew Brzezinski, one of the intellectual leaders of the school.

Brzezinski is describing a nightmare that he calls the "technetronic society" (the word, like the concept, is a pastiche of technology and electronics). This society will be characterized, he argues, by the application of ". . . the principle of equal opportunity for all but . . . special opportunity for the singularly talented few." It will thus combine ". . . continued *respect* for the popular will with an increasing *role* in the key decision-making institutions of individuals with special intellectual and scientific attainments." [Italics added.] Naturally, "The educational and social systems [will make] it increasingly attractive and easy for those meritocratic few to develop to the fullest of their special potential."

However, while it will be ". . . necessary to require everyone at a sufficiently responsible post to take, say, two years of [scientific and technical] retraining every ten years . . .," the rest of us can develop a new ". . . interest in the cultural and humanistic aspects of life, *in addition to purely hedonistic preoccupations*." [Italics added.] The latter, he is careful to point out, "would serve as a social valve, reducing tensions and political frustration."

Is it not fair to ask how much respect we carefree pleasure lovers and culture consumers will get from the hardworking bureaucrats, going to night school two years in every ten, while working like beavers in the "key decision-making institutions"? The altruism of our bureaucrats has a heavy load to bear.

Stripped of their euphemisms, these are simply arguments that enhance the social legitimacy of the interests of new technical and scientific elites and detract from the interests of the rest of us. . . .

As has already been made clear, the *laissez innover* school accepts as inevitable and desirable the centralizing tendencies of technology's social organization, and they accept as well the mystification that comes to surround the management process. Thus, equality of opportunity, as they understand it, has precious little to do with creating a more egalitarian society. On the contrary, it functions as an indispensable feature of the highly stratified society they envision for the future. For in their society of meritocratic hierarchy, equality of opportunity assures that talented young meritocrats (the word is no uglier than the social system it refers to) will be able to climb into the "key decision-making" slots reserved for trained talent and thus generate the success of the new society and its cohesion against popular "tensions and political frustration."

The structures that formerly guaranteed the rule of wealth, age, and family will not be destroyed (or at least not totally so). They will be firmed up and rationalized by the perpetual addition of trained (and, of course, acculturated) talent. In technologically advanced societies, equality of opportunity functions as a hierarchical principle, in opposition to the egalitarian social goals it pretends to serve. To the extent that is has already become the kind of "equality" we seek to institute in our society, it is one of the main factors contributing to the widening gap between the cultures of upper- and lower-class America.

V

. . . *Laissez innover* is now the premier ideology of the technological impulse in American society, which is to say, of the institutions that monopolize and profit from advanced technology and of the social classes that find in the free exploitation of their technology the most likely guarantee of their power, status, and wealth.

This said, it is important to stress both the significance and limitations of what has in fact been said. Here, Mesthene's distinction between the positive opportunities and negative "externalities" inherent in technological change is pivotal; for everything else that I've argued follows inferentially from the actual social meaning of that distinction. As my analysis of the Vietnam bombing program suggested, those technological effects that are sought after as positive opportunities and those that are dismissed as negative externalities are decisively influenced by the fact that this distinction between positive and negative within advanced technological organizations tends to be made among the planners and managers themselves. Within these groups there are, as was pointed out, extremely powerful organizational, hierarchical, doctrinal, and other "technical" factors, which tend by design to filter out "irrational" demands from below, substituting for them the "rational" demands of technology itself. As a result, technological rationality is as socially neutral today as market rationality was a century ago. . . .

This analysis lends some weight (though perhaps no more than that) to a number of wide-ranging and unorthodox conclusions about American society today and the directions in which it is tending. . . .

First, and most important, technology should be considered as an institutional system, not more and certainly not less. Mesthene's definition of the subject is inadequate, for it obscures the systematic and decisive social changes, especially their political and cultural tendencies, that follow the widespread application of advanced technological systems. At the same time, technology is less than a social system per se, though it has many elements of a social system, viz., an elite, a group of linked institutions, an ethos, and so forth. Perhaps the best summary statement of the case resides in an analogy — with all the vagueness and imprecision attendant on such things: today's technology stands in relation to today's capitalism as, a century ago, the latter stood to the free market capitalism of the time. . . .

A second major hypothesis would argue that the most important dimension of advanced technological institutions is the social one, that is, the institutions are agencies of highly centralized and intensive social control. Technology conquers nature, as the saying goes. But to do so it must first conquer man. More precisely, it demands a very high degree of control over the training, mobility, and skills of the work force. The absence (or decline) of direct controls or of coercion should not serve to obscure from our view the reality and intensity of the social controls that are employed (such as the internalized belief in equality of opportunity, indebtedness through credit, advertising, selective service channeling, and so on).

Advanced technology has created a vast increase in occupational specialties, many of them requiring many, many years of highly specialized training. It must motivate this training. It has made ever more complex and "rational" the ways in which these occupational specialties are combined in our economic and social life. It must win passivity and obedience to this complex activity. Formerly, technical rationality had been employed only to organize the production of rather simple physical objects, for example, aerial bombs. Now, technical rationality is increasingly employed to organize all of the processes necessary to the utilization of physical objects, such as bombing systems. For this reason, it seems a mistake to argue that we are in a "postindustrial" age, a concept favored by the *laissez innover* school. On the contrary, the rapid spread of technical in organizational and economic life and, hence, into social life is more aptly described as a second and much more intensive phase of the industrial revolution. One might reasonably suspect that it will create analogous social problems.

Accordingly, a third major hypothesis would argue that there are very profound social antagonisms or contradictions not less sharp or fundamental than those ascribed by Marx to the development of nineteenth-century industrial society. The general form of the contradictions might be described as follows: A society characterized by the employment of advanced technology requires an ever-more socially disciplined population, yet retains an ever-declining capacity to enforce the required discipline. . . .

These are brief and, I believe, barely adequate reviews of extremely complex hypotheses. But, in outline, each of these contradictions appears to bear on roughly the same group of the American population: a technological underclass. If we assume this to be the case, a fourth hypothesis would follow, namely that technology is creating the basis for new and sharp class conflict in our society. That is, technology is creating its own working and managing classes, just as earlier industrialization created its working and owning classes. Perhaps this suggests a return to the kind of class-based politics that characterized the U.S. in the last quarter of the nineteenth century, rather than the somewhat more ambiguous politics that was a feature of the second quarter of this century. I am inclined to think that this is the case, though I confess the evidence for it is as yet inadequate.

This leads to a final hypothesis, namely that *laissez innover* should be frankly recognized as a conservative or right-wing ideology. . . .

The point of this final hypothesis is not primarily to reimpress the language of European politics on the American scene. Rather, it is to summarize the fact that many of the forces in American life hostile to the democratic ethos have enrolled under the banner of *laissez innover*. Merely to grasp this is already to take the first step toward a politics of radical reconstruction and against the malaise, irrationality, powerlessness, and official violence that characterize American life today.

NOTE

1. For a more complete statement of the argument that follows, see Suzanne Keller, *Beyond the Ruling Class* (New York: Random House, 1963).

PART III
ALTERNATIVE PERSPECTIVES ON TECHNOLOGY

Is it possible to reshape technological systems in ways that reflect a different set of interests and perspectives than those served by existing mainstream industrial technology? Is it possible to see and direct technological development from a fundamentally different point of view? Those who approach technology from alternative perspectives are not interested in abstract critiques. Some are concerned with the practical, long-term viability of contemporary industrial society in the face of growing population, resource constraints, and the potential for human actions to cause long-term, possibly irreversible damage to the global environment. Others focus on the equity implications of current technological systems — for example, the impacts of such systems on women and racial minorities. Still others see the need for reforms to the policy-making apparatus by which technological development is governed. All would alter the directions of technological change to better accommodate these alternative perspectives.

Central to the first two readings in this section is the notion of alternative or appropriate technology. This concept, which in the United States was associated with the counterculture of the 1960s and 1970s, is a way of looking at technology itself rather than at a specific type of hardware. It is a set of design criteria that stress simplicity, individual self-worth and self-reliance, labor intensiveness rather than capital intensiveness, minimum energy use, consistency with environmental quality, and decentralization rather than centralization.

The authors of the first two chapters are two of the best known and most creative thinkers on the subject of technological alternatives: E. F. Schumacher and Paul Goodman. Schumacher's name is practically synonymous with appropriate technology, especially as it applies to Third World development. His essay, "Buddhist Economics," though more than twenty-five years old, is still as thought provoking as it is original. Paul Goodman's paper, "Can Technology Be Humane?" which actually predates Schumacher's by several years, provides an idea of what the philosophical underpinnings of a really different style of technology might be like.

The next five chapters discuss the redirection of technology from somewhat different angles. Richard Sclove's recent essay, "Technological Politics As If Democracy Really Mattered," updates some of Goodman's ideas and suggests ways in which technological decision making can be made more democratic and technology can be used to create a more democratic society. Ziauddin Sardar, a noted Muslim intellectual, critiques futures studies and the technological wizardry that many of them espouse from a non-Western standpoint. Timothy Jenkins takes a fresh look at technology from an African American perspective in his 1997 book (coauthored by Khafra K. Om-Ra-Seti), *Black Futurists in the Information Age*. How can new technologies be made to serve the interests of the black community, he asks, and how can the members of that community seize the initiative?

Australian sociologist Judy Wajcman critiques mainstream technology from a feminist standpoint, suggesting along the way how a technology based on women's values might look. Finally, in one of his many provocative essays on technology, Langdon Winner asks whether certain technological systems by their nature determine particular arrangements of power and authority among people. Understanding the significance of this and related questions is essential, Winner would argue, to maintaining (or perhaps restoring) democratic control over the course of technological and social development.

8. Buddhist Economics

E. F. SCHUMACHER

More than any other single individual, E. F. Schumacher is responsible for popularizing the notion of appropriate technology. It may seem strange that a man who was once chief economist of Britain's National Coal Board emerged as intellectual parent of a movement that seeks the radical restructuring of the whole essence of economics, but Schumacher was also a longtime advocate of organic farming, a student of Gandhi, and an activist for political decentralization.

Schumacher was born in Germany in 1911, trained in economics, and came to England as a Rhodes scholar. Like many Germans living in Britain, he was interned for a long time during World War II. Later, he was released to do farmwork, an experience that strongly influenced his later work. While pursuing a career as a government economist, he became involved in organic farming, became president of the Soil Association, and in 1966 founded the Intermediate Technology Development Group, an organization that promotes small-scale technology tailored to the needs of specific developing countries. Schumacher died in 1977, not long after a visit to the United States in which he was accorded the recognition of a meeting with President Jimmy Carter to discuss his ideas.

His book, Small Is Beautiful, *from which the brilliant essay "Buddhist Economics" is taken, became an underground classic soon after its publication in the early 1970s. As effective an introduction as can be found to the ideas of appropriate technology, "Buddhist Economics" provides Schumacher's answer to the question Leo Marx asks in the opening chapter of this book, "Does Improved Technology Mean Progress?"*

"Right Livelihood" is one of the requirements of the Buddha's Noble Eightfold Path. It is clear, therefore, that there must be such a thing as Buddhist economics.

Buddhist countries have often stated that they wish to remain faithful to their heritage. So Burma: "The New Burma sees no conflict between religious values and economic progress. Spiritual health and material well-being are not enemies: they are natural allies."[1] Or "We can blend successfully the religious and spiritual values of our heritage with the benefits of modern technology."[2] Or: "We Burmans have sacred duty to conform both our dreams and our acts to our faith. This we shall ever do."[3]

All the same, such countries invariably assume that they can model their economic development plans in accordance with modern economics, and they call upon modern economists from so-called advanced countries to advise them, to formulate the policies to be pursued, and to construct the grand design for development, the Five-Year Plan or whatever it may be called. No one seems to think that a Buddhist way of life would call for Buddhist economics, just as the modern materialist way of life has brought forth modern economics.

Economists themselves, like most specialists, normally suffer from a kind of metaphysical blindness, assuming that theirs is a science of absolute and invariable truths, without any presuppositions. Some go as far as to claim that economic laws are as free from "metaphysics" or "values" as the law of gravitation. We need not, however, get involved in arguments of methodology. Instead, let us take some fundamentals and see what they look like when viewed by a modern economist and a Buddhist economist.

There is universal agreement that a fundamental source of wealth is human labor. Now, the modern economist has been brought up to consider "labor" or work as little more than a necessary evil. From the point of view of the employer, it is in any case simply an item of cost, to be reduced to a minimum if it cannot be eliminated altogether, say, by automation. From the point of view of the workman, it is a "disutility"; to work is to make a sacrifice of one's leisure and comfort, and wages are a kind of compensation for the sacrifice. Hence, the ideal from the point of view of the employer is to have output without employees, and the ideal from the point of view of the employee is to have income without employment.

The consequences of these attitudes both in theory and in practice are, of course, extremely far-reaching. If the ideal with regard to work is to get rid of it, every method that "reduces the work load" is a good thing. The most potent method, short of automation, is the so-called "division of labor," and the classical example is the pin factory eulogized in Adam Smith's *Wealth of Nations*. Here, it is not a matter of ordinary specialization, which humankind has practiced from time immemorial, but of dividing up every complete process of production into minute parts, so that the final product can be produced at great speed without anyone having had to contribute more than a totally insignificant and, in most cases, unskilled movement of his limbs.

The Buddhist point of view takes the function of work to be at least threefold: to give a man a chance to utilize and develop his faculties, to enable him to overcome his egocenteredness by joining with other people in a common task, and to bring forth the goods and services needed for a becoming existence. Again, the consequences that flow from this view are endless. To organize work in such a manner that it becomes meaningless, boring, stultifying, or nerve wracking for the worker would be little short of criminal; it would indicate a greater concern with goods than with people, an evil lack of compassion and a soul-destroying degree of attachment to the most primitive side of this worldly existence. Equally, to strive for leisure as an alternative to work would be considered a complete misunderstanding of one of the basic truths of human existence, namely that work and leisure are complementary parts of the same living process and cannot be separated without destroying the joy of work and the bliss of leisure.

From the Buddhist point of view, there are therefore two types of mechanization, which must be clearly distinguished: one that enhances a man's skill and power and one that turns the work of man over to a mechanical slave, leaving man in a position of having to serve the slave. How to tell the one from the other? "The craftsman himself," says Ananda Coomaraswamy, a man equally competent to talk about the modern West as the ancient East, "can always, if allowed to, draw the delicate distinction between the machine and the tool. The carpet loom is a tool, a contrivance for holding warp threads at a stretch for the pile to be woven round them by the craftsmen's fingers; but the power loom is a machine, and its significance as a destroyer of culture lies in the fact that it does the essentially human part of the work."[4] It is clear, therefore, that Buddhist economics must be very different from the economics of modern materialism, since the Buddhist sees the essence of civilization not in a multiplication of wants but in the purification of human character. Character, at the same time, is formed primarily by a man's work. And work, properly conducted in conditions of human dignity and freedom, blesses those who do it and equally their products. The Indian philosopher and economist J. C. Kumarappa sums the matter up as follows:

> If the nature of the work is properly appreciated and applied, it will stand in the same relation to the higher faculties as food is to the physical body. It nourishes and enlivens the higher man and urges him to produce the best he is capable of. It directs his free will along the proper course and disciplines the animal in him into progressive channels. It furnishes an excellent background for man to display his scale of values and develop his personality.[5]

If a man has no chance of obtaining work, he is in a desperate position, not simply because he lacks an income but because he lacks this nourishing and enlivening factor of disciplined work, which nothing can replace. A modern economist may engage in highly sophisticated calculations on whether full employment "pays" or whether it might be more "economic" to run an economy at less than full employment so as to ensure a greater mobility of labor, a better stability of wages, and so forth. His fundamental criterion of success is simply the total quantity of goods produced during a given period of time. "If the marginal urgency of goods is low," says Professor Galbraith in *The Affluent Society,* "then so is the urgency of employing the last man or the last million men in the labor force."[6] And again: "If . . . we can afford some unemployment in the interest of stability — a proposition, incidentally, of impeccably conservative antecedents — then we can afford to give those who are unemployed the goods that enable them to sustain their accustomed standard of living."

From a Buddhist point of view, this is standing the truth on its head by considering goods as more important than people and consumption as more important than creative activity. It means shifting the emphasis from the worker to the product of work, that is, from the human to the subhuman, a surrender to the forces of evil. The very start of Buddhist economic planning would be a planning for full employment, and the primary purpose of this would in fact be employment for everyone who needs an "outside" job: It would not be the maximization of employment nor the maximization of production. Women, on the whole, do not need an "outside" job, and the large-scale employment of women in offices or factories would be considered a sign of serious economic failure. In particular, to let mothers of young children work in factories while the children run wild would be as uneconomic in the eyes of a Buddhist economist as the employment of a skilled worker as a soldier in the eyes of a modern economist.

While the materialist is mainly interested in goods, the Buddhist is mainly interested in liberation. But Buddhism is "The Middle Way" and therefore in no way antagonistic to physical well-being. It is not wealth that stands in the way of liberation but the attachment to wealth; not the enjoyment of pleasurable things but the craving for them. The keynote of Buddhist economics, therefore, is simplicity and nonviolence. From an economist's point of view, the marvel of the Buddhist way of life is the utter rationality of its pattern — amazingly small means leading to extraordinarily satisfactory results.

For the modern economist, this is very difficult to understand. He is used to measuring the "standard of living" by the amount of annual consumption, assuming all the time that a man who consumes more is "better off" than a man who consumes less. A Buddhist economist would consider this approach excessively irrational: Since consumption is merely a means to human well-being, the aim should be to obtain the maximum of well-being with the minimum of consumption. Thus, if the purpose of clothing is a certain amount of temperature comfort and an attractive appearance, the task is to attain this purpose with the smallest possible effort; that is, with the smallest annual destruction of cloth and with the help of designs that involve the smallest possible input of toil. The less toil there is, the more time and strength are left for artistic creativity. It would be highly uneconomic, for instance, to go in for complicated tailoring, like the modern West, when a much more beautiful effect can be achieved by the skillful draping of uncut material. It would be the height of folly to make material so that it should wear out quickly and the height of barbarity to make anything ugly, shabby, or mean. What has just been said about clothing applies equally to all other human requirements. The ownership and the consumption of goods are a means to an end, and Buddhist economics is the systematic study of how to attain given ends with the minimum means.

Modern economics, on the other hand, considers consumption to be the sole end and purpose of all economic activity, taking the factors of production—land, labor, and capital — as the means. The former, in short, tries to maximize human satisfactions by the optimal pattern of consumption, while the latter tries to maximize consumption by the optimal pattern of productive effort. It is easy to see that the effort needed to sustain a way of life that seeks to attain the optimal pattern of consumption is likely to be much smaller than the effort needed to sustain a drive for maximum consumption. We need not be surprised, therefore, that the pressure and strain of living are very much less in, say, Burma than they are in the United States, in spite of the fact that the amount of labor-saving machinery used in the former country is only a minute fraction of the amount used in the latter.

Simplicity and nonviolence are obviously closely related. The optimal pattern of consumption, producing a high degree of human satisfaction by means of a relatively low rate of consumption, allows people to live without great pressure and strain and to fulfill the primary injunction of Buddhist teaching: "Cease to do evil; try to do good." As physical resources are everywhere limited, people satisfying their needs by means of a modest use of resources are obviously less likely to be at each other's throats than people depending upon a high rate of use. Equally, people who live in highly self-sufficient local communities are less likely to get involved in large-scale violence than people whose existence depends on world-wide systems of trade.

From the point of view of Buddhist economics, therefore, production from local resources for local needs is the most rational way of economic life, while dependence on imports from afar and the consequent need to produce for export to unknown and distant peoples is highly uneconomic and justifiable only in exceptional cases and on a small scale, just as the modern economist would admit that a high rate of consumption of transport services between a man's home and his place of work signifies a misfortune and not a high standard of life, so the Buddhist economist would hold that to satisfy human wants from faraway sources rather than from sources nearby signifies failure rather than success. The former tends to take statistics showing an increase in the number of tons/miles per head of the population carried by a country's transport system as proof of economic progress, while to the latter—the Buddhist economist — the same statistics would indicate a highly undesirable deterioration in the *pattern* of consumption.

Another striking difference between modern economics and Buddhist economics arises over the use of natural resources. Bertrand de Jouvenel, the eminent French political philosopher, has characterized "Western man" in words that may be taken as a fair description of the modern economist:

> He tends to count nothing as an expenditure, other than human effort; he does not seem to mind how much mineral matter he wastes and, far worse, how much living matter he destroys. He does not seem to realize at all that human life is a dependent part of an ecosystem of many different forms of life. As the world is ruled from towns where men are cut off from any form of life other than human, the feeling of belonging to an ecosystem is not revived. This results in a harsh and improvident treatment of things upon which we ultimately depend, such as water and trees.[7]

The teaching of the Buddha, on the other hand, enjoins a reverent and non-violent attitude not only to all sentient beings but also, with great emphasis, to trees. Every follower of the Buddha ought to plant a tree every few years and look after it until it is safely established, and the Buddhist economist can demonstrate without difficulty that the universal observation of this rule would result in a high rate of genuine economic development independent of any foreign aid. Much of the economic decay of southeast Asia (as of many other parts of the world) is undoubtedly due to a heedless and shameful neglect of trees.

Modern economics does not distinguish between renewable and nonrenewable materials, as its very method is to equalize and quantify everything by means of a money price. Thus, taking various alternative fuels, like coal, oil, wood, or water-power: The only difference between them recognized by modern economics is relative cost per equivalent unit. The cheapest is automatically the one to be preferred, as to do otherwise would be irrational and "uneconomic." From a Buddhist point of view, of course, this will not do; the essential difference between nonrenewable fuels like coal and oil on the one hand and renewable fuels like wood and waterpower on the other cannot simply be overlooked. Nonrenewable goods must be used only if they are indispensable, and then only with the greatest care and the most meticulous concern for conservation. To use them heedlessly or extravagantly is an act of violence, and while complete nonviolence may not be attainable on this earth, there is nonetheless an ineluctable duty on man to aim at the ideal of nonviolence in all he does.

Just as a modern European economist would not consider it a great economic achievement if all European art treasures were sold to America at attractive prices, so the Buddhist economist would insist that a population basing its economic life on nonrenewable fuels is living parasitically, on capital instead of income. Such a way of life could have no permanence and could therefore be justified only as a purely temporary expedient. As the world's resources of nonrenewable fuels — coal, oil, and natural gas — are exceedingly unevenly distributed over the globe and undoubtedly limited in quantity, it is clear that their exploitation at an ever-increasing rate is an act of violence against nature, which must almost inevitably lead to violence between men.

This fact alone might give food for thought even to those people in Buddhist countries who care nothing for the religious and spiritual values of their heritage and ardently desire to embrace the materialism of modern economics at the fastest possible speed. Before they dismiss Buddhist economics as nothing better than a nostalgic dream, they might wish to consider whether the path of economic development outlined by modern economics is likely to lead them to places where they really want to be. Toward the end of his courageous book, *The Challenge of Man's Future*, Professor Harrison Brown of the California Institute of Technology gives the following appraisal:

> Thus we see that, just as industrial society is fundamentally unstable and subject to reversion to agrarian existence, so within it the conditions which offer individual freedom are unstable in their ability to avoid the conditions which impose rigid organization and totalitarian control. Indeed, when we examine all of the foreseeable difficulties which threaten the survival of industrial civilization, it is difficult to see how the achievement of stability and the maintenance of individual liberty can be made compatible.[8]

Even if this were dismissed as a long-term view, there is the immediate question of whether "modernization," as currently practiced without regard to religious and spiritual values, is actually producing agreeable results. As far as the masses are concerned, the results appear to be disastrous — a collapse of the rural economy, a rising tide of unemployment in town and country, and the growth of a city proletariat without nourishment for either body or soul.

It is in the light of both immediate experience and long-term prospects that the study of Buddhist economics could be recommended, even to those who believe that economic growth is more important than any spiritual or religious values. For it is not a question of choosing between "modern growth" and "traditional stagnation." It is a question of finding the right path of development, the Middle Way between materialist heedlessness and traditionalist immobility, in short, of finding "Right Livelihood."

NOTES

1. *The New Burma* (Economic and Social Board, Government of the Union of Burma, 1954).
2. Ibid.
3. Ibid.
4. Ananda K. Coomaraswamy, *Art and Swadeshi* (Madras: Ganesh & Co.).
5. J. C. Kumarappa, *Economy of Permanence* (Sarva-Seva Sangh Publication, Rajghat, Kashi, 4th ed., 1958).
6. John Kenneth Galbraith, *The Affluent Society* (London: Penguin Books Ltd., 1962).
7. Richard B. Gregg, *A Philosophy of Indian Economic Development* (Ahmedabad: Navajivan Publishing House, 1958).
8. Harrison Brown, *The Challenge of Man's Future* (New York: The Viking Press, 1954).

9. Can Technology Be Humane?

PAUL GOODMAN

In his essay "Technology: The Opiate of the Intellectuals" (which appears in Part II of this book), John McDermott despairs of the possibility of creating a humane technology within our present system. In a footnote to a section not included in this book, he writes, "Any discussion of the reorganization of technology to serve human needs seems, at this point, so utopian that it robs one of the conviction necessary to shape a believable vision." Paul Goodman, unwilling to accept such a hopeless view, asks in the title of his selection, "Can Technology Be Humane?"

In developing his response to this question, Goodman admits there is no certainty that technology will become humane. Yet, in the classic style of a prophet — partly predictive and partly prescriptive — he asserts that our society is "on the eve of a new Protestant Reformation, and no institution or status will go unaffected." In this selection, he offers a number of suggestions for channeling the energies of this Reformation into directions that he sees as critical to its success: prudence in the application of technology, an ecological viewpoint, and decentralization. Although the term appropriate technology *was barely known when Goodman first published this essay in the late 1960s, it is easy to see its roots in his prescription for reshaping technology.*

Paul Goodman (1911–1972) was a philosopher and humanist whose book Growing Up Absurd *established him as "the philosopher of the New Left" in the 1960s. His work ranged widely, from* Communitas *(1947), a classic of community planning written with his brother, Percival Goodman, to* Gestalt Therapy *(1951), written with F. S. Perls and Ralph Hefferline. Goodman was an anarchist and a pacifist, very active in the antiwar movement of the sixties. He wrote theoretical and practical treatises on politics, education, language, and literature, but his own judgment was that his literary work — novels, stories, poems, and plays — was his best. He was born in Manhattan, attended City College of New York, and was trained in philosophy at the University of Chicago.*

On March 4, 1969, there was a "work stoppage" and teach-in initiated by dissenting professors at the Massachusetts Institute of Technology and followed at thirty other major universities and technical schools across the country, against misdirected scientific research and the abuse of scientific technology. Here I want to consider this event in a broader context than the professors did, indeed as part of a religious crisis. For an attack on the American scientific establishment is an attack on the worldwide system of belief. I think we are on the eve of a new Protestant Reformation, and no institution or status will go unaffected.

March 4 was, of course, only [one] of a series of protests in the [over] twenty-five years since the Manhattan Project to build the atom bomb, during which time the central funding of research and innovation has grown so enormously and its purposes have become so unpalatable. In 1940, the federal budget for research and development was less than 100 million dollars; in 1967, 17 billion.* Hitler's war was a watershed of modern times. We are accustomed, as H. R. Trevor-Roper has pointed out, to write Hitler off as an aberration, of little political significance. But, in fact, the military emergency that he and his Japanese allies created confirmed the worst tendencies of the giant states, till now they are probably irreversible by ordinary political means.

After Hiroshima, there was the conscience-stricken movement of the Atomic Scientists and the founding of their *Bulletin*. The American Association for the Advancement of Science pledged itself to keep the public informed about the dangerous bearings of new developments. There was the Oppenheimer incident. Ads of the East Coast scientists successfully stopped the bomb shelters, warned about the fallout, and helped produce the test ban. There was a scandal about the bombardment of the Van Allen belt. Scientists and technologists formed a powerful (and misguided) ad hoc group for Johnson in the 1964 election. In some universities, sometimes with bitter struggle, classified contracts have been excluded. There is a Society for Social Responsibility in Science. Rachel Carson's book on the pesticides caused a stir, until the Department of Agriculture rescued the manufacturers and plantation owners. Ralph Nader has been on his rampage. Thanks to spectacular abuses like smog, strip-mining, asphalting, pesticides, and oil pollution, even ecologists and conservationists have been getting a hearing. Protest against the boom has slowed up the development of the supersonic transport [particularly in the United States]. Most recent has been the concerned outcry against the antiballistic missiles.

The target of protest has become broader and the grounds of complaint deeper. The target is now not merely the military, but the universities, commercial corporations, and government. It is said that money is being given by the wrong sponsors to the wrong people for the wrong purposes. In some of the great schools, such funding is the main support (e.g., at MIT, 90 percent of the research budget is from the government, and 65 percent of that is military).

Inevitably, such funding channels the brainpower of most of the brightest science students, who go where the action is, and this predetermines the course of American science and technology for the foreseeable future. At present, nearly 200,000 American engineers and scientists spend all their time making weapons, which is a comment on, and perhaps explanation for, the usual statement that more scientists are now alive than since Adam and Eve. And the style of such research and development is not good. It is dominated by producing hardware, figuring logistics, and devising salable novelties. Often, there is secrecy, always nationalism. Since the grants go overwhelmingly through a very few corporations and universities, they favor a limited number of scientific attitudes and preconceptions, with incestuous staffing. There is a premium on "positive results"; surprising "failures" cannot be pursued, so that science ceases to be a wandering dialogue with the unknown.

*R&D in the fiscal year 2003 federal budget is estimated at well over $100 billion — ED.

The policy is economically wasteful. A vast amount of brains and money is spent on crash programs to solve often essentially petty problems, and the claim that there is a spin-off of useful discoveries is derisory, if we consider the sums involved. The claim that research is neutral, and it doesn't matter what one works on, is shabby, if we consider the heavy funding in certain directions. Social priorities are scandalous: Money is spent on overkill, supersonic planes, brand-name identical drugs, annual model changes of cars, new detergents, and color television, whereas water, air space, food, health, and foreign aid are neglected. And much research is morally so repugnant (e.g., chemical and biological weapons) that one dares not humanly continue it.

The state of the behavioral sciences is, if anything, worse. Their claim to moral and political neutrality becomes, in effect, a means of diverting attention from glaring social evils, and they are in fact used — or would be if they worked — for warfare and social engineering, manipulation of people for the political and economic purposes of the powers that be. This is an especially sad betrayal since, in the not-too-distant past, the objective social sciences were developed largely to dissolve orthodoxy, irrational authority, and taboo. They were heretical and intellectually revolutionary, as the physical sciences had been in their own Heroic Age, and they weren't getting government grants.

This is a grim indictment. Even so, I do not think the dissenting scientists understand how deep their trouble is. They still take themselves too much for granted. Indeed, a repeated theme of the March 4, [1969,] complaints was that the science budget was being cut back, especially in basic research. The assumption was that though the sciences are abused, Science would rightly maintain and increase its expensive preeminence among social institutions. Only Science could find the answers.

But, underlying the growing dissent, there is a historical crisis. There has been a profound change in popular feeling, more than among the professors. Put it this way: Modern societies have been operating as if religion were a minor and moribund part of the scheme of things. But this is unlikely. Men do not do without a system of "meanings" that everybody believes and puts his hope in even if, or especially if, he doesn't know anything about it; what Freud called a "shared psychosis," meaningful because shared, and with the power that resides in dream and longing. In fact, in advanced countries it is science and technology themselves that have gradually and finally triumphantly become the system of mass faith, not disputed by various political ideologies and nationalism that have also been mass religions. Marxism called itself "scientific socialism" as against moral and utopian socialisms, and movements of national liberation have especially promised to open the benefits of industrialization and technological progress when once they have gotten rid of the imperialists.

For 300 years, science and scientific technology had an unblemished and justified reputation as a wonderful adventure, pouring out practical benefits, and liberating the spirit from the errors of superstition and traditional faith. During this century, they have finally been the only generally credited system of explanation and problem-solving. Yet, in our generation, they have come to seem to many, and to very many of the best of the young, as essentially inhuman, abstract, regimenting, hand-in-glove with Power, and even diabolical. Young people say that science is antilife, it is a Calvinist obsession, it has been a weapon of white Europe to subjugate colored races, and manifestly — in view of recent scientific technology — people who think that way become insane. With science, the other professions are discredited, and the academic "disciplines" are discredited.

The immediate reasons for this shattering reversal of values are fairly obvious. Hitler's ovens and his other experiments in eugenics, the first atom bombs and their frenzied subsequent developments, the deterioration of the physical environment and the destruction of the biosphere, the catastrophes impending over the cities because of technological failures and psychological stress, the prospect of a brainwashed and drugged 1984. Innovations yield diminishing returns in enhancing life. And, instead of rejoicing, there is now widespread conviction that beautiful advances in genetics, surgery, computers, rocketry, or atomic energy will surely only increase human woe.

In such a crisis, in my opinion, it will not be sufficient to ban the military from the universities, and it will not even be sufficient, as liberal statesmen and many of the big corporations envisage, to beat the swords into ploughshares and turn to solving problems of transportation, desalinization, urban renewal, garbage disposal, and cleaning up the air and water. If the present difficulty is religious and historical, it is necessary to alter the entire relationship of science, technology, and social needs both in men's minds and in fact. This involves changes in the organization of science, in scientific education, and in the kinds of men who make scientific decisions.

In spite of the fantasies of hippies, we are certainly going to continue to live in a technological world. The question is a different one: Is that workable?

PRUDENCE

Whether or not it draws on new scientific research, technology is a branch of moral philosophy, not of science. It aims at prudent goods for the commonweal and to provide efficient means for these goods. At present, however, "scientific technology" occupies a bastard position in the universities, in funding, and in the public mind. It is half tied to the theoretical sciences and half treated as mere know-how for political and commercial purposes. It has no principles of its own. To remedy this — so Karl Jaspers in Europe and Robert Hutchins in America have urged — technology must have its proper place on the faculty as a learned profession important in modern society, along with medicine, law, the humanities, and natural philosophy, learning from them and having something to teach them. As a moral philosopher, a technician should be able to criticize the programs given him to implement. As a professional in a community of learned professionals, a technologist must have a different kind of training and develop a different character than we see at present among technicians and engineers. He should know something of the social sciences, law, the fine arts, and medicine, as well as relevant natural sciences.

Prudence is foresight, caution, utility. Thus, it is up to the technologists, not to regulatory agencies of the government, to provide for safety and to think about remote effects. This is what Ralph Nader is saying and Rachel Carson used to ask. An important aspect of caution is flexibility, to avoid the pyramiding catastrophe that occurs when something goes wrong in interlocking technologies, as in urban power failures. Naturally, to take responsibility for such things often requires standing up to the front office and urban politicians, and technologists must organize themselves in order to have power to do it.

Often, it is clear that a technology has been oversold, like the cars. Then, even though the public, seduced by advertising, wants more, technologists must balk, as any professional does when his client wants what isn't good for him. We are now repeating the same self-defeating congestion with the planes and airports: The more the technology is oversold, the less immediate utility it provides, the greater the costs, and the more damaging the remote effects. As this becomes evident, it is time for technologists to confer with sociologists and economists and ask deeper questions. Is so much travel necessary? Are there ways to diminish it? Instead, the recent history of technology has consisted largely of a desperate effort to remedy situations caused by previous overapplication of technology.

Technologists should certainly have a say about simple waste, for even in an affluent society there are priorities — consider the supersonic transport, which has little to recommend it. But the moon shot has presented the more usual dilemma of authentic conflicting claims. I, myself, believe that space exploration is a great human adventure, with immense aesthetic and moral benefits, whatever the scientific or utilitarian uses. Yet, it is amazing to me that the scientists and technologists involved have not spoken more insistently for international cooperation instead of a puerile race. But I have heard some say that except for this chauvinist competition, Congress would not vote any money at all.

Currently, perhaps the chief moral criterion of a philosophic technology is modesty, having a sense of the whole and not obtruding more than a particular function warrants. Immodesty is always a danger of free enterprise, but when the same disposition is financed by big corporations, technologists rush into production with neat solutions that swamp the environment. This applies to packaging products and disposing of garbage, to freeways that bulldoze neighborhoods, high-rises that destroy landscape, wiping out a species for a passing fashion, strip mining, scrapping an expensive machine rather than making a minor repair, draining a watershed for irrigation because (as in Southern California) the cultivable land has been covered by asphalt. Given this disposition, it is not surprising that we defoliate a forest in order to expose a guerrilla and spray tear gas from a helicopter on a crowded campus.

Since we are technologically overcommitted, a good general maxim in advanced countries at present is to innovate in order to simplify the technical system, but otherwise to innovate as sparingly as possible. Every advanced country is overtechnologized; past a certain point, the quality of life diminishes with new "improvements." Yet no country is rightly technologized, making efficient use of available techniques. There are ingenious devices for unimportant functions, stressful mazes for essential functions, and drastic dislocation when anything goes wrong, which happens with increasing frequency. To add to the complexity, the mass of people tend to become incompetent and dependent on repairmen — indeed, unrepairability except by experts has become a desideratum of industrial design.

When I speak of slowing down or cutting back, the issue is not whether research and making working models should be encouraged or not. They should be, in every direction, and given a blank check. The point is to resist the temptation to apply every new device without a second thought. But the big corporate organization of research and development makes prudence and modesty very difficult; it is necessary to get big contracts and rush into production in order to pay the salaries of the big team. Like other bureaucracies, technological organizations are run to maintain themselves, but they are more dangerous because, in capitalist countries, they are in a competitive arena.

I mean simplification quite strictly, to simplify the technical system. I am unimpressed by the argument that what is technically more complicated is really economically or politically simpler (e.g., by complicating the packaging we improve the supermarkets, by throwing away the machine rather than repairing it, we give cheaper and faster service all around, or even by expanding the economy with trivial innovations, we increase employment, allay discontent, save on welfare). Such ideas may be profitable for private companies or political parties, but for society they have proved to be an accelerating rat race. The technical structure of the environment is too important to be a political or economic pawn; the effect on the quality of life is too disastrous, and the hidden social costs are not calculated — the auto graveyards, the torn-up streets, the longer miles of commuting, the advertising, the inflation, etc. As I pointed out in *People or Personnel*, a country with a fourth of our per capita income, like Ireland, is not necessarily less well off; in some respects, it is much richer, in some respects, a little poorer. If possible, it is better to solve political problems by political means. For instance, if teaching machines and audiovisual aids are indeed educative, well and good, but if they are used just to save money on teachers, then not good at all — nor do they save money.

Of course, the goals of right technology must come to terms with other values of society. I am not a technocrat. But the advantage of raising technology to be a responsible learned profession with its own principles is that it can have a voice in the debate and argue for its proper contribution to the community. Consider the important case of modular sizes in building, or prefabrication of a unit bathroom: These conflict with the short-run interests of manufacturers and craft unions, yet to deny them is technically an abomination. The usual recourse is for a government agency to set standards; such agencies accommodate to interests that have a strong voice, and at present technologists have no voice.

The crucial need for technological simplification, however, is not in the advanced countries—which can afford their clutter and probably deserve it — but in underdeveloped countries which must rapidly innovate in order to diminish disease, drudgery, and deepening starvation. They cannot afford to make mistakes. It is now widely conceded that the technological aid we have given to such areas according to our own high style — a style usually demanded by the native ruling groups—has done more harm than good. Even when, as frequently if not usually, aid has been benevolent, without strings attached, not military, and not dumping, it has nevertheless disrupted ways of life, fomented tribal wars, accelerated urbanization, decreased the food supply, gone wasted for lack of skills to use it, developed a do-nothing elite.

By contrast, a group of international scientists called Intermediate Technology argue that what is needed is techniques that use only native labor, resources, traditional customs, and teachable know-how, with the simple aim of remedying drudgery, disease, and hunger, so that people can then develop further in their own style. This avoids cultural imperialism. Such intermediate techniques may be quite primitive, on a level unknown among us for a couple of centuries, and yet they may pose extremely subtle problems, requiring exquisite scientific research and political and human understanding, to devise a very simple technology. Here is a reported case (which I trust I remember accurately): In Botswana, a very poor country, pasture was overgrazed, but the economy could be salvaged if the land were fenced. There was no local material for fencing, and imported fencing was prohibitively expensive. The solution was to find the formula and technique to make posts out of mud and a pedagogic method to teach people how to do it.

In *The Two Cultures*, C. P. Snow berated the humanists for their irrelevance when two-thirds of mankind is starving and what is needed is science and technology. They have perhaps been irrelevant, but unless technology is itself more humanistic and philosophical, it is of no use. There is only one culture.

Finally, let me make a remark about amenity as a technical criterion. It is discouraging to see the concern about beautifying a highway and banning billboards, and about the cosmetic appearance of the cars, when there is no regard for the ugliness of bumper-to-bumper traffic and the suffering of the drivers. Or the concern for preserving a historical landmark while the neighborhood is torn up and the city has no shape. Without moral philosophy, people have nothing but sentiments.

ECOLOGY

The complement to prudent technology is the ecological approach to science. To simplify the technical system and modestly pinpoint our artificial intervention in the environment makes it possible for the environment to survive in its complexity evolved for a billion years, whereas the overwhelming instant intervention of tightly interlocked and bulldozing technology has already disrupted many of the delicate sequences and balances. The calculable consequences are already frightening, but of course we don't know enough, and won't in the foreseeable future, to predict the remote effects of much of what we have done. The only possible conclusion is to be prudent; when there is serious doubt, to do nothing.

Cyberneticists — I am thinking of Gregory Bateson — come to the same cautious conclusion. The use of computers has enabled us to carry out crashingly inept programs on the bases of willful analyses. But we have also become increasingly alert to the fact that things respond, systematically, continually, cumulatively; they cannot simply be manipulated or pushed around. Whether bacteria or weeds or bugs or the technologically unemployed or unpleasant thoughts, they cannot be eliminated and forgotten; repressed, the nuisances return in new forms. A complicated system works most efficiently if its parts readjust themselves decentrally, with a minimum of central intervention or control, except in case of breakdown. Usually, there is an advantage in a central clearinghouse of information about the gross total situation, but decision and execution require more minute local information. The fantastically simulated moon landing hung on a last split-second correction on the spot. In social organization, deciding in headquarters means relying on information that is cumulatively abstract and irrelevant, and chain-of-command execution applies standards that cumulatively do not fit the concrete situation. By and large it is better, given a sense of the whole picture, for those in the field to decide what to do and do it.

But with organisms too, this has long been the bias of psychosomatic medicine, the Wisdom of the Body, as Cannon called it. To cite a classical experiment of Ralph Hefferline of Columbia: A subject is wired to suffer an annoying regular buzz, which can be delayed and finally eliminated if he makes a precise but unlikely gesture, say by twisting his ankle in a certain way; then it is found that he adjusts quicker if he is not told the method and it is left to his spontaneous twitching than if he is told and tries deliberately to help himself. He adjusts better without conscious control, his own or the experimenter's.

Technological modesty, fittingness, is not negative. It is the ecological wisdom of cooperating with Nature rather than trying to master her. (The personification of "Nature" is linguistic wisdom.) A well-known example is the long-run superiority of partial pest control in farming by using biological deterrents rather than chemical ones. The living defenders work harder, at the right moment, and with more pinpointed targets. But let me give another example because it is so lovely — though I have forgotten the name of my informant: A tribe in Yucatan educates its children to identify and pull up all weeds in the region; then, what is left is a garden of useful plants that have chosen to be there and now thrive.

In the life sciences, there is at present a suggestive bifurcation in methodology. The rule is still to increase experimental intervention, but there is also a considerable revival of old-fashioned naturalism, mainly watching and thinking, with very modest intervention. Thus, in medicine, there is new diagnostic machinery, new drugs, spectacular surgery; but there is also a new respect for family practice with psychosomatic background, and a strong push, among young doctors and students, for a social-psychological and sociological approach, aimed at preventing disease and building up resistance. In psychology, the operant conditioners multiply and refine their machinery to give maximum control of the organism and the environment (I have not heard of any dramatic discoveries, but perhaps they have escaped me). On the other hand, the most interesting psychology in recent years has certainly come from animal naturalists (e.g., pecking order, territoriality, learning to control aggression, language of the bees, overcrowding among rats, trying to talk to dolphins).

On a fair judgment, both contrasting approaches give positive results. The logical scientific problem that arises is, What is there in the nature of things that makes a certain method, or even moral attitude, work well or poorly in a given case? This question is not much studied. Every scientist seems to know what "the" scientific method is.

Another contrast of style, extremely relevant at present, is that between Big Science and old-fashioned shoestring science. There is plenty of research, with corresponding technology, that can be done only by Big Science; yet much, and perhaps most, of science will always be shoestring science, for which it is absurd to use the fancy and expensive equipment that has gotten to be the fashion.

Consider urban medicine. The problem, given a shortage of doctors and facilities, is how to improve the level of mass health, the vital statistics, and yet to practice medicine, which aims at the maximum possible health for each person. Perhaps the most efficient use of Big Science technology for the general health would be compulsory biennial checkups, as we inspect cars, for early diagnosis and to forestall chronic conditions with accumulating costs. Then, an excellent machine would be a total diagnostic bus to visit the neighborhoods, as we do [with] chest X rays. On the other hand, for actual treatment and especially for convalescence, the evidence seems to be that small, personalized hospitals are best. And to revive family practice, maybe the right idea is to offer a doctor a splendid suite in a public housing project.

Our contemporary practice makes little sense. We have expensive technology stored in specialists' offices and big hospitals, really unavailable for mass use in the neighborhoods; yet every individual, even if he is quite rich, finds it almost impossible to get attention to himself as an individual whole organism in his setting. He is sent from specialist to specialist and exists as a bag of symptoms and a file of test scores.

In automating, there is an analogous dilemma of how to cope with masses of people and get economies of scale without losing the individual at great consequent human and economic cost. A question of immense importance for the immediate future is, "Which functions should be automated or organized to use business machines, and which should not?" This question also is not getting asked, and the present disposition is that the sky is the limit for extraction, refining, manufacturing, processing, packaging, transportation, clerical work, ticketing, transactions, information retrieval, recruitment, middle management, evaluation, diagnosis, instruction, and even research and invention. Whether the machines can do all these kinds of jobs and more is partly an empirical question, but it also partly depends on what is meant by doing a job. Very often (e.g., in college admissions), machines are acquired for putative economies (which do not eventuate), but the true reason is that an overgrown and overcentralized organization cannot be administered without them. The technology conceals the essential trouble (e.g., that there is no community of scholars and students are treated like things). The function is badly performed, and finally the system breaks down anyway. I doubt that enterprises in which interpersonal relations are important are suited to much programming.

But, worse, what can happen is that the real function of the enterprise is subtly altered so that it is suitable for the mechanical system (e.g., "information retrieval" is taken as an adequate replacement for critical scholarship). Incommensurable factors, individual differences, the local context, the weighing of evidence are quietly overlooked though they may be of the essence. The system, with its subtly transformed purposes, seems to run very smoothly; it is productive, and it is more and more out of line with the nature of things and the real problems. Meantime, it is geared in with other enterprises of society (e.g., major public policy may depend on welfare or unemployment statistics, which, as they are tabulated, are blind to the actual lives of poor families). In such a case, the particular system may not break down, the whole society may explode.

I need hardly point out that American society is peculiarly liable to the corruption of inauthenticity, busily producing phony products. It lives by public relations, abstract ideals, front politics, show-business communications, mandarin credentials. It is preeminently overtechnologized. And computer technologists especially suffer for the euphoria of being in a new and rapidly expanding field. It is so astonishing that the robot can do the job at all or seem to do it, that it is easy to blink at the fact that it is doing it badly or isn't really doing quite that job.

DECENTRALIZATION

The current political assumption is that scientists and inventors, and even social scientists, are "value neutral," but their discoveries are "applied" by those who make decisions for the nation. Counter to this, I have been insinuating a kind of Jeffersonian democracy or guild socialism, that scientists and inventors and other workmen are responsible for the uses of the work they do and ought to be competent to judge these uses and have a say in deciding them. They usually are competent. To give a striking example, Ford assembly-line workers, according to Harvey Swados, who worked with them, are accurately critical of the glut of cars, but they have no way to vent their dissatisfactions with their useless occupation except to leave nuts and bolts to rattle in the body.

My bias is also pluralistic. Instead of the few national goals of a few decision-makers, I propose that there are many goals of many activities of life, and many professions and other interest groups each with its own criteria and goals that must be taken into account. A society that distributes power widely is superficially conflictful but fundamentally stable.

Research and development ought to be widely decentralized, the national fund for them being distributed through thousands of centers of initiative and decision. This would not be chaotic. We seem to have forgotten that for 400 years Western science majestically progressed with no central direction whatever, yet with exquisite international coordination, little duplication, almost nothing getting lost, in constant communication despite slow facilities. The reason was simply that all scientists wanted to get on with the same enterprise of testing the boundaries of knowledge, and they relied on one another.

What is noteworthy is that something similar holds also in invention and innovation, even in recent decades when there has been such a concentration of funding and apparent concentration of opportunity. The majority of big advances have still come from independents, partnerships, and tiny companies. (Evidence published by the Senate Subcommittee on Antitrust and Monopoly, May 1965.) To name a few, jet engines, xerography, automatic transmission, cellophane, air conditioning, quick freeze, antibiotics, and tranquilizers. The big technological teams must have disadvantages that outweigh their advantages, like lack of singlemindedness, poor communications, awkward scheduling. Naturally, big corporations have taken over the innovations, but the Senate evidence is that ninety percent of the government subsidy has gone for last-stage development for production, which they ought to have paid out of their own pockets.

We now have a theory that we have learned to learn, and that we can program technical progress, directed by a central planning board. But this doesn't make it so. The essence of the new still seems to be that nobody has thought of it, and the ones who get ideas are those in direct contact with the work. Too precise a pre-conception of what is wanted discourages creativity more than it channels it, and bureaucratic memoranda from distant directors don't help. This is especially true when, as at present, so much of the preconception of what is wanted comes from desperate political anxiety in emergencies. Solutions that emerge from such an attitude rarely strike out on new paths, but rather repeat traditional thinking with new gimmicks; they tend to compound the problem. A priceless advantage of widespread decentralization is that it engages more minds, and more mind, instead of a few panicky (or greedy) corporate minds.

A homespun advantage of small groups, according to the Senate testimony, is that coworkers can talk to one another, without schedules, reports, clock watching, and face saving.

An important hope from decentralizing science is to develop knowledgeable citizens, and provide not only a bigger pool of scientists and inventors, but also a public better able to protect itself and know how to judge the enormous budgets asked for. The safety of the environment is too important to be left to scientists, even ecologists. During the last decades of the nineteenth century and the first decade of the twentieth, the heyday of public faith in the beneficent religion of science and invention, say from Pasteur and Huxley to Edison and the Wright brothers, philosophers of science had a vision of a "scientific way of life," one in which people would be objective, respectful of evidence, accurate, free of super-stition and taboo, immune to irrational authority, experimental. All would be well, is the impression one gets from Thomas Huxley, if everybody knew the splendid Ninth Edition of the *Encyclopaedia Britannica* with its articles by Darwin and Clerk Maxwell. Veblen put his faith in the modesty and matter-of-factness of engineers to govern. Sullivan and Frank Lloyd Wright spoke for an austere func-tionalism and respect for the nature of materials and industrial processes. Patrick Geddes thought that new technology would finally get us out of the horrors of the Industrial Revolution and produce good communities. John Dewey devised a sys-tem of education to rear pragmatic and experimental citizens to be at home in the new technological world rather than estranged from it. Now, fifty years later, we are in the swamp of a scientific and technological environment and there are more scientists alive, etc., etc. But the mention of the "scientific way of life" seems like black humor.

Many of those who have grown up since 1945 and have never seen any other state of science and technology assume that rationalism itself is totally evil and dehumanizing. It is probably more significant than we like to think that they go in for astrology and the Book of Changes, as well as inducing psychedelic dreams by technological means. Jacques Ellul, a more philosophic critic, tries to show that technology is necessarily overcontrolling, standardizing, and voraciously inclusive, so that there is no place for freedom. But I doubt that any of this is intrinsic to science and technology. The crude history has been, rather, that they have fallen willingly under the dominion of money and power. Like Christianity or communism, the scientific way of life has never been tried.

THE NEW REFORMATION

To satisfy the March 4 dissenters, to break the military-industrial corporations and alter the priorities of the budget, would be to restructure the American economy almost to a revolutionary extent. But to meet the historical crisis of science at present, for science and technology to become prudent, ecological, and decentralized, requires a change that is even more profound, a kind of religious transformation. Yet there is nothing untraditional in what I have proposed: Prudence, ecology, and decentralization are indeed the high tradition of science and technology. Thus, the closest analogy I can think of is the Protestant Reformation, a change of moral allegiance, liberation from the Whore of Babylon, return to the pure faith.

Science has long been the chief orthodoxy of modern times and has certainly been badly corrupted, but the deepest flaw of the affluent societies that has alienated the young is not, finally, their imperialism, economic injustice, or racism, bad as these are, but their nauseating phoniness, triviality, and wastefulness, the cultural and moral scandal that Luther found when he went to Rome in 1510. And precisely science, which should have been the wind of truth to clear the air, has polluted the air, helped to brainwash, and provided weapons for war. I doubt that most young people today have even heard of the ideal of the dedicated researcher, truculent and incorruptible, and unrewarded, for instance the "German scientist" that Sinclair Lewis described in *Arrowsmith*. Such a figure is no longer believable. I don't mean, of course, that he doesn't exist; there must be thousands of him, just as there were good priests in 1510.

The analogy to the Reformation is even more exact if we consider the school system, from educational toys and Head Start up through the universities. This system is staffed by the biggest horde of monks since the time of Henry VIII. It is the biggest industry in the country. I have heard the estimate that forty percent of the national product is in the Knowledge Business. It is mostly hocus-pocus. Yet, the belief of parents in this institution is quite delusional and school diplomas are in fact the only entry to licensing and hiring in every kind of job. The abbots of this system are the chiefs of science (e.g., the National Science Foundation) who talk about reform but work to expand the school budgets, step up the curriculum, and inspire the endless catechism of tests.

These abuses are international, as the faith is. For instance, there is no essential difference between the military-industrial or the school systems of the Soviet Union and the United States. There are important differences in way of life and standard of living, but the abuses of technology are very similar: pollution, excessive urbanization, destruction of the biosphere, weaponry, and disastrous foreign aid. Our protesters naturally single out our own country, and the United States is the most powerful country, but the corruption we are speaking of is not specifically American nor even capitalist; it is a disease of modern times.

But the analogy is to the Reformation, it is not to primitive Christianity or some other primitivism, the abandonment of technological civilization. There is indeed much talk about the doom of Western civilization, and a few Adamites actually do retire into the hills; but for the great mass of humankind, and myself, that's not where it's at. There is not the slightest interruption to the universalizing of Western Civilization, including most of its delusions, into the so-called Third World. (If the atom bombs go off, however?)

Naturally, the exquisitely interesting question is whether or not this Reformation will occur, how to make it occur, against the entrenched worldwide system of corrupt power that is continually aggrandizing itself. I don't know. In my analogy, I have deliberately been choosing the date 1510, Luther in Rome, rather than 1517 when, in the popular story, he nailed his Theses on the cathedral door. There are everywhere contradictory signs and dilemmas. The new professional and technological class is more and more entangled in the work, statuses, and rewards of the system, and yet this same class, often the very same people, are more and more Protestant. On the other hand, the dissident young, who are unequivocally for radical change, are so alienated from occupation, function, knowledge, or even concern, that they often seem to be simply irrelevant to the underlying issues of modern times. The monks keep "improving" the schools and getting bigger budgets to do so, yet it is clear that high schools will be burned down, twelve-year-olds will play truant in droves, and the taxpayers are already asking what goes on and voting down the bonds.

The interlocking of technologies and all other institutions makes it almost impossible to reform policy in any part, yet this very interlocking that renders people powerless, including the decision-makers, creates a remarkable resonance and chain reaction if any determined group, or even determined individual, exerts force. In the face of overwhelmingly collective operations like space exploration, the average person must feel that local or grassroots efforts are worthless, there is no science but Big Science, and no administration but the State. And yet there is a powerful surge of localism, populism, and community action, as if people were determined to be free even if it makes no sense. A mighty empire is stood off by a band of peasants, and neither can win — This is even more remarkable than if David beats Goliath; it means that neither principle is historically adequate. In my opinion, these dilemmas and impasses show that we are on the eve of a transformation of conscience.

10. Technological Politics As If Democracy Really Mattered

RICHARD SCLOVE

"Of all the social impacts of technology," writes Richard Sclove in the following selection, "perhaps the most worrisome are the adverse effects on democracy." Sclove believes that technologies as diverse as microwave ovens, air conditioning, and urban sewage systems all have aspects that can prove detrimental to human communities and to democracy. He has no desire to reject all technology outright, however. Rather, he would like us "to become more discriminating in how we design, choose, and use technologies" — a course that might force us to give democracy priority over short-run economic goals.

How would democratic technologies look? Sclove proposes a set of design criteria. He gives examples, including several from Scandinavian nations, of technologies that meet these criteria. And he suggests some of the ways in which our political system and the nation's R&D enterprise might contribute to the development and promotion of democratic technologies. Sclove's essay comes from the "progressive left" political tradition. Some might regard it as hopelessly idealistic, particularly in view of current political trends in the United States that seem to run in the opposite direction. Nevertheless, it is a provocative piece that should give readers from all parts of the political spectrum much food for thought.

Richard Sclove, former executive director of the Loka Institute in Amherst, Massachusetts, is the author of Democracy and Technology *(Guilford Press, 1995). He is also the founder of the Federation of Activists on Science and Technology Network (FASTnet). Sclove, whose education combines a B.A. in environmental studies with a graduate degree in nuclear engineering and Ph.D. in political science from MIT, founded the Loka Institute in 1987 as a vehicle to carry on his work, which is dedicated to making science and technology more responsive to democratically decided social and environmental concerns. He is a popular lecturer and serves as a consultant to a variety of organizations.*

A century and a half ago, Alexis de Tocqueville described a politically exuberant United States in which steaming locomotives could not restrain citizens' enthusiasm to involve themselves in politics and community life:

> In some countries the inhabitants seem unwilling to avail themselves of the political privileges which the law gives them; it would seem that they set too high a value upon their time to spend it on the interests of the community; and they shut themselves up in a narrow selfishness. . . . But if an American were condemned to confine his activity to his own affairs, he would be robbed of

From *Technology for the Common Good*, Michael Shuman and Julia Sweig (eds.). "Technological Politics As If People Mattered: Choices Confronting Progressives." Copyright © 1993 by Richard Sclove. Reprinted with permission of Richard Sclove.

one-half of his existence; he would feel an immense void in the life which he is accustomed to lead, and his wretchedness would be unbearable.[1]

That is not today's United States, in which a bare majority of eligible voters participate in presidential elections while usually even fewer engage in local politics.[2] The causes of Americans' political disengagement are complex, but one culprit, more significant and intricate than commonly believed, is technology. Consider an instructive story from across the Atlantic.

During the early 1970s, running water was installed in the houses of Ibieca, a small village in northeast Spain. With pipes running directly to their homes, Ibiecans no longer had to fetch water from the village fountain. Families gradually purchased washing machines, and women stopped gathering to scrub laundry by hand at the village washbasin. Arduous tasks were rendered technologically superfluous, but village social life was unexpectedly altered. The public fountain and washbasin, once scenes of vigorous social interaction, became nearly deserted. Men began losing their sense of familiarity with the children and donkeys that once helped them haul water. Women stopped gathering at the washbasin to intermix scrubbing with politically empowering gossip about men and village life. In hindsight, the installation of running water helped break down the Ibiecans' strong bonds — with one another, with their animals, and with the land — that had knit them together as a community.[3] Painful in itself, such loss of community carries a specific political cost as well: As social ties weaken, so does a people's capacity to mobilize for political action.[4]

Is this a parable for our time? Like Ibiecans, we acquiesce in seemingly benign or innocuous technological changes. Ibiecans opted for technological innovations promising convenience, productivity, and economic growth. But they did not anticipate the hidden costs: greater inequality, social alienation, and steps toward community disintegration and political disempowerment. Does technological change invariably embody a Faustian trade-off between economic reward and sociopolitical malaise? No, not invariably. But the best hope for escaping such trade-offs is to develop a full-blown democratic politics of technology — something that even political progressives have not begun to conceive.

* * *

TECHNOLOGY AND DEMOCRACY

The approach to technology policy proposed here is grounded morally in the belief that people should be able to shape the basic social circumstances of their lives. It is aimed at organizing society along relatively equal and participatory lines, at achieving a system of egalitarian decentralization and confederation that Rutgers political scientist Benjamin Barber calls "strong democracy."[5] Historic examples of strong democracy include New England town meetings, the confederation of self-governing Swiss villages and cantons, and the tradition of trial by a jury of peers. Strong democracy also is apparent in the methods or aspirations of various social movements, such as the late nineteenth-century American Farmers Alliance, the 1960s Civil Rights movement, and the 1980s uprising of Solidarity in Poland.[6] In each of these cases, ordinary people claimed the rights and responsibilities of active citizenship.

If citizens ought to be empowered to participate in determining their society's basic structure and if technologies are an important part of that structure, it follows that technological design and practice should be democratized. Substantively, technologies must be compatible with our fundamental interest in strong democracy. And, procedurally, people from all walks of life must have expanding opportunities to shape the evolving technological order.

DESIGN CRITERIA FOR DEMOCRATIC TECHNOLOGIES

Table 1 presents some criteria for distinguishing among technologies based on their compatibility with democracy. The criteria are labeled "provisional" because they are neither complete nor definitive. Rather, they are intended to provoke political debate that can lead to an improved set of criteria.

Each criterion is intended to fulfill the institutional requirements for strong democracy: democratic community, democratic work, or democratic politics.[7]

TABLE 1.   A Provisional System of Design Criteria for Democratic Technologies

TOWARD DEMOCRATIC COMMUNITY

A.   Seek a balance among communitarian/cooperative, individualized, and inter-community technologies. Avoid technologies that establish authoritarian social relationships.

TOWARD DEMOCRATIC WORK

B.   Seek a diverse array of flexibly schedulable, self-actualizing technological practices. Avoid meaningless, debilitating, or otherwise autonomy-impairing technological practices.

TOWARD DEMOCRATIC POLITICS

C.   Seek technologies that can enable disadvantaged individuals and groups to participate fully in social and political life. Avoid technologies that support illegitimately hierarchical power relations between groups, organizations, or polities.

TO SECURE DEMOCRATIC SELF-GOVERNANCE

D.   Keep the potentially adverse consequences (e.g., environmental or social harms) of technologies within the boundaries of local political jurisdictions.

E.   Seek local economic self-reliance. Avoid technologies that promote dependency and loss of local autonomy.

F.   Seek technologies (including an architecture of public space) compatible with globally aware, egalitarian political decentralization and federation.

TO PERPETUATE DEMOCRATIC SOCIAL STRUCTURES

G.   Avoid technologies that are ecologically unsustainable or destructive of human health, survival, and the perpetuation of democratic institutions.

Technological decisions should attend initially and foremost to strengthening democracy, because democracy provides the necessary circumstances for deciding freely and fairly what other considerations must be taken into account in technological (and nontechnological) decision making. Until we do this, technologies will continue to hinder the advancement of other social objectives in subtle yet significant ways.

A series of examples can help explain these criteria and the feasibility of designing technologies that can satisfy them. Before proceeding, however, one clarifying note is in order. Each of the following examples illustrates a worthy social and democratic goal in its own right. However, isolated technological changes of this sort cannot be expected to represent a significant improvement in the overall democratization of society. The latter result will require multiple democratic design criteria, applied simultaneously to diverse technologies by citizens who employ broadly democratized processes of technological decision making. In other words, all the elements of a complete democratic politics of technology should converge at one time.

Criterion A: Technology and Democratic Community

Egalitarian community life is important to strong democracy because it enhances citizens' mutual respect, shared understanding, political equality, and social commitment. It empowers individuals within collectivities to challenge unjust concentrations of power. Unfortunately, diverse technological developments have contributed to the decline of community. The noise and danger of automobile traffic, detached single-family homes, air conditioning, and television all have isolated families away from one another and undermined a sense of collective purpose. This has been exacerbated by the loss of public spaces (with, for instance, town commons being supplanted by shopping malls).[8]

Are these plausible alternatives? Zurich, Switzerland, has promoted a partial antidote by providing neighborhoods with legal advice and architectural assistance aimed at increasing community interaction.[9] Thanks to the program, neighbors have begun to remove backyard fences; to build new walkways, gardens, and other community facilities; and generally to refashion a system of purely private yards into a well-balanced blend of private, semipublic, and public spaces.[10]

A housing movement born in Denmark in the mid-1960s seeks, more ambitiously, to integrate desirable aspects of traditional village life with such contemporary realities as urbanization, smaller families, single-parent or working-parent households, and greater sexual equality. The result is "co-housing" — resident-planned communities ranging today from six to eighty households. More than 100 such communities now exist in Denmark and the Netherlands, and they are spreading to the United States and elsewhere.

The Trudeslund co-housing community, located near Copenhagen, comprises thirty-three families. Homes for each family cluster along two garden-lined pedestrian streets and are surrounded by ample open space and forested areas.

Each home has its own kitchen, living room, and bedrooms, though these rooms have been somewhat downsized so that the savings can be used to construct and maintain common facilities. The latter include picnic tables, sandboxes, a parking lot, and, most importantly, a "common house" with a large kitchen and dining room, playrooms, a darkroom, a workshop room, a laundry room, and a community store. Each night, residents have the option of eating in the common dining room; cooking responsibilities rotate among all adults in the community (which means everyone cooks one evening a month). Because the community is designed to have residents walk past the common house on the way from the parking lot to any house, the common house becomes a natural gathering spot.

Trudeslund is successful by many measures. The common facilities save time and money, day care and baby-sitting flow naturally from the pattern of community life, social interaction flourishes without sacrificing privacy, and safety and conviviality both prosper by banishing cars to the outskirts of the community. Over time, cooperation has grown, with resident families choosing to purchase and share collectively tools, a car, a sailboat, and a vacation home. Rather than becoming insular, residents are actively involved in social and political life outside Trudeslund, with the common house serving as an organizing base for other activities.[11]

Insofar as mutual respect and equality are fundamental democratic values, an egalitarian community represents a democratic gain in its own right. Moreover, if one could envision creating an interacting network of such communities, one could expect to see greater respect, tolerance, and commonality emerging between communities, with beneficial implications for democratization on a broader scale.[12]

Criterion B: Democratic Work

Social scientists have hypothesized that the quality of our work life influences our moral development and our readiness to function as engaged citizens — that is, as active participants in a strong democracy.[13] Technology, in turn, plays a critical role in shaping our work experiences. Some years ago, sociologist and one-time union organizer Robert Schrank discussed alternative work arrangements with a group of union representatives at the General Motors Corporation. After describing several experiments in Scandinavian factories that permitted more interesting work routines and greater worker involvement in the day-to-day decision making, Schrank asked the men to imagine how they might redesign their own factories if given a chance. Their response was skeptical and unenthusiastic. Later Schrank reflected, "[T]he frame of reference of these workers was the linear assembly line as they experienced it. Even to think beyond that seemed difficult."[14]

Linear assembly lines not only tend to restrict possibilities for worker self-management, conviviality, and meaningful work but also to impair the ability of workers to envision technological alternatives. Schrank, however, was eventually able to show the GM workers more democratic automobile manufacturing technologies that have been in use for some years. For example, an innovative Volvo factory in Kalmar, Sweden, uses independently movable electronic dollies — each carrying an individual auto chassis — in place of a traditional assembly line. The dollies enable small teams of workers to plan and vary their daily routines for assembling automobile subsystems.[15]

A more creative and self-managed workplace "is democratically desirable in itself. But it also can help workers develop the moral commitment, skills, and confidence to participate politically beyond the workplace."

Criterion C: Technology and Power

While political equality is essential for strong democracy, all contemporary political systems encompass groups whose opportunities for participating in social and political life are circumscribed. Today's technologies help reproduce this inequitable constellation of power. For instance, the technologies and architecture with which women must cope every day often help exclude them from the corridors of power. "Labor-saving" appliances "liberate" many wives to do housework that was once performed by other family members. (During the bygone era of open-hearth cooking, for example, men chopped wood and children hauled water, thus contributing more equally to household maintenance.)[16] Likewise, modern neighborhood designs often isolate women socially, heighten their risk of physical abuse, and limit their opportunities to organize child care. The typical suburb lacks sidewalks, common gathering spaces, or the opportunity to work within a short distance of home.[17] Most public-transit systems have been designed without regard to women's typical social responsibilities. How is a mother supposed to get a baby carriage up onto a traditional bus or down the steps of a New York City subway station?[18] Many workplaces have jobs stereotyped as female that carry special risks of isolation, domination, stress, or harm. Secretaries and keypunch operators, who are preponderantly female, suffer unusually high levels of stress-related emotional and physical disorders. The marketing techniques of the mass media often degrade women and erect punishingly unattainable beauty standards.[19]

All of these consequences of technology limit women's opportunities to participate on equal terms in social and political life — including technological decision making. To explain these results, one need not invoke theories of misogyny or conspiracy (although the temptation may be strong). Generally, it seems more plausible to blame the indifference and insensitivity of male-dominated institutions and design professions, in which women's evaluations of their own needs rarely qualify as even a discussion topic.

Criterion D: Translocal Harms

Local self-governance is a key building block for strong democracy. The average citizen can exert much more influence locally than nationally, and local political equality and autonomy provide crucial opportunities for citizens to influence translocal politics.

Technologies can affect a community's ability to govern itself in several ways. For example, a technology that harms people in neighboring communities can provoke intercommunity conflict, which in turn can precipitate intervention by higher political authorities that subverts local self-governance. In the late nineteenth and early twentieth centuries, American cities imported clean water, or filtered and treated incoming water, while discharging raw sewage into rivers and lakes. Various methods of sewage treatment were known or under development, but few cities adopted them (unless the raw sewage caused local harm). As the buildup of sewage increased illness and death in downstream communities, state governments passed preemptive laws protecting water quality, established state boards of health to help administer the laws, and created new regional governmental authorities ("special districts") charged with integrating and managing the systems of water supply and sewage treatment. The result of this state intervention was that water quality and public health dramatically improved — but local autonomy dramatically declined. Indeed, regional water management set a precedent that influenced the development of institutions governing transportation, electrification, and telephone communication. The failure of municipal governments to assume technological responsibility toward neighboring communities wound up subverting their own autonomy and the tradition of local self-governance.[20]

Today, a related pattern continues to play out as large corporations repeatedly use cross-border pollution as a rationale to justify environmental regulation at ever higher levels of political aggregation (shifting, that is, from local to state, national, and, ultimately, international authorities). When "successful," this reallocation of power has transposed environmental decision making to arenas relatively inaccessible to grassroots participation, where corporations have secured weak environmental standards that preempt stronger standards favored at the local level. This logic helps to explain industry support for the 1970 U.S. Clean Air Act and for the 1990 amendments to the Montreal Protocol (a treaty that regulates emissions of industrial chemicals hazardous to the earth's atmospheric ozone shield).[21] The erosion of local authority to control pollution has thus led to a violation of Criterion G in Table 1 — "seek ecological sustainability."

Criterion E: Local Economic Self-Reliance

How can citizens meaningfully decide the fate of their community if economic survival depends on institutions or forces utterly beyond their control? Just as a measure of local political autonomy is essential for strong democracy, so, in turn, is a measure of local and regional economic self-reliance essential for political autonomy. Many modern technologies, however, can subvert self-reliance.

A century ago, London differed from other leading world cities in eschewing reliance on a single major electric company, large generating plants, or even a city-wide electric grid. Instead, there were dozens of small electric companies scattered throughout London — some privately owned, some public — deploying a diverse array of small-scale electrical generating technologies. Was London just backward and irrational, as engineers from elsewhere commonly supposed? Not obviously. London's electric companies operated at a profit and provided reliable and affordable power adapted to local needs. London's borough governments, perceiving their own political significance and autonomy as inextricable from the infrastructures upon which they depended economically, consistently opposed Parliamentary efforts to consolidate the grid. The boroughs favored a highly decentralized electrical system that each could control more easily.[22]

For analogous reasons, a number of American cities, towns, and neighborhoods have begun to develop locally owned businesses oriented toward production for nearby markets. The Rocky Mountain Institute has developed an analytical process, along with supporting instructional materials, which a growing number of towns in economic difficulty are using to reduce their consumption of imported energy, water, and food (rather than to depend on distant supplies) and to reinvest local capital (rather than to put it in the hands of bankers thousands of miles away).[23] Once these communities are more secure against distant market forces or multinational corporate decisions, they are more empowered to conceive and undertake local democratic initiatives.[24]

This strategy of self-reliance contrasts strikingly with the prevalent strategy used by communities — self-defeating when it is not futile — of using concessionary tax breaks, waivers on environmental standards or the promise of low wages to try to entice geographically fickle corporations. While generally decrying these corporate inducements, most proposed progressive technological strategies nonetheless remain preoccupied with advancing U.S. international competitiveness in ways that will assuredly erode local self-reliance. [25]

DEMOCRATIC DESIGN VERSUS PROGRESSIVE PROPOSALS

Several of the preceding examples suggest an important deficiency in the familiar progressive call to "rebuild America's crumbling technological infrastructure."[26] If our infrastructure needs repair or modernization, shouldn't we rebuild it in ways amenable to local democratic governance? For instance, there are technologies for managing industrial and municipal waste and conserving energy that can be deployed and administered with extensive local involvement.[27] Facilities to store solar energy for heating homes and buildings, as pioneered in Scandinavia, comprise another example of neighborhood-scale technology. Indeed, unless localities regain more control of their own infrastructures, there will be diminished incentive for the kind of grassroots political involvement essential to strong democracy. People only will participate in local politics when they have the power to affect important local decisions.

Another significant feature of all the preceding criteria is that they are designed to work together as a complementary system applied to an entire technological order. This, too, can improve the technology policies advocated by progressives. For instance, advocates of workplace democracy aim admirably to fulfill Criteria A and B, but generally fail to inquire whether the resulting goods and services are socially benign.[28] If we competitively and democratically produce democratically dubious technologies — say, chemical weapons, or certain consumer electronics like Walkmen that erode social interaction and solidarity — are we really making progress?[29]

Similarly, in an era of growing popular concern over acid rain, atmospheric ozone depletion, and global warming, few doubt the necessity of devising more ecologically sustainable technologies (Criterion G). Yet environmentalists sometimes imagine that sustainability alone is a sufficient basis for technological design.[30] To see the incompleteness here, recall the old sewage system configurations that both protected public health and subverted local self-governance, or consider Singapore's relatively stringent environmental policies that are coupled with a starkly authoritarian political regime.[31] In evaluating technology, we must learn to take into account all technologies, all their focal and nonfocal effects, and all the manifold ways in which technologies influence political relations.

TOWARD A DEMOCRATIC POLITICS OF TECHNOLOGY

Democratic design criteria are essential to a democratic politics of technology, but only if coupled with institutions for greater popular involvement in all domains of technological decision making. This suggests the need to establish new opportunities for popular participation to contest and apply the design criteria (in communities, workplaces, and other social realms), to set research and development (R&D) priorities, and to govern important technological systems. For instance, perhaps corporate R&D tax credits could be scaled up if a business introduces a democratic process or uses democratic design criteria to guide its R&D.

Our basic goal must be to open, democratize, and partly decentralize pertinent government agencies, to create avenues for worker and community involvement in corporate R&D and strategic planning, and to strengthen the capabilities of public institutions to monitor and, as needed, guide the political and social consequences of technology. We also need political strategies to accomplish these objectives, preferably built on popular movements and technological initiatives that already exist.[32]

One pertinent example of how to democratize technological decision making began in the early 1970s, when natural gas was found beneath the frigid and remote northwest corner of Canada. Energy companies soon proposed building a high-pressure, chilled pipeline across thousands of miles of wilderness, the traditional home of the Inuit (Eskimos) and various Indian tribes. At that point, a government ministry, anticipating significant environmental and social repercussions, initiated a public inquiry under the supervision of a respected Supreme Court justice, Thomas R. Berger.

The MacKenzie Valley Pipeline Inquiry opened its preliminary hearings to any Canadian who felt remotely affected by the proposal. Berger and his staff developed a novel format to encourage a thorough, open, and accessible inquiry. Formal, quasijudicial hearings were held that combined conventional expert testimony with cross-examination. Berger also conducted a series of informal "community hearings." Traveling 17,000 miles to thirty-five remote villages and settlements, the MacKenzie Inquiry took testimony from nearly 1,000 native witnesses. And it provided funding to disadvantaged groups to support travel and legal counsel for more competent participation. The Canadian Broadcasting Company carried daily radio summaries of all the hearings in English and in six native languages.

One of the MacKenzie Inquiry's important lessons was that laypeople can produce useful social and technical information. According to one technical adviser:

> Input from nontechnical people played a key role in the Inquiry's deliberations over even the most highly technical and specialized scientific and engineering subjects. . . . [The final report] discusses the biological vulnerability of the Beaufort Sea based not only on the evidence of the highly trained biological experts who testified at the formal hearings but also on the views of the Inuit hunters who spoke at the community hearings. . . . [Moreover,] when discussion turned to . . . complex socioeconomic issues of social and cultural impact, [native] land claims, and local business involvement — it became apparent that the people who live their lives with the issues are in every sense the experts. . . . Their perceptions provided precisely the kind of information necessary to make an impact assessment.[33]

Quoting generously from expert and citizen witnesses, Berger's final report became a national best-seller. Within months, the original pipeline proposal was rejected, and the Canadian Parliament instead approved an alternate route paralleling the existing Alaska Highway.[34] One can fault the MacKenzie Inquiry for depending so much on the democratic sensibilities and good faith of one man — Judge Berger—rather than empowering the affected native groups to play a role in formulating the conclusions. But the process was nevertheless vastly more open and egalitarian than comparable decision-making efforts in other industrial societies.[35]

There are many other prototypes for institutions or processes that enable greater popular involvement in technological decisions. For instance, the nascent Community Health Decisions (CHD) movement has developed grassroots procedures to forge popular consensus on ethical principles governing medical policy and technology. One of the accomplishments of the movement has been to organize dozens of community meetings throughout Oregon to debate proposed reforms in the state's health care system.[36] The CHD movement could provide a model for future forums in which citizens debate more general democratic design criteria for technology.

In several states, including Maine, Washington, and California, coalitions of peace activists, labor unions, business leaders, community groups, and government officials have created democratic processes to wean regional economies away from their dependence on military production. For example, responding to grassroots pressure, the state of Washington has established a citizen advisory group that monitors military spending in the state, assesses post–Cold War economic needs and opportunities, and promulgates action plans to help defense-dependent communities diversify their productive base.[37] This shows how a region can use social criteria to evaluate and redirect an entire technological order.

During the past twenty years, the Dutch have developed a network of street-corner "science shops," supported by nearby university staff and students, where citizen groups receive free assistance to address social issues with technical components. One science shop helped a local environmental group document the contamination of heavy metals in vegetables, which pressured the Dutch government to sponsor a major cleanup in metalworking plants. The science shops have empowered citizens to participate in technological decision making so successfully that they have prompted similar efforts throughout much of Western Europe.[38]

Traditional Amish communities, often misperceived as technologically naive or backward, have pioneered popular deliberative processes for screening technologies based on their cumulative social impacts, in effect attending to many of the criteria listed in Table 1. One of their methods is to place the adoption of a new technology on probation for one year to discover what the social effects might be. For instance, Amish dairy communities in east-central Illinois ran a one-year trial with diesel-powered bulk milk tanks before judging them socially acceptable; other Amish communities used social trials to prohibit once-probationary household telephones or personal computers.[39]

The preceding examples are, of course, atypical. Most technological choices are made by experts, bureaucratic machination, or unregulated market interactions. But the exceptions provide crucial evidence that, given the right institutional circumstances, lay citizens can make reasonable technological decisions reflecting their own priorities. Even federal agencies, such as the [now defunct] Office of Technology Assessment, the National Science Foundation, and the National Institutes of Health (NIH), have occasionally supported or incorporated citizen participation in their decision-making procedures.[40] For instance, the NIH has used both expert and lay advisory panels to evaluate research proposals. The experts judge the scientific merits, while laypeople help weigh the social value, political import, or ethical propriety. One can envision a wide range of private or public institutions using such models to develop a new system of democratic procedures for choosing among technological alternatives.

PARTICIPATORY RESEARCH, DEVELOPMENT, AND DESIGN

Democratic processes for technological choice and oversight are vital, yet hardly worth the effort unless participants have a broad range of alternative technologies from which to choose. Hence, it is essential to weave democracy into the fabric of technological research, development, and design (RD&D).[41] Consider four examples of how this has been done.

Democratic Design of Workplace Technology

In Scandinavia during the early 1980s, unionized newspaper-graphics workers —
in collaboration with sympathetic university researchers, a Swedish government
laboratory, and a state-owned publishing company — succeeded in inventing a
form of computer software unique in its day. Instead of following trends toward
routinized or mechanized newspaper layout, this software contained some of the
capabilities later embodied in desktop-publishing programs that enable printers
and graphic artists to exercise considerable creativity in page design.[42] Known as
UTOPIA, this project demonstrated how broadened participation in the RD&D
process could lead to a design innovation that, in turn, supported one condition
of democracy — creative work (Criterion B).

UTOPIA is less ambitious than several other attempts at participatory design
within the workplace. For example, in the 1970s workers at Britain's Lucas Aerospace Corporation sought not only to democratize their own work processes but
also to produce more socially useful products.[43] But UTOPIA demonstrated that
workers could go beyond just developing prototypes. It also should be noted that
this instance of collaboration between workers and technical experts — initially
limited to a single technology within a single industry — occurred under unusually favorable social and political conditions. Sweden's workforce is eighty-five
percent unionized, and the nation's pro-labor Social Democratic party has held
power during most of the past fifty years.

Participatory Architecture

Compared with the relatively few examples of participatory design of machinery,
appliances, or technical infrastructure, there is a rich history of citizen participation in architectural design. One example is the "Zone Sociale" at the Catholic
University of Louvain Medical School in Brussels. In 1969, students insisted that
new university housing mitigate the alienating architecture of the adjacent hospital. Architect Lucien Kroll established an open-ended, participatory design
process that elicited intricate organic forms (e.g., support pillars shaped like
gnarled tree trunks), richly diverse patterns of social interaction (e.g., a nursery
school situated near administrative offices and a bar), and a dense network of
pedestrian paths, gardens, and public spaces. Walls and floors of dwellings were
movable so that students could design their own living spaces. Construction
workers were given design principles and constraints rather than finalized blueprints, and they were encouraged to create and display their own sculptures.
Initially baffled by the level of spontaneity and playfulness, the project's structural engineers gradually adapted themselves to the diversity of competent
participants.

Everything proceeded splendidly for some years until the university administration became alarmed at the extent to which they could not control the
process. When the students were away on vacation, they fired Kroll and halted
further construction.[44]

Feminist Design

What would happen if women played a greater part in RD&D? One answer comes from feminists who have long been critical of housing designs and urban layouts that reinforce the social isolation and the low, unpaid status of women as housewives.[45] If women were more actively engaged in community design, they might set up more shared neighborhood facilities for day care, laundry, or food preparation, or they might locate homes, workplaces, stores, and public facilities more closely together. Realized examples of feminist design exist in London, Stockholm, and Providence, Rhode Island.[46]

Another approach has been pioneered by an artist and former overworked mother named Frances Gabe, who devoted several decades to inventing a self-cleaning house. "In Gabe's house," according to author Jan Zimmerman, "dishes are washed in the cupboard, clothes are cleaned in the closets, and the rest of the house sparkles after a humid misting and blow dry!"[47]

Other feminists have established women's computer networks and designed alternatives to dreary female office work and to transportation networks insensitive to women's needs.[48] An explicit feminist complaint against current reproductive technologies — such as infertility treatments, surrogate mothering, hysterectomy, and abortion — is that women have played a negligible role in guiding the medical RD&D agendas which have imposed on women agonizing moral dilemmas that might otherwise be averted or structured differently.[49]

Barrier-Free Design

During the past two decades, there has been substantial innovation in the design of "barrier-free" equipment, buildings, and public spaces responsive to the needs of people with physical disabilities. Much of the impetus came from disabled citizens who organized themselves to assert their needs or helped invent design solutions. For example, prototypes of the Kurzweil Reading Machine, which uses computer voice-synthesis to read typed text aloud, were tested by over 150 blind users. In an eighteen-month period, these users made over a hundred recommendations, many of which were incorporated into later versions of the device.[50]

Technology by the People

All these examples of participatory design demonstrate that it is possible to have a much wider range of people participating in technological research, development, and design.[51] Moreover, participatory design broadens the menu of technological choices. But many participatory design exercises also have encountered fierce opposition from powerful institutions — opposition engendered, not because the exercises were failing, but because they were succeeding.

Still, some advocates of participatory RD&D have elected to state their case entirely in terms of the material interests of the nonparticipants. Others have noted the contribution that participation can make to improved productivity or to better design solutions. These are all fair and reasonable arguments. What is rarely articulated is the specific moral argument that the opportunity to participate in RD&D should be a matter of right, because it is essential to individual moral autonomy, to human dignity, and to democratic self-governance.

A powerful moral case for participatory design has been made by people with disabilities who have demanded barrier-free design. The movement's achievements are now apparent in the profusion of ramps and modified rest rooms in public places (responsive to Criterion C), and they will soon become even more apparent with the promulgation of new regulations under the Americans with Disabilities Act of 1990. The movement not only opposes antidemocratic design but also has a constructive, hopeful thrust. Nonmarket, democratic design criteria — often formulated and applied by disabled laypeople — are now being used to define individual and collective needs, including access to public spaces. Moreover, participants do not evaluate just one technology at a time — the norm in conventional technology assessment — but entire technological and architectural environments. When the range of democratic criteria broadens and when the participants expand beyond the disabled population, we will be well on our way toward ensuring that our technology is compatible with democracy.

CONCLUSION

Current technological orders are generally short on communitarian or cooperative activities and long on isolation and authoritarianism (violating Criterion A). Work is frequently stultifying and tends to impair moral growth and political efficacy (violating Criterion B). Illegitimate power asymmetries are reproduced through technological means (violating Criterion C.)

The opportunity to engage in a vibrant civic life is often preempted by shopping malls, suburban subdivisions, unconstrained automobilization, and an explosive proliferation in home entertainment devices. Thus, we have diminished access to local mediating institutions or to public spaces that could support democratic empowerment within the broader society (violating Criteria A and F). The need to manage translocal harms, coupled with widespread dependence on centrally managed technological systems and with the growing integration of the global economy, has helped render local governments relatively powerless, thereby reducing anyone's incentive to participate (violating Criteria D, E, and F). Meanwhile, there is little compensating incentive to engage directly in national politics, which television reduces to a passive spectator sport, where powerful corporations exert disproportionate influence, where deep questions of social structure are slighted, and where the average citizen has negligible effect.

While it is not always easy to establish causal connections running from structural deficiencies to other social ills, it hardly seems conceivable that weak community ties, atrophied local political capabilities, and authoritarian and degraded work processes have had no influence upon illiteracy, stress, illness, divorce rates, teen pregnancy, crime, drug abuse, psychological disorders, and so on. Perhaps, as de Tocqueville foresaw, many of us do sometimes feel shut up in a narrow selfishness, robbed of one-half of our existence, left with an immense void in our lives.

Progressive technological strategists face a dilemma. We can couch our nostrums in terms of prevailing economic goals like competitiveness and try to win short-run victories. Or we can strive for a world worthy of our ideals. But we can no longer pretend that the progressive policies so far proposed for improving national economic performance, any more than conservative policies, are going to avoid exacerbating the United States's most profound social and political maladies. Has not the time arrived to mobilize for a democratic politics of technology?

NOTES

1. Alexis de Tocqueville, *Democracy in America,* ed. Phillips Bradley, rev. ed. (1848; reprint, New York: Vintage Books, 1954), Vol. 1, p. 260.
2. John J. Kushma, "Participation and the Democratic Agenda: Theory and Praxis," in Marc V. Levine et al. *The State and Democracy: Revitalizing America's Government* (New York: Routledge, 1988), pp. 14–48. According to the Harwood Group, many Americans would like to be more involved in public affairs, but feel locked out of the current system. See *Citizens and Politics: A View from Main Street America* (Dayton, OH: The Kettering Foundation, 1991).
3. Susan Friend Harding, *Remaking Ibieca: Rural Life in Aragon under Franco* (Chapel Hill: University of North Carolina Press, 1984).
4. Samuel Bowles and Herbert Gintis, *Democracy and Capitalism: Property, Community, and the Contradictions of Modern Social Thought* (New York: Basic Books, 1986). The converse causal tie between community strength and political empowerment is suggested, for instance, by solidaristic Amish communities' success in resisting mandatory public schooling, military conscription, and participation in the federal social security system. See Donald B. Kraybill, *The Riddle of Amish Culture* (Baltimore: Johns Hopkins University Press, 1989).
5. Benjamin Barber, *Strong Democracy: Participatory Politics for a New Age* (Berkeley: University of California Press, 1984).
6. See, for example, Sara M. Evans and Harry C. Boyte, *Free Spaces: The Sources of Democratic Change in America* (New York: Harper and Row, 1986).
7. For the complete derivation and justification for these and additional democratic design criteria, see Richard E. Sclove, *Democracy and Technology* (New York: Guilford Press, 1995).
8. See, for example, Kenneth T. Jackson, *Crabgrass Frontier: The Suburbanization of the United States* (New York: Oxford University Press, 1985); and Barber, *Strong Democracy* pp. 267–73, 305–6.
9. I define technology broadly as material artifacts and the practices or beliefs that accompany their creation or use. Hence, I regard architecture and community planning as a subdomain of technology.
10. Dolores Hayden, *Redesigning the American Dream: The Future of Housing, Work, and Family Life* (New York: W. W. Norton, 1984), pp. 189–91.
11. Kathryn McCamant and Charles Durrett, *Cohousing: A Contemporary Approach to Housing Ourselves* (Berkeley, CA: Habitat Press, 1988).
12. Some supporting evidence can be found in the emerging international network of "sister cities." See, for example, Michael Shuman, "From Charity to Justice," *Bulletin of Municipal Foreign Policy* 2:4 (Autumn 1988), pp. 50–59.
13. Edward S. Greenberg, *Workplace Democracy: The Political Effects of Participation* (Ithaca, NY: Cornell University Press, 1986); William M. Lafferty, "Work as a Source of Political Learning among Wage-Laborers and Lower-Level Employees," in *Political Learning in*

Adulthood: A Sourcebook of Theory and Research, ed. Roberta S. Sigel (Chicago: University of Chicago Press, 1989), pp. 102–42; Melvin L. Kohn et al., "Position in the Class Structure and Psychological Functioning in the United States, Japan, and Poland," *American Journal of Sociology* 95:4 (January 1990), pp. 964–1008.

14. Robert Schrank, *Ten Thousand Working Days* (Cambridge, MA: MIT Press, 1978), p. 226.

15. Ibid., pp. 221–27. On remaining democratic shortcomings in the Volvo factories, see Stephen Hill, *Competition and Control at Work: The New Industrial Sociology* (Cambridge, MA: MIT Press, 1981), pp. 39 and 104–5. For further recent examples of both democratic and nondemocratic workplace technology, see Shoshana Zuboff, *In the Age of the Smart Machine: The Future of Work and Power* (New York: Basic Books, 1988). Excerpted in Part VI of this book.

16. See Ruth Schwartz Cowan, *More Work for Mother: The Ironies of Household Technology from the Open Hearth to the Microwave* (New York: Basic Books, 1983).

17. Hayden, *Redesigning the American Dream;* Ray Oldenburg, *The Great Good Place: Cafes, Coffee Shops, Community Centers, Beauty Parlors, General Stores, Bars, Hangouts, and How They Get You through the Day* (New York: Paragon House, 1989).

18. See Women and Transport Forum, "Women on the Move: How Public Is Public Transport?" in *Technology and Women's Voices: Keeping in Touch,* ed. Cheris B. Kramarae (New York: Routledge & Kegan Paul, 1988), pp. 116–34.

19. Barbara Drygulski Wright, *Women, Work, and Technology: Transformations* (Ann Arbor: University of Michigan Press, 1987); Naomi Wolf, *The Beauty Myth: How Images of Beauty Are Used against Women* (New York: William Morrow, 1991).

20. See Joel A. Tarr, "Sewerage and the Development of the Networked City in the United States, 1850–1930," in *Technology and the Rise of the Networked City,* ed. Joel A. Tarr and Gabriel Dupuy (Philadelphia: Temple University Press, 1988), pp. 159–85; and Gerald E. Frug, "The City as a Legal Concept," *Harvard Law Review* 93:6 (April 1980), pp. 1057–154.

21. See Samuel P. Hays, *Beauty, Health, and Permanence: Environmental Politics in the United States, 1955–1985* (Cambridge: Cambridge University Press, 1987), pp. 443–5, 456–7; Gareth Porter and Janet Welsh Brown, *Global Environmental Politics* (Boulder, CO: Westview Press, 1991), pp. 64, 66; Wolfgang Sachs, "Environment and Development: The Story of a Dangerous Liaison," *The Ecologist* 21:6 (November/December 1991), pp. 252–7. Local ability to pressure corporations to reduce pollution could be much advanced by supportive legislation, such as the Environmental Bill of Rights proposed in Samuel Bowles, David M. Gordon, and Thomas E. Weisskopf, *Beyond the Wasteland: A Democratic Alternative to Economic Decline* (Garden City, NY: Anchor Press/Doubleday, 1983), pp. 344–6.

22. Thomas Parke Hughes, *Networks of Power: Electrification in Western Society, 1880–1930* (Baltimore: Johns Hopkins University Press, 1983), Chapter 9.

23. See Robert Gilman, "Four Steps to Self-Reliance: The Story behind Rocky Mountain Institute's Economic Renewal Project," *In Context* 14 (Autumn 1986), pp. 41–46; Barbara A. Cole, *Business Opportunities Casebook* (Snowmass, CO: Rocky Mountain Institute, 1988); and David Morris, "Self-Reliant Cities: The Rise of the New City-States," in *Resettling America: Energy, Ecology, and Community* ed. Gary J. Coates (Andover, MA: Brick Housing Publishing Co., 1981), pp. 240–62.

24. See John Gaventa, *Power and Powerlessness: Quiescence and Rebellion in an Appalachian Valley* (Urbana: University of Illinois Press, 1980), Chapter 8; and Gerald E. Frug, "The City as a Legal Concept," *Harvard Law Review* 93:6 (April 1980), pp. 1057–154.

25. See, for example, Stephen S. Cohen and John Zysman, *Manufacturing Matters: The Myth of the Post-Industrial Economy* (New York: Basic Books, 1987); Michael L. Dertouzos, Richard K. Lester, Robert M. Solow, and the MIT Commission on Industrial Competitiveness, *Made in America: Regaining the Productive Edge* (Cambridge, MA: MIT Press, 1989); Lester C. Thurow, *The Zero-Sum Solution: Building a World-Class American Economy* (New York: Simon & Schuster, 1985); and Joel S. Yudken and Michael Black, "Targeting National Needs: A New Direction for Science and Technology Policy," *World Policy Journal* 7:2 (Spring 1990), pp. 282–3. While sharply critical of economic nationalism, Robert B. Reich's *The Work of Nations* (New York: Vintage Books, 1992) assumes increased integra-

tion into an ever-more-intensively globalized economy. On the importance of granting greater local power over national self-reliance, see Ann J. Tickner, *Self-Reliance versus Power Politics: The American and Indian Experiences in Building Nation States* (New York: Columbia University Press, 1987).

26. See, for example, Bowles et al., *Beyond the Wasteland;* Yudken and Black, "Targeting National Needs"; and Robert B. Reich, "The Real Economy," *Atlantic Monthly* 267:2 (February 1991), pp. 35–52.

27. Amory B. Lovins, *Soft Energy Paths: Toward a Durable Peace* (Cambridge, MA: Ballinger, 1977); National Center for Appropriate Technology, *Wastes to Resources: Appropriate Technologies for Sewage Treatment and Conversion,* DOE/CE/15095-2 (Washington, DC: U.S. Government Printing Office, July 1983); Ken Darrow and Mike Saxenian, *Appropriate Technology Sourcebook: A Guide to Practical Books for Village and Small Community Technology* (Stanford, CA: Volunteers in Asia, 1986); Valjean McLenighan, *Sustainable Manufacturing: Saving Jobs, Saving the Environment* (Chicago: Center for Neighborhood Technology, 1990).

28. See, for example, Michael J. Piore and Charles F. Sabel, *The Second Industrial Divide: Possibilities for Prosperity* (New York: Basic Books, 1984); Cohen and Zysman, *Manufacturing Matters.*

29. David F. Noble's deservedly influential essay, "Social Choice in Machine Design: The Case of Automatically Controlled Machine Tools," lauds Norwegian factory worker involvement in technology choices that helped workers maintain autonomy and creativity. True enough, but the factory in question was a state-owned weapons production plant. In *Case Studies on the Labor Process,* ed. Andrew Zimbalist (New York: Monthly Review Press, 1979), pp. 18–50.

30. See, for example, John Todd and Nancy Jack Todd, *Bioshelters, Ocean Arks, City Farming: Ecology as the Basis of Design* (San Francisco: Sierra Club Books, 1984).

31. Stan Sesser, "A Reporter at Large: A Nation of Contradictions," *The New Yorker* (13 January 1992), pp. 37–68.

32. See Richard E. Sclove, "The Nuts and Bolts of Democracy: Toward a Democratic Politics of Technological Design," in *Critical Perspectives on Non-Academic Science and Engineering,* ed. Paul T. Durbin (Bethlehem, PA: Lehigh University Press, 1991), pp. 239–62; and Sclove, *Technology and Freedom.*

33. D. J. Gamble, "The Berger Inquiry: An Impact Assessment Process," *Science* 199:4332 (3 March 1978), pp. 950–1.

34. Ibid., pp. 946–52; Thomas R. Berger, *Northern Frontier, Northern Homeland: The Report of the MacKenzie Valley Pipeline Inquiry,* 2 vols. (Ottawa: Minister of Supply and Services, Canada, 1977); Organisation for Economic Cooperation and Development (OECD), *Technology on Trial. Public Participation in Decision-Making Related to Science and Technology* (Paris: OECD, 1979).

35. See, for example, Barry M. Casper and Paul David Wellstone, *Powerline: The First Battle of America's Energy War* (Amherst: University of Massachusetts Press, 1981); David Dickson, *The New Politics of Science* (Chicago: University of Chicago Press, 1988).

36. Bruce Jennings et al., "Grassroots Bioethics Revisited: Health Care Priorities and Community Values," *Hastings Center Report* 20:5 (September/October 1990), pp. 16–23.

37. Kevin J. Cassidy, "Defense Conversion: Economic Planning and Democratic Participation," *Science, Technology, and Human Values* 17:3 (Summer 1992), pp. 334–48.

38. Seth Shulman, "Mr. Wizard's Wetenschapswinkel," *Technology Review* 91:5 (July 1988), pp. 8–9.

39. On Amish technological decision making see, for example, Marc A. Olshan, "Modernity, the Folk Society, and the Old Order Amish: An Alternative Interpretation," *Rural Sociology* 46:2 (Summer 1981), pp. 297–309; Victor Stoltzfus, "Amish Agriculture: Adaptive Strategies for Economic Survival of Community Life," *Rural Sociology* 38:2 (Fall 1973), pp. 196–206; Kraybill, *The Riddle of the Amish Culture.*

40. See for example, U.S. Congress, Office of Technology Assessment, *Coastal Effects of Offshore Energy Systems* (Washington, DC: U.S. Government Printing Office, 1976); Rachelle

Hollander, "Institutionalizing Public Service Science: Its Perils and Promise," in *Citizen Participation in Science Policy,* ed. James C. Petersen (Amherst: University of Massachusetts Press, 1984), pp. 75–95.

41. For additional arguments in support of participatory design, see Richard E. Sclove, "The Nuts and Bolts of Democracy: Democratic Theory and Technological Design," in *Democracy in Technological Society,* ed. Langdon Winner (Dordrecht, Netherlands: Kluwer Academic Publisher, 1992), pp. 132–57.

42. Andrew Martin, "Unions, the Quality of Work, and Technological Change in Sweden," in *Worker Participation and the Politics of Reform,* ed. Carmen Sirianni (Philadelphia: Temple University Press, 1987), pp. 99–139.

43. Hilary Wainwright and Dave Elliott, *The Lucas Plan. A New Trade Unionism in the Making?* (London: Allison and Busby, 1982).

44. Lucien Kroll, "Anarchitecture," in *The Scope of Social Architecture,* ed. Richard C. Hatch (New York: Van Nostrand Reinhold, 1984), pp. 166–85.

45. Hayden, *Redesigning the American Dream,* Chapter 4.

46. Ibid., pp. 163–70.

47. Jan Zimmerman, *Once Upon the Future: A Woman's Guide to Tomorrow's Technology* (New York: Pandora, 1986), pp. 36–37.

48. Wright, *Women, Work, and Technology*; Kramarae, *Technology and Women's Voices.*

49. See Sarah Franklin and Maureen McNeil, "Reproductive Futures: Recent Literature and Current Feminist Debates on Reproductive Technologies," *Feminist Studies* 14:3 (Fall 1988), pp. 545–60.

50. See Michael Hingson, "The Consumer Testing Project for the Kurzweil Reading Machine for the Blind," pp. 89–90, and Raymond Kurzweil, "The Development of the Kurzweil Reading Machine," pp. 94–96, in Virginia W. Stern and Martha Ross Redden, (eds.), *Technology for Independent Living: Proceedings of the 1980 Workshops on Science and Technology for the Handicapped.* (Washington, DC: American Association for the Advancement of Science, 1982).

51. For a number of additional examples, see Sclove, "The Nuts and Bolts of Democracy: Toward a Democratic Politics of Technological Design," or contact the Loka Institute, P.O. Box 355, Amherst, MA 01004; e-mail: Loka@amherst.edu.

11. Western Colonization of the Future

ZIAUDDIN SARDAR

Ziauddin Sardar has seen the future and he doesn't like it. It's much like the present, only more so. It is a future cast in the mold of the West. Technology has created a "self-perpetuating momentum that has locked us in a linear, one-dimensional trajectory" that is leading the world to a Western vision of the future. Large corporations create desires and fulfill those desires with new products. Globalization means shaping the world in the image of Western culture and civilization. The future has been "colonized" by the West. The rest of the world, led by Asia, must break the cycle of colonization if it is going to shape a future that reflects a wider range of values.

Sardar is a distinguished Muslim writer, cultural critic, and intellectual. He is consulting editor of Futures *and the author of over 200 papers, essays, and articles and many books, including* Thomas Kuhn and the Science Wars *(2000),* Postmodernism and the Other *(1998), and* Introducing Muhammad *(1994). He is currently visiting professor of science policy at Middlesex University in London. The following selection is drawn from his edited volume,* Rescuing All Our Futures: The Future of Futures Studies *(1999), a collection of essays that discuss the application of multiculturalism to the study of the future.*

It is simple. The future has been colonized. It is already an occupied territory whose liberation is the most pressing challenge for the people of the non-West if they are to inherit a future made in their own likeness.

Even though thinking about the future is a tricky and hazardous business, it has become big business. Tricky because our conventional way of thinking does not normally incorporate the future — It requires considerable conscious effort to imagine how the future may unfold, what anticipated and unexpected possibilities lurk on distant horizons. Hazardous because the probability of getting one's forecasts wrong is very high. But this has not stopped the business of forecasting from spreading like a global fire. Anticipating the future nowadays means little more than forecasting the future. And forecasting is one of the major tools by which the future is colonized. No matter how sophisticated the technique—and techniques are becoming more and more refined and complex—forecasting simply ends up by projecting the (selected) past and the (often-privileged) present onto a linear future.

Despite numerous failures, unfulfilled promises, and misplaced optimism about the ability of technology to usher in a more humane and sane future, technological trends dominate the business of forecasting. The future is little more than the transformation of society by new Western technologies. We are bombarded by this message constantly from a host of different directions. The advertisements on television and radio, in newspapers and magazines, for new models of computers, cars, mobile phones, digital and satellite consumer goods — all ask us to reflect on how new technologies will transform not just our social and cultural environments but the very idea of what it is to be human. "The future," according to a mobile phone company, "is Orange." According to a car manufacturer, "The future is Vauxhall Vectra." And computer junkies sing in unison, "The future is the World Wide Web."

It is highly significant that the filler material, what appears between programs broadcast by satellite all over Asia, relies heavily on supposedly informative vignettes wherein Western experts reiterate the message of high technology as the creative potential of the future. The subtext is that the future technologies are the resource of the West, which will enable the non-West to have a future; the future it will have is a clone of the Western future. If that seems empowering and inclusive, it is only an illusory surface seduction that obfuscates how that future is made.

Business and corporate books, available globally and at any airport, tell us how we will all be Internetted, tuned in to hundreds of channels, working from home, and generally living in a technological bliss in the decades to come. For example, John Naisbitt's *Megatrends*[1] tells us that global trends are moving us from industrial to information age, national to world economy, representative to participatory democracy (where on earth can you find even an inkling of a participatory democracy?), and from either/or to multiple logic. The future will thus be better all around and for everyone. (Richard Slaughter has shown that Naisbitt's megatrends are half-truths that cannot be clearly discerned, and the book itself amounts to little more than a brochure for liberal capitalism.[2]) Peter Drucker's *Managing for the Future*[3] advises corporate types to hang on to their culture as the future is already with us. No need to contemplate what could or would happen in the next decades as they have already collapsed on us. And in *Rethinking the Future,*[4] we are told how the new science of complexity will enable us to manage uncertainty and generate new methods for creating tomorrow's advantages and strategies for growth and reinvent the basis for competition. The future, therefore, will not be much different in at least one respect: Corporations will continue to dominate and they will have new theories and tools to maintain their domination.

The messages of such works are translated into visual metaphors by global television programs, such as CNN's "Future Watch" and BBC's "Tomorrow's World." The sheer repetition and the intellectual and visual power with which this message is hammered home have profound consequences for our future-consciousness. It is thus not surprising that the vast majority of humanity thinks of the future only in terms of advertisement clichés, corporate strategies, and gee-whiz technological gadgets. But "reality" at ground level also comes wrapped in this notation. Consider the most profound developments of recent years. The information and communication revolution owes everything to advancements in technology. The cloning of Dolly the sheep is a wonder of bioengineering — a short step from cloning man and not too far from redefining the whole notion of humanity. The eradication of dreaded diseases like smallpox and the containment of AIDS with a cocktail of new drugs are achievements of technology-based medicine. Moreover, technology is providing choices where there were none. A host of new fertility treatments now enables barren women to have a much-wanted child (or two, three, or more), even choose the baby's sex; and in the not-too-distant future, its physical qualities, features, and character could also be selected. All these developments make someone genuinely happy — and hold the rest of us in awe, imprisoned in the glare of technological advancements.

The inherent problem of the information revolution, however, is that most information is recycled in new packaged forms that are rigorously selected. To make children computer literate is a worldwide aspiration — to do the best for the future generation. In the non-West, it is seen as an imperative. Yet this well-intentioned determination not to be left behind again becomes the prime means of foreclosing the future. The resources available, the learning programs students can run on their computers, are more dominated by the West's selective vision than any library, bookstore, or school yet devised. To surf the Net is to immerse one's self in the worldview and interests of white male American college students. The grand strategies being offered of cheap technology that instantly circumvents marginality and exclusion (though it is not cheap enough to include the poor) again foster the idea that the world of all the knowledge that matters can by brought direct to classroom and home in the non-West instantly. Indeed, information can be delivered — but it will have less non-Western content, more seductive clone-making intent than was ever conceived possible in the headiest days of the development decades.

There is thus an in-built momentum that seems to take us toward a single, determined future. Technology is projected as an autonomous and desirable force. Its desirable products generate more desire; its second-order side-effects require more technology to solve them. There is thus a perpetual feedback loop. One need not be a technological determinist to appreciate the fact that this self-perpetuating momentum has locked us in a linear, one-dimensional trajectory that has actually foreclosed the future. This trajectory is in fact an arch-ideology, and like all ideologies, it is inverse to the truth. An illusion of accelerated movement is created to shroud the fact that we are at best standing still, if not actually retarding. Faster and faster cars are actually not taking us anywhere but straight to a gridlock. No wonder concerned citizens in the West are giving up their cars for bicycles. Faster, intelligent, and perfect computers are not solving any problems but creating newer ones. Being connected is a substitute for being a real community. All biotechnological advances have nightmarish underbellies and generate ethical paradoxes that are almost impossible to solve.

The reality is that we have reached a technological plateau. The futuristic revolution turns out to have had very little conception of the future — Witness the billions that will have to be spent because computer programs cannot recognize dates beyond the year 1999. The millennium was beyond the consciousness of those who wrote and manufactured more and more sophisticated computer programs; instant solutions foreclose the future more effectively than planned ones. The future has been made only by projecting instant technological answers, and that means pushing forward the desires of the powerful. New technologies may appear to be better, faster, and more promising, but in reality they do not improve our lives or deliver greater material benefits to most of humanity or make us happier. While the belief in the power of technology to rescue our future continues to gain more ground, it is, in fact, a dangerously obsolete ideology. The future is thus waiting to explode.

The future is being colonized by yet another force. Conventionally, this force was called "Westernization," but now it goes under the rubric of "globalization." It may be naive to equate the former with the latter — but the end product is the same: The process that is transforming the world into the proverbial "global village," rapidly shrinking distances, compressing space and time, is also shaping the world in the image of a single culture and civilization.

Globalization can be identified with (at least) two main elements. The first is the economic wave of liberalization that began in the 1980s and achieved global proportions after the fall of communism. Markets are becoming free from all state constraints, and capital can now move across borders with ease. Multinational corporations move from country to country in their quest for cheap labor and tax exemptions. Globalization has meant that a single consumer product, such as a computer, may actually be made in segments in several different places and put together in yet another place. While the management remains in the industrialized world, many sectors of manufacturing industry are now being located offshore in developing countries, where corporations can take advantage of cheap labor, lower taxes, and liberal labor-protection and environmental-protection regimes. On the whole, manufacturing facilities play very little part in fueling the economy of the developing countries. Global capital is now shifting from resource-based and market-seeking investment to spatial optimization and absolute maximization of profit opportunities. The end result is that the economies of most countries, both industrialized and developing, are becoming dominated by consumer and lifestyle choices, production is being replaced by consumption as the central economic activity, and privatization is becoming the norm.

Second, the wide acceptance of liberal democracy across cultures from Eastern Europe to Africa is leading to a total embrace of Western culture. Even though the trend toward universalization of Western culture is actively contested, it has become the dominant norm, encouraged and aided by Hollywood, television, satellite, pop music, fashion, and global news networks such as CNN, News International, and BBC World. Thus, globalization maintains all the well-known patterns of Western economic and cultural imperialism and goes further. It promotes a dominant set of cultural practices and values, one vision of how life is to be lived, at the expense of all others. And it has serious practical consequences: Not only does it erode non-Western local traditions and cultural practices, but it kills non-Western future options. Once again, the future is locked into a single, linear projection.

Furthermore, the future is being colonized in the way futures studies itself is being shaped into a discipline, with fixed boundaries, a set of basic principles and assumptions, and all the other trappings of a crystallized discipline: established authorities, designated areas of research and thought, learned and professional organizations, bibliographic tools, and study guides. As yet, futures studies is not a fully fledged discipline, although it has acquired the trappings of a discipline.

Traditionally, futures studies — like cultural studies — developed as an intellectual and social movement emphasizing the plurality of futures, with a particular accent on alternative futures. As futures studies was domesticated and institutionalized, particularly in the corridors of American and European corporations, that emphasis began to evaporate. In this organizational framework, futures studies is synonymous with Western interests. The aim here is to preserve a future landscape where technological advances can be employed to maintain the hegemony of the West.

A direct outcome of the corporatization of futures studies is the belief that America is the locus not just for futures studies but for the future itself. This is the basic assumption and prime principle of much of the futures thought that emanates from even the grassroots American organizations, such as the Washington-based World Future Society (WFS). The Society's monthly journal *The Futurist,* bimonthly abstract journal *Futures Survey,* and the learned journal *Futures Research Quarterly* are tools consciously designed to create a professional discipline that, like anthropology and Orientalism, serves the interests of the dominant culture. *The Futurist* regularly offers a comatosed vision of how technology will make our life better in — perhaps I am being charitable here — an unconscious attempt to validate the most debilitating forms of technological consumerism. *Futures Survey,* the most important bibliographic tool in futures studies, seems to be totally blind to anything relating to the future that does not yield some kind of dividend or early warning signal for multinational corporations. The textbooks produced by WFS, like Edward Cornish's *The Study of the Future,*[5] set the worldview of *The Futurist* and *Futures Survey* in disciplinary stone.

On the whole, futures studies is sponsored by scholars who are not just totally divorced from any political and cultural movements, but are quite unaware of the fact that the future has anything to do with critical questions of power, history, and politics. Indeed, of the numerous intellectual movements that have swept American social sciences since the 1970s, few could be described as so utterly shallow and xenophobic, so opportunistically unreflective toward the non-West and so ahistorical in their analysis. The recently published *Encyclopedia of the Future*[6] sums up the whole argument. Brief entries for countries such as India and civilizations such as Islam are there only as a necessary evil. Other countries involved in serious future planning, such as Malaysia, are conspicuous by their absence. There is absolutely no awareness of the numerous non-Western notions of the future, time, being, or knowing. The list of the "100 most influential futurists" contains only one person from the non-West. Clearly, the future is a Western territory that has no place for the non-West.

This is not to say that there are no Western futurists who use non-Western philosophies and modes of knowing as the basis for constructing alternative visions of the future. But even here both the research and the vision are strictly enframed within the European tradition of humanism — a tradition that is totally enveloped in the secularist worldview. The end-products of their labor are often a grotesque parody of non-Western thought, philosophy, and tradition. As such, even the "new spirituality" and "values" that these more aware futurists offer ultimately conform to the dictates of Western secularism. Hence, it is always the secular forms of Eastern mysticism — like Zen Buddhism — with which these futurists find sympathy. The vast corpus of nonsecular non-Western traditions is almost totally ignored. There is also the added irony of the product of Western humanism borrowing "traditional thought" from a non-Western culture and subsequently presenting the repackaged confection to the natives. At best, the appropriation of non-Western ideas and thought amounts to little more than a second-hand regurgitation of "Eastern mysticism," as in the case, for example, of the "small is beautiful" guru E. F. Schumacher. But whatever his standing in the West, as a mystic in the Eastern tradition, Schumacher is decidedly an infant: the non-West has greater minds and a long historical tradition to learn from. At worst, non-Western ideas are used in an opportunistic exercise to make dubious reputations, as is the case with Fritjof Capra.

Thus, even when futures studies is allegedly borrowing and incorporating non-Western thought into its framework, it remains rooted firmly in Western philosophical ideas. All the future alternatives are actually worked out within this single, dominating, philosophical outlook. Other cultures are there, at best, for decorative purposes, or worse, to be used to prop up a system of thought and action that is actually responsible for the present dire predicament of humanity.

Of course, there is nothing special in the way futures studies has developed and is evolving toward a discipline. It is following a well-trodden path laid out in history by anthropology and Oriental studies and in more modern times by development studies. It is worth noting that these disciplines are remarkably similar in how they approach the non-West. Operating within a linear teleology that makes Western civilization the yardstick for measuring progress, norms, and values, these disciplines have evolved by using non-Western cultures and societies to define themselves and to develop and grow. In following suit, futures studies has not only colonized the future, it is itself becoming an instrument for maintaining and enlarging that colonization. Futures studies thus has an unsavory underside that is — ultimately — much darker than those of mere anthropology or Orientalism.

Elsewhere, I have compared the evolution of futures studies with the unfolding of development studies:

> In that field, Western "authorities" were first created by citation analysis, literature surveys, and study guides, and the boundaries of the discipline were pegged to the research interests of these "authorities." The textbooks produced by these authorities became the essential teaching instruments in the Third World, while the masters of the discipline went to the Third World as consultants and authors of national development plans. It is only a matter of time until the "experts" (identified in the *Encyclopaedia of the Future* and other disciplinary texts) make their appearance in the Third World as consultants to set up university departments and long-range future plans. Already the signs are ominous. Just as the "national development plans" of so many developing

countries reflect little concern or respect for indigenous culture and local needs, so many of the national future plans reflect the concern and interests of Western futurists rather than hopes and aspiration of the local population. The priorities of such future studies as Malaysia's Vision 2020, China 2000, Mexico 2000 have been set not by local populations but by the U.S. Global 2000 report.[7]

The colonization of the future by these powerful forces means that the future ceases to be an arena of action. We are in the domains of a new kind of colonization that goes beyond physical and mental occupation to the seizure of our being and hence total absorption. Modernity tolerated our existence as an appendage to Western civilization. But the postmodern future is less tolerant — it will settle for nothing less than complete assimilation of all non-Western societies into Western civilization. Modernity raised the question, "Can the non-Western societies actually survive the future with their sanity and cultures intact?" The colonized horizon of the future forces us to ask a new question: "Can we survive as distinctive entities, as something different, other than the Western civilization?"

Given the myopic vision and one-dimensional logic with which Western civilization pursues its goals, and given the lack of concern for the future among non-Western intellectuals and thinkers and the consequent (almost) total lack of future-consciousness in many non-Western societies, my contention is that the prognosis is grim — unless we start to think more concretely and imaginatively about the future, unless we transform the future into a site of both real and symbolic struggles, and hence change the future by opening it to non-Western possibilities and move from the future to a plethora of futures. Changing the future means both questioning and resisting the forces, and the values and canonical myths associated with them, that have colonized the future.

Surviving the future thus involves confronting the deterministic, Western future and altering the political and intellectual landscape of the future. The non-Western intellectual project of futures must insist on exposing the political dimension of all knowledge relating to the future and cast the future not as an autonomous and inevitable domain but as a contested arena of conflictual practices — technological, global, and scholarly — bound up with the perpetual expansion of the West. In theoretical terms, the project involves studying not what the future could or would be, but how new alternatives and options could be made to emerge and how alternative futures could be shaped according to the desires and visions of non-Western societies. In practical terms, the project has to focus on evolving a discourse of social involvement: in raising the future-consciousness of communities (including communities of intellectuals and academics), in articulating visions of societies, and in involving citizens in efforts to shape their own futures.

In liberating the future, the non-West has a number of significant disadvantages. A great deal of emancipatory thought in recent years has concentrated on recovery of a discrete past. The non-West is coming to appreciate the creativity of its own traditions, and halting steps are being taken toward studying that creativity as a dynamic concept. However, that still leaves the problem of dislocation between past and present, let alone past and future. The past becomes, and for many Asian conceptual traditions has always been, a lacuna where ideals and aspirations reside. So a chasm is opened between appreciation of tradition and the imaginative capacity to think traditions forward. The imaginative leap is made even harder by the limitations of the language and techniques of futures studies and methodologies. A perception of a discrete past was intended to bolster the search for alternatives to Western dominance, to provide a means for continuity of values so that the non-West could move forward with its identity intact. However, it is a moot point whether the search for alternatives has not generated a public perception in the non-West of being the equivalent of opting out of the future altogether. Tradition is sold outside the technological wizardry of today and tomorrow. It provides perhaps a comforting answer to the dire needs of poverty, not a handle on power. Alternative technology became technology for the poor, while the mainstream concern of "real" development was getting a handle on modern Western technology. Critique of Western technology has so far failed to develop a concerted field of alternative technology products that offer a new nexus of possible life-styles with market possibilities either for the non-West or the "New Age" markets of the West.

The recovery of history has been a truncated endeavor in the non-West. Yet, it does have the potential to upset the limited vision and self-satisfied composure of the future-forecasters. History holds a model for a different perspective on what is actually happening today, and from this can come new questions about how the future can be created. Corporate future-forecasters have leaped to embrace the so-called Pacific Century, the Pacific-Rim-centered view of the future. Much of Asia is preparing to dismemorialize the arrival of Vasco da Gama and incidentally recover the world his arrival disrupted. What stands behind this is an Indian-Ocean-centered vision of the world, its history, and interconnections that opens a new perspective not merely on the distant past but also on present trends and hence the potential to engineer different, plural futures. Yet, how many alternative thinkers in the non-West are prepared to jettison the West as an integral part of their thinking and the center of their future-consciousness? The trading world of Asia operated irrespective of the minor and distant European market. The trading world of Asia worked through plurality and interconnection through difference. Once more the trading world of Asia has the potential for sustained long-term growth by trading within itself. The fulcrum in the past was the Southeast Asian archipelago; today that again is a source of dynamic growth that can ripple and interconnect the old world of Asian interconnection. This is a rich topic for integration of past and future thought, but it has been analyzed so meagerly that it has failed to generate much of an output to challenge the might of "official" futures thinking. It is a timely conceptual basis from which to subvert the whole "official" idea of how the future was made and will be shaped.

From this perspective, futures studies is not and cannot be a discipline in the conventional sense. Indeed, if futures studies was to become a fully fledged discipline, it would follow in the footsteps of ecology, cultural studies, and feminist studies and be totally domesticated. Awareness of the future involves rescuing futures studies from any disciplinary constraints and from the clutches of tame professionals and academic bureaucrats. Futures studies must be openly incomplete, unpredictable, and thus function as an intellectual movement rather than a closed discipline. It must work in opposition to the dominant politics and culture of our time, resist and critique science and technology (the most powerful agents of change and thought), globalization (the most powerful process of homogenization), and linear, deterministic projections (the official orthodoxy of the future) of the future itself. It must, in the words of Ashis Nandy, become "a game of dissenting visions," an attempt to widen human choices, by reconceptualizing political, social, and cultural ends; by identifying emerging or previously ignored social pathologies that have to be understood, contained, or transcended; by linking up the fates of different polities and societies through envisioning their common fears and hopes.[8]

For the genuine transformation of futures studies into a movement for resisting the status quo, its conceptual language has to change. Futures studies will remain alien to the non-West as long as its basic concepts and categories are those of the dominant civilization. This is why in non-Western societies, despite the best intentions of its practitioners, it often ends up subverting indigenous visions and futures. If the future is a state of awareness, then that awareness can have genuine meaning only if it emanates from the indigenous depths of a culture. This means that there have to be a whole variety of futures studies, each using the conceptual tools of a particular culture and thus reflecting the intrinsic values and concerns of that culture. The plurality of futures has to be reflected in the plurality of futures studies.

Thus, intellectuals in non-Western societies will have to take the future seriously or become prisoners of someone else's future. They have to change the actualized future by changing the future-consciousness of their societies and by articulating the visions of their cultures in terms of their own notions and categories. It is probable that futures studies in different cultures will not be fully comprehensible across cultural borders, or, more particularly, that there will be incommensurability, in a Kuhnian sense, between indigenous notions of non-Western futures studies and Western futures studies. This incommensurability will arise from different norms and cognitive values, as well as different experiences, and it will be a product of the fact that many non-Western concepts and categories cannot really be rendered in English. Moreover, the incommensurability will itself be a source of resistance ensuring both a multiform of dissent and plurality of options for the future. Futures studies could thus become a genuinely high adventure generating a kaleidoscope of visions and fusing other imaginations and moral concerns with political activism.

Problems often contain the seeds of their own solutions. Our awareness of the colonization of the future arrives at a key moment in history, when the colonizing civilization has reached the end of its golden age. As ibn Khaldun would have said, the West, like all other civilizations, must now decline to rise again in some far distant future. The present phase of the cycle of rise and decline of civilizations favors the Asian civilizations. The next century belongs to Asia in general and India and China in particular. The center of world trade has already moved to the Pacific Basin — the economic problems of Southeast Asia at the tail end of the twentieth century notwithstanding. For the West, the growth of Asia could mean a return to a future of a thousand years ago. Both India and China, poised to become global civilizations, stand at the beginning of a cycle that could last a millennium; Western civilization stands at the end of a cycle that is already a thousand years old.

But it is insufficient merely to accept the growth potential of Asia, enormous as that is and even though it is reconceptualized in the language of cycles. Alternative futures will genuinely emerge when Asia starts to think afresh by marginalizing the West. That is the kind of equation Western dominance is working tirelessly to maintain as nonthought. Southeast Asia and the high-performing economies of East Asia were insulated from the recession of the 1980s by the potency of their growing economic interaction. This is a topic that does not figure largely in official futures thought. But it must be a starting point for us, a willingness of Asia to think the unthinkable. Rather than be a victim of a totally colonized future, Asia needs to imagine that it can be a source of its own alternatives, that it can generate its own power base. The story so far is that those Asian countries that have most confidence in their long-term growth potential are also most in thrall to the power complex of the West; they are least able to see even their own power other than in Western terms and the language of Western futures studies. It seems that colonialism has predisposed the colonized to think only in colonial terms. That is the cycle that must be broken.

NOTES

1. Warner Books, 1984.
2. Richard Slaughter, "Looking for the Real 'Megatrends,'" *Futures*, 25(8), October 1993.
3. Oxford: Butterworth, 1992.
4. Edited by Rowen Gibson, London: Nicholas Brealey, 1996.
5. Bethesda, MD: World Future Society, 1977.
6. Edited by George Thomas Kurian and Graham T. T. Molitor, 2 vols., New York: Macmillan, 1996.
7. "Colonizing the Future: The 'Other' Dimension of Future Studies," *Futures* 25(3), April 1993.
8. "Bearing Witness to the Future," *Futures* 28(6–7), August–September 1996.

12. Black Futurists in the Information Age

TIMOTHY L. JENKINS

The new technologies of the Information Age offer great promise to African Americans, according to Timothy L. Jenkins. They present the prospect of a more level playing field on which ideas can stand or fall on their own merits, regardless of the economic power of those who propose them, and out of which a freer and more egalitarian society can evolve. But such an outcome is not foreordained. In fact, there are many reasons to believe that Information Age technologies could bring new woes to already disadvantaged minorities. "Left to their own devices," says Jenkins, "minorities are most likely to be the major roadkill of the Information Superhighway."

Black Futurists in the Information Age, from which this selection is taken, is intended as a wake-up call to black leadership in the United States. Jenkins and volume coauthor Khafra K. Om-Ra-Seti would have these leaders move from being gatekeepers—mediators of information from other areas of society—to gatecrashers—"opening up new lines of thinking and new avenues of public policy." They call for no less than a scientific and technological revolution in the African American world, advising its leaders to focus their attention on economic and technology progress.

Timothy L. Jenkins is chairman and CEO of Unlimited Vision, Inc., a multimedia firm. He was instrumental in creating the first all-black on-line forum on the Internet. Jenkins holds a J.D. degree from Yale University Law School and served as chief lobbyist for the Student Nonviolent Coordinating Committee for five years.

THE FAR SIDE OF THE MOUNTAIN

It has been a source of amazement and alarm that, in spite of the roar of public attention surrounding the advent of the Information Age as the explosive successor to the Industrial Era, the leadership of the African American community has yet to broadly interpret the Age's far-reaching implications for the vital interests of their constituents. The delinquency of their silence has been all the more profound because of the palpable evidence that, without major interventions, the utopian predictions of the Information Age for the society as a whole will paradoxically result in a doomsday scenario for the masses of black people. Alternatively, a clear understanding of the broad implications and susceptibilities of these tools of modern communications, coupled with information science, has the clear potential to foster unheard-of strategies of liberation. The burden of [the book from which this essay was excerpted] has been to articulate a new vision for African Americans in the Information Age.

The benefit and the burden of being black in America arise from the ability and the necessity to view the same things the rest of society sees differently. This difference is born of bitter experience, that popular propaganda is seldom predicated on the best interests of black people in particular or humanity in general. Moreover, black people harbor a justifiable skepticism that the larger society is equipped to interpret or even understand the best interests of those elements of the population it has excluded from so many of its inner sanctums. Ironically, by the very reason of such exclusion, the social perceptions black leaders hold sometimes allow them insights that are clearer and more reliable reflections of reality for the larger society as well. Contributing factors in the black/white leadership divide come from the material differences in their resources and power. In almost every sphere of life, the historic status of blacks increases their vulnerability. Statistics affirm these differences in economics, education, health, social mobility, and even in certain areas of historical and philosophical aspirations.

Because of these increased vulnerabilities, many stresses that the majority easily survives exceed the level of tolerance for blacks. In this sense, observing the effects of certain conditions on blacks may predict the later ramifications on the general public. Black people, suffering economically in the early stages of the Information Age, may be like the canary in a coal mine, forecasting climactic dangers before they become a general manifestation. Thus, as the euphoria sweeps the nation regarding the exciting expectations of the Information Age, African Americans must sound the alarm on the dangers of systematic exclusion.

On the surface, every reason exists to celebrate the proliferation of Information Age technologies. But it does not follow that information by itself can guarantee an improved quality of life or more secure democratic rights. Nor do the international migrations of information industries assure that the result will not be the lowest common denominator in wages and jobs. The propagandists insist that universally available information leads inexorably toward democracy, but they seldom acknowledge the megadisparities that exist in the corporate versus citizens' ability to gather, manipulate, and interpret information in politically relevant ways.

Confronted by these pressing issues, black leaders must now move forward in a new role with specific agendas, promoting the development and advocacy of reform policies and programs that can wisely pick and choose among the probable social effects of the Information Age. The result could be an early wake-up call for our nation, hopefully before the negative effects of telecybernetics become irreversible. By fulfilling their role, black leaders can move from being gatekeepers to gatecrashers, opening up new lines of thinking and new avenues of public policy. The beneficiaries of their interventions will not only be blacks, but workers of all races, ages, and their institutions. By the same token, if, at the end of the day, technology will only provide an economic haven for the brightest and the best of us—regardless of race—then we will have cold and shallow comfort in the toll that this direction will have on our society. If those of us who care exercise influence sufficient to force the agenda of our interest on the application of technology, then we should have our fortunes rise with the whole of humankind.

It is still too early to know which will be the predominant result. In the meantime, we must do all in our power to assure that we are technically aware of technology's positives and negatives as each public decision is made in response to the rapidly changing world of *The Age of Light.* And woe be unto us if Marshall McLuhan was right when he said "the medium is the message," for most of us are likely to be left out of understanding or enjoying a vital economic connection with either.

In the final analysis, the essence of technology ought to be service. Judged from that perspective, it remains to be seen whether the interests of the black community are served or sacrificed. Absent purposeful leadership involvement, either could be true. The deciding factor will be the extent to which those who both understand and influence the direction of technology take into account the peculiar interests of the black community, as they may well harbinger society's interests in general. If its prime effect is to reduce the labor force to an absolute minimum in order to maximize profits or to allow jobs to follow tax breaks and the lowest wages wherever they might lead, then technology, while benefiting some, will have failed us all.

DEDICATED TO THE FUTURE

This [chapter] is, therefore, dedicated to the future — not an inevitable future — but rather the future that we can design. Never before has there been a time when so much could be achieved in leveling the playing field of life through pluralistic imagination and commercial creativity, as modern, computer-driven technological genius has now made possible. But we will first have to be open to a personal as well as an institutional need to change, before we can use technology to counteract social, economic, and intellectual inertia on the matters of race and ethnicity in America. Indeed, the refusal to open our minds to the discomfort of change may be the largest obstacle yet to our ultimate empowerment through technology.

In spite of its many positive potentials, the unfolding of the decade that closes the twentieth century and opens the twenty-first is at best neutral. With equal facility, this epoch can irrevocably alter for good or ill the intellectual and economic disparities born of race, as well as spatial and social realities. The exercise of values in our allocation of relevant technological resources will be the critical challenge.

The factors that make these next ten years [1997–2007] so critical are both the unprecedented pace of emergent telecommunications and computer innovations, as well as the recognition that, unlike the agricultural and industrial revolutions, those who are left behind this time may never be able to catch up again. Moreover, the Information Age promises to impact monumentally on every area of human life, especially our social and commercial organizations, where the impact will be far-reaching and pervasive. Emergent technologies will be the keys for determining economic and employment opportunity, freedom of expression, educational attainment, and meaningful political participation, all of which are tantamount to deciding who will exercise predominant power for the next hundred years. As such, we stand on the threshold of the invention of what may well become a new worldwide class distinction, or technological caste system.

While the coming of this New Age is a matter of prolific study and investigation in all of these areas, ironically it has been left to the fringe elements of the nation's counterculture to examine its revolutionary implications for America's black, red, and brown minorities. Indeed, if one were to judge by mainstream portrayals of high-tech beneficiaries, it would be easy to conclude that cultural "homogeneity" is to be the uniform requirement of the next century, rather than an increase in diversity implicit in the national demographic shifts in which the minorities of today will become the population majority of tomorrow. Overwhelmingly, the computer icons, advertisements, spokespersons, and media campaigns are standardized to look, feel, and act like their industrial creators, resulting in their not being user-friendly to minorities or their unique cultural interests. We have not only seen the creation of the Information Age invisible man, but also the invisible interests and concerns of racial and ethnic diversity excluded from high-tech images. As a result, *Star Treks I* and *II* notwithstanding, we might be led subliminally to conclude that the future belongs to only the information industry's chosen few rather than the whole population.

Article 17 of the Universal Declaration of Human Rights asserts that access to technology is a fundamental entitlement, yet nowhere is such an "entitlement" given universal access. Accordingly, those of us who have been to a different mountain and seen a different promised land must now declare a different vision. Ours is a vision in which American society as well as world culture, through the marvels of technology, open themselves up to beneficial change based on a deeper and more intimate understanding of the creative differences of which they are comprised. With an appreciation for the enormity of the coming change in information access, this decade represents the last, best hope to challenge the patterns of social exclusion from the past being extended and reinforced by technology into the future. The information and telecommunications revolution promises brand new games, which require that we invent new rules by which they can be played for life-quality improvements rather than mere quantitative accelerations. Only then can the inherent power for change — implicit in high-technology communications — yield results that alleviate rather than further degrade our communities. In essence, we as black people must shape and mold the emergent Information Age revolution into our own image, and establish values and morals that are consistent with our historical traditions, to ultimately benefit the world. For example, it will not be appropriate to follow the pattern of mindlessly creating video games on CD-ROM that simply entertain people in the sport of killing the enemy. We need to rethink the possibilities of such tools, so they can help to produce a generation of enlightened people.

Alas, any hope of playing by a set of new rules demands intellectual as well as behavioral modifications of today's leadership, not only on explicit matters of race and ethnicity in America, but the ingenuous ways in which seemingly neutral trends can help to perpetuate inequalities. In spite of the loudest protests to the contrary, minority group leaders and majority group power-holders have both grown used to slow dancing with each other, while they are increasingly distanced from the growing economic and social insecurities that plague their constituents. Although it tends to be less frequently noted, educated white elites often display as little real appreciation for the material and emotional needs lying below them as certain miseducated elite black escapees from the ghetto. Hence, the expressions of political and editorial surprise at the electoral revolts that have occurred throughout the nation in recent years, when blue-collar constituencies have rejected predicted group behavior and voted with the opposition, or when opinion polls fly in the face of predictions from would-be pundits and opinion-makers.

The establishment just doesn't get it: The majority of people feel betrayed by both their leaders and institutions. Almost nowhere, except in dark alleys, poorly lit parking lots, or celebrated talk shows, does the world of most black leaders and white power-holders come together with the alienated underclass and its seething social rebellion. These social and economic distances are seriously exacerbated by mainstream communication barriers that provide little or no ongoing dialogue. The heated debates regarding black rap lyrics, as well as the librettos of white heavy-metal ballads, vividly illustrate the symptoms of such class warfare.

For the first time, however, walking in another class's shoes is becoming feasible. On-line computer networks can offer a new town hall. Desktop publishing promises a new public forum. Civic teleconferencing can become a new vehicle for group dialogue. Distance learning will allow a classroom to be worldwide. No longer must music, art, and theater suffer an unnatural fence. The libraries and museums of the world can be available to the most remote corners of the earth for the first time in history. Diagnostic health care can now be distributed without regard to distance between patients and national hospital specialists. Soon, with everyone able to be his or her own publisher, the means for truth-telling as an everyday Internet exchange, rather than the occasional moment, can be at hand. While the uncensored picture that emanates from down under may not always be exactly pretty, it at least promises to be far more honest and realistic than the polished products of editorial middlemen with their own hidden agendas.

Few will deny that the instant presence of television has made a tremendous difference politically during the past thirty years, whether evidenced in the civil rights marches or the fall of the Berlin Wall. By way of parallel, the problem will now be assuring that unrestrained market forces alone are not the only forces left to determine individual and group access to knowledge or set the speed limits of the Information Superhighway. This calls for the development of enlightened public policies that balance the bargaining power among the players and provide a level playing field. On such a playing field the merits of an idea will be able to withstand the onslaught of superior economic power, and this can lead to a freer and more egalitarian society than the cash register alone is likely to foster.

But before we get euphoric over these grand possibilities, we need the sobering recognition that such progress is not a self-evident truth nor a historical imperative. On the contrary, if the old rules of means tests, class advantage, ethnicity, and geographical preferences are applied to these new technologies, the result will not only be the perpetuation of existing disparities, but their indelible reinforcement. And based on emerging patterns to date, the perpetuation of the old rules is clearly at work. Low-income children are half as likely to have access to computers at home or in school. Students at historically black colleges and universities are substantially less likely to have high-tech facilities, equipment, and technological programs of equal quality. Minority workers are disproportionately relegated to the tedious low end of automated systems, if they have any access at all. The geographical areas slated to enjoy entree to these marvelous new and costly communications systems are those least likely to include minority or low-income households. In this regard, it is useful to be reminded that the majority of the world's population has yet to be able to place its first telephone call. In the United States population, pockets exist that have actually lost ground in their access to telephones in the years from 1985 to 1995, and many of these are in the very cities that boast the most advanced forms of progress in telecommunications.

All of this suggests that this new information and communications revolution could easily bypass the minority communities of America, just like the infamous interstate highways of old, providing few or no meaningful access ramps unless they are carefully designed into the plans taking shape now. Indeed, it has been graphically suggested that, left to their own devices, minorities are most likely to be the major roadkill of the Information Superhighway, with jobs flowing abroad, while those remaining in the country have unreachable high-tech entry requirements or offer a new form of housebound peonage without hard-won worker fringe benefits or long-term job security. All of this makes the coming decade of pivotal importance, for the next ten years will determine who goes up and who goes down on the technology seesaw. Because we share a stake in the design of the future, we must exercise the option to modify these outcomes based on direct participation in the decision-making processes that are bringing about the construction of the new Information Superhighway. But to do this we must first reinvent our leaders.

One of the most astonishing discoveries we encountered [in the research for the book from which this article was excepted] was the private-sector indifference shown by the various Fortune 500 computer hardware, software, and telecommunications companies; there is essentially a lack of concern not only toward the underserved information needs of black people in general, but also toward the $450 billion appeal of the African American market. Having participated in or been aware of efforts to induce such companies to expand their high-tech marketing outreach into minority consumer niches, with only three exceptions, we have witnessed a response that has been uniformly negative. When approached, such companies retort that either blacks aren't interested in high-tech telecommunication devices and computers or those that are so inclined can be readily reached through a generalized mainstream outreach.

This behavior flies in the face of the great weight of professional marketing in other areas, which shows the importance of special niche market identification and promotion. Such indifference also underestimates the extent to which upper-income black consumers not only exceed the general population in brand-name loyalties, but also in the mainstream consumption of sophisticated electronic equipment. The consumer areas in question include CDs, hi-fi and stereo equipment buying, as well as VCRs and video cameras, all of which aggregated to a $6 billion electronic market among minorities in 1994, well above the comparable per capita expenditure of the general U.S. population. Indeed, the black-market penetration of VCRs is greater than that for the household population as a whole. Consider what this might imply for CD-ROM products and other software capable of appealing to this same audience.

In a larger sense, this backward corporate attitude poses an additional threat to the long-term economic and social health of the nation based on technology diffusion. Corporate negativity toward the high-tech minority market suggests the specter of an ever-increasing racial and ethnic divide in technology usage, due to ineffective promotion among minorities, leading to a permanently uneven computer and telecommunication diffusion throughout the population to the [detriment of the nation through] a less competitive workforce and less just society. All of this is to underscore the fact that, left to the traditional market forces of today, those who know and those who know not will translate to a schism of those employable or unemployable along racial and ethnic lines comparable to a distinction of class or caste. One would have hoped for a more forward-looking response from that very segment of the economy that prides itself most on its creative alliance with the future. But, alas, even the industrial gatekeepers who stand to collect the tolls to the Information Superhighway have shown themselves unwilling to attract additional road traffic from the minority community. This only reinforces the urgency for the black community's internal mobilization to assure its access to the Information Superhighway and the policies that shape its path, as Malcolm X once said, "by any means necessary."

LOOKING BACK TO MOVE FORWARD

The Adinkra peoples of West Africa have a symbol called Sankofa, of a bird in full flight with its head turned backward. Sankofa signifies the truth that no people can know where it is going if it cannot look backward from whence it came. This may be the classic recognition of all culture. Visionary black leadership will be of critical importance in how we chart our future course. Therefore, we need to be reminded of some of the historic leadership strengths and weaknesses in our community to be able to discern the one from the other in the future. Because of the peculiar ways in which our traditions of leadership have been fashioned, such hegemony may itself represent a temporary impasse to the free flow of benefits from the info-revolution. Such an examination may also identify patterns and practices that are no longer affordable in the face of current requirements. At the same time, it can highlight unique strengths to which we must hold and carry forward for future progress.

From Colonial days to the present, black leadership has primarily been a matter of damage control or the juggling of crises. Limited to operating with inadequate resources against superior material odds, faced with an ever-present urgency that defied long-term planning and originally surrounded by a constituency with limited understanding, black leaders developed peculiar leadership styles. For most, day-to-day survival was [their major preoccupation]. Their coping with leadership responsibilities without any management tutelage was like having to learn to read without either a dictionary or the formal rules of grammar. Trial and error mixed with innate talent and personal fortitude often led to highly subjective, if not dogmatic, management styles.

Understandably, not only did the cult of personality sometimes become a problem, but also the requirement for self-reliance was frequently at war with democratic procedures. Moreover, the role of leadership carried with it the conflicting need to project one set of characteristics to black constituents and another to the hostile white world outside the community. Accordingly, it remained for black leaders historically to adapt to special balancing acts for survival.

The traditional procession of leaders has been first preachers, then teachers, and lastly doctors and lawyers. Each succeeding wave of such leaders has had to master the means of walking in two directions at once and the ability to "hit straight licks with crooked sticks" in order to meet the approval of two racially antagonistic audiences for their every act. Preachers were the first to be mutually acceptable in both worlds because they could disguise their temporal leadership as otherworldly guidance. Teachers became acceptable because they were usually controllable public employees. Lawyers and doctors were safe agents of change in the eyes of a dominant majority because of the constraints of their essentially conservative professional guilds. Along the way, sprinkles of more radical writers, entrepreneurs, or labor leaders have come to the fore, but, for the most part, the traditional professions historically comprised the dominant leadership profiles within the black community. This is not to deny that sports, theater, and screen celebrities were briefly elevated to leadership roles; rather, it is to recognize that the principal flow of direction associated with large-scale membership and affinity groups with mass self-help agendas has come from the same basic professional core, which for the most part had the credentials of higher education as the prerequisite for its status. Through the accident of such education passed on to their children, an almost hereditary leadership class developed, which has benignly perpetuated itself from the employment differentiations of old until now, with the ever-present potential for gradual estrangement from its constituency.

Such leadership has accordingly mastered those messianic arts and crafts required of [it]. Typically, some measure of entrepreneurship and personal economic success, along with a mastery of oratory and audience appeal, were their principal instruments of influence. They exercised persuasion as charismatic spokespersons or grievance-brokers with power centers. Serving as middlemen and -women between two worlds, the perpetuation of their own leadership roles was sometimes as subtle a goal as the objective improvement of their followers. This irony has been aptly described in such works as Carter G. Woodson's *The Mis-education of the Negro*, W. E. B. DuBois's early treatise, *The Philadelphia Negro*, E. Franklin Frazier's *Black Bourgeoisie*, and other analytic works that followed these pioneering publications.

Historically, this duality was maintained easily when the discriminations faced were palpable and universal both in law as well as in fact, as so vividly described in Gunnar Myrhdal's *American Dilemma*. But with the incremental and some-times sweeping changes brought about by a steady march of victories over de jure segregation and discrimination born of civil rights protests, litigation, and legisla-tion, a new set of inequality challenges, not easily addressed by the traditional leadership styles, arose; the creation of a veritable "underclass," the name first given the phenomena by Douglas Glasgow in his seminal book of the same name. This signaled the demarcation of a new substrata of characteristics reinforcing the factor of race as a barrier to advancement such as welfare dependence, unem-ployability, and the alienation from middle-class ideals, values, and aspirations.

With this metamorphosis has come a kind of leadership dislocation, whereby the alternate traditions of managed protest and accommodation (which had been the black leadership's hallmarks from precolonial days) are less certain or margin-ally applicable strategies. Now the issues are not petitioning for or even obtaining equality before the law, but obtaining equality in fact. With this bold reality has come the need for greater empowerment from within the black community, based on the mechanisms of self-reliance and self-improvement.

In spite of this need for a shift in emphasis, too often the traditional leadership in the black community has continued to emphasize *pro forma* legal remedies, which leave factual inequities beyond their reach. The cynical suggested that this resistance to change was more the result of conflicting interests between tradi-tional leaders and those outside their social and economic class. But a more charitable view is that established leaders may have inadvertently either lost touch with the full weight of the social and economic forces newly confronting their constituents or be at an intellectual loss for better strategies. The leader-ship's personal misperceptions may be further influenced by their own relatively stable economic circumstances, which are at stark variance with the increas-ing numbers of those for whom they would speak. These are problems easily addressed by honest dialogue and the reconsideration of the facts, but first they must be jointly acknowledged.

Because of the many bad experiences of hostile "divide and conquer" strategies as well as leadership assassinations (both real and figurative), a general reluc-tance to criticize or even challenge leadership figures from within the community has arisen. Those with the temerity to challenge such blind silence frequently have become objects of criticism themselves, branded as disloyalists or, worse, agents provocateur for sinister as well as invisible racist forces. Such conspiracy theories are all the more easily promoted when partisan, regional, and monetary considerations are part of the mix. The resulting differences have led to addi-tional strains when both sides have resorted to name calling and mutual castiga-tion of one another's motives, rather than addressing relevant issues objectively or collaboratively. This caused even further confusion, with the suggestion that many of the traditional civil rights remedies disproportionately benefit the tradi-tional reformers rather than their down-and-out constituencies. Hence, we wit-ness the pro and con affirmative action arguments addressed by Tony Brown in his book, *Black Lies, White Lies*, as part of this ongoing dialogue. In addition, demagogues aplenty have practiced patterns of factual denial that have made race and racial inequality the sole culprit for every conceivable social ill in the black community, whether substance abuse, the high rates of crime, school dropout rates, low reading scores, teenage pregnancies, job unreadiness, [or] other social pathologies. These often radical voices have promoted a fatalistic generic excuse for failures, rather than their being attributed to personal inadequacies capable of reform and correction.

As if this were not sufficiently confusing, now comes a new breed of minstrel-like propagandists and politicians from the right, whose profession it is to heap self-blame on blacks for each and every one of their social pathologies. For these neo-apologists, the holocaust of slavery either never existed or, if it did, it was primarily the fratricidal African's fault. Equally unfortunate, these distorted voices have been adopted by major political conservatives as their favorite Negroes and given talk shows, widespread media access, highly visible political appointments and the like. Throughout this process, the practice is to rely on the time-honored tools of hyperbolic rhetoric, *ad hominem,* and emotionalism, at the cost of clarity, precision, and objective debate on racial matters. Although thoughtful analysts, thinkers, and writers have existed in the black community throughout, these more measured voices have seldom had a platform off campus or beyond the pages of scholarly journals and outside the covers of thick volumes in fine print.

Sadly, not enough of the existing cadre of brand-name leadership in the black community are describable in terms of the future analytic needs. Too often, they are content with their select roles as middlemen and -women within the power centers. Some are seduced with personal benefits or benefits for those who mirror themselves, without comparable attention to those below them economically and socially with different needs. They are too preoccupied with an assured leadership status throughout their lifetimes to be concerned with development of a leadership transition system within their institutions, which prepares younger and equally capable leaders to take on leadership roles after their timely retirement.

Many among this current black-leadership generation, like their role models before them, have little or no appreciation for the discipline of managing information in the work they pursue. To many, personal [and] institutional decisions are indistinguishable. Few of them consult quantitative data as a required tool for strategy development. Their preference is for speculation, intuition, subjective past experience, and anecdotal information. They are content to employ statistical data only for rhetorical effect, without ever documenting the factual basis for their citations. Take, for example, the frequently mouthed shibboleth that, "there are more black men in prisons than there are enrolled in higher education." To the contrary, there are far more blacks in colleges and universities and only a minority in confinement, but it is more dramatic to use shock rhetoric over the truth. An information-based, scientific approach to leadership would prevent such excess.

A rigorous review of the institutions and organizations of the black community reveals a consistent absence of other systems controls common to modern institutional management. Typically, this improvised approach has left key leadership figures open to willful charges of graft or financial irregularities, even when there can be no showing of criminal intent. From Marcus Garvey to the latest sensation of laid-back approaches to financial accountability, these problems seem to be endemic to black institutions.

One finds similar disregard in personnel matters and staff planning. The functions of recruitment, hiring, evaluation, compensation, promotion, and dismissal in staff procedures cannot be assumed as a matter of formal routine. Typically, whatever exists in the way of written policies are rife with exceptions. All too frequently, nepotism, sexism, conflicts of interest, technical incompetence, and marginal productivity are shown a blind eye in favor of personal loyalties, congenial personalities, and all-absolving "good intentions," reminiscent of Sterling Brown's indulgent encomium, "he mean good, even if he do so doggone po!" Because of the absence of planned maintenance, human resources and capital equipment are frequently consumed prematurely, rather than refurbished and scheduled for upgrading or timely replacement to maximize their useful lives. As a result, age-old crisis management is constantly required to meet what could be routine occurrences, leading to uncertainty, program disruptions, and recurring episodes of organizational disruption.

Similarly, local public agencies controlled by people who profess a commitment to high-minded service objectives sometimes reflect the same shortcomings. These occasionally destabilized institutions include housing authorities, welfare agencies, churches, colleges and universities, labor unions, civic and social organizations, health centers, public school systems, business enterprises, professional organizations, and a myriad of charitable activities. The ultimate price of this approach to management and operations is less effective organizations and institutions. It comes as no small wonder then that most of our leadership has been taken unawares by the revolutionary sweep of information systems and the managerial implications they generate. In large part, the crux of the problem is a lack of awareness of the necessary connection between valid information management and desired outcomes. While not universally applicable, having participated in all these activities for many years, we are embarrassed by the truth of this as well as the inveterate resistance to improvement by the very leaders who would benefit most from reform. Unless reformed from within, such leadership itself will be a principal impediment to community development and advancement. And, unless reformed, such leadership will be unable to lead the black community into the Information Age.

Criticism of such practices should not be taken as personal attacks or forbidden in the name of aiding and abetting our enemies. Investigative journalism and oversight of leadership are just as indispensable within the black community as in society at large. Writers must not be expected to play the ancient role of the African "praise singers," highlighting or magnifying accomplishments and following a code of silence on anything negative. The results will only be continued widespread organizational dysfunction in a community trapped in the denial of its procedural problems, given to a collective avoidance of the responsibility for internal reform, and prone to attributing any and all shortcomings on the single external cause of racism. Most importantly, denial will serve to stifle the diffusion of information systems throughout our institutions.

With the coming of program analysis, better communications, and information systems to the black community, many of these historic proclivities will be objectively challenged. Simple computer-generated spreadsheets of comparative daily, weekly, monthly, quarterly, annual, and biannual financial and performance results, correlated to particular organizational units or individuals, will be able to objectify mission accomplishments alongside particularized costs. Structured reporting relationships and formal report dissemination, as well as documented peer reviews and quantitative evaluations as standard management procedures based on objective criteria and accountabilities, will go a long way to overcome subjective indulgences that cost productivity. The customary distribution of routine information to all appropriately interested parties will further enhance checks and balances on personal excesses and lead to greater confidence in the operations of the institutions we own and care about.

All of these management and information tools, while routine throughout the broader society, are still in their infancy in too many organizations and institutions within the black community. When these are newly introduced, they should not just come on the heels of a major scandal or after protracted litigation or bureaucratic guerrilla warfare. Instead, they should be routine assurances of willingly adopted group accountability consistent with modern management. In all of this, the tools of personal computers and telecommunications offer important improvements. . . .

Furthermore, with the coming of the Information Age's instant media blend of news as entertainment, a heightened mischief will result from having community spokespersons and organizations that easily lend themselves to sitcom caricatures for managerial incompetence. Therefore, an urgent need exists to identify and promote a new paradigm in community leadership of those who can master the newly available information tools and the management capacities they offer. Moreover, given the increasing complexities of the economic, social, and political issues facing the community, we are compelled to seek and promote new voices which speak in factual, managerial, and quantitative terms as additional spokespersons. Existing leaders need to attract these new voices as valuable assets for their effectiveness.

Our leaders need to be aware of the new high-tech avenues through which to talk sense with the masses and to enable these new players to assist in that mission. Equally important are the means to simplify and present complex data and concepts through desktop publishing so that the man in the street can understand, as Marvin Gaye would say, "what's going on." The support of black technologists must be mobilized to combat the distortions of the right wing on complex social, economic, and political issues. We need a different type of black talk-show participant than those most frequently called upon now. Fiery sound bites need to be replaced with sober analysis of the kind that only information analysts can provide. While either possibility might not have been feasible with the gatekeeper controls of traditional media (with its inherently high costs and exclusivity due to scarcity), it is now highly possible with the technological explosion of multimedia outlets.

Revolutionary multimedia systems and state-of-the-art telecommunications technologies include the low costs for the production and distribution of videos, upscale publications, color-coded graphs, CD-ROM presentations, animation, e-mail, on-line networks, and teleconferencing, as well as the rapid transmission of personal computer data and text. Using state-of-the-art Internet and World Wide Web electronic delivery techniques can mean less time and less censorship of these new voices. . . . These are the new means by which the old gatekeepers can be turned into gatecrashers. All of this means that traditional leadership talent must now be enhanced by additional technology training and exposure to be able to understand and relate to different, more analytic, and more quantitatively verifiable requirements with which to influence public policy as well as manage community institutions. Also, they need to seek out and work with those holding such technological training and talents as a matter of routine.

While the community might well be content with an evolutionary approach to making the managerial and system reforms discussed in this book, national political realities foreclose that genteel option. With the coming of the 104th Congress of the United States on November 6, 1994, many of the public-policy assumptions in favor of continued external support for African American interests were turned upside down. For example, a public monopoly for primary and secondary education, which had been the mainstay for upward mobility, is no longer a foregone conclusion. Unending welfare support can no longer be the economic staple for one-third of the black community. The expectation of affirmative action to address past inequities through access to higher education, jobs, and public procurement contracts seems to be on its deathbed. The steady increase in elective political power through national, state, and local office holders may be in jeopardy of a Second Reconstruction era.

The steady erosion of economic viability in our high-density urban centers sounds parallel alarms. The aggravated tendency toward one-party politics within and without our communities poses a long-term threat of our political isolation. The loss of employment opportunities for unskilled, or even skilled, labor, as it has been known traditionally, promises a worldwide shift in unemployment and employability likely to be catastrophic to certain segments of the black workforce and threatens permanent Depression-like conditions. These are the external factors that give added impetus to the need to reexamine the ways in which leadership is exhibited and exercised within the black community. With such broad-sweeping changes in required perspectives, traditional leadership types will need to undergo a radical metamorphosis to understand the rules of management, systems analysis, computer literacy, multimedia, and telecommunications, as well as their importance to understanding the domestic connection to worldwide labor and capital markets.

Hopefully, this will also call attention to the necessity for a more dedicated effort to recycle the purchasing power and economic resources within the black community to replace the diminished resources artificially supplied from outside sources. Indeed, the lessening of support from public spending, external philanthropy, and remedial public policy ought to now lead to the resurgence of long-forgotten economic self-reliance, which fell dormant when the walls of segregation began to crumble. While much of our leadership's energy has routinely made the case for greater external public and private support, too little emphasis has been devoted to recycling our own $450 billion in earnings and consumer power to provide the response to community self-needs. Effecting this shift in emphasis away from external dependency to internal self-help will require a massive and deep reordering of leadership priorities.

Through C-Span, CNN, and other twenty-four-hour vehicles of instant access to congressional and state and local legislative proceedings, the leadership role as information middlemen will naturally erode. As a result, only value-added interpreters who can build upon commonly known information with new and meaningful understandings and strategies will be able to justify attention or a popular following.

With this proliferation of media outlets, even in the face of more highly concentrated ownership patterns devolving to a handful of international megacorporations, there will undoubtedly emerge more cost-effective means through which diverse voices can be heard. This will be the inevitable result of media channel supply exceeding the demand for its use. But to succeed effectively in accessing these new modes of expression will require higher sophistication than that commonly available among our traditional leaders.

Additional forms of leadership must arise to address the issues critical to the competitive interests of the black community. High-tech educators, entrepreneurs, and finance brokers, as well as systems managers and planners, are needed in countless locations throughout black society. For the most part, these will be professionals who have grown up in the Information Age, learned state-of-the-art computer tools of work, and had an opportunity for hands-on experience within the belly of one of the major commercial structures that are at the center of the Information Age. These will be the very people least likely to have had leadership roles in the old paradigm.

This new generation of role models must see themselves as more than conspicuous consumers, with a recognition of the interaction of their material resources and skills with the security and well-being of the black masses. Hopefully, they will be more inclined to participate out of self-interest in the social and economic uplift of that third of the population falling below the poverty line than many of their miseducated predecessors were typically willing to do. This new generation of "haves" will be the backbone for reform in public education, as well as the invention of private means of education through alternative education systems, and will craft the paths by which black youth can be prepared for modern employment through applied forms of learning technology. The coming generation will see church resources as more than private holdings and connect them with community renewal projects. They will also be able to negotiate better terms by which jobs and business opportunities are coupled with the grant of consumer patronage. Finally, this new generation must appreciate the age-old reality that one cannot take without giving back lest the source of the bounty not be renewable. In addition, this new generation leadership must be at pains to groom their own successors as soon as they assume office, lest the ruin of discontinuity undermine every new level of their accomplishments. The education of successors requires a role reversal for those who are the first to get into racially restricted positions. Leaders must see themselves as pathfinders for others, instead of barring the door after themselves to assure their continued uniqueness and prestige.

Contrary to the doomsday predictions of some, black people can have confidence in the revitalization required by these changes in circumstances. Based on a bedrock of self-esteem through accomplishments during the worst of times in yesteryear, our community has what it takes to reinvent its institutions and restore the ladders of hope that sustained past progress. Drug addiction and the other attendant pathologies are the symptoms, not the disease. The disease is the despairing inability to fashion the realistic course of survival through self-controlled improvement. Too little has also been devoted to naming those who are the detractors within our ranks for their contribution to the plight of the village. Now this misdirected practice of silent indulgence must stop. It must stop now, not just because of the internal ethical appeals that have been heard for the past fifty years, but because of the imminent cutoff of prior support that was coming by external hands.

The challenge is to use this pivotal decade that spans the end of this century and the beginning of the next to replace the old style of gatekeeping with a new role of gatecrashers to the throughway to the future known as the Information Superhighway. It means retooling the educational engines of our communities. It means assuring internal economic benefit from the billions of dollars that mark the black community as the twelfth largest economy in the world. It means zero tolerance for waste and dysfunctional self-seeking of select institutional leadership. It calls for a deeper celebration of self that is not predicated on a put-down or even a protest against others, but calls for constructive criticism. It means a new message of concern and participation in educational development and communal parenting for our lost youth.

Fortunately, the genius of modern-day science and technology of the Information Age offers tools needed for this kind of broad-sweeping change. The demand is that we step up and seize the opportunities inherent in the world reordering that will inevitably result through the communications revolution and the industrial, economic, and social ripples resulting in its wake. We must replace rhetoric with analysis, mere opinions with factual documentation, speculation with studied probabilities, procrastination with real-time initiatives, the historical with the futuristic, the haphazard with the calculated, the emotional with the deliberative, and even representation must be replaced by the direct participation of the actual stakeholders themselves, through ongoing and direct means of communications. Our organizational behavior will not change, however, if the people at the top are not personally knowledgeable, committed, and actively given to the demonstration of modern managerial leadership. Simply giving lip service to the importance of computers in information and management sciences will simply generate lip service in response.

Equally important is the assurance that senior executives have the understanding and ability to manage others who are using these new tools. In learning what is and is not possible with personal computers, executives learn to gauge what they can expect from others. The great generals are those familiar with the perspective of the foot soldiers. The object is to make the tools of this complex new world an enhancement to intuition, not its denial. The reinvention of our leadership is a two-way street; it will also introduce something new to the world of cybernetics, computational science, and enhanced multimedia applications. For too long, such scientific innovations have simply been viewed in quantitative terms to make life faster and more materially profitable without improving goals, purposes, or quality.

Because the historic strength of black leadership has been the advocacy of values, it should use this skill to refine the interpretation of cybernetics. By doing so, black people can give a voice and direction that goes beyond engineering for engineering's sake. In this way, different and more people-oriented discussions can emerge to complement the language of science. Such a blend of sensitivity with knowledge is what much of the world of cybernetics has repeatedly shown to be lacking. It has known a great deal about how, but not enough about why. Black leadership is ideally positioned to add a high touch of the world of high-tech. By "high touch" we mean a personal and caring dimension that assures equal access, affordability, and applications for technology relevant to the disadvantaged elements of society.

13. Feminist Perspectives on Technology

JUDY WAJCMAN

The study of the relationship between gender and technology has received increasing attention in recent years as feminists (both scholars and activists) have become concerned with the impact of new technology on women's lives and work, while "social constructionist" researchers on technology (see Chapter 2) have begun to examine how women's roles have influenced the evolution of technologies. This selection, "Feminist Perspectives on Technology," by Judy Wajcman, provides an overview of this area of study.

In order to understand the relationship between women and technology, it is important, first of all, to distinguish between science and technology and to be sensitive to the different layers of meaning of "technology." Women have contributed to the development of technology not just in terms of their conventional inventive activity but in terms of other kinds of activities in which they have engaged, but which may not have been recognized as "technological" in a gender-stereotyped view of technology. The emerging sociology of technology lacks a gender dimension, which Wajcman aims to provide both by the conceptual analysis presented here (and in her book, Feminism Confronts Technology, *from which this essay is taken), and by her own sociological research.*

Judy Wajcman is a professor of sociology at the Research School of Social Sciences at the Australian National University in Canberra. Recently, she held the Visiting Centennial Professorship in the Gender Institute of the London School of Economics. She has also been a research fellow at the Industrial Relations Research Unit at the University of Warwick in England, where she studied the differing experiences of men and women who are senior managers. She has been active in the women's movement in both Britain and Australia. In addition, she is coeditor, with Donald MacKenzie, of The Social Shaping of Technology *(1985).*

FROM SCIENCE TO TECHNOLOGY

While there has been a growing interest in the relationship of science to society over the last decade, there has been an even greater preoccupation with the relationship between technology and social change. Debate has raged over whether the "white heat of technology" is radically transforming society and delivering us into a postindustrial age. A major concern of feminists has been the impact of new technology on women's lives, particularly on women's work. The introduction of word processors into the office provided the focus for much early research. The recognition that housework was also work, albeit unpaid, led to studies on

Originally titled "Feminist Critiques of Science and Technology." From *Feminism Confronts Technology.* © by Judy Wajcman 1991. Reproduced by permission of the publisher.

how the increasing use of domestic technology in the home affected the time spent on housework. The exploitation of Third World women as a source of cheap labor for the manufacture of computer components has also been scrutinized. Most recently there has been a vigorous debate over developments in reproductive technology and the implications for women's control over their fertility.

Throughout these debates there has been a tension between the view that technology would liberate women — from unwanted pregnancy, from housework, and from routine paid work — and the obverse view that most new technologies are destructive and oppressive to women. For example, in the early seventies, Shulamith Firestone (1970) elaborated the view that developments in birth technology held the key to women's liberation through removing from them the burden of biological motherhood. Nowadays, there is much more concern with the negative implications of the new technologies, ironically most clearly reflected in the highly charged debate over the new reproductive technologies.

A key issue here is whether the problem lies in men's domination of technology or whether the technology is in some sense inherently patriarchal. If women were in control, would they apply technology to more benign ends? In the following discussion on gender and technology, I will explore these and related questions.

An initial difficulty in considering the feminist commentary on technology arises from its failure to distinguish between science and technology. Feminist writing on science has often construed science purely as a form of knowledge, and this assumption has been carried over into much of the feminist writing on technology. However, just as science includes practices and institutions, as well as knowledge, so too does technology. Indeed, it is even more clearly the case with technology, because technology is primarily about the creation of artifacts. This points to the need for a different theoretical approach to the analysis of the gender relations of technology from that being developed around science.

Perhaps this conflation of technology with science is not surprising given that the sociology of scientific knowledge over the last ten years has contested the idea of a noncontroversial distinction between science and technology. John Staudenmaier (1985, pp. 83–120) comments that although the relationship between science and technology has been a major theme in science and technology studies, the discussion has been plagued by a welter of conflicting definitions of the two basic terms. The only consensus to have emerged is that the way in which the boundaries between science and technology are demarcated, and how they are related to each other, change from one historical period to another.

In recent years, however, there has been a major reorientation of thinking about the form of the relationship between science and technology. The model of the science–technology relationship that enjoyed widespread acceptance over a long period was the traditional hierarchical model, which treats technology as applied science. This view that science discovers and technology applies this knowledge in a routine, uncreative way is now in steep decline. "One thing which practically any modern study of technological innovation suffices to show is that far from applying, and hence depending upon, the culture of natural science, technologists possess their own distinct cultural resources, which provide the principal basis for their innovative activity" (Barnes and Edge, 1982, p. 149). Technologists build on, modify, and extend existing technology, but they do this by a creative and imaginative process. And part of the received culture technologists inherit in the course of solving their practical problems is nonverbal; nor can it be conveyed adequately by the written word. Instead, it is the individual practitioner who transfers practical knowledge and competence to another. In short, the current model of the science–technology relationship characterizes science and technology as distinguishable subcultures in an interactive, symmetrical relationship.

Leaving aside the relationship between technology and science, it is most important to recognize that the word *technology* has at least three different layers of meaning. Firstly, "technology" is a form of knowledge, as Staudenmaier emphasizes.[1] Technological "things" are meaningless without the "know-how" to use them, repair them, design them, and make them. That know-how often cannot be captured in words. It is visual, even tactile, rather than simply verbal or mathematical. But it can also be systematized and taught, as in the various disciplines of engineering.

Few authors, however, would be content with this definition of technology as a form of knowledge. "Technology" also refers to what people do as well as what they know. An object such as a car or a vacuum cleaner is a technology, rather than an arbitrary lump of matter, because it forms part of a set of human activities. A computer without programs and programmers is simply a useless collection of bits of metal, plastic, and silicon. "Steelmaking," say, is a technology, but this implies that the technology includes what steelworkers do, as well as the furnaces they use. So "technology" refers to human activities and practices. And, finally, at the most basic level, there is the "hardware" definition of technology, in which it refers to sets of physical objects, for example, cars, lathes, vacuum cleaners, and computers.

In practice, the technologies dealt with here cover all three aspects, and often it is not useful to separate them further. My purpose is not to attempt to refine a definition. These different layers of meaning of "technology" are worth bearing in mind in what follows.

The rest of this [essay] will review the theoretical literature on gender and technology, which in many cases mirrors the debates about science outlined above. However, feminist perspectives on technology are more recent and much less theoretically developed than those that have been articulated in relation to science. One clear indication of this is the preponderance of edited collections that have been published in this area.[2] As with many such collections, the articles do not share a consistent approach or cover the field in a comprehensive fashion. Therefore, I will be drawing out strands of argument from this literature rather than presenting the material as coherent positions in a debate.

HIDDEN FROM HISTORY

To start with, feminists have pointed out the dearth of material on women and technology, especially given the burgeoning scholarship in the field of technology studies. Even the most perceptive and humanistic works on the relationship between technology, culture, and society rarely mention gender. Women's contributions have by and large been left out of technological history. Contributions to *Technology and Culture*, the leading journal of the history of technology, provide one accurate barometer of this. Joan Rothschild's (1983, pp. xii–xiv) survey of the journal for articles on the subject of women found only four in twenty-four years of publishing. In a more recent book about the journal, Staudenmaier (1985, p. 180) also notes the extraordinary bias in the journal toward male figures and the striking absence of a women's perspective. The history of technology represents the prototype inventor as male. So, as in the history of science, an initial task of feminists has been to uncover and recover the women hidden from history who have contributed to technological developments.

There is now evidence that during the Industrial Era, women invented or contributed to the invention of such crucial machines as the cotton gin, the sewing machine, the small electric motor, the McCormick reaper, and the Jacquard loom (Stanley, 1992). This sort of historical scholarship often relies heavily on patent records to recover women's forgotten inventions. It has been noted that many women's inventions have been credited to their husbands, because they actually appear in patent records in their husbands' names. This is explained in terms of women's limited property rights, as well as the general ridicule afforded women inventors at that time (Pursell, 1981; Amram, 1984; Griffiths, 1985). Interestingly, it may be that even the recovery of women inventors from patent records seriously underestimates their contribution to technological development. In a recent article on the role of patents, Christine MacLeod (1987) observes that, prior to 1700, patents were not primarily about the recording of the actual inventor, but were instead sought in the name of financial backers.[3] Given this, it is even less surprising that so few women's names are to be found in patent records.

For all but a few exceptional women, creativity alone was not sufficient. In order to participate in the inventive activity of the Industrial Revolution, capital as well as ideas were necessary. It was only in 1882 that the Married Women's Property Act gave English women legal possession and control of any personal property independently of their husbands. Dot Griffiths (1985) argues that the effect of this was to virtually exclude women from participation in the world of the inventor–entrepreneur. At the same time, women were being denied access to education and specifically to the theoretical grounding in mathematics and mechanics upon which so many of the inventions and innovations of the period were based. As business activities expanded and were moved out of the home, middle-class women were increasingly left to a life of enforced leisure. Soon, the appropriate education for girls became "accomplishments" such as embroidery and music — accomplishments hardly conducive to participation in the world of the inventor–entrepreneur. In the current period, there has been considerable interest in the possible contributions that Ada Lady Lovelace, Grace Hopper, and other women may have made to the development of computing. Recent histories of computer programming provide substantial evidence for the view that women played a major part.[4]

To fully comprehend women's contributions to technological development, however, a more radical approach may be necessary. For a start, the traditional conception of technology too readily defines technology in terms of male activities. As I have pointed out above, the concept of technology is itself subject to historical change, and different epochs and cultures had different names for what we now think of as technology. A greater emphasis on women's activities immediately suggests that females, and in particular black women, were among the first technologists. After all, women were the main gatherers, processors, and storers of plant food from earliest human times onward. It was therefore logical that they should be the ones to have invented the tools and methods involved in this work, such as the digging stick, the carrying sling, the reaping knife and sickle, pestles, and pounders. In this vein, Autumn Stanley (1992) illustrates women's early achievements in horticulture and agriculture, such as the hoe, the scratch plow, grafting, hand pollination, and early irrigation.

If it were not for the male bias in most technology research, the significance of these inventions would be acknowledged. As Ruth Schwartz Cowan notes:

> The indices to the standard histories of technology . . . do not contain a single reference, for example, to such a significant cultural artifact as the baby bottle. Here is a simple implement . . . which has transformed a fundamental human experience for vast numbers of infants and mothers, and been one of the more controversial exports of Western technology to underdeveloped countries — yet it finds no place in our histories of technology. (1979, p. 52)

There is important work to be done not only in identifying women inventors, but also in discovering the origins and paths of development of "women's sphere" technologies that seem often to have been considered beneath notice.

▲ TECHNOLOGY BASED ON WOMEN'S VALUES?

During the eighties, feminists began to focus on the gendered character of technology itself. Rather than asking how women could be more equitably treated within and by a neutral technology, many feminists now argue that Western technology itself embodies patriarchal values. This parallels the way in which the feminist critique of science evolved from asking the "woman question" in science to asking the more radical "science question" in feminism. Technology, like science, is seen as deeply implicated in the masculine project of the domination and control of women and nature.[5] Just as many feminists have argued for a science based on women's values, so too has there been a call for a technology based on women's values. In Joan Rothschild's (1983) preface to a collection on feminist perspectives on technology, she says that, "Feminist analysis has sought to show how the subjective, intuitive, and irrational can and do play a key role in our science and technology." Interestingly, she cites an important male figure in the field, Lewis Mumford, to support her case. Mumford's linking of subjective impulses, life-generating forces, and a female principle is consistent with such a feminist analysis, as is his endorsement of a more holistic view of culture and technological developments.

Other male authors have also advocated a technology based on women's values. Mike Cooley is a well-known critic of the current design of technological systems, and he has done much to popularize the idea of human-centered technologies. In *Architect or Bee?* (1980, p. 43) he argues that technological change has "male values" built into it: "the values of the White Male Warrior, admired for his strength and speed in eliminating the weak, conquering competitors and ruling over vast armies of men who obey his every instruction. . . . Technological change is starved of the so-called female values, such as intuition, subjectivity, tenacity, and compassion." Cooley sees it as imperative that more women become involved in science and technology to challenge and counteract the built-in male values: that we cease placing the objective above the subjective, the rational above the tacit, and the digital above analogical representation. In *The Culture of Technology*, Arnold Pacey (1983) devotes an entire chapter to "Women and Wider Values." He outlines three contrasting sets of values involved in the practice of technology — first, those stressing virtuosity, second, economic values, and third, user or need-oriented values. Women exemplify this third "responsible" orientation, according to Pacey, as they work with nature in contrast to the male interest in construction and the conquest of nature.

Ironically, the approach of these male authors is in some respects rather similar to the eco-feminism that became popular among feminists in the eighties. This marriage of ecology and feminism rests on the "female principle," the notion that women are closer to nature than men and that the technologies men have created are based on the domination of nature in the same way that they seek to dominate women. Eco-feminists concentrated on military technology and the ecological effects of other modern technologies. According to them, these technologies are products of a patriarchal culture that "speaks violence at every level" (Rothschild, 1983, p. 126). An early slogan of the feminist antimilitarist movement, "Take the Toys from the Boys," drew attention to the phallic symbolism in the shape of missiles. However, an inevitable corollary of this stance seemed to be the representation of women as inherently nurturing and pacifist. The problems with this position have been outlined [here] in relation to science based on women's essential values. We need to ask how women became associated with these values. The answer involves examining the way in which the traditional division of labor between women and men has generally restricted women to a narrow range of experience concerned primarily with the private world of the home and family.

Nevertheless, the strength of these arguments is that they go beyond the usual conception of the problem as being women's exclusion from the processes of innovation and from the acquisition of technical skills. Feminists have pointed to all sorts of barriers — in social attitudes, girls' education, and the employment policies of firms — to account for the imbalance in the number of women in engineering. But rarely has the problem been identified as the way engineering has been conceived and taught. In particular, the failure of liberal and equal opportunity policies has led authors such as Cynthia Cockburn (1985) to ask whether women actively resist entering technology. Why have the women's training initiatives designed to break men's monopoly of the building trades, engineering, and information technology not been more successful? Although schemes to channel women into technical trades have been small scale, it is hard to escape the conclusion that women's response has been tentative and perhaps ambivalent.

I share Cockburn's view that this reluctance "to enter" is to do with the sex-stereotyped definition of technology as an activity appropriate for men. As with science, the very language of technology, its symbolism, is masculine. It is not simply a question of acquiring skills, because these skills are embedded in a culture of masculinity that is largely coterminous with the culture of technology. Both at school and in the workplace, this culture is incompatible with femininity. Therefore, to enter this world, to learn its language, women have first to forsake their femininity.

TECHNOLOGY AND THE DIVISION OF LABOR

I will now turn to a more historical and sociological approach to the analysis of gender and technology. This approach has built on some theoretical foundations provided by contributors to the labor process debate of the 1970s. Just as the radical science movement had sought to expose the class character of science, these writers attempted to extend the class analysis to technology. In doing so, they were countering the theory of "technological determinism" that remains so widespread.

According to this account, changes in technology are the most important cause of social change. Technologies themselves are neutral and impinge on society from the outside; the scientists and technicians who produce new technologies are seen to be independent of their social location and above sectional interests. Labor-process analysts were especially critical of a technicist version of Marxism in which the development of technology and productivity is seen as the motor force of history. This interpretation represented technology itself as beyond class struggle.

With the publication of Harry Braverman's *Labor and Monopoly Capital* (1974), there was a revival of interest in Marx's contribution to the study of technology, particularly in relation to work. Braverman restored Marx's critique of technology and the division of labor to the center of his analysis of the process of capitalist development. The basic argument of the labor-process literature that developed was that capitalist–worker relations are a major factor affecting the technology of production within capitalism. Historical case studies of the evolution and introduction of particular technologies documented the way in which they were deliberately designed to deskill and eliminate human labor.[6] Rather than technical inventions developing inexorably, machinery was used by the owners and managers of capital as an important weapon in the battle for control over production. So, like science, technology was understood to be the result of capitalist social relations.

This analysis provided a timely challenge to the notion of technological determinism and, in its focus on the capitalist division of labor, it paved the way for development of a more sophisticated analysis of gender relations and technology. However, the labor process approach was gender blind, because it interpreted the social relations of technology in exclusively class terms. Yet, as has been well established by the socialist feminist current in this debate, the relations of production are constructed as much out of gender divisions as class divisions. Recent writings (Cockburn, 1983, 1985; Faulkner and Arnold, 1985; McNeil, 1987) in this historical vein see women's exclusion from technology as a consequence of the gender division of labor and the male domination of skilled trades that developed under capitalism. In fact, some argue that, prior to the Industrial Revolution, women had more opportunities to acquire technical skills and that capitalist technology has become more masculine than previous technologies.

I have already described how, in the early phases of industrialization, women were denied access to ownership of capital and access to education. Shifting the focus, these authors show that the rigid pattern of gender divisions that developed within the working class in the context of the new industries laid the foundation for the male dominance of technology. It was during this period that manufacturing moved into factories and home became separated from paid work. The advent of powered machinery fundamentally challenged traditional craft skills, because tools were literally taken out of the hands of workers and combined into machines. But, as it had been men who on the whole had technical skills in the period before the Industrial Revolution, they were in a unique position to maintain a monopoly over the new skills created by the introduction of machines.

Male craft workers could not prevent employers from drawing women into the new spheres of production. So instead they organized to retain certain rights over technology by actively resisting the entry of women to their trades. Women who became industrial laborers found themselves working in what were considered to be unskilled jobs for the lowest pay. "It is the most damning indictment of skilled working-class men and their unions that they excluded women from membership and prevented them gaining competences that could have secured them a decent living" (Cockburn, 1985, p. 39). This gender division of labor within the factory meant that the machinery was designed by men with men in mind, either by the capitalist inventor or by skilled craftsmen. Industrial technology from its origins thus reflects male power as well as capitalist domination.

The masculine culture of technology is fundamental to the way in which the gender division of labor is still being reproduced today. By securing control of key technologies, men are denying women the practical experience upon which inventiveness depends. I noted earlier the degree to which technical knowledge involves tacit, intuitive knowledge and "learning by doing." New technology typically emerges not from sudden flashes of inspiration but from existing technology, by a process of gradual modification to, and new combinations of, that existing technology. Innovation is, to some extent, an imaginative process, but that imagination lies largely in seeing ways in which existing devices can be improved and in extending the scope of techniques successful in one area into new areas. Therefore, giving women access to formal technical knowledge alone does not provide the resources necessary for invention. Experience of existing technology is a precondition for the invention of new technology.

The nature of women's inventions, like that of men's, is a function of time, place, and resources. Segregated at work and primarily confined to the private sphere of household, women's experience has been severely restricted and therefore so too has their inventiveness. An interesting illustration of this point lies in the fact that women who were employed in the munitions factories during the First World War are on record as having redesigned the weaponry they were making.[7] Thus, given the opportunity, women have demonstrated their inventive capacity in what now seems the most unlikely of contexts.

MISSING: THE GENDER DIMENSION IN THE SOCIOLOGY OF TECHNOLOGY

The historical approach is an advance over essentialist positions that seek to base a new technology on women's innate values. Women's profound alienation from technology is accounted for in terms of the historical and cultural construction of technology as masculine. I believe that women's exclusion from, and rejection of, technology is made more explicable by an analysis of technology as a culture that expresses and consolidates relations among men. If technical competence is an integral part of masculine gender identity, why should women be expected to aspire to it?

Such an account of technology and gender relations, however, is still at a general level.[8] There are few cases where feminists have really got inside the "black box" of technology to do detailed empirical research, as some of the most recent sociological literature has attempted. Over the last few years, a new sociology of technology has emerged, which is studying the invention, development, stabilization, and diffusion of specific artifacts.[9] It is evident from this research that technology is not simply the product of rational technical imperatives. Rather, political choices are embedded in the very design and selection of technology.

Technologies result from a series of specific decisions made by particular groups of people in particular places at particular times for their own purposes. As such, technologies bear the imprint of the people and social context in which they developed. David Noble (1984, p. xiii) expresses this point succinctly as follows: "Because of its very concreteness, people tend to confront technology as an irreducible brute fact, a given, a first cause, rather than as hardened history, frozen fragments of human and social endeavor." Technological change is a process subject to struggles for control by different groups. As such, the outcomes depend primarily on the distribution of power and resources within society.

There is now an extensive literature on the history of technology and the economics of technological innovation. Labor historians and sociologists have investigated the relationship between social change and the shaping of production processes in great detail and have also been concerned with the influence of technological form upon social relations. The sociological approach has moved away from studying the individual inventor and from the notion that technological innovation is a result of some inner technical logic. Rather, it attempts to show the effects of social relations on technology that range from fostering or inhibiting particular technologies, through influencing the choice between competing paths of technical development, to affecting the precise design characteristics of particular artifacts. Technological innovation now requires major investment and has become a collective, institutionalized process. The evolution of a technology is thus the function of a complex set of technical, social, economic, and political factors. An artifact may be looked on as the "congealed outcome of a set of negotiations, compromises, conflicts, controversies, and deals that were put together between opponents in rooms filled with smoke, lathes, or computer terminals" (Law, 1987, p. 406).

Because social groups have different interests and resources, the development process brings out conflicts between different views of the technical requirements of the device. Accordingly, the stability and form of artifacts depend on the capacity and resources that the salient social groups can mobilize in the course of the development process. Thus, in the technology of production, economic and social class interests often lie behind the development and adoption of devices. In the case of military technology, the operation of bureaucratic and organizational interests of state decision making will be identifiable. Growing attention is now being given to the extent to which the state sponsorship of military technology shapes civilian technology.

So far, however, little attention has been paid to the way in which technological objects may be shaped by the operation of gender interests. This blindness to gender issues is also indicative of a general problem with the methodology adopted by the new sociology of technology. Using a conventional notion of technology, these writers study the social groups that actively seek to influence the form and direction of technological design. What they overlook is the fact that the absence of influence from certain groups may also be significant. For them, women's absence from observable conflict does not indicate that gender interests are being mobilized. For a social theory of gender, however, the almost complete exclusion of women from the technological community points to the need to take account of the underlying structure of gender relations. Preferences for different technologies are shaped by a set of social arrangements that reflect men's power in the wider society. The process of technological development is socially structured and culturally patterned by various social interests that lie outside the immediate context of technological innovation.

More than ever before, technological change impinges on every aspect of our public and private lives, from the artificially cultivated food that we eat to the increasingly sophisticated forms of communication we use. Yet, in common with the labor process debate, the sociology of technology has concentrated almost exclusively on the relations of paid production, focusing in particular on the early stages of product development. In doing so [it has] ignored the spheres of reproduction, consumption, and the unpaid production that takes place in the home. By contrast, feminist analysis points us beyond the factory gates to see that technology is just as centrally involved in these spheres.

Inevitably perhaps, feminist work in this area has so far raised as many questions as it has answered. Is technology valued because it is associated with masculinity or is masculinity valued because of the association with technology? How do we avoid the tautology that "technology is masculine because men do it"? Why is women's work undervalued? Is there such a thing as women's knowledge? Is it different from "feminine intuition"? Can technology be reconstructed around women's interests? These are the questions that abstract analysis has so far failed to answer. The character of salient interests and social groups will differ depending on the particular empirical sites of technology being considered. Thus, we need to look in more concrete and historical detail at how, in specific areas of work and personal life, gender relations influence the technological enterprise. . . . [In the book from which this chapter is drawn I stress] that a gendered approach to technology cannot be reduced to a view which treats technology as a set of neutral artifacts manipulated by men in their own interests. While it is the case that men dominate the scientific and technical institutions, it is perfectly plausible that there will come a time when women are more fully represented in these institutions without transforming the direction of technological development. To cite just one instance, women are increasingly being recruited into the American space-defense program, but we do not hear their voices protesting about its preoccupations. Nevertheless, gender relations are an integral constituent of the social organization of these institutions and their projects. It is impossible to divorce the gender relations that are expressed in, and shape technologies from, the wider social structures that create and maintain them. In developing a theory of the gendered character of technology, we are inevitably in danger of either adopting an essentialist position that sees technology as inherently patriarchal or losing sight of the structure of gender relations through an overemphasis on the historical variability of the categories of "women" and "technology." [My work seeks] to chart another course.

NOTES

1. Staudenmaier (1985, pp. 103–20) outlines four characteristics of technological knowledge—scientific concepts, problematic data, engineering theory, and technological skill.
2. A good cross-section of this material can be found in Trescott (1979), Rothschild (1983), Faulkner and Arnold (1985), McNeil (1987) and Kramarae (1988). McNeil's book is particularly useful as it contains a comprehensive bibliography, which is organized thematically.
3. MacLeod (1987) suggests that although George Ravenscroft is credited in the patent records with being the "heroic" inventor of lead-crystal glass, he was rather the purchaser or financier of another's invention. This study alerts us to the danger of assuming that patent records have always represented the same thing.
4. For a biography of Lady Lovelace, which takes issue with the view of her as a major contributor to computer programming, see Stein (1985). However, both Kraft (1977) and, more recently, Giordano (1988) have documented the extensive participation of women in the development of computer programming.
5. Technology as the domination of nature is also a central theme in the work of critical theorists, such as Marcuse, for whom it is capitalist relations (rather than patriarchal relations) that are built into the very structure of technology. "Not only the application of technology but technology itself is domination (of nature and men) — methodical, scientific, calcu-

lated, calculating control. Specific purposes and interests of domination are not foisted upon technology 'subsequently' and from the outside; they enter the very construction of the technical apparatus" (Marcuse, 1968, pp. 223–4).
6. This point is elaborated in Chapter 2 of *Feminism Confronts Technology*. See also Part Two of MacKenzie and Wajcman (1985) for a collection of these case studies.
7. Amram (1984) provides a selection of the patents granted to women during the First World War.
8. Cockburn's (1983, 1985) work is one important exception discussed at greater length in Chapter 2 of *Feminism Confronts Technology*.
9. For an introduction to this literature, see MacKenzie and Wajcman (1985) and Bijker, Hughes, and Pinch (1987).

REFERENCES

Amram, F. 1984. "The Innovative Woman." *New Scientist* 24 May 1984, 10–12.

Barnes, Barry, and David Edge, eds. 1982. *Science in Context: Readings in the Sociology of Science*. Milton Keynes, England: Open University Press/Cambridge, MA: MIT Press.

Bijker, Wiebe E., Thomas P. Hughes, and Trevor J. Pinch, eds. 1987. *The Social Construction of Technological Systems*. Cambridge, MA: MIT Press.

Braverman, Harry. 1974. *Labor and Monopoly Capital: The Degradation of Work in the Twentieth Century*. New York: Monthly Review Press.

Cockburn, Cynthia. 1985. *Machinery of Dominance: Women, Men, and Technical Know-How*. London: Pluto Press.

Cockburn, Cynthia. 1983. *Brothers: Male Dominance and Technical Change*. London: Pluto Press.

Cooley, Mike. 1980. *Architect or Bee? The Human/Technology Relationship*. Slough, England: Langley Technical Services.

Cowan, Ruth S. 1979. "From Virginia Dare to Virginia Slims: Women and Technology in American Life." *Technology and Culture* 20; 51–63.

Faulkner, Wendy, and Erik Arnold, eds. 1985. *Smothered by Invention: Technology in Women's Lives*. London: Pluto Press.

Firestone, Shulamith. 1970. *The Dialectic of Sex*. New York: William Morrow & Co.

Giordano, R. 1988. *The Social Context of Innovation: A Case History of the Development of COBOL Programming Language*. Columbia University Department of History.

Griffiths, Dot. 1985. "The Exclusion of Women from Technology." In Faulkner and Arnold, op. cit.

Kraft, P. 1977. *Programmers and Managers: The Routinization of Computer Programming in the United States*. New York: Springer Verlag.

Kramarae, Chris, ed. 1988. *Technology and Women's Voices*. New York: Routledge & Kegan Paul.

Law, John. 1987. Review Article: "The Structure of Sociotechnical Engineering — A Review of the New Sociology of Technology." *Sociological Review* 35; 404–25.

MacKenzie, Donald, and Judy Wajcman, eds. 1985. *The Social Shaping of Technology: How the Refrigerator Got Its Hum*. Milton Keynes, England: Open University Press.

MacLeod, Christine. 1987. "Accident or Design? George Ravenscroft's Patent and the Invention of Lead-Crystal Glass." *Technology and Culture* 28, 4:776–803.

Marcuse, H. 1968. *Negations*. London: Allen Lane.

McNeil, Maureen, ed. 1987. *Gender and Expertise*. London: Free Association Books.

Noble, David. 1984. *Forces of Production: A Social History of Industrial Automation*. New York: Knopf.

Pacey, Arnold. 1983. *The Culture of Technology*. Oxford, England: Basil Blackwell/Cambridge, MA: MIT Press.

Pursell, C. 1981. "Women Inventors in America." *Technology and Culture* 22, 3:545–9.

Rothschild, Joan, ed. 1983. *Machina ex Dea: Feminist Perspectives on Technology*. New York: Pergamon Press.

Stanley, Autumn. 1992. *Mothers and Daughters of Invention: Notes for a Revised History of Technology*. Metuchen, NJ: Scarecrow Press.

Staudenmaier, John M. 1985. *Technology Storytellers: Reweaving the Human Fabric*. Cambridge, MA: MIT Press.

Stein, D. 1985. *Ada: A Life and Legacy*. Cambridge, MA: MIT Press.

Trescott, Martha M., ed. 1979. *Dynamos and Virgins Revisited: Women and Technological Change in History*. Metuchen, NJ: Scarecrow.

14. Do Artifacts Have Politics?

LANGDON WINNER

Do the properties of technological systems embody specific kinds of power and authority relationships? Are nuclear power systems inherently centralizing and authoritarian? Are solar power systems, as some of their advocates claim, more democratic and consistent with the values of pluralistic societies? Langdon Winner looks for answers to questions such as these in the following essay, originally published in a 1980 symposium issue of the journal Daedalus *devoted to "Modern Technology: Problem or Opportunity?" Winner believes that, indeed, technological choices do have political consequences. He cites many examples, including a particularly egregious one: Robert Moses designed bridges over his parkways on Long Island too low for buses in order to keep members of the urban lower classes (who couldn't afford private automobiles) from crowding the suburban parks and beaches.*

"Technologies," Winner concludes, "are ways of building order in our world," which, by their nature, influence the way people live and work over long periods of time. We need to study and understand their consequences and to develop means of making technological choices in a more open and participatory fashion if we are to maintain a democratic society.

A prolific writer whose works have appeared in both scholarly and popular publications and who served as contributing editor to Rolling Stone *magazine from 1969 to 1971, Langdon Winner is professor of political science in the Department of Science and Technology Studies at Rensselaer Polytechnic Institute (RPI) in Troy, New York. Prior to coming to RPI in 1985, he taught at the Massachusetts Institute of Technology, the University of Leiden (in the Netherlands), and the University of California at Berkeley and at Santa Cruz. Among Winner's books are* Autonomous Technology *(1977) and* The Whale and the Reactor *(1988).*

In controversies about technology and society, there is no idea more provocative than the notion that technical things have political qualities. At issue is the claim that the machines, structures, and systems of modern material culture can be accurately judged not only for their contributions of efficiency and productivity, not merely for their positive and negative environmental side effects, but also for the ways in which they can embody specific forms of power and authority. Since ideas of this kind have a persistent and troubling presence in discussions about the meaning of technology, they deserve explicit attention.[1]

Writing in *Technology and Culture* almost two decades ago, Lewis Mumford gave classic statement to one version of the theme, arguing that "from late neolithic times in the Near East, right down to our own day, two technologies

"Do Artifacts Have Politics?" Reprinted by permission of *Daedalus*, Journal of the American Academy of Arts and Sciences, from the issue entitled, "Modern Technology: Problem or Opportunity?" Winter 1980, Vol. 109, No. 1.

have recurrently existed side by side: one authoritarian, the other democratic, the first system centered, immensely powerful, but inherently unstable, the other man centered, relatively weak, but resourceful and durable."[2] This thesis stands at the heart of Mumford's studies of the city, architecture, and the history of technics and mirrors concerns voiced earlier in the works of Peter Kropotkin, William Morris, and other nineteenth-century critics of industrialism. More recently, antinuclear and prosolar energy movements in Europe and America have adopted a similar notion as a centerpiece in their arguments. Thus, environmentalist Denis Hayes concludes, "The increased deployment of nuclear power facilities must lead society toward authoritarianism. Indeed, safe reliance upon nuclear power as the principal source of energy may be possible only in a totalitarian state." Echoing the views of many proponents of appropriate technology and the soft energy path, Hayes contends that "dispersed solar sources are more compatible than centralized technologies with social equity, freedom, and cultural pluralism."[3]

An eagerness to interpret technical artifacts in political language is by no means the exclusive property of critics of large-scale, high-technology systems. A long lineage of boosters have insisted that the "biggest and best" that science and industry made available were the best guarantees of democracy, freedom, and social justice. The factory system, automobile, telephone, radio, television, the space program, and, of course, nuclear power itself have all at one time or another been described as democratizing, liberating forces. David Lilienthal, in *T.V.A.: Democracy on the March*, for example, found this promise in the phosphate fertilizers and electricity that technical progress was bringing to rural Americans during the 1940s.[4] In a recent essay, *The Republic of Technology*, Daniel Boorstin extolled television for "its power to disband armies, to cashier presidents, to create a whole new democratic world — democratic in ways never before imagined, even in America."[5] Scarcely a new invention comes along that someone does not proclaim it the salvation of a free society.

It is no surprise to learn that technical systems of various kinds are deeply interwoven in the conditions of modern politics. The physical arrangements of industrial production, warfare, communications, and the like have fundamentally changed the exercise of power and the experience of citizenship. But to go beyond this obvious fact and to argue that certain technologies in themselves have political properties seems, at first glance, completely mistaken. We all know that people have politics, not things. To discover either virtues or evils in aggregates of steel, plastic, transistors, integrated circuits, and chemicals seems just plain wrong, a way of mystifying human artifice and of avoiding the true sources, the human sources of freedom and oppression, justice and injustice. Blaming the hardware appears even more foolish than blaming the victims when it comes to judging conditions of public life.

Hence, the stern advice commonly given those who flirt with the notion that technical artifacts have political qualities: What matters is not technology itself, but the social or economic system in which it is embedded. This maxim, which in a number of variations is the central premise of a theory that can be called the social determination of technology, has an obvious wisdom. It serves as a needed corrective to those who focus uncritically on such things as "the computer and its social impacts" but who fail to look behind technical things to notice the social circumstances of their development, deployment, and use. This view provides an antidote to naive technological determinism — the idea that technology develops as the sole result of an internal dynamic, and then, unmediated by any other influence, molds society to fit its patterns. Those who have not recognized the ways in which technologies are shaped by social and economic forces have not gotten very far.

But the corrective has its own shortcomings; taken literally, it suggests that technical things do not matter at all. Once one has done the detective work necessary to reveal the social origins — power holders behind a particular instance of technological change — one will have explained everything of importance. This conclusion offers comfort to social scientists: It validates what they had always suspected, namely, that there is nothing distinctive about the study of technology in the first place. Hence, they can return to their standard models of social power — those of interest group politics, bureaucratic politics, Marxist models of class struggle, and the like — and have everything they need. The social determination of technology is, in this view, essentially no different from the social determination of, say, welfare policy or taxation.

There are, however, good reasons technology has of late taken on a special fascination in its own right for historians, philosophers, and political scientists, good reasons the standard models of social science only go so far in accounting for what is most interesting and troublesome about the subject. In another place I have tried to show why so much of modern social and political thought contains recurring statements of what can be called a theory of technological politics, an odd mongrel of notions often crossbred with orthodox liberal, conservative, and socialist philosophies.[6] The theory of technological politics draws attention to the momentum of large-scale sociotechnical systems, to the response of modern societies to certain technological imperatives, and to the all-too-common signs of the adaptation of human ends to technical means. In so doing, it offers a novel framework of interpretation and explanation for some of the more puzzling patterns that have taken shape in and around the growth of modern material culture. One strength of this point of view is that it takes technical artifacts seriously. Rather than insist that we immediately reduce everything to the interplay of social forces, it suggests that we pay attention to the characteristics of technical objects and the meaning of those characteristics. A necessary complement to, rather than a replacement for, theories of the social determination of technology, this perspective identifies certain technologies as political phenomena in their own right. It points us back, to borrow Edmund Husserl's philosophical injunction, to the things themselves.

In what follows, I shall offer outlines and illustrations of two ways in which artifacts can contain political properties. First are instances in which the invention, design, or arrangement of a specific technical device or system becomes a way of settling an issue in a particular community. Seen in the proper light, examples of this kind are fairly straightforward and easily understood. Second are cases of what can be called inherently political technologies, man-made systems that appear to require, or to be strongly compatible with, particular kinds of political relationships. Arguments about cases of this kind are much more trouble-some and closer to the heart of the matter. By "politics," I mean arrangements of power and authority in human associations as well as the activities that take place within those arrangements. For my purposes, "technology" here is under-stood to mean all of modern practical artifice,[7] but to avoid confusion I prefer to speak of technologies, smaller or larger pieces or systems of hardware of a specific kind. My intention is not to settle any of the issues here once and for all, but to indicate their general dimensions and significance.

TECHNICAL ARRANGEMENTS AS FORMS OF ORDER

Anyone who has traveled the highways of America and has become used to the normal height of overpasses may well find something a little odd about some of the bridges over the parkways on Long Island, New York. Many of the overpasses are extraordinarily low, having as little as nine feet of clearance at the curb. Even those who happened to notice this structural peculiarity would not be inclined to attach any special meaning to it. In our accustomed way of looking at things like roads and bridges we see the details of form as innocuous and seldom give them a second thought.

It turns out, however, that the 200 or so low-hanging overpasses on Long Island were deliberately designed to achieve a particular social effect. Robert Moses, the master builder of roads, parks, bridges, and other public works from the 1920s to the 1970s in New York, had these overpasses built to specifications that would discourage the presence of buses on his parkways. According to evi-dence provided by Robert A. Caro in his biography of Moses, the reasons reflect Moses's social-class bias and racial prejudice. Automobile-owning whites of "upper" and "comfortable middle" classes, as he called them, would be free to use the parkways for recreation and commuting. Poor people and blacks, who nor-mally used public transit, were kept off the roads because the twelve-foot-tall buses could not get through the overpasses. One consequence was to limit access of racial minorities and low-income groups to Jones Beach, Moses's widely acclaimed public park. Moses made doubly sure of this result by vetoing a pro-posed extension of the Long Island Railroad to Jones Beach.[8]

As a story in recent American political history, Robert Moses's life is fascinat-ing. His dealings with mayors, governors, and presidents, and his careful manipu-lation of legislatures, banks, labor unions, the press, and public opinion, are all matters that political scientists could study for years. But the most important and enduring results of his work are his technologies, the vast engineering projects that give New York much of its present form. For generations after Moses has gone and the alliances he forged have fallen apart, his public works, especially the highways and bridges he built to favor the use of the automobile over the devel-opment of mass transit, will continue to shape that city. Many of his monumental structures of concrete and steel embody a systematic social inequality, a way of engineering relationships among people that, after a time, becomes just another part of the landscape. As planner Lee Koppleman told Caro about the low bridges on Wantagh Parkway, "The old son-of-a-gun had made sure that buses would never be able to use his goddamned parkways."[9]

Histories of architecture, city planning, and public works contain many examples of physical arrangements that contain explicit or implicit political purposes. One can point to Baron Haussmann's broad Parisian thoroughfares, engineered at Louis Napoleon's direction to prevent any recurrence of street fighting of the kind that took place during the revolution of 1848. Or one can visit any number of grotesque concrete buildings and huge plazas constructed on American university campuses during the late 1960s and early 1970s to defuse student demonstrations. Studies of industrial machines and instruments also turn up interesting political stories, including some that violate our normal expectations about why technological innovations are made in the first place. If we suppose that new technologies are introduced to achieve increased efficiency, the history of technology shows that we will sometimes be disappointed. Technological change expresses a panoply of human motives, not the least of which is the desire of some to have dominion over others, even though it may require an occasional sacrifice of cost cutting and some violence to the norm of getting more from less.

One poignant illustration can be found in the history of nineteenth-century industrial mechanization. At Cyrus McCormick's reaper manufacturing plant in Chicago in the middle 1880s, pneumatic molding machines, a new and largely untested innovation, were added to the foundry at an estimated cost of $500,000. In the standard economic interpretation of such things, we would expect that this step was taken to modernize the plant and achieve the kind of efficiencies that mechanization brings. But historian Robert Ozanne has shown why the development must be seen in a broader context. At the time, Cyrus McCormick II was engaged in a battle with the National Union of Iron Molders. He saw the addition of the new machines as a way to "weed out the bad element among the men," namely, the skilled workers who had organized the union local in Chicago.[10] The new machines, manned by unskilled labor, actually produced inferior castings at a higher cost than the earlier process. After three years of use, the machines were, in fact, abandoned, but by that time they had served their purpose — the destruction of the union. Thus, the story of these technical developments at the McCormick factory cannot be understood adequately outside the record of workers' attempts to organize, police repression of the labor movement in Chicago during that period, and the events surrounding the bombing at Haymarket Square. Technological history and American political history were at that moment deeply intertwined.

In cases like those of Moses's low bridges and McCormick's molding machines, one sees the importance of technical arrangements that precede the use of the things in question. It is obvious that technologies can be used in ways that enhance the power, authority, and privilege of some over others, for example, the use of television to sell a candidate. To our accustomed way of thinking, technologies are seen as neutral tools that can be used well or poorly, for good, evil, or something in between. But we usually do not stop to inquire whether a given device might have been designed and built in such a way that it produces a set of consequences logically and temporally prior to any of its professed uses. Robert Moses's bridges, after all, were used to carry automobiles from one point to another; McCormick's machines were used to make metal castings; both technologies, however, encompassed purposes far beyond their immediate use. If our moral and political language for evaluating technology includes only categories having to do with tools and uses, if it does not include attention to the meaning of the designs and arrangements of our artifacts, then we will be blinded to much that is intellectually and practically crucial.

Because the point is most easily understood in the light of particular intentions embodied in physical form, I have so far offered illustrations that seem almost conspiratorial. But to recognize the political dimensions in the shapes of technology does not require that we look for conscious conspiracies or malicious intentions. The organized movement of handicapped people in the United States during the 1970s pointed out the countless ways in which machines, instruments, and structures of common use — buses, buildings, sidewalks, plumbing fixtures, and so forth — made it impossible for many handicapped persons to move about freely, a condition that systematically excluded them from public life. It is safe to say that designs unsuited for the handicapped arose more from long-standing neglect than from anyone's active intention. But now that the issue has been raised for public attention, it is evident that justice requires a remedy. A whole range of artifacts are now being redesigned and rebuilt to accommodate this minority.

Indeed, many of the most important examples of technologies that have political consequences are those that transcend the simple categories of "intended" and "unintended" altogether. These are instances in which the very process of technical development is so thoroughly biased in a particular direction that it regularly produces results counted as wonderful breakthroughs by some social interests and crushing setbacks by others. In such cases, it is neither correct nor insightful to say, "Someone intended to do somebody else harm." Rather, one must say that the technological deck has been stacked long in advance to favor certain social interests and that some people were bound to receive a better hand than others.

The mechanical tomato harvester, a remarkable device perfected by researchers at the University of California from the late 1940s to the present, offers an illustrative tale. The machine is able to harvest tomatoes in a single pass through a row, cutting the plants from the ground, shaking the fruit loose, and, in the newest models, sorting the tomatoes electronically into large plastic gondolas that hold up to twenty-five tons of produce headed for canning. To accommodate the rough motion of these "factories in the field," agricultural researchers have bred new varieties of tomatoes that are hardier, sturdier, and less tasty. The harvesters replace the system of handpicking, in which crews of farmworkers would pass through the fields three or four times putting ripe tomatoes in lug boxes and saving immature fruit for later harvest.[11] Studies in California indicate that the machine reduces costs by approximately five to seven dollars per ton as compared to hand harvesting.[12] But the benefits are by no means equally divided in the agricultural economy. In fact, the machine in the garden has in this instance been the occasion for a thorough reshaping of social relationships of tomato production in rural California.

By their very size and cost, more than $50,000 each to purchase, the machines are compatible only with a highly concentrated form of tomato growing. With the introduction of this new method of harvesting, the number of tomato growers declined from approximately 4,000 in the early 1960s to about 600 in 1973, yet with a substantial increase in tons of tomatoes produced. By the late 1970s, an estimated 32,000 jobs in the tomato industry had been eliminated as a direct consequence of mechanization.[13] Thus, a jump in productivity to the benefit of very large growers has occurred at a sacrifice to other rural agricultural communities.

The University of California's research and development on agricultural machines like the tomato harvester is at this time the subject of a lawsuit filed by attorneys for California Rural Legal Assistance, an organization representing a group of farmworkers and other interested parties. The suit charges that University officials are spending tax monies on projects that benefit a handful of private interests to the detriment of farmworkers, small farmers, consumers, and rural California generally and asks for a court injunction to stop the practice. The University has denied these charges, arguing that to accept them "would require elimination of all research with any potential practical application."[14]

As far as I know, no one has argued that the development of the tomato harvester was the result of a plot. Two students of the controversy, William Friedland and Amy Barton, specifically exonerate both the original developers of the machine and the hard tomato from any desire to facilitate economic concentration in that industry.[15] What we see here instead is an ongoing social process in which scientific knowledge, technological invention, and corporate profit reinforce each other in deeply entrenched patterns that bear the unmistakable stamp of political and economic power. Over many decades, agricultural research and development in American land-grant colleges and universities has tended to favor the interests of large agribusiness concerns.[16] It is in the face of such subtly ingrained patterns that opponents of innovations like the tomato harvester are made to seem "antitechnology" or "antiprogress." For the harvester is not merely the symbol of a social order that rewards some while punishing others; it is in a true sense an embodiment of that order.

Within a given category of technological change there are, roughly speaking, two kinds of choices that can affect the relative distribution of power, authority, and privilege in a community. Often the crucial decision is a simple "yes or no" choice — Are we going to develop and adopt the thing or not? In recent years, many local, national, and international disputes about technology have centered on "yes or no" judgments about such things as food additives, pesticides, the building of highways, nuclear reactors, and dam projects. The fundamental choice about an ABM or an SST is whether or not the thing is going to join society as a piece of its operating equipment. Reasons for and against are frequently as important as those concerning the adoption of an important new law.

A second range of choices, equally critical in many instances, has to do with specific features in the design or arrangement of a technical system after the decision to go ahead with it has already been made. Even after a utility company wins permission to build a large electric power line, important controversies can remain with respect to the placement of its route and the design of its towers; even after an organization has decided to institute a system of computers, controversies can still arise with regard to the kinds of components, programs, modes of access, and other specific features the system will include. Once the mechanical tomato harvester had been developed in its basic form, design alteration of critical social significance — the addition of electronic sorters, for example — changed the character of the machine's effects on the balance of wealth and power in California agriculture. Some of the most interesting research on technology and politics at present focuses on the attempt to demonstrate in a detailed, concrete fashion how seemingly innocuous design features in mass transit systems, water projects, industrial machinery, and other technologies actually mask social choices of profound significance. Historian David Noble is now studying two kinds of automated machine tool systems that have different implications for the relative power of management and labor in the industries that might employ them. He is able to show that, although the basic electronic and mechanical components of the record/playback and numerical control systems are similar, the choice of one design over another has crucial consequences for social struggles on the shop floor. To see the matter solely in terms of cost cutting, efficiency, or the modernization of equipment is to miss a decisive element in the story.[17]

From such examples I would offer the following general conclusions. The things we call "technologies" are ways of building order in our world. Many technical devices and systems important in everyday life contain possibilities for many different ways of ordering human activity. Consciously or not, deliberately or inadvertently, societies choose structures for technologies that influence how people are going to work, communicate, travel, consume, and so forth over a very long time. In the processes by which structuring decisions are made, different people are differently situated and possess unequal degrees of power, as well as unequal levels of awareness. By far the greatest latitude of choice exists the very first time a particular instrument, system, or technique is introduced. Because choices tend to become strongly fixed in material equipment, economic investment, and social habit, the original flexibility vanishes for all practical purposes once the initial commitments are made. In that sense, technological innovations are similar to legislative acts or political foundings that establish a framework for public order that will endure over many generations. For that reason, the same careful attention one would give to the rules, roles, and relationships of politics must also be given to such things as the building of highways, the creation of television networks, and the tailoring of seemingly insignificant features on new machines. The issues that divide or unite people in society are settled not only in the institutions and practices of politics proper, but also, and less obviously, in tangible arrangements of steel and concrete, wires and transistors, nuts and bolts.

INHERENTLY POLITICAL TECHNOLOGIES

None of the arguments and examples considered thus far address a stronger, more troubling claim often made in writings about technology and society — the belief that some technologies are by their very nature political in a specific way. According to this view, the adoption of a given technical system unavoidably brings with it conditions for human relationships that have a distinctive political cast — for example, centralized or decentralized, egalitarian or inegalitarian, repressive or liberating. This is ultimately what is at stake in assertions like those of Lewis Mumford that two traditions of technology, one authoritarian, the other democratic, exist side by side in Western history. In all the cases I cited, the technologies are relatively flexible in design and arrangement and variable in their effects. Although one can recognize a particular result produced in a particular setting, one can also easily imagine how a roughly similar device or system might have been built or situated with very much different political consequences. The idea we must now examine and evaluate is that certain kinds of technology do not allow such flexibility and that to choose them is to choose a particular form of political life.

A remarkably forceful statement of one version of this argument appears in Friedrich Engels's little essay "On Authority," written in 1872. Answering anarchists who believed that authority is an evil that ought to be abolished altogether, Engels launches into a panegyric for authoritarianism, maintaining, among other things, that strong authority is a necessary condition in modern industry. To advance his case in the strongest possible way, he asks his readers to imagine that the revolution has already occurred. "Supposing a social revolution dethroned the capitalists, who now exercise their authority over the production and circulation of wealth. Supposing, to adopt entirely the point of view of the antiauthoritarians, that the land and the instruments of labor had become the collective property of the workers who use them. Will authority have disappeared or will it have only changed its form?"[18]

His answer draws upon lessons from three sociotechnical systems of his day: cotton-spinning mills, railways, and ships at sea. He observes that, on its way to becoming finished thread, cotton moves through a number of different operations at different locations in the factory. The workers perform a wide variety of tasks, from running the steam engine to carrying the products from one room to another. Because these tasks must be coordinated, and because the timing of the work is "fixed by the authority of the steam," laborers must learn to accept a rigid discipline. They must, according to Engels, work at regular hours and agree to subordinate their individual wills to the persons in charge of factory operations. If they fail to do so, they risk the horrifying possibility that production will come to a grinding halt. Engels pulls no punches. "The automatic machinery of a big factory," he writes, "is much more despotic than the small capitalists who employ workers ever have been."[19]

Similar lessons are adduced in Engels's analysis of the necessary operating conditions for railways and ships at sea. Both require the subordination of workers to an "imperious authority" that sees to it that things run according to plan. Engels finds that, far from being an idiosyncrasy of capitalist social organization, relationships of authority and subordination arise "independently of all social organization, [and] are imposed upon us together with the material conditions under which we produce and make products circulate." Again, he intends this to be stern advice to the anarchists who, according to Engels, thought it possible simply to eradicate subordination and superordination at a single stroke. All such schemes are nonsense. The roots of unavoidable authoritarianism are, he argues, deeply implanted in the human involvement with science and technology. "If man, by dint of his knowledge and inventive genius, has subdued the forces of nature, the latter avenge themselves upon him by subjecting him, insofar as he employs them, to a veritable despotism independent of all social organization."[20]

Attempts to justify strong authority on the basis of supposedly necessary conditions of technical practice have an ancient history. A pivotal theme in *The Republic* is Plato's quest to borrow the authority of techne and employ it by analogy to buttress his argument in favor of authority in the state. Among the illustrations he chooses, like Engels, is that of a ship on the high seas. Because large sailing vessels by their very nature need to be steered with a firm hand, sailors must yield to their captain's commands; no reasonable person believes that ships can be run democratically. Plato goes on to suggest that governing a state is rather like being captain of a ship or like practicing medicine as a physician. Much the same conditions that require central rule and decisive action in organized technical activity also create this need in government.

In Engels's argument, and arguments like it, the justification for authority is no longer made by Plato's classic analogy, but rather directly with reference to technology itself. If the basic case is as compelling as Engels believed it to be, one would expect that, as a society adopted increasingly complicated technical systems as its material basis, the prospects for authoritarian ways of life would be greatly enhanced. Central control by knowledgeable people acting at the top of a rigid social hierarchy would seem increasingly prudent. In this respect, his stand in "On Authority" appears to be at variance with Karl Marx's position in Volume One of *Capital*. Marx tries to show that increasing mechanization will render obsolete the hierarchical division of labor and the relationships of subordination that, in his view, were necessary during the early stages of modern manufacturing. The "Modern Industry," he writes, ". . . sweeps away by technical means the manufacturing division of labor, under which each man is bound hand and foot for life to a single detail operation. At the same time, the capitalistic form of that industry reproduces this same division of labor in a still more monstrous shape; in the factory proper, by converting the workman into a living appendage of the machine.[21] In Marx's view, the conditions that will eventually dissolve the capitalist division of labor and facilitate proletarian revolution are conditions latent in industrial technology itself. The differences between Marx's position in *Capital* and Engels's in his essay raise an important question for socialism: What, after all, does modern technology make possible or necessary in political life? The theoretical tension we see here mirrors many troubles in the practice of freedom and authority that have muddied the tracks of socialist revolution.

Arguments to the effect that technologies are in some sense inherently political have been advanced in a wide variety of contexts, far too many to summarize here. In my reading of such notions, however, there are two basic ways of stating the case. One version claims that the adoption of a given technical system actually requires the creation and maintenance of a particular set of social conditions as the operating environment of that system. Engels's position is of this kind. A similar view is offered by a contemporary writer who holds that "if you accept nuclear power plants, you also accept a techno-scientific-industrial-military elite. Without these people in charge, you could not have nuclear power."[22] In this conception, some kinds of technology require their social environments to be structured in a particular way in much the same sense that an automobile requires wheels in order to run. The thing could not exist as an effective operating entity unless certain social as well as material conditions were met. The meaning of "required" here is that of practical (rather than logical) necessity. Thus, Plato thought it a practical necessity that a ship at sea have one captain and an unquestioningly obedient crew.

A second, somewhat weaker, version of the argument holds that a given kind of technology is strongly compatible with, but does not strictly require, social and political relationships of a particular stripe. Many advocates of solar energy now hold that technologies of that variety are more compatible with a democratic, egalitarian society than energy systems based on coal, oil, and nuclear power; at the same time, they do not maintain that anything about solar energy requires democracy. Their case is, briefly, that solar energy is decentralizing in both a technical and political sense: Technically speaking, it is vastly more reasonable to build solar systems in a disaggregated, widely distributed manner than in large-scale, centralized plants; politically speaking, solar energy accommodates the attempts of individuals and local communities to manage their affairs effectively because they are dealing with systems that are more accessible, comprehensible, and controllable than huge centralized sources. In this view, solar energy is desirable not only for its economic and environmental benefits, but also for the salutary institutions it is likely to permit in other areas of public life.[23]

Within both versions of the argument there is a further distinction to be made between conditions that are internal to the workings of a given technical system and those that are external to it. Engels's thesis concerns internal social relations said to be required within cotton factories and railways, for example; what such relationships mean for the condition of society at large is for him a separate question. In contrast, the solar advocate's belief that solar technologies are compatible with democracy pertains to the way they complement aspects of society removed from the organization of those technologies as such.

There are, then, several different directions that arguments of this kind can follow. Are the social conditions predicated said to be required by, or strongly compatible with, the workings of a given technical system? Are those conditions internal to that system or external to it (or both)? Although writings that address such questions are often unclear about what is being asserted, arguments in this general category do have an important presence in modern political discourse. They enter into many attempts to explain how changes in social life take place in the wake of technological innovation. More importantly, they are often used to buttress attempts to justify or criticize proposed courses of action involving new technology. By offering distinctly political reasons for or against the adoption of a particular technology, arguments of this kind stand apart from more commonly employed, more easily quantifiable claims about economic costs and benefits, environmental impacts, and possible risks to public health and safety that technical systems may involve. The issue here does not concern how many jobs will be created, how much income generated, how many pollutants added, or how many cancers produced. Rather, the issue has to do with ways in which choices about technology have important consequences for the form and quality of human associations.

If we examine social patterns that comprise the environments of technical systems, we find certain devices and systems almost invariably linked to specific ways of organizing power and authority. The important question is: Does this state of affairs derive from an unavoidable social response to intractable properties in the things themselves, or is it instead a pattern imposed independently by a governing body, ruling class, or some other social or cultural institution to further its own purposes?

Taking the most obvious example, the atom bomb is an inherently political artifact. As long as it exists at all, its lethal properties demand that it be controlled by a centralized, rigidly hierarchical chain of command closed to all influences that might make its workings unpredictable. The internal social system of the bomb must be authoritarian; there is no other way. The state of affairs stands as a practical necessity independent of any larger political system in which the bomb is embedded, independent of the kind of regime or character of its rulers. Indeed, democratic states must try to find ways to ensure that the social structures and mentality that characterize the management of nuclear weapons do not "spin off" or "spill over" into the polity as a whole.

The bomb is, of course, a special case. The reasons very rigid relationships of authority are necessary in its immediate presence should be clear to anyone. If, however, we look for other instances in which particular varieties of technology are widely perceived to need the maintenance of a special pattern of power and authority, modern technical history contains a wealth of examples.

Alfred D. Chandler in *The Visible Hand,* a monumental study of modern business enterprise, presents impressive documentation to defend the hypothesis that the construction and day-to-day operation of many systems of production, transportation, and communication in the nineteenth and twentieth centuries require the development of a particular social form — a large-scale, centralized, hierarchical organization administered by highly skilled managers. Typical of Chandler's reasoning is his analysis of the growth of the railroads:

> Technology made possible fast, all-weather transportation; but safe, regular, reliable movement of goods and passengers, as well as the continuing maintenance and repair of locomotives, rolling stock, and track, roadbed, stations, roundhouses, and other equipment, required the creation of a sizable administrative organization. It meant the employment of a set of managers to supervise these functional activities over an extensive geographical area; and the appointment of an administrative command of middle and top executives to

monitor, evaluate, and coordinate the work of managers responsible for the day-to-day operations.[24]

Throughout his book, Chandler points to ways in which technologies used in the production and distribution of electricity, chemicals, and a wide range of industrial goods "demanded" or "required" this form of human association. "Hence, the operational requirements of railroads demanded the creation of the first administrative hierarchies in American business."[25]

Were there other conceivable ways of organizing these aggregates of people and apparatus? Chandler shows that a previously dominant social form, the small traditional family firm, simply could not handle the task in most cases. Although he does not speculate further, it is clear that he believes there is, to be realistic, very little latitude in the forms of power and authority appropriate within modern sociotechnical systems. The properties of many modern technologies — oil pipelines and refineries, for example — are such that overwhelmingly impressive economies of scale and speed are possible. If such systems are to work effectively, efficiently, quickly, and safely, certain requirements of internal social organization have to be fulfilled; the material possibilities that modern technologies make available could not be exploited otherwise. Chandler acknowledges that as one compares sociotechnical institutions of different nations, one sees "ways in which cultural attitudes, values, ideologies, political systems, and social structure affect these imperatives."[26] But the weight of argument and empirical evidence in *The Visible Hand* suggests that any significant departure from the basic pattern would be, at best, highly unlikely.

It may be that other conceivable arrangements of power and authority, for example, those of decentralized, democratic worker self-management, could prove capable of administering factories, refineries, communications systems, and railroads as well as or better than the organizations Chandler describes. Evidence from automobile assembly teams in Sweden and worker-managed plants in Yugoslavia and other countries is often presented to salvage these possibilities. I shall not be able to settle controversies over this matter here, but merely point to what I consider to be their bone of contention. The available evidence tends to show that many large, sophisticated technological systems are in fact highly compatible with centralized, hierarchical managerial control. The interesting question, however, has to do with whether or not this pattern is in any sense a requirement of such systems, a question that is not solely an empirical one. The matter ultimately rests on our judgments about what steps, if any, are practically necessary in the workings of particular kinds of technology and what, if anything, such measures require of the structure of human associations. Was Plato right in saying that a ship at sea needs steering by a decisive hand and that this could only be accomplished by a single captain and an obedient crew? Is Chandler correct in saying that the properties of large-scale systems require centralized, hierarchical, managerial control?

To answer such questions, we would have to examine in some detail the moral claims of practical necessity (including those advocated in the doctrines of economics) and weigh them against moral claims of other sorts, for example, the notion that it is good for sailors to participate in the command of a ship or that workers have a right to be involved in making and administering decisions in a factory. It is characteristic of societies based on large, complex technological systems, however, that moral reasons other than those of practical necessity appear increasingly obsolete, "idealistic," and irrelevant. Whatever claims one may wish to make on behalf of liberty, justice, or equality can be immediately neutralized when confronted with arguments to the effect: "Fine, but that's no way to run a railroad" (or steel mill, or airline, or communications system, and so on). Here we encounter an important quality in modern political discourse and in the way people commonly think about what measures are justified in response to the possibilities technologies make available. In many instances, to say that some technologies are inherently political is to say that certain widely accepted reasons of practical necessity — especially the need to maintain crucial technological systems as smoothly working entities — have tended to eclipse other sorts of moral and political reasoning.

One attempt to salvage the autonomy of politics from the bind of practical necessity involves the notion that conditions of human association found in the internal workings of technological systems can easily be kept separate from the polity as a whole. Americans have long rested content in the belief that arrangements of power and authority inside industrial corporations, public utilities, and the like have little bearing on public institutions, practices, and ideas at large. That "democracy stops at the factory gates" was taken as a fact of life that had nothing to do with the practice of political freedom. But can the internal politics of technology and the politics of the whole community be so easily separated? A recent study of American business leaders, contemporary exemplars of Chandler's "visible hand of management," found them remarkably impatient with such democratic scruples as "one man, one vote." If democracy doesn't work for the firm, the most critical institution in all of society, American executives ask, how well can it be expected to work for the government of a nation — particularly when that government attempts to interfere with the achievements of the firm? The authors of the report observe that patterns of authority that work effectively in the corporation become for businessmen "the desirable model against which to compare political and economic relationships in the rest of society."[27] While such findings are far from conclusive, they do reflect a sentiment increasingly common in the land: What dilemmas like the energy crisis require is not a redistribution of wealth or broader public participation but, rather, stronger, centralized, public management — President Carter's proposal for an Energy Mobilization Board and the like.

An especially vivid case in which the operational requirements of a technical system might influence the quality of public life is now at issue in debates about the risks of nuclear power. As the supply of uranium for nuclear reactors runs out, a proposed alternative fuel is the plutonium generated as a by-product in reactor cores. Well-known objections to plutonium recycling focus on its unacceptable economic costs, its risks of environmental contamination, and its dangers in regard to the international proliferation of nuclear weapons. Beyond these concerns, however, stands another, less widely appreciated set of hazards — those that involve the sacrifice of civil liberties. The widespread use of plutonium as a fuel increases the chance that toxic substance might be stolen by terrorists, [members of] organized crime, or other persons. This raises the prospect, and not a trivial one, that extraordinary measures would have to be taken to safeguard plutonium from theft and to recover it if ever the substance were stolen. Workers in the nuclear industry, as well as ordinary citizens outside, could well become subject to background security checks, covert surveillance, wiretapping, informers, and even emergency measures under martial law — all justified by the need to safeguard plutonium.

Russell W. Ayres's study of the legal ramifications of plutonium recycling concludes, "With the passage of time and the increase in the quantity of plutonium in existence will come pressure to eliminate the traditional checks the courts and legislatures place on the activities of the executive and to develop a powerful central authority better able to enforce strict safeguards." He avers that "once a quantity of plutonium had been stolen, the case for literally turning the country upside down to get it back would be overwhelming." Ayres anticipates and worries about the kinds of thinking that, I have argued, characterize inherently political technologies. It is still true that, in a world in which human beings make and maintain artificial systems, nothing is "required" in an absolute sense. Nevertheless, once a course of action is under way, once artifacts like nuclear power plants have been built and put in operation, the kinds of reasoning that justify the adaptation of social life to technical requirements pop up as spontaneously as flowers in the spring. In Ayres's words, "Once recycling begins and the risks of plutonium theft become real rather than hypothetical, the case for governmental infringement of protected rights will seem compelling."[28] After a certain point, those who cannot accept the hard requirements and imperatives will be dismissed as dreamers and fools.

* * *

The two varieties of interpretation I have outlined indicate how artifacts can have political qualities. In the first instance, we noticed ways in which specific features in the design or arrangement of a device or system could provide a convenient means of establishing patterns of power and authority in a given setting. Technologies of this kind have a range of flexibility in the dimensions of their material form. It is precisely because they are flexible that their consequences for society must be understood with reference to the social actors able to influence which designs and arrangements are chosen. In the second instance, we examined ways in which the intractable properties of certain kinds of technology are strongly, perhaps unavoidably, linked to particular institutionalized patterns of power and authority. Here, the initial choice about whether or not to adopt something is decisive in regard to its consequences. There are no alternative physical designs or arrangements that would make a significant difference; there are, furthermore, no genuine possibilities for creative intervention by different social systems — capitalist or socialist — that could change the intractability of the entity or significantly alter the quality of its political effects.

To know which variety of interpretation is applicable in a given case is often what is at stake in disputes, some of them passionate ones, about the meaning of technology for how we live. I have argued a "both/and" position here, for it seems to me that both kinds of understanding are applicable in different circumstances. Indeed, it can happen that within a particular complex of technology — a system of communication or transportation, for example — some aspects may be flexible in their possibilities for society, while other aspects may be (for better or worse) completely intractable. The two varieties of interpretation I have examined here can overlap and intersect at many points.

These are, of course, issues on which people can disagree. Thus, some proponents of energy from renewable resources now believe they have at last discovered a set of intrinsically democratic, egalitarian, communitarian technologies. In my best estimation, however, the social consequences of building renewable energy systems will surely depend on the specific configurations of both hardware and the social institutions created to bring that energy to us. It may be that we will find ways to turn this silk purse into a sow's ear. By comparison, advocates of the further development of nuclear power seem to believe that they are working on a rather flexible technology whose adverse social effects can be fixed by changing the design parameters of reactors and nuclear waste disposal systems. For reasons indicated above, I believe them to be dead wrong in that faith. Yes, we may be able to manage some of the "risks" to public health and safety that nuclear power brings. But as society adapts to the more dangerous and apparently indelible features of nuclear power, what will be the long-range toll in human freedom?

My belief that we ought to attend more closely to technical objects themselves is not to say that we can ignore the contexts in which those objects are situated. A ship at sea may well require, as Plato and Engels insisted, a single captain and obedient crew. But a ship out of service, parked at the dock, needs only a caretaker. To understand which technologies and which contexts are important to us, and why, is an enterprise that must involve both the study of specific technical systems and their history as well as a thorough grasp of the concepts and controversies of political theory. In our times, people are often willing to make drastic changes in the way they live to accord with technological innovation at the same time they would resist similar kinds of changes justified on political grounds. If for no other reason than that, it is important for us to achieve a clearer view of these matters than has been our habit so far.

NOTES

1. I would like to thank Merritt Roe Smith, Leo Marx, James Miller, David Noble, Charles Weiner, Sherry Turkle, Loren Graham, Gail Stuart, Dick Sclove, and Stephen Graubard for their comments and criticisms on earlier drafts of this essay. My thanks also to Doris Morrison of the Agriculture Library of the University of California, Berkeley, for her bibliographical help.
2. Lewis Mumford, "Authoritarian and Democratic Technics," *Technology and Culture* 5 (1964): 1–8.
3. Denis Hayes, *Rays of Hope: The Transition to a Post-Petroleum World* (New York: W. W. Norton, 1977), pp. 71, 159.
4. David Lilienthal, *T.V.A.: Democracy on the March* (New York: Harper and Brothers, 1944), pp. 72–83.
5. Daniel J. Boorstin, *The Republic of Technology* (New York: Harper & Row, 1978), p. 7.

6. Langdon Winner, *Autonomous Technology: Technics-out-of-Control as a Theme in Political Thought* (Cambridge, MA: M.I.T. Press, 1977).
7. The meaning of "technology" I employ in this essay does not encompass some of the broader definitions of that concept found in contemporary literature, for example, the notion of "technique" in the writings of Jacques Ellul. My purposes here are more limited. For a discussion of the difficulties that arise in attempts to define "technology," see Winner, *Autonomous Technology*, pp. 8–12.
8. Robert A. Caro, *The Power Broker: Robert Moses and the Fall of New York* (New York: Random House, 1974), pp. 318, 481, 514, 546, 951–8.
9. Ibid., p. 952.
10. Robert Ozanne, *A Century of Labor–Management Relations at McCormick and International Harvester* (Madison: University of Wisconsin Press, 1967), p. 20.
11. The early history of the tomato harvester is told in Wayne D. Rasmussen, "Advances in American Agriculture: The Mechanical Tomato Harvester as a Case Study," *Technology and Culture* 9 (1968): 531–43.
12. Andrew Schmitz and David Seckler, "Mechanized Agriculture and Social Welfare: The Case of the Tomato Harvester," *American Journal of Agricultural Economics* 52 (1970): 569–77.
13. William H. Friedland and Amy Barton, "Tomato Technology," *Society* 13:6 (September/October 1976). See also William H. Friedland, *Social Sleepwalkers: Scientific and Technological Research in California Agriculture*, University of California, Davis, Department of Applied Behavioral Sciences, Research Monograph No. 13, 1974.
14. University of California Clip Sheet, 54:36, May 1, 1979.
15. Friedland and Barton, "Tomato Technology."
16. A history and critical analysis of agricultural research in the land-grant colleges is given in James Hightower, *Hard Tomatoes, Hard Times* (Cambridge, MA: Schenkman, 1978).
17. David Noble, "Social Change in Machine Design: The Case of Automatically Controlled Machine Tools," in *Case Studies in the Labor Process* (New York: Monthly Review Press, 1981).
18. Friedrich Engels, "On Authority" in *The Marx-Engels Reader*, 2nd ed., ed. Robert Tucker (New York: W. W. Norton, 1978), p. 731.
19. Ibid.
20. Ibid., pp. 732, 731.
21. Karl Marx, *Capital*, vol. 1, 3rd ed., trans. Samuel Moore and Edward Aveling (New York: The Modern Library, 1906), p. 530.
22. Jerry Mander, *Four Arguments for the Elimination of Television* (New York: William Morrow, 1978), p. 44.
23. See, for example, Robert Argue, Barbara Emanuel, and Stephen Graham, *The Sun Builders: A People's Guide to Solar, Wind, and Wood Energy in Canada* (Toronto: Renewable Energy in Canada, 1978). "We think decentralization is an implicit component of renewable energy; this implies the decentralization of energy systems, communities and of power. Renewable energy doesn't require mammoth generation sources or disruptive transmission corridors. Our cities and towns, which have been dependent on centralized energy supplies, may be able to achieve some degree of autonomy, thereby controlling and administering their own energy needs" (p. 16).
24. Alfred D. Chandler, Jr., *The Visible Hand: The Managerial Revolution in American Business* (Cambridge, MA: Belknap, Harvard University Press, 1977), p. 244.
25. Ibid.
26. Ibid., p. 500.
27. Leonard Silk and David Vogel, *Ethics and Profits: The Crisis of Confidence in American Business* (New York: Simon & Schuster, 1976), p. 191.
28. Russell W. Ayres, "Policing Plutonium: The Civil Liberties Fallout," *Harvard Civil Rights–Civil Liberties Law Review* 10 (1975): 374, 413–4, 443.

PART IV
DILEMMAS OF NEW TECHNOLOGY: VULNERABILITY

The terrorist attacks on the United States of September 11, 2001, awakened the world to an aspect of technology that previously had not received much attention — the vulnerability of the technological systems that sustain our society. This was not the first instance that might have made this vulnerability apparent. The November 9, 1965, blackout that plunged thirty million people in the northeastern part of the United States and southern Canada into darkness for several hours; the OPEC oil embargo of 1973; the viruses, worms, and denial of service attacks that have bedeviled the Internet since it became a public utility; and the earthquakes and other natural disasters that strike repeatedly in various parts of the world all have served to demonstrate how fragile our large-scale technologies are.

Nevertheless, the complete destruction of New York's World Trade Center and the deaths of several thousand innocent people brought about by a small number of terrorists from a distant country who turned the tools of everyday technology into deadly weapons in an absurdly simple way highlighted this issue as never before. The security measures subsequently adopted around the world, but especially by the United States, are keeping this vulnerability in sharp focus. Can the United States and other industrialized countries maintain their high-technology systems in the framework of an open society that embodies democratic values, a substantial degree of personal privacy, and all of the other elements of contemporary life to which we have grown accustomed?

The answer is not at all clear, but one thing can be said for certain. These issues are bound to be in the public eye for years to come, and they will undoubtedly influence the course of technological development. To the extent that medical research and development in the United States is directed toward fighting bioterrorism, for example, it may slow progress in preventing and curing diseases. To the extent that resources are devoted to airport and aircraft security, they may be diverted from other aspects of aviation safety.

The study of technology and society will also be affected as studies of this issue become more fashionable. Some researchers, however, began looking at technological vulnerability years ago. Among them are Amory and Hunter Lovins of the Rocky Mountain Institute in Colorado and Brian Martin of the University of Wollongong in New South Wales, Australia, whose writings are included in this part of *Technology and the Future*. The

Lovinses' article, written in late 2001, after the terrorist attacks, responds directly to some of the issues those attacks raised. In doing so, however, the authors refer back to a study they conducted for the Department of Defense in 1982, which looked at the vulnerability — or "brittleness," as they call it — of the highly centralized U.S. energy system. Martin's article dates from 1996 and, while it deals with a subject that has immediate and direct application, it is a more conceptual piece, laying out a way to think about the vulnerability of technological systems.

15. Terrorism and Brittle Technology

AMORY B. LOVINS AND L. HUNTER LOVINS

"The United States is extremely vulnerable, not just because it's a free and open society, but also because of the fragile architecture of its complex, centralized, inter-dependent technical systems — gigantic pipelines, powerlines, dams, refineries, chemical and nuclear complexes." So write Amory and Hunter Lovins, well-known advocates of decentralization and alternative energy technologies. The idea of technological vulnerability is not new to them. They wrote about it in a 1982 Pentagon study, Brittle Power. *They see the terrorist attacks of September 11, 2001, as a terrible tragedy, of course, but also as a wake-up call to which the nation needs to respond, not just by tightening security, but by making fundamental changes in the structure of its technological systems as well as in its posture toward the rest of the world, particularly the poor nations.*

Amory Lovins is cofounder and CEO (Research) of the Rocky Mountain Institute, a nonprofit applied research center in Snowmass, Colorado. He first came to public notice when he published an article on alternative energy entitled "Soft Energy Paths," in the prestigious journal, Foreign Affairs, *in 1976. He has received numerous awards, seven honorary degrees, and a MacArthur Fellowship. L. Hunter Lovins is cofounder and CEO (Strategy) of the Rocky Mountain Institute. She has also received numerous awards and was named a "Hero of the Planet" by* Time *magazine in 2000. The article below was originally published in the Rocky Mountain Institute's Newsletter (Fall/Winter 2001).*

From its inception, Rocky Mountain Institute has worked to promote a secure, prosperous, and life-sustaining world. On 11 September, those goals came under attack — magnifying their importance and urgency. We can best honor the thousands of victims, citizens of over eighty nations throughout the world, by recommitting to create such a future.

A handful of people with plastic knives and box cutters seized four airplanes and wreaked havoc. A week later, their violence was threatening to hijack much of U.S. policy. Their attack so outrages common decency as to tempt reactions that Americans would abhor in normal times — bombing civilians ruled by despots considered complicit, eroding civil liberties, blaming anyone who looks or thinks differently, rushing to military and energy choices that would be repented at leisure. But, if policy simply reacts to the terrorists, they win. America and the world need rather to address root causes: to reassume global leadership in helping all people to fulfill their legitimate aspirations for a safe and decent life.

From "Brittle Times, RMI's Response," in *RMI Solutions*, Vol. XVII, No. 3 (Fall 2000), p. 1–3.

The terrorist attack elicited wide agreement on some obvious but sometimes overlooked points:

- Murdering innocent people is a supreme evil in the eyes of every religion, emphatically including Islam. This applies to terrorism — and to America's response to it.
- The perpetrators must be brought to justice under the rule of law and with great care not to harm the innocent. Indiscriminately violent retaliation would undermine all we're fighting for. A world of justice and compassion is morally, as well as practically, better than a world of revenge. Amidst talk of technology and retribution, we need understanding and transformation.
- America's distinctive strengths flow from her diversity, freedom, and tolerance — precisely the qualities that are most under attack, most precious, and most vital not to impair. Terrorists succeed if they drive us to deny our values and diminish our freedoms.
- The attackers hope to provoke a jihad/crusade confrontation between America and Islam and more broadly to inflame tensions between the powerful and the dispossessed. We defeat this goal if we instead build a new solidarity between those working to achieve a just and sustainable society and those for whom it is a distant abstraction. Terrorists are bred amid social and economic conditions that create despair and fury. To the extent that enhancing sustainability can relieve those conditions, we both do right and increase everyone's security.
- Many people in the world are profoundly angry at America, and it would be wise to understand why. *Wall Street Journal* correspondent Jonathan Kwitney, in his disquieting book, *Endless Enemies: The Making of an Unfriendly World*, chronicles scores of countries where venal, stupid, or insensitive U.S. behavior, over decades, turned potential friends into foes. If we want other countries to think well of us, he concludes, we should be the kind of people one would like to do business with and should ensure that whoever comes to power in other countries has never been shot at by an American gun. That seems simple and effective, pragmatic and principled. As we seek to understand other cultures, honor their differences, and respect social goals that may diverge widely from our own, we need to hear the reasons for the anger of those who do not feel heard. As a Muslim prayer reminds us, "Praise be to the Lord of the Universe who has created us and made us into tribes and nations / That we may know each other, not that we may despise each other . . . And the servants of God, most gracious are those who walk on the Earth in humility, and when we address them, we say 'Peace.'"
- The United States is extremely vulnerable, not just because it's a free and open society, but also because of the fragile architecture of its complex, centralized, interdependent technical systems — gigantic pipelines, powerlines, dams, refineries, chemical and nuclear complexes. This vulnerable design makes future attacks both more probable and potentially far worse. We've long been surprised these weaknesses weren't exploited sooner and more

fully. A great deal more work is needed to identify these vulnerabilities and design them out.

Consider, for example, the opportunistically renewed push for uneconomic and extraordinarily vulnerable energy technologies, such as expanded dependence on the Trans-Alaska Pipeline (*RMI Solutions*, Vol. 17, No. 1, Spring '01) and on nuclear power, which holds billions of curies of releasable radioactivity — rivaling the fallout from a megaton-range groundburst — upwind of many American cities. For example, *The Nation* (16 September) and *U.S. News and World Report* (17 September) report that over half of U.S. nuclear plants routinely fail basic site-security tests, even when given advance notice. (They just went on maximum alert, but that doesn't mean they could repel a competent attack.) It doesn't take a crashing widebody jet to unleash their lethal inventories (though that would); a few people could do it on the ground, in some cases without entering the plant's site. Despite this threat and nuclear power's disastrous economics (see "Gone Fission," p. 11), its proponents nonetheless want, and have so far gotten, even bigger subsidies to support expansion, and seem about to win renewal of their liability exemption. In contrast, as David Lochbaum of the Union of Concerned Scientists noted, nobody is asking about terrorist threats to windmills — which also produce power sooner and cheaper.

Our 1982 Pentagon study *Brittle Power: Energy Strategy for National Security*, still the definitive unclassified work, showed how accepting market verdicts could gradually, steadily, turn vulnerability into resilience. The foundation of a secure energy system is to need less energy in the first place, then to get it from sources that are inherently invulnerable because they're diverse, dispersed, renewable, and mainly local. They're secure not because they're American but because of their design. Any highly centralized energy system — pipelines, nuclear plants, refineries — invites devastating attack. But invulnerable alternatives don't, and can't, fail on a large scale. Ignored in the current debate but available in the marketplace, they're also cheaper and more reliable. In time, they can make major energy interruptions impossible. Thus, real energy security comes from choosing the best buys first, not bailing out market failures, building a balanced portfolio of competitive demand and supply-side investments, and preferring energy options invulnerable to cutoff by accident or malice. Happily, all these virtues coincide in the same technologies — the ones current policy disfavors. Why should some of the gravest threats to national energy security come from the energy policy of our own government?

To some extent, RMI can offer these answers. In other realms, we have only just begun to pose the questions. For example, the work that Hunter Lovins and Walter Link of the Global Academy have been doing on globalization raises some intriguing issues. As their recent paper for the United Nations pointed out, the world is profoundly different from the mental model most of us carry of an effective community of national governments. In fact, power now resides in three sectors: governments, corporations, and civil society. As newspapers blare that we are at war, it is worth asking, "with whom?" Is this the first major conflict between a globalized network and a national government? In the new tripolar world, where power resides in governments, corporations, and civil society, this network of self-organized individuals empowered by satellite phones, e-mail, and FedEx to pursue their agenda aren't playing by governments' rules, but they're highly effective. Similarly, solutions to the many global challenges will only arise if collaboration between the three sectors creates new networks dedicated to finding and implementing solutions.

The question that has guided RMI's work from its inception is how can Americans, and all people, be safe and feel safe in ways that work better and cost less than present arrangements? Recent events have been called the first war of the twenty-first century. Unfortunately, that "honor" goes to the many conflicts that continue to take lives around the world. Security — freedom from fear of attack or privation — is best achieved from the bottom up, not from the top down; by means that are the province of every citizen, not the monopoly of national governments; and without needing to use or threaten violence. It comes from making others more secure, not less, whether on the scale of the village or the globe. It is rooted in conflict avoidance or prevention; bolstered by conflict resolution; and backstopped by nonprovocative defense, which can reliably defeat aggression without threatening others. This new security triad from *Security Without War* — a prescient 1993 RMI book by Hal Harvey and Mike Shuman — suggests that though there is a vital role for the military professionals with whom RMI has long worked (see "Battling Fuel Waste in the Military," p. 6), that role is poised for profound change in an increasingly dangerous, multipolar, and polarized world.

The foundation of real security is global good-citizenship, fully engaged within an interdependent world of mutual interests. World War II arose from a resentful Germany punished for World War I. George Marshall didn't repeat that error; he strengthened and rebuilt Germany as a bulwark of democracy. We have vast rebuilding to do to reverse the poverty, inequity, and injustice that make people feel angry, powerless, and resentful. As Jeff Raskin remarks, "Putting the billions recently allocated [for military strikes] into feeding the hungry, teaching the undereducated, and healing the sick around the world would go further toward minimizing terrorism than anything else we could do with the money."

John Wimberly, of Western Presbyterian Church in Washington, D.C., writes of the spiritual dimensions of this challenge:

Regardless of where one stands in the debate about the causes of wealth and poverty, Tuesday's terrorism leaves us no choice but to admit that fear, hatred, and violence increasingly define the relations between the rich and poor.

Those who don't have wealth fear that their children's lives will be worse than their own. Anger grows as they watch their loved ones die of diseases that disappeared years ago in developed nations. Leaders who foster hatred of the developed nations suddenly sound reasonable.

Those who have wealth grow increasingly fearful of the masses of poor people. They become resentful that their wealth does not give them the freedom and safety they once assumed it would create. Leaders who tell them that the poor are a threat to their well-being suddenly sound reasonable.

It is a recipe for madness. A blueprint for mutual self-destruction. Where does it end? The world's major religions all agree that it is the responsibility of those who have to help those who do not . . . What we do or don't do with our money is an issue of profound spiritual significance. The strong are supposed to help the weak.

And isn't the well-being of others an important aspect of good economic policy as well? Impoverished people don't buy products. Uneducated people don't constitute a good workforce. Strong economies produce jobs that can enable the poor to build a better future . . . Long-term economic self-interest requires attention to the needs of others.

If both economists and the world's religions agree that self-interest and the interest of all are inseparably intertwined, what is the problem? The problem is fear, fear that morphs into hostility . . .

The opposite of fear is faith. Our daily lives are built on hundreds of large and small acts of faith. We have faith that when we get on a plane, it will take us to the scheduled destination; that when we sit in an office, we are safe; that the sun will set tonight and rise tomorrow.

What is at stake today is whether we will live lives of fear or lives of faith. We live in a national and personal moment of truth."

We all have much work to do.

16. Technological Vulnerability

BRIAN MARTIN

While there is literature on technological accidents, on risk, on complex organizations and their problems, and on the impacts of natural disasters, relatively few people have thought systematically about the problem of technological vulnerability. Brian Martin is one who has. He views technological vulnerability as "the chance that a technological system may fail due to outside impacts." His analysis suggests that interest groups play a role in vulnerability, sometimes because they engage in practices that cause vulnerabilities, sometimes because they have vested interests in maintaining the vulnerabilities themselves. Martin's work suggests that dealing with technological vulnerabilities may be more difficult than just identifying them and finding straightforward ways of addressing them. It suggests yet another of the many ways in which technology and the institutions of society interact with and shape one another.

Brian Martin is an associate professor in the Program on Science, Technology, and Society at the University of Wollongong in New South Wales, Australia, where he has been a member of the faculty since 1986. Among the most recent of his many books are Technology and Public Participation *(1999) and* Technology for Nonviolent Struggle *(2001). He holds a Ph.D. in theoretical physics from the University of Sydney.*

INTRODUCTION

Every new technology seems to bring with it some new vulnerability for its users, a vulnerability to accident, disease, environmental degradation, or social disruption. With the automobile came traffic accidents. With electric appliances came exposure to electromagnetic fields. With the burning of fossil fuels came the greenhouse effect. With nuclear weapons came the possibility of megadeath.

The usual approach to these issues is through the concept of risk, which deals with the chance that specified adverse effects may occur due to operation or breakdown of the technology.[1] Risk is a useful concept, especially when events are well specified and can be quantified, as in the cases of the collapse of a bridge or loss of power in an electricity grid. But, for other purposes, the concept of vulnerability can be more illuminating.

To take an example, industrialized societies are becoming ever more dependent on computers and hence highly vulnerable to disruption of computer-based services. Intentional sabotaging of vital computer programs in telephone systems, banks, or factories could bring much commerce to a halt. More dramatically, a

From "Technology Vulnerability" in *Technology in Society*, Vol. 18, No. 4, 1996. Reprinted with permission of Elsevier Science.

nuclear explosion high in the atmosphere would produce a continent-wide pulse of electromagnetic energy that could disrupt all sorts of microcircuits temporarily or even permanently.[2] New infectious diseases could arise and spread rapidly due to urbanization, poverty, new patterns of sexual activity, and other changes creating an ecology favorable to certain microbes.[3] These sorts of contingencies, in which the possible consequences are enormous but the chance of an occurrence is difficult to determine because the cause is due primarily to social processes outside the system under threat, are usefully approached using the idea of vulnerability.

In the next section, I give a more precise definition of *technological vulnerability*. Then I turn to frameworks for classifying technological vulnerabilities, presenting a framework that distinguishes between vulnerable systems according to whether there are groups with an interest in perpetuating the vulnerabilities themselves. The focus is on large-scale vulnerabilities to which there has been relatively little attention.[4]

THE NATURE OF TECHNOLOGICAL VULNERABILITY

To define *technological vulnerability* it is helpful to draw on systems theory and distinguish between a technological system and its environment.[5] The technological system might be, for example, a clothing factory or water supply system. The system includes artifacts (e.g., cloth and sewing machines, dams and pipes), relevant humans (factory workers, civil engineers), and associated skills and routines.[6] The "environment" is everything outside the technological system and can include things like financial markets and earthquakes.

To achieve its intended purposes, a technological system requires certain inputs (raw materials, replacement workers, education, etc.) and produces certain outputs (finished clothing, water for consumers). The system's vulnerability can be defined as the chance that a specified change in the environment leads to disruption of the usual purposes of the system. For example, the threat to the clothing factory might be competition from imports, a strike by workers, or a flood. The threat to the water supply system might be sabotage or a drought.

A technological system can be said to be resilient in the face of a particular threat if it is capable of maintaining its purposes when the threat is realized.[7] For example, the clothing factory will be more resilient in the face of a strike if there are other workers available with the skills required to keep production going. The water supply system will be more resilient against the destruction of a dam if no single dam provides a large percentage of water for the system.

To quantify vulnerability and resilience, it would be necessary to provide much more detailed specifications of various components in these definitions, including the distinction between the technological system and its environment, the nature of the threat, and what is meant by the system "maintaining its purposes." Such precision is not necessary for the purposes here, which is to highlight significant features of technological vulnerability.

With the above definition, the distinction between technological risk and vulnerability becomes clearer. Technological risk usually refers to the danger to the public from technological systems, whether due to breakdowns or normal operations.[8] Examples are aircraft crashes and emissions from microwave ovens. Technological vulnerability, by contrast, refers to the chance of failure of an entire technological system due to outside events. Nevertheless, there is a close connection between the concepts of risk and vulnerability. Among other things, a system collapse resulting from exploitation of a vulnerability typically leads to the sorts of consequences analyzed in studies of risks.

CLASSIFICATION OF TECHNOLOGICAL VULNERABILITIES

There are quite a few ways to classify vulnerabilities, each of which is useful for some purposes but limited for others. Here I give a brief overview of a number of common frameworks before introducing yet another one.

It is commonplace to discuss risks and vulnerabilities according to the type of technology involved. For example, chemical plants are vulnerable to malfunction, as in the cases of Seveso and Bhopal. Nuclear power plants are subject to core meltdowns, terrorist attack, and military attack, among other things. In recent years, there has been considerable attention to the vulnerabilities of computer systems.[9] Focusing on a type of technology has the obvious advantage of grouping systems with certain similar features. The complexities of large computer programs mean that certain types of failures are common wherever such programs are used.[10] On the other hand, focusing on a type of technology artificially divides common areas, such as energy systems, including hydro, fossil fuel, and nuclear components, where different types of technology combine to serve a single purpose.

Another approach is to divide vulnerabilities according to scale, namely the "size" of the disaster that might occur. When a software glitch in a radiotherapy machine causes a lethal overdose of radiation to a patient, a single person, or at most a sequence of patients, is affected. In an aircraft crash, a large number of passengers and crew can die. Then there are global processes, such as reduction in stratospheric ozone due to emissions of chlorofluorocarbons and other chemicals, leading to an increase in skin cancer in many parts of the world, among other effects. In some cases, the scale of a vulnerability is not clear-cut. Automobile accidents seldom kill more than a few people at a time, yet in total such accidents leave many tens of thousands of people dead each year, which can be attributed to the technological system of car-based travel. The scale of consequences is an obvious way to classify vulnerabilities, but it is not so clear what insights this provides.

Another framework commonly used refers to the type of problem involved in causing a technological breakdown, such as human error, mechanical failure, shortcoming in system design, or excessive complexity.[11] This sort of analysis can be very useful in focusing on areas where changes can be made to reduce the risks of a breakdown.

These different frameworks each have their advantages when dealing with technological risk, but they are of limited value for elucidating technological vulnerability. As noted above, vulnerability is defined in relation to a particular threat. In the classification schemes based on type of technology, scale, or type of problem, the threat varies from case to case. Indeed, classifying vulnerabilities by type of problem is really, in a sense, classifying them according to different threats. None of these classification schemes really says much about the nature of system breakdown, especially when the system is large scale, such as the food system or health system.

Because vulnerabilities are defined in relation to particular threats, it might seem that the only way forward is to look at particular cases. For example, in looking at the vulnerability of the entire system of road transport against breakdown, one might investigate threats due to a blockade of oil imports, terrorist attacks on petroleum refineries, or global economic collapse. In each of these examples, the basic problem is a shortage of reasonably priced fuel for vehicles.

A general method of analyzing technological vulnerabilities is as follows. First, write down every conceivable threat to the operation of the system in question. For each threat, write down the possible consequences. Next, write down possible responses to prevent or reduce the effect of each of the consequences. An example would be to look at the vulnerability of a country's computer networks to attack. Threats would include widespread sabotage, military takeover, and nuclear electromagnetic pulse. Consequences would include disabling of software, central political control, and physical destruction. Responses would include tighter security, unbreakable encryption, and shielding against EMP. A much more detailed analysis has been made of the vulnerability of steel production to military threats.[12]

Although an analysis of vulnerabilities requires looking at specific threats, making generalizations would seem to be difficult. There are various ways around this obstacle. The approach adopted here is to look at interest groups and vulnerabilities to see whether there are interests in maintaining the vulnerabilities. This allows generalizations, since the key question is whether there is a feedback loop between the vulnerability and its cause.

INTERESTS AND VULNERABILITY

The concept of "interest" is used to indicate that an individual or group has something to gain from a course of action, policy, or practice.[13] For example, a scientist has an interest in being an author of a paper reporting a discovery, a pharmaceutical company has an interest in a patented drug, a government has an interest in the perceived legitimacy of taxation. When interests are institutionalized through law or custom, they are commonly referred to as "vested interests."

My concern here is with vulnerabilities that are perpetuated because of strong interests, not just in practices causing the vulnerabilities but in the existence of vulnerabilities themselves. Some examples will help explain this phenomenon.

Consider the impact of chlorofluorocarbons on stratospheric ozone, setting aside other human processes that affect ozone.[14] Companies that produce aerosol sprays, refrigerants, and the like have an interest in continuing production, sales, and profits from these chemicals, but they certainly have no interest in the vulnerability of stratospheric ozone to chemical depletion. If this vulnerability did not exist, their corporate existence would be much more secure. The vulnerability of ozone to chlorofluorocarbons, then, is a case where there are no obvious interests in the vulnerability itself, though clearly there are corporate interests in activities that cause a hazard, "exploiting" the vulnerability.

Of course, there might be some groups with an interest in the existence of this vulnerability of stratospheric ozone. Perhaps some environmental groups might be upset if the chlorofluorocarbon-ozone link were disproved, though it seems more likely that they would simply move on to other issues. Perhaps some manufacturers of sunscreens have an interest in worries about ozone depletion, which they can use to promote their products, though presumably other advertising angles could easily be found. The upshot is that it may be possible to unearth some individuals or groups with an interest in this particular vulnerability, but that the main relevant group — the chlorofluorocarbon industry — has no interest in it.

Most examples are like this: There are interests whose activities cause hazards, but these interests do not benefit from the existence of the hazard. In other words, there are no institutionalized interests in vulnerability itself. Producers and users of fossil fuels have an interest in practices that contribute to the greenhouse effect, but they have no obvious interest in the vulnerability of the earth's climate to human inputs of carbon dioxide and other chemicals. Manufacturers of motor vehicles have an interest in continuing use of these vehicles that happens to lead to tens of thousands of deaths on the road each year, yet these manufacturers have no interest in the vulnerability of road transport to accidents. Indeed, they have made considerable investments in methods of reducing accidents and their consequences, though not as many efforts as critics would like.[15] The same sort of analysis applies to innumerable risks and vulnerabilities more local in scale. Producers of microwave ovens have an interest in maintaining sales of a technology that poses a certain risk to health, but have no interest in the vulnerability of the human body to exposure to microwave radiation.

There are, though, a few cases in which it can be argued that there are strong interests in maintaining certain types of vulnerabilities. These cases are inherently contentious, since few groups ever admit — to themselves or anyone else — that they foster vulnerabilities, especially when their rationale is to overcome these very vulnerabilities. Let me start then with an example — terrorism — that conforms to common viewpoints before turning to more significant ones that challenge conventional wisdom.

Terrorism can be defined as the use of threats or attacks on a population to cause fear and obtain compliance with demands. Nonstate terrorists[16] often exploit technological vulnerabilities, such as the vulnerability of an aircraft, passengers, and crew to a bomb or a few armed individuals. These terrorists have an interest in maintaining this vulnerability. But they have little say in the perpetuation of the vulnerability, since they do not control aircraft manufacture, choice of transport mode, etc. Thus, while terrorists have an interest in technological vulnerability, they have little control over the existence of the vulnerability itself.

For a more comprehensive and challenging example, consider the system of liquid-fuel-based road transport, including cars, trucks, roads, oil companies, automobile manufacturers, and government transport departments, among others. This technological system is highly vulnerable to a shortage or cut-off of oil, which might be caused by sabotage of petroleum refineries, strikes by oil company workers, a blockade of oil imports, or war in oil-producing regions.[17]

There are various ways to reduce this vulnerability or, in other words, to increase the resilience of the transport system in the face of a cut-off of oil supplies. Possibilities include stockpiling fuel, developing diversified sources of supply, preparing rationing systems, and promoting fuel efficiency. These provide some cushion against emergencies but do not remove the underlying vulnerability.

Another approach is to move toward a transport system that relies far less on liquid fuel. This could include dramatically improved public transport, telecommuting, and redesign of cities so that most trips can conveniently be made by walking or cycling. Such an alternative has often been advocated, and a number of cities have made moves in this direction,[18] but the vulnerability remains a significant one. Why?

The interests behind a transport system based on oil are enormous: oil companies, car manufacturers, road-building industries, and government roads departments, among many others. This is one of the most powerful industrial-bureaucratic complexes in the world.[19] Parts of this complex have an interest in selling oil products, selling cars, building roads, and so forth. Can it also be said that they have an interest in the vulnerability of a transport system to shortages of liquid fuel?

The case for this is especially strong in the United States, which has massive oil reserves of its own. Nevertheless, U.S. production is not enough to serve the country's huge consumption of cheap oil, and there is massive importation of oil, especially from Gulf states. Even very moderate conservation measures, such as switching to smaller and more efficient vehicles like those commonly in use in Europe and Japan, would eliminate the need for oil imports to the United States, eliminating its dependence and hence one vulnerability. But this path has not been adopted. Instead, national policy has centered on maintaining access to cheap overseas oil. This has meant putting pressure on foreign governments, occasionally conspiring to overthrow them and going to war.[20] A very risky and interventionist foreign policy has been adopted, which would be quite unnecessary if some simple conservation measures were adopted.[21]

There are various ways to understand this promotion of energy vulnerability. One is to argue that U.S.–based oil companies seek to maximize their share of the world market by controlling foreign oil fields and have directly or indirectly shaped the U.S. policy-making agenda to serve their interests in this respect.[22] It is also possible to delve more deeply and to argue that both corporations and states prefer energy options that make consumers dependent on their services. Reserves of liquid fuels are very unevenly distributed over the globe, and this means that small groups can easily take control over them; they have an interest in making others dependent on these fuels. By contrast, solar energy is relatively evenly distributed and much harder to monopolize, hence the much lower interest by corporations.[23] A similar set of arguments applies to governments. Raising revenue is much more straightforward when the population is dependent for survival on commodities that are controlled by government or large corporations.[24] The liquid-fuel-based transport system is ideal for collecting taxes on fuel, vehicles, etc. The prospects for taxation on travel when town planning allows people to walk to work are much less.

A little reflection reveals that these arguments apply to centralized energy sources of all kinds. For example, in the production of electricity, large hydroelectric plants, nuclear power, and large fossil-fuel plants are all vulnerable to terrorism, sabotage, and military attack in a way that microhydro, passive solar design, and local solar and wind electricity systems are not. Arguably, there is more involved here than simply efficiency considerations. In early 1950s, the U.S. Paley Commission recommended increased use of solar energy, but instead major investments were poured into nuclear power.[25] This sort of choice can be analyzed at several levels. For organizations administering technological systems for large populations — energy or water boards, for example — it is "easier" to deploy experts, raise funds, and mobilize political support for large-scale projects than to foster a process of small-scale change. A new dam is built rather than fix leaky faucets throughout the city; a new power plant is built rather than install energy-efficient heaters and air conditioners.[26] To say that building new centralized capacity is an "easier" option hides a key factor: This approach makes necessary the central administering organization itself. Associated with this, it requires the attention of experts, including financial managers, engineers, and police (the latter to protect against attacks on vulnerable systems). More generally, centralized energy production is congruent with the centralized administrative apparatuses associated with the state.[27]

I have devoted considerable attention to features of centralized energy systems, presenting the argument that certain groups have an interest in vulnerabilities of these systems, namely those vulnerabilities that are linked to the population's dependence on centralized provision of energy. Much more could be said about this issue without necessarily resolving it. My point is that there is a case that some powerful groups may have an interest in maintaining technological vulnerabilities. The following examples are outlined even more briefly.

Among the salient vulnerabilities of every society today is vulnerability to military attack. This includes attacks by a country's own military on indigenous populations, civil war, invasion, and the consequences of global nuclear war. Many of these threats are created or perpetuated at least in part by the very institutions designed to oppose them. The most familiar is nuclear deterrence: Nuclear weapons pose a threat to other countries, justifying acquisition of nuclear forces by other governments, thereby justifying the need for nuclear weapons in the first place. But the phenomenon of military races applies much more widely, of course.

Looking more deeply, the very possession of armed forces has been described as a "protection racket."[28] The military must be funded, typically requiring a sizable slice of the government budget. Those who refuse to pay their taxes are compelled to by the police power of the state, ultimately backed up by the military. In many countries, militaries are irrelevant or inadequate for defense against outside attack. Their main purpose is to prop up the ruling regime, sometimes with murderous consequences.

This view of the military is of course completely at variance with the usual idea of "defense." Interest groups linked to the military naturally foster a belief system — in which they themselves believe implicitly — that sees military forces as essential to protect against both enemy troops and internal subversives. It is well known that militaries are prone to exaggerate the threat from potential enemies. From their point of view, it is best to be prepared for the worst contingencies; others perceive a self-serving element. Whatever the motivation, militaries by their existence serve to create vulnerabilities to military attack.

Military-induced vulnerabilities are increasingly technological. Vast investments are made in research, development, and production of ever more sophisticated weapons systems.[29] Many of these weapons, especially the potentially offensive ones such as bombers and missiles, create greater vulnerability, since the ability to attack is seen as a deterrent.[30] The nuclear arms race is the ultimate in self-justifying technological vulnerability.

Alternatives to militaries have received little attention, certainly far less than alternatives to centralized energy supplies. One possibility is nonviolent defense based on civilian action using techniques such as strikes, boycotts, sit-ins, and noncooperation.[31] The case for such an alternative cannot be canvassed here; suffice it to say that, on the basis of many studies and actual uses of nonviolent action, it seems worthy of attention but has received very little, least of all in terms of developing technology for nonviolent struggle. One plausible reason for this is the strong interests behind maintaining military systems and their associated vulnerabilities.

Another example where there seem to be significant interests in maintaining vulnerabilities involves the complex issue of cash crops in the Third World. When farmers grow food that they can eat themselves or sell locally, this provides communities some degree of resilience against the vagaries of international markets. To increase export income, many Third World governments have promoted production of crops for export, such as coffee, tea, or bananas. This can increase incomes, at least of some farmers, but at the expense of increased vulnerabilities. A political factor becomes prominent here. Many Third World countries are run by repressive rulers, either military dictatorships or figurehead democracies. These regimes are maintained by force, not least against any challenge to prevailing economic inequalities. It is easier to maintain repressive rule when the population is not self-reliant.[32] Producing cash crops makes it harder for popular opposition movements to build support. This process is fostered by the so-called structural adjustment programs commonly imposed by the World Bank and International Monetary Fund as a condition for providing finance. Technology enters this complex process through the dependence of cash crops on pesticides, artificial fertilizers, and genetically engineered seeds.

The Third World agriculture package fosters vulnerability of farmers to both repression and interruption of technological inputs through the interlinked interests of international financial systems and repressive rulers. Without exports of cash crops, rulers cannot pay for imports of goods from the First World, including military and police technology used to maintain their rule.

Illegal drugs provide another case where it can be argued that there are interests in maintaining vulnerabilities. The issue of whether specific drugs should be legal or illegal — with various shades of gray in terms of types and degrees of regulation — is highly contentious on its own, not to mention the argument here that certain groups have interests in maintaining vulnerability to drug-related hazards. Nevertheless, let me present the argument. A number of researchers have argued that society would be better off if certain drugs, now illegal, were decriminalized or legalized.[33] The paradigm case is marijuana.[34] A complex of interests maintains the current legal regime, including politicians who campaign on drug scares and some enforcement agencies. More diffuse is the interest of a broad cross-section of the population in the stigmatizing of users of currently illegal drugs. Because of highly selective enforcement of drug laws, it is primarily the poor, unemployed, and minority groups that are arrested and jailed for drug use or sales. The enormous and continually growing prison population in the United States is partly attributable to a prison-industrial complex that owes much to drug policies.[35]

Many of the health hazards of illegal drugs are due to their illegality. Legal drugs are obtainable in reliable and unadulterated doses; quality control of illegal drugs is difficult. Many middle-class doctors maintain opioid habits for years with no physical or legal problems; street users are likely to suffer overdoses and arrests. Crime associated with illegal drugs is aggravated by enforcement policies: Police seizures of drugs drive up prices, leading to greater involvement by criminals willing to take greater risks.

To be sure, there is a counterargument to be made about the greater hazards from legalization of currently illegal drugs. The point here is that it can be argued that certain drug-related vulnerabilities — the vulnerability of individual drug users to impure drugs and to arrest and the vulnerability of society to drug-related criminal activity — persist because it is in the interest of certain groups to maintain these vulnerabilities.

As mentioned at the outset, it is difficult to provide convincing examples of vulnerabilities that are perpetuated by vested interests, because of entrenched belief systems that these very interests are necessary to protect against the vulnerabilities. Centralized energy sources seem to be required to provide the reliability in energy supplies that people have come to expect, military forces seem to be required to protect against military attack, cash cropping seems to be necessary to provide income for survival and prosperity, laws against drugs seem to be necessary to prevent even greater hazards from uncontrolled drug use. At one level, these beliefs are correct. The vulnerabilities associated with these systems have grown along with the systems themselves and cannot be banished by any quick fix. It is tempting to call these vulnerabilities "self-reproducing" in that sociotechnical systems help create the demand for their own existence. Since this terminology might suggest that this process is autonomous, perhaps a better description is the clumsy "interest-reproducing vulnerabilities."

CONCLUSION

There is far more attention given to technological risk, namely the consequences of the failure of technological systems, especially hazards to the public, than to technological vulnerability, which focuses more on how a technological system may fail due to outside impacts. The most interesting, important, and challenging vulnerabilities are ones associated with large-scale systems, such as energy, agriculture, and economics. How should such vulnerabilities be studied? Typical approaches divide risks and vulnerabilities according to the type of technology, the scale of the hazard, or the modes of failure. Each of these approaches has advantages, but none provides much insight into the persistence of significant vulnerabilities of large-scale systems.

Analysis of interests provides a useful method of analysis. In a first category of cases, no major group is linked to the vulnerability. In such cases, a rational examination of the issues and responses faces fewest obstacles, though action may be stymied by disputes over what, if any, preventive measures should be taken and who will pay for them.

In a second category of cases, vulnerabilities are associated with the activities of powerful interests but the dangers do not serve these interests. In such cases, such as factory hazards and the greenhouse effect, agreement on the value of reducing the vulnerability is relatively easy; disagreement occurs over the trade-off between the costs and benefits of hazard reduction, whether this is installation of safety equipment in factories or reducing use of fossil fuels. The path for hazard reduction is clear: The debate is over how far down it has to travel.

In a third category of cases, it can be argued that powerful groups have an interest not just in maintaining practices that lead to a danger but in maintaining vulnerability itself. For example, militaries justify their existence by the need to protect against threats that are partly provoked by their existence in the first place. This sort of analysis is inherently contentious since no interest group is likely to welcome a conclusion that it is responsible for maintaining a vulnerability that it is supposedly there to overcome or limit.

Analyzing the role of interests in vulnerabilities carries with it the implicit suggestion that overcoming these vulnerabilities requires a challenge to the interests; rational persuasion is unlikely to be successful on its own. Even when there is no interest in a vulnerability, the interests involved can be incredibly powerful, as in the case of fossil-fuel producers and users in the case of the greenhouse effect. Yet there is an extra dimension to the task facing those who wish to tackle vulnerabilities in which interests have a stake, such as military vulnerabilities. This extra dimension is the deep-seated beliefs in systems that create the need for their services.[36] This extra dimension also makes the task in this paper of presenting a case that such vulnerabilities exist a challenging one.

NOTES

1. See, for example, Susan L. Cutter, *Living with Risk: The Geography of Technological Hazards* (London: Edward Arnold, 1993); Theodore S. Glickman and Michael Gough (eds.), *Readings*

in Risk (Washington, DC: Resources for the Future, 1990); William W. Lowrance, *Of Acceptable Risk: Science and the Determination of Safety* (Los Altos, CA: William Kaufmann, 1976).

2. Manuel Wik et al., "URSI Factual Statement on Nuclear Electromagnetic Pulse (EMP) and Associated Effects," *International Union of Radio Science Information Bulletin*, Vol. 232 (March 1985), pp. 4–12.

3. Laurie Garrett, *The Coming Plague: Newly Emerging Diseases in a World Out of Balance* (New York: Farrar, Straus & Giroux, 1994). It is conceivable that new diseases may arise due to medical procedures. See, for example, B. F. Elswood and R. B. Stricker, "Polio Vaccines and the Origin of AIDS," *Medical Hypotheses*, Vol. 42 (1994), pp. 347–54.

4. Colin Kearton and Brian Martin, "Technological Vulnerability: A Neglected Area in Policy-Making," *Prometheus*, Vol. 7 (June 1989), pp. 49–60.

5. F. E. Emery (ed.), *Systems Thinking* (Harmondsworth: Penguin, 1981).

6. I take it as a given that "technology" includes both technical and social aspects. A "technological system" could also be called a "sociotechnical ensemble."

7. Depending on the threat, flexible systems — see David Collingridge, *The Social Control of Technology* (London: Frances Pinter, 1980) — are more likely to be resilient.

8. Accidents can be considered to be a normal part of the operation of any system, as argued by Charles Perrow, *Normal Accidents* (New York: Basic Books, 1984).

9. Jacques Berleur, Colin Beardon, and Romain Laufer (eds.), *Facing the Challenge of Risk and Vulnerability in an Information Society* (Amsterdam: North-Holland, 1993); Peter G. Neumann, *Computer-Related Risks* (New York: ACM Press, 1995).

10. Bev Littlewood and Lorenzo Stringini, "The Risks of Software," *Scientific American*, Vol. 267 (November 1992), pp. 38–43.

11. See Perrow, op. cit.

12. Colin Kearton and Brian Martin, "The Vulnerability of Steel Production to Military Threats," *Materials and Society*, Vol. 14, no. 1 (1990), pp. 11–44.

13. See, for example, Barry Barnes, *Interests and the Growth of Knowledge* (London: Routledge and Kegan Paul, 1977).

14. A nice treatment of the interaction of interests and knowledge in the ozone debate is given by Lydia Dotto and Harold Schiff, *The Ozone War* (Garden City, NY: Doubleday, 1978).

15. See, for example, Alan Irwin, *Risk and the Control of Technology: Public Policies for Road Safety in Britain and the United States* (Manchester: Manchester University Press, 1985).

16. Contrary to popular opinion, most terrorism is carried out or sponsored by major governments, not the small groups or renegade regimes that are the focus of most attention. See Edward S. Herman, *The Real Terror Network: Terrorism in Fact and Fiction* (Boston: South End Press, 1982).

17. Walter Carsnaes, *Energy Vulnerability and National Security: The Energy Crises, Domestic Policy Responses, and the Logic of Swedish Neutrality* (London: Pinter, 1988); Wilson Clark and Jake Page, *Energy, Vulnerability, and War: Alternatives for America* (New York: Norton, 1981); Amory B. Lovins and L. Hunter Lovins, *Brittle Power: Energy Strategy for National Security* (Boston: Brick House, 1982); James L. Plummer (ed.), *Energy Vulnerability* (Cambridge, MA: Ballinger, 1982).

18. Terrence Bendixson, *Instead of Cars* (London: Maurice Temple Smith, 1974); Colin Ward, *Freedom to Go: After the Motor Age* (London: Freedom Press, 1991).

19. James J. Flink, *The Car Culture* (Cambridge, MA: MIT Press, 1975); Delbert A. Taebel and James V. Cornehls, *The Political Economy of Urban Transportation* (Port Washington, NY: Kennikat Press, 1977).

20. The most well-known examples are the CIA-assisted overthrow of the Iranian government in 1953 and the 1991 Gulf War.

21. This argument has been made best by Lovins and Lovins, op. cit. See also Amory B. Lovins, *Soft Energy Paths: Toward a Durable Peace* (Harmondsworth: Penguin, 1977).

22. It may not be necessary for powerful groups to make active efforts in order for others to serve their interests. See Matthew A. Crenson, *The Un-Politics of Air Pollution: A Study of Nondecisionmaking in the Cities* (Baltimore: Johns Hopkins University Press, 1971).

23. Godfrey Boyle, *Living on the Sun: Harnessing Renewable Energy for an Equitable Society* (London: Calder and Boyars, 1975), pp. 14, 16, 58.
24. On the link between the rise and survival of the state and the power to extract resources from the economy, see for example Henry Jacoby, *The Bureaucratization of the World* (Berkeley: University of California Press, 1973); Margaret Levi, *Of Rule and Revenue* (Berkeley: University of California Press, 1988).
25. Ralph Nader and John Abbotts, *The Menace of Atomic Energy* (Collingwood, Victoria: Outback Press, 1977), pp. 29–31.
26. Mans Lönnroth, Peter Steen, and Thomas B. Johansson, *Energy in Transition: A Report on Energy Policy and Future Options* (Uddevalla, Sweden: Secretariat for Future Studies, 1977), pp. 13–14, make this point in relation to Swedish energy policy in the 1950s, namely that from the point of view of central administration it is more complicated to administer a policy of energy conservation than one of increasing energy supply.
27. See, for example, André Gorz, *Ecology as Politics* (Boston: South End Press, 1980); Robert Jungk, *The New Tyranny: How Nuclear Power Enslaves Us* (New York: Grosset & Dunlap, 1979); Lawrence Solomon, *Energy Shock: After the Oil Runs Out* (Toronto: Doubleday, 1980).
28. Charles Tilly, "War Making and State Making as Organized Crime," in Peter B. Evans, Dietrich Rueschemeyer, and Theda Skocpol (eds.), *Bringing the State Back In* (Cambridge, MA: Cambridge University Press, 1985), pp. 169–91. See also Ekkehart Krippendorff, *Staat und Krieg: Die Historische Logik Politischer Unvernunft* (Frankfurt: Suhrkamp, 1985), as reviewed by Johan Galtung, "The State, the Military, and War," *Journal of Peace Research*, Vol. 26 (1989), pp. 101–5; Bruce D. Porter, *War and the Rise of the State: The Military Foundations of Modern Politics* (New York: Free Press, 1994); Charles Tilly, Coercion, *Capital, and European States, AD 990–1992* (Cambridge, MA: Blackwell, 1992).
29. See, for example, Everett H. Mendelsohn, Merritt Roe Smith, and Peter Weingart (eds.), *Science, Technology, and the Military* (Dordrecht: Kluwer, 1988).
30. An exception to this is so-called nonoffensive defense, which relies on weapons that are not easy to use for attack, such as short-range fighter aircraft. Only a few governments have seriously investigated this sort of defense system.
31. See, for example, Anders Boserup and Andrew Mack, *War Without Weapons: Non-violence in National Defence* (London: Frances Pinter, 1974); Michael Randle, *Civil Resistance* (London: Fontana, 1994); Adam Roberts (ed.), *The Strategy of Civilian Defence: Non-violent Resistance to Aggression* (London: Faber and Faber, 1967); Gene Sharp with the assistance of Bruce Jenkins, *Civilian-Based Defense: A Post-Military Weapons System* (Princeton, NJ: Princeton University Press, 1990).
32. Douglas V. Porpora, *How Holocausts Happen: The United States in Central America* (Philadelphia: Temple University Press, 1990), Chapter 4 points out how the social structures of dependence and inequality — including cash-cropping — lead to mass hunger. On the state as a hazard, specifically the link between government repression, technological vulnerability, and famine in the Third World, see Ben Wisner, "Disaster Vulnerability: Scale, Power, and Daily Life," *GeoJournal*, Vol. 30 (1993), pp. 127–40.
33. James B. Bakalar and Lester Grinspoon, *Drug Control in a Free Society* (Cambridge, MA: Cambridge University Press, 1984); Steven B. Duke and Albert C. Gross, *America's Longest War: Rethinking Our Tragic Crusade against Drugs* (New York: G. P. Putnam's Sons, 1993).
34. Lester Grinspoon, *Marijuana Reconsidered* (Cambridge, MA: Harvard University Press, 1971).
35. Nils Christie, *Crime Control as Industry: Towards Gulags, Western Style* (London: Routledge, 1994, second edition).
36. This is a theme running through the incisive critiques of education, energy, health, and other systems by Ivan Illich. See *Deschooling Society* (London: Calder & Boyars, 1971); *Energy and Equity* (London: Calder & Boyars, 1974); *Medical Nemesis: The Appropriation of Health* (London: Calder & Boyars, 1975); *The Right to Useful Unemployment and Its Professional Enemies* (London: Marion Boyars, 1978).

PART V
Dilemmas of New Technology: Bioethics

Some of the most dramatic — and controversial — developments in late-twentieth and early-twenty-first-century technology have come from the life sciences. The event that captured the most headlines was undoubtedly the disclosure, in February 1997, that Ian Wilmut, a Scottish scientist, had succeeded in cloning a sheep (which he named Dolly after Dolly Parton) from the mammary cell of an adult ewe. The success of that experiment, marking the first time a large mammal had been cloned from an adult cell, brought an onslaught of speculation about the prospects and problems of cloning human beings.

But Dolly was only one of a series of remarkable scientific and technological developments that have cascaded out of the discovery, by James Watson and Francis Crick in the early 1950s, of the structure of DNA, the molecule fundamental to most forms of life on earth. This discovery has allowed researchers to unravel the biochemical basis of genes, those units within cells that transmit traits (e.g., eye color, height, and susceptibility to particular diseases) from one generation to the next. It has also led to the isolation, in 1998, of human embryonic stem cells — cells which can theoretically differentiate into virtually any kind of cell in the human body, from brain to skin to blood. What sets these developments apart from most other areas of science and technology are the ethical, philosophical, and religious issues they raise, as well as, for some, the potential to change the course of human evolution.

In Part V of *Technology and the Future,* we examine a specific area of technology and its relations to society with several articles related to biomedical developments and their ethical and social implications. An essay by Robert Weinberg, an eminent molecular biologist, opens the section with a cautionary note about the potential outcomes of the Human Genome Initiative, a government-funded effort to decode the entire genetic makeup of the human organism. This effort climaxed in June 2000 with the announcement that a "working draft" sequence of the human genome had been completed, followed in February 2001 by the simultaneous publication by two competing teams of the sequence itself. In his article, which was written several years earlier, anticipating the success of this effort, Weinberg expresses hope about the prospects for preventing and treating disease and alleviating human suffering, but he is also deeply worried about the potential misuse of genetic knowledge for socially destructive ends.

The two chapters that follow present the text of an unprecedented nationally televised speech by President George W. Bush on August 9, 2001, on the subject of stem cell research and a response to the president by Thomas Murray, a distinguished bioethicist. What led the president to make this speech was the dispute over federal financing of stem cell research, which had been percolating through the federal government for several years. On one side are those who oppose the use of human embryonic stem cells in research, because doing so would cause the destruction of embryos, which are seen as having the potential to become human beings. On the other are those who see stem cell research as offering the possibility of major advances in the fight against disease and debilitating injuries, a consideration they feel outweighs concerns about the use of embryos.

In his address, President Bush announced the formation of a council to advise him on issues of bioethics, including stem cell research. He named biomedical ethicist Leon Kass to chair the council. In Chapter 20, which follows and which dates from 1998, Kass takes up the issue of whether to ban human cloning. The stakes are very high, he says; indeed, "the future of humanity hangs in the balance." Kass asserts that there are good reasons for the repugnance we feel toward the idea of cloning humans and we should heed them rather than allowing ourselves to become slaves to unregulated technological progress. Finally, physician-writer Jerome Groopman takes a critical look at Kass's views as they might affect his role as chair of the National Bioethics Council. The issues raised by these five chapters are central to the future of this key area of technology, to our ethical and moral self-concept, and, finally, to the future of the human race.

17. The Dark Side of the Genome

ROBERT A. WEINBERG

Among the most rapid and important scientific advances of the past two decades have been developments in molecular biology. The breaking of the genetic code and the development of new techniques to analyze genetic materials have given scientists the ability to understand the relationship between the biochemical building blocks of cells and the traits and characteristics of living organisms, including humans.

During the past several years, life scientists in several countries have conducted a coordinated, systematic effort to create a complete biochemical description of the human genome (i.e., the DNA contained in the chromosomes in human cells) and to develop a map or atlas indicating which components of this genetic material determine which human traits, from susceptibility to particular disorders to eye color to mathematical or artistic ability. A "working draft" of the sequence of the human genome was published in February 2001. While much work remains to be done to associate the genes in this sequence with specific traits and functions, geneticists have already identified the location of genes associated with dozens of disorders, including cystic fibrosis, fragile-X syndrome (a form of mental retardation), and Huntington's disease.

These new capabilities offer the prospect of eliminating a great deal of human suffering, but they also present some serious ethical dilemmas and risks to society. Use of genetic information by insurance companies, by employers, and by government agencies could infringe on individual rights to privacy and could even make it difficult for some people to get health insurance, find employment, or find a marriage partner.

Robert A. Weinberg, one of the leading figures in molecular genetics, discusses some of these perplexing issues in his essay, "The Dark Side of the Genome" Along the way, he gives a lucid introduction to the fundamentals of molecular genetics. Weinberg is a professor of biology at the Massachusetts Institute of Technology and a member of the Whitehead Institute for Biomedical Research. His laboratory was among the first to recognize the existence of human oncogenes, which are responsible for converting normal cells into cancer cells. Weinberg holds a Ph.D. in biology from MIT. He is a member of the National Academy of Sciences and the recipient of a long list of honors, scientific prizes, and honorary degrees, including, in 1997, the National Medal of Science.

In the past 10 years, biology has undergone a revolution that has repeatedly attracted wide attention. At first, controversy swirled over whether the genetic cloning technology that powers this revolution could create new and possibly dangerous forms of life. These fears have dissipated as thousands of investigators

From *Technology Review* (April 1991). © 1991 *Technology Review*. Reprinted with permission.

have found that the organisms created by gene splicing pose no threat to human health or the ecosystem around us.

A much larger stream of headlines next touted the power of genetic engineering to produce great quantities of valuable medical and agricultural products cheaply. Without doubt, over the next decades these fruits of biotechnology will enormously benefit health and economic productivity.

Largely lost amidst these stories, however, are developments that will ultimately have a far larger social impact. Recently gained abilities to analyze complex genetic information, including our own, will soon allow us to predict human traits from simple DNA tests. [In just a few years], routine tests will detect predispositions to dozens of diseases, as well as indicate a wide range of normal human traits. We have only begun to confront the problems engendered by the power of genetic diagnosis.

Consider, for example, the societal problems that will likely develop from the recent isolation of the gene that in a defective form causes cystic fibrosis. Genetic counselors can now trace that version of the gene in families, thereby revealing those couples who could have children with cystic fibrosis. While providing extraordinarily useful information for cystic fibrosis carriers, this technique raises questions about the marriageability and reproductive decisions of gene carriers and the terms under which their offspring will be able to obtain health and life insurance.

Individual successes like the isolation of the cystic fibrosis gene will soon be overshadowed by the avalanche of genetic information flowing out of research labs. The engine that will drive these advances in gene analysis is the biologists' moonshot, the Human Genome Project. (See box.) The ambitious goal of this international effort is to read out the sequence of the three billion bases of DNA that, strung end to end, carry the information of all the body's genes. Given a clear, easily read atlas of our genetic endowment, researchers will be able to accelerate the rate at which they discover important genes — now several dozen each year — by tenfold and eventually maybe even hundredfold. Scientists will then be able to study how the normal versions of these genes work, and how their aberrant versions cause disease.

Some fear that by reading through the entire library of human gene sequences we will rapidly come to understand the ultimate secrets of life and the essence of our humanity. For my part, such fears are far astray of the mark. Our bodies function as complex networks of interacting components that are often influenced by our variable environment. By enumerating and studying individual components — genes, in this case — we will only begin to scratch the surface of our complexity. Nonetheless, certain genes can be especially influential in determining one or another aspect of human form and function. Herein lie the seeds of the substantial problems we will begin to encounter over the next decade.

MAPPING THE GENETIC TERRAIN

Ten to fifteen years from now — barring unforeseen technical obstacles — scientists will have described every bump in our complex genetic terrain. Yet, long before this project is finished, information yielded by "mapping" this landscape — breaking it into sectors of manageable size and placing them in a logical array — will make possible powerful genetic analysis techniques. These, in turn, will engender a host of ethical issues.

DNA and Babylonian Tablets

To find every human gene, scientists will have to determine the sequence of the three billion characters in our DNA that together form the genetic blueprint known as the human genome. One can convey how daunting the effort will be by comparing the genome to a Babylonian library uncovered in some nineteenth-century archeological dig.

Imagine tens of thousands of clay tablets — individual genes — scattered about, each inscribed with thousands of cuneiform characters in a language with few known cognates. The library's chaos mirrors that encountered when the precisely ordered array of DNA molecules that is present in a living cell is extracted and introduced into a test tube. Imagine, too, that the library's full meaning will be understood only when most of its tablets have been deciphered.

Geneticists today have ways of laboriously sifting through heaps of "tablets" to find certain genes of special interest. Once a gene is located and retrieved, or "cloned," the sequence of its 5,000 or more bases of DNA — our cuneiform characters — can be determined.

While biologists are proud of having sequenced more than one percent of the "tablets" so far, these achievements represent only a piecemeal solution to a very large problem. Gene cloning and sequencing techniques developed in the 1970s are so time-consuming and painstaking that systematic searches for many genes have been impossible.

A better answer, in the form of the human genome project, will begin by mapping the genome — cataloguing all the Babylonian tablets. In effect, geneticists will gather and systematically shelve the scattered tablets, reconstructing their original order.

Initially, groups of tablets (DNA fragments) thought to derive from a common section (chromosomal region) of the library will be placed together on a shelf. Then geneticists will order the tablets within a group and give each a label. They will do so without any understanding of the tablets' contents.

How is this possible? Imagine that our Babylonian scribes have used the final phrases at the end of one tablet as the opening phrases of the next one. Short, redundant strings of characters would enable tablets to be shelved in the right order without any knowledge of the bulk of the text. Long, carefully ordered lists of the labels identifying individual tablets, in effect a complete library catalog, will compose the human genome map.

Only after this work is completed can the reading of all the characters in each tablet proceed — the sequencing of the DNA bases. Great technical progress will be required before the work becomes economically viable. Sequencing a 1,000-base stretch of DNA now costs $5,000 to $10,000. And some genes are giants; the one involved in muscular dystrophy was recently found to encompass two million bases. The cost will have to drop by a factor of ten through automation before sequencing can begin in earnest.

Think of the technology required to develop automated readers that could photograph 3,000-year-old tablets, analyze and read the characters with greater than 99 percent accuracy, flag ambiguous ones, and introduce everything into a computerized database. The details of the automated DNA-sequencing equipment under development differ, but the technical problems are no less challenging. — *Robert A. Weinberg*

To understand why, it is important to know a little about the underlying biology. The human genetic landscape — our genome — consists of all the DNA information carried on the twenty-two pairs of chromosomes in our cells, plus the X and Y chromosomes involved in determining sex. Each chromosome carries a linear molecule of DNA ranging in size from 50 million to 250 million pairs of four kinds of chemical bases. They are commonly referred to by the letters A, C, G, and T. In all, three billion base pairs of DNA lie on the chromosomes. Some 50,000 to 100,000 discrete segments of DNA — each several thousand or more base pairs long — constitute the genes that store our genetic information. The trick is to figure out where these genes lie and what information each encodes.

As a first step in understanding this enormous information base, investigators have started mapping each chromosome by labeling small segments along its length. The labels used are actually built-in features of the genome. They consist of minor genetic variations called polymorphisms that occur frequently throughout human DNA sequences and distinguish one person's DNA from another's. For example, at a certain chromosomal site, one person's DNA bases may read AAGCTT, while a second person's may read AAGTTT. Such polymorphisms, widely scattered throughout the genome, are readily detected using existing techniques, even without any knowledge of the genome's detailed structure.

Polymorphisms are not only important for their usefulness in marking the genome at specific places. The location of a particular gene in the human genome is usually obscure. Geneticists can track down such a gene by localizing it near one or another polymorphic marker. To do this, they ascertain the presence of markers in DNA samples collected from members of large families and even large, unrelated populations.

Researchers have already used a polymorphic marker to determine the rough location of the gene that in one variant form, or "allele," leads to Huntington's disease. This illness appears as a severe neurological deterioration in midlife. Within a large kin group studied in Venezuela, all the relatives showing the disease were found to carry a distinct polymorphic marker on a particular chromosome, while their middle-aged, disease-free relatives did not. This concordance means that the still unknown gene lies close to the polymorphic marker on that chromosome, and therefore that detection of the marker signals the presence of the gene that causes the disease. The marker will prove invaluable in helping researchers to directly identify the Huntington's gene, isolation of which offers the only real hope for understanding and treating the disease.

Genes linked to terrible diseases are not the only ones geneticists study. During the next ten years, researchers may well make associations between polymorphic markers and normal, highly variable traits such as height, eye color, hair shape, and even foot width without knowledge of the genes that serve as blueprints for these traits. Not much farther down the road, scientists may uncover links between certain markers and more complex, subtle traits, such as aspects of physical coordination, mood, and maybe even musical ability. At that point, we will confront social problems that will bedevil us for decades to come.

Imagine that investigators could predict with some accuracy certain aspects of intelligence through simple analysis of an individual's DNA. Consider the power this would give some people and the vulnerable position in which it would put others.

The magnitude of the problems of genetic diagnosis depends on one's view of how many complex human traits will be successfully associated with polymorphic markers. Some observers, such as geneticists Richard Lewontin and Jonathan Beckwith of Harvard University, believe that few such associations will be made correctly. Some people argue that traits such as perfect pitch and mathematical ability depend on the workings of dozens of genes. Yet others think that the contributions of nature and nurture can never be teased apart.

Most likely, the doubters will be correct in many cases but wrong in others. Mathematical analysis has led some geneticists to conclude that the expression of many complex traits is strongly influenced by the workings of a few genes operating amid a large number of more silent collaborators. Moreover, scientists can most easily explain rapid organismic evolution, such as humans have experienced over the last several million years, by attributing important roles to a small number of especially influential genes. According to this hypothesis, each such gene has undergone alterations over the course of evolution that have in turn resulted in profound changes in our embryological development and adult functioning.

For these reasons, I believe that a number of genetic markers will be strongly linked to certain discrete aspects of human behavior and mental functioning. Yet other traits will, as some argue, prove to be influenced by many interacting genes and the environment and will not lend themselves to the genetic analysis soon to be at our fingertips.

What type of higher functions will be understood and predictable by genetic methods? One can only speculate. The list of possibilities — say, shyness, aggressiveness, foreign-language aptitude, chess-playing ability, heat tolerance, or sex drive — is limited only by one's imagination. Likewise, the consequences of one or another identification — and there will surely be some successes — can barely begin to be foreseen.

THE LONG REACH OF GENETIC SCREENING

From cradle to grave — even from conception to grave — the coming genetic diagnostic technology will have profound effects on our descendants' lives. Parents-to-be in the latter part of the 1990s will confront an ever-lengthening menu of prenatal genetic tests that will affect a variety of reproductive decisions. Terminating a pregnancy may come relatively easily to some whose offspring carry genes dooming them to crippling diseases that appear early in life, such as Tay-Sachs and cystic fibrosis. But the mutant gene leading to Huntington's disease usually permits normal life until one's forties or fifties, typically after the trait has been passed on to half of the next generation. Will its detection in a fetus justify abortion?

As the years pass, this gray area of decision making will widen inexorably. Sooner or later, an enterprising graduate student will uncover a close association between a polymorphic marker and some benign aspect of human variability, like eye color or body shape. And then genetic decision making will hinge on far more than avoiding dread disease.

Such knowledge and the tests it makes possible could lead to eugenics through elective abortion. In India, thousands of abortions are said to be performed solely on the basis of fetal sex. It would seem to be but a small step for many to use the genetic profile of a fetus to justify abortion for a myriad of other real or perceived genetic insufficiencies.

This prospect may appear remote, seemingly encumbered by complicated laboratory procedures that will limit these analyses to a privileged elite. And the revulsion built up against eugenics would seem to present a significant obstacle. But the onward march of technology will change all this. Current programs for developing new diagnostic instruments should, by the end of this decade, yield machines able to automatically detect dozens of markers in a single, small DNA sample. As genetic diagnosis becomes more automated, it will become cheap and widely available. And the responsibility for children's genetic fitness will shift from the uncontrollable hand of fate into the hands of parents. [Within a few years], the birth of a cystic fibrosis child will, in the minds of many, reflect more the negligence of parents than God's will or the whims of nature.

Still other specters loom as the coming generation matures. Twenty-five years hence, educators and guidance counselors intent on optimizing educational "efficiency" could find children's genetic profiles irresistible tools. Once correlations are developed between performance and the frequency of certain genetic sequences — and once computers can forecast the interactions of multiple genes — such analyses could be used in attempts to predict various aspects of cognitive function and general educability.

The dangers here are legion. Some will use tests that will at best provide only probabilistic predictors of performance as precise gauges of competence. And factors strongly affecting education, including personality and environment, will likely be overlooked, leading to gross misreadings of individual ability.

Only slightly less insidious could be the effects of genetic analysis on future marriages. Will courtships be determined by perceptions of the genetic fitness of prospective partners? Over the past decade, how many Jewish couples who have discovered that their children could be born with Tay-Sachs disease, and black couples with similar concerns about sickle-cell anemia, have opted to forgo marriage altogether? As we uncover genes affecting traits that fall well within the range of normal variability, will these, too, become the object of prenuptial examination?

Once again, such an Orwellian vision would seem to reach far beyond current realities. Yet nightmares have already occurred. Two decades ago, genetic screening among the population in central Greece for the blood disease sickle-cell anemia revealed a number of normal individuals carrying genes that predispose their offspring to the disease. Because the test results were inappropriately disclosed, these individuals became publicly identified and stigmatized and formed an unmarriageable genetic underclass.

Along with facing new issues around marriage, young adults with unfavorable constellations of genes may be limited in their employment possibilities. Employers want to hire productive, intelligent people. Will they exploit genetic screening to decide how rapidly a prospective employee will adapt to a new job or contribute to a company's productivity?

Even more likely will be attempts to use genetic markers to predict susceptibility to dangers in the workplace. People have different tolerances to on-the-job chemical exposures, dictated by their genetic variability. There is therefore great interest in uncovering polymorphic markers that would allow companies to predict employees' susceptibility to certain chemicals encountered in the workplace.

Employers will also feel pressure to use the expanding powers of genetic diagnosis to predict lifelong disease susceptibility among workers. The staggering rise in health-insurance costs has already generated strong economic incentives for employers to improve the health of their workers by promoting smoke-free environments, routine medical screening, and healthy life-styles. Hiring only those people who pass genetic profile tests might be seen as a means to reduce health-insurance costs further.

Most employers have until now been unwilling to enter so deeply into employees' private lives. But insurance providers have shown no such reticence. For example, many have been interested in learning whether their insured carry the AIDS virus. Genetic tests predicting heart disease at an early age or susceptibility to cancer will be tempting targets for insurance companies intent on establishing allocation of risk and premiums as precisely as possible. Such logic might dictate that the risks now shared within large insurance pools should be allocated instead on the basis of individual genetic profiles.

Genetic profiles could be widely available by the year 2000, when many primary-care physicians will routinely order certain genetic tests along with the usual blood pressure reading and urinalysis. Overlooking a standard genetic test will increasingly be seen as tantamount to malpractice. And as genetic profiles are routinely entered into health records, limiting insurers' access to such data may prove difficult.

Surely legislation could limit the direct viewing of confidential genetic data by insurers, but they might circumvent even the best attempts at regulation. Imagine the health policy of 2001 that offers substantially reduced premiums to non-smokers having a desirable genetic makeup. Such incentives will drive many people to flaunt their DNA profiles. As the genetically fit flock to the low-risk, low-premium pool, those left behind will have to pay higher premiums or even forgo insurance. In time, the concept of pooling genetic risk will seem a quaint relic of a pretechnological era.

While these developments are unsettling and even frightening, they pale beside the possibility that our ever-advancing understanding of human genetics could stoke the fires of racism.

Imagine in the not-so-distant future a survey of the prevalence of certain polymorphic alleles among different ethnic and racial groups. Ten years from now, will our enterprising graduate student find a polymorphic marker correlated with acute visual perception that is unusually common among Tibetans, or another correlated with impaired mathematical ability that crops up frequently among coastal Albanians? Given the vagaries of human history and population genetics, it is more than likely that different versions of genes are unevenly distributed throughout the human species.

Will such ostensibly innocent measurements of distributions of polymorphic markers ultimately provide a scientific basis for the type of virulent racism that inflamed Europe a half-century ago? Nazi racial theories were based on a pseudo-science that today looks ludicrous. But surely some observed variations in gene frequencies will place solid scientific data in the hands of those with an openly racist agenda.

BEYOND LEGISLATION

Policies governing the use of genetic information need to be debated and put in place early in this decade, not after problems emerge. Bioethics is already a thriving cottage industry, but the problems many of its practitioners wrestle with — issues like surrogate motherhood and in vitro fertilization — will be dwarfed by those surrounding genetic analysis. The groups organizing the human genome project have already assembled experts to confront the ethical, legal, and social dimensions of this work. But these individuals have yet to plumb the depths of the problems.

Even if we as a society can anticipate and rein in most misuse of genetic data, we will also need to address a more insidious and ultimately far more corrosive problem of DNA profiling: the rise of an ethic of genetic determinism.

For the past century, the prevailing winds of ideology have largely driven the ebb and flow of the nature versus nurture debate. A widespread reaction against social Darwinism and Nazi racism buoyed the strong nurturist sentiments of the past half-century, but the tide is turning, pushed by the ever more frequent success of genetics. As this decade progresses, a growing proportion of the lay public will come to accept genes as the all-powerful determinants of the human condition. This uncritical embrace of genetics will not be deterred by scientists' reminders that the powers of genetic predictions are limited.

Even some experts who, through appropriate channels, will gain access to genetic profiles may overinterpret the data. DNA profiles will never be clear, fully reliable predictors of all traits. For many complex traits, such as those involved in behavior and cognition, genetics will at best provide only a probability of development. After all, many traits are governed by the interplay between genetics and the environment. Environmental variations can cause genetically similar individuals to develop in dramatically different ways. Interpreters of genetic information who overlook this fact will repeatedly and disastrously misjudge individual ability.

What a tragedy this would be. The world we thrive in was built by many people who were not shackled by their pedigrees. They saw their origins as vestiges to be transcended. By and large, we Americans have viewed our roots as interesting historical relics, hardly as rigid molds that dictate all that we are and will be. What will come of a worldview that says people live and struggle to fulfill an agenda planned in detail by their genes? Such a surrender to genetic determinism may disenfranchise generations of children who might come to believe that genes, rather than spunk, ambition, and passion, must guide their life course.

A belief that each of us is ultimately responsible for our own behavior has woven our social fabric. Yet in the coming years, we will hear more and more from those who write off bad behavior to the inexorable forces of biology and who embrace a new astrology in which alleles rather than stars determine individuals' lives. It is hard to imagine how far this growing abdication of responsibility will carry us.

As a biologist, I find this prospect a bitter pill. The biological revolution of the past decades has proven extraordinarily exciting and endlessly fascinating, and it will, without doubt, spawn enormous benefit. But, as with most new technologies, we will pay a price unless we anticipate the human genome project's dark side. We need to craft an ethic that cherishes our human ability to transcend biology, that enshrines our spontaneity, unpredictability, and individual uniqueness. At the moment, I find myself and those around me ill equipped to respond to the challenge.

18. Remarks by the President on Stem Cell Research

PRESIDENT GEORGE W. BUSH

The notion of an American president devoting an entire speech, nationally televised and in prime time, to a topic as arcane as human embryonic stem cell research seems almost incredible. Yet, President George W. Bush, who, as a candidate, had barely mentioned science or technology, did exactly that on August 9, 2001. The speech culminated a long process of deliberation within the Bush administration on how to handle this delicate issue. Many Americans, particularly those who oppose abortion (which the president also opposes) are uneasy about research using human embryos because these embryos represent potential human lives. They oppose the use of federal government funds for such research.

Yet, research with stem cells derived from human embryos has opened the prospect of remarkable progress in the battle against many diseases, including diabetes, Alzheimer's, and Parkinson's. And advocates for stem cell research point out that the embryos that are used in such research are frozen excess embryos, produced in fertility clinics that are destined to be discarded in any case. In this address, President Bush describes how he has wrestled with this issue and announces his decision to go forward with it, but under severe limitations.

George Walker Bush is the forty-third president of the United States. The son of George H. W. Bush, who served as the nation's forty-first president, he was elected in 2000. He is a graduate of Yale University and holds an M.B.A. from Harvard Business School. He was elected governor of Texas from 1994 and won reelection in 1998.

Good evening. I appreciate you giving me a few minutes of your time tonight so I can discuss with you a complex and difficult issue, an issue that is one of the most profound of our time.

The issue of research involving stem cells derived from human embryos is increasingly the subject of a national debate and dinner-table discussions. The issue is confronted every day in laboratories as scientists ponder the ethical ramifications of their work. It is agonized over by parents and many couples as they try to have children, or to save children already born.

The issue is debated within the church, with people of different faiths, even many of the same faith coming to different conclusions. Many people are finding that the more they know about stem cell research, the less certain they are about the right ethical and moral conclusions.

My administration must decide whether to allow federal funds, your tax dollars, to be used for scientific research on stem cells derived from human embryos.

A large number of these embryos already exist. They are the product of a process called in vitro fertilization, which helps so many couples conceive children. When doctors match sperm and egg to create life outside the womb, they usually produce more embryos than are planted in the mother. Once a couple successfully has children, or if they are unsuccessful, the additional embryos remain frozen in laboratories.

Some will not survive during long storage; others are destroyed. A number have been donated to science and used to create privately funded stem cell lines. And a few have been implanted in an adoptive mother and born and are today healthy children.

Based on preliminary work that has been privately funded, scientists believe further research using stem cells offers great promise that could help improve the lives of those who suffer from many terrible diseases — from juvenile diabetes to Alzheimer's, from Parkinson's to spinal cord injuries. And while scientists admit they are not yet certain, they believe stem cells derived from embryos have unique potential.

You should also know that stem cells can be derived from sources other than embryos — from adult cells, from umbilical cords that are discarded after babies are born, from human placenta. And many scientists feel research on these types of stem cells is also promising. Many patients suffering from a range of diseases are already being helped with treatments developed from adult stem cells.

However, most scientists, at least today, believe that research on embryonic stem cells offer the most promise, because these cells have the potential to develop in all of the tissues in the body.

Scientists further believe that rapid progress in this research will come only with federal funds. Federal dollars help attract the best and brightest scientists. They ensure new discoveries are widely shared at the largest number of research facilities and that the research is directed toward the greatest public good.

The United States has a long and proud record of leading the world toward advances in science and medicine that improve human life. And the United States has a long and proud record of upholding the highest standards of ethics as we expand the limits of science and knowledge. Research on embryonic stem cells raises profound ethical questions, because extracting the stem cell destroys the embryo and thus destroys its potential for life. Like a snowflake, each of these embryos is unique, with the unique genetic potential of an individual human being.

As I thought through this issue, I kept returning to two fundamental questions: First, are these frozen embryos human life and therefore something precious to be protected? And second, if they're going to be destroyed anyway, shouldn't they be used for a greater good, for research that has the potential to save and improve other lives?

I've asked those questions and others of scientists, scholars, bioethicists, religious leaders, doctors, researchers, members of Congress, my Cabinet, and my friends. I have read heartfelt letters from many Americans. I have given this issue a great deal of thought, prayer, and considerable reflection. And I have found widespread disagreement.

On the first issue, are these embryos human life — well, one researcher told me he believes this five-day-old cluster of cells is not an embryo, not yet an individual, but a pre-embryo. He argued that it has the potential for life, but it is not a life because it cannot develop on its own.

An ethicist dismissed that as a callous attempt at rationalization. Make no mistake, he told me, that cluster of cells is the same way you and I, and all the rest of us, started our lives. One goes with a heavy heart if we use these, he said, because we are dealing with the seeds of the next generation.

And to the other crucial question, if these are going to be destroyed anyway, why not use them for good purpose — I also found different answers. Many argue these embryos are by-products of a process that helps create life, and we should allow couples to donate them to science so they can be used for good purpose instead of wasting their potential. Others will argue there's no such thing as excess life, and the fact that a living being is going to die does not justify experimenting on it or exploiting it as a natural resource.

At its core, this issue forces us to confront fundamental questions about the beginnings of life and the ends of science. It lies at a difficult moral intersection, juxtaposing the need to protect life in all its phases with the prospect of saving and improving life in all its stages.

As the discoveries of modern science create tremendous hope, they also lay vast ethical mine fields. As the genius of science extends the horizons of what we can do, we increasingly confront complex questions about what we should do. We have arrived at that brave new world that seemed so distant in 1932, when Aldous Huxley wrote about human beings created in test tubes in what he called a "hatchery."

In recent weeks, we learned that scientists have created human embryos in test tubes solely to experiment on them. This is deeply troubling and a warning sign that should prompt all of us to think through these issues very carefully.

Embryonic stem cell research is at the leading edge of a series of moral hazards. The initial stem cell researcher was at first reluctant to begin his research, fearing it might be used for human cloning. Scientists have already cloned a sheep. Researchers are telling us the next step could be to clone human beings to create individual designer stem cells, essentially to grow another you, to be available in case you need another heart or lung or liver.

I strongly oppose human cloning, as do most Americans. We recoil at the idea of growing human beings for spare body parts or creating life for our convenience. And while we must devote enormous energy to conquering disease, it is equally important that we pay attention to the moral concerns raised by the new frontier of human embryo stem cell research. Even the most noble ends do not justify any means.

My position on these issues is shaped by deeply held beliefs. I'm a strong supporter of science and technology and believe they have the potential for incredible good — to improve lives, to save life, to conquer disease. Research offers hope that millions of our loved ones may be cured of a disease and rid of their suffering. I have friends whose children suffer from juvenile diabetes. Nancy Reagan has written me about President Reagan's struggle with Alzheimer's. My own family has confronted the tragedy of childhood leukemia. And, like all Americans, I have great hope for cures.

I also believe human life is a sacred gift from our Creator. I worry about a culture that devalues life and believe as your President I have an important obligation to foster and encourage respect for life in America and throughout the world. And while we're all hopeful about the potential of this research, no one can be certain that the science will live up to the hope it has generated.

Eight years ago, scientists believed fetal tissue research offered great hope for cures and treatments — yet, the progress to date has not lived up to its initial expectations. Embryonic stem cell research offers both great promise and great peril. So I have decided we must proceed with great care.

As a result of private research, more than sixty genetically diverse stem cell lines already exist. They were created from embryos that have already been destroyed, and they have the ability to regenerate themselves indefinitely, creating ongoing opportunities for research. I have concluded that we should allow federal funds to be used for research on these existing stem cell lines, where the life-and-death decision has already been made.

Leading scientists tell me research on these sixty lines has great promise that could lead to breakthrough therapies and cures. This allows us to explore the promise and potential of stem cell research without crossing a fundamental moral line, by providing taxpayer funding that would sanction or encourage further destruction of human embryos that have at least the potential for life.

I also believe that great scientific progress can be made through aggressive federal funding of research on umbilical cord placenta, adult and animal stem cells which do not involve the same moral dilemma. This year, your government will spend $250 million on this important research.

I will also name a President's council to monitor stem cell research, to recommend appropriate guidelines and regulations, and to consider all of the medical and ethical ramifications of biomedical innovation. This council will consist of leading scientists, doctors, ethicists, lawyers, theologians, and others and will be chaired by Dr. Leon Kass, a leading biomedical ethicist from the University of Chicago.

This council will keep us apprised of new developments and give our nation a forum to continue to discuss and evaluate these important issues. As we go forward, I hope we will always be guided by both intellect and heart, by both our capabilities and our conscience.

I have made this decision with great care, and I pray it is the right one.

Thank you for listening. Good night, and God bless America.

19.   Hard Cell: A Commentary on the President's Stem Cell Address

THOMAS H. MURRAY

The president's stem cell decision was a compromise. While neither side in the dispute rejected it outright, neither was particularly pleased, either. The opponents of stem cell research were displeased that the president was willing to allow it to proceed at all. The advocates were concerned with the restrictions, particularly the president's announcement that only cell lines (the sources from which researchers obtain the cells they use in research) in existence before he began his speech (at 9 p.m. Eastern Daylight Time on August 9) could be used. Although the president said that sixty such lines were in existence, scientists immediately questioned that number. In addition, they wondered aloud about the conditions under which the sixty-plus cell lines were derived and about the wisdom of placing such restrictions on federally funded research, which is accountable to the public and open to scrutiny by government officials, while allowing privately funded research to continue without such restrictions.

Thomas Murray examines these matters in his critique of the president's address, originally published in The American Prospect *in September 2001. Murray is president of the Hastings Center in Garrison, New York, a think tank devoted to bioethics. He was formerly director of the Center for Biomedical Ethics in the School of Medicine at Case Western Reserve University in Cleveland. He has written, spoken, consulted, and testified extensively on issues of bioethics and served as a member of the National Bioethics Advisory Commission, the precursor to the new council announced by President Bush in his speech. He holds a Ph.D. in social psychology from Princeton University.*

President George W. Bush's August 9, 2001, address to the nation on embryonic stem cells was an exercise in politico-moral bumper bowling. He acknowledged the hopes of desperate patients and their families, then bounced across the alley to embrace the moral arguments of right-to-life allies. It was fascinating to watch this slow, lurching journey down the lane and to wonder where the ball would actually strike. The biggest surprise was not that he offered a compromise on research with embryonic stem cells but rather his claim that sixty cell lines had already been created and were potential candidates for research grants from the U.S. National Institutes of Health (NIH). Most scientists were aware of only a dozen lines at most; hearing that there were many times that number was startling.

The official number is now sixty-four. Lana Skirboll, associate director for science policy at NIH and a well-respected scientist and administrator, was the source for the figure, which was based on an exhaustive worldwide search to find

Reprinted with permission from *The American Prospect* Vol. 12, No. 17 (September 24 - October 8, 2001). *The American Prospect*, 5 Broad Street, Boston, MA 02109. All rights reserved.

any possible embryonic stem cell line. Dr. Skirboll found them in Israel, India, Australia, Sweden, and the United States. Sixty-four lines met the criteria set by the Bush administration: They were derived from embryos in excess of those needed for a couple's reproductive purposes, the couple who authorized their creation consented for the embryo to be used for research, the embryo had not originally been created for research, and no monetary or other inducements had been offered for the embryo. The president added an additional condition: Destruction of the embryo must have been initiated by 9:00 P.M. on August 9, 2001.

The president's announcement did not please everyone. That was always an impossibility given the mutually incompatible goals. On the side favoring research funding were patients and their advocacy organizations, who see stem cells as a bright new hope for afflictions like Parkinson's disease, spinal-cord injuries, and diabetes. On the same side were scientists fiercely resistant to what they view as politically inspired limitations on embryonic stem cell research. Arrayed against them were the forces of the right-to-life movement, some of whom saw in embryonic stem cell research an issue that might cause Americans to think hard, perhaps for the first time, about the moral significance of the earliest human embryos. As it happened, some of the Americans who engaged in those reflections were reliably antiabortion politicians, and so the debate over embryonic stem cells has fractured the pro-life movement itself.

Whether Bush's announced policy was a political masterstroke, a muddled but serviceable compromise, or a latent disaster waiting to unfold, time will reveal. Whatever its apparent appeal, the president's policy has four significant defects: It alters previously proposed ethical standards for embryonic stem cell lines, it reinforces an oligopoly over the existing lines, it is inherently unstable given likely scientific developments and the prospect of future experimental stem cell therapies, and it drives a wedge into the heart of the pro-life movement. (This last will not be seen as a defect in all quarters.)

Make no mistake, there are vexing ethical questions concerning how we treat human embryos and about the new powers our investigations into embryonic stem cells may give us to manipulate or genetically select our future children. But these moral misgivings would never have derailed the enthusiasm for such research. Disease causes such misery and grief for so many families that research on stem cells, with its great promise (though no certainty) of success, was supported by most Americans — and passionately so by many. No, the principal political roadblock to such research was fierce opposition by those in the antiabortion community for whom human embryos are full moral persons, end of story.

Because most of the notable battles fought by right-to-life groups concerned much later stages of prenatal human development — "late-term abortion," for example — the right-to-life movement has successfully avoided calling public attention to implications of its views about the earliest days of embryonic life. Among these implications is the startling inference that common practices at fertility clinics amount to mass murder (more about that later). Public support for embryonic stem cell research posed a quandary for antiabortion leaders: If the president banned all public monies for the research, it would have been inescapably clear that the right-to-life movement had imposed its minority view on the majority of Americans — an obstructionism likely to anger many people.

On the other hand, if the president permitted any public funding, that would amount to complicity with evil: If you believe that destroying an embryo is murder, and if the creation of embryonic stem cell lines can only be accomplished by destroying embryos, then it is difficult to see how you can escape the charge of complicity with that murder, whether it was done before or after an arbitrary deadline of 9:00 P.M. on August 9, 2001. A number of pro-life leaders have already reached that conclusion.

AN ETHICS OF CONVENIENCE

What the president offered allowed the pro-life movement to escape public opprobrium for favoring a disputable metaphysical view that favored the moral status of embryos over relief of palpable human suffering. Beyond that, it is difficult to see what ethical reasoning would commend a policy that takes as its central distinction the time chosen for political convenience to deliver a presidential address. Human embryos will continue to be destroyed in large numbers in fertility clinics. Some fraction of those will be donated to research, and a smaller number still will be used to make stem cell lines, all with private money. This would have been the case whatever the president had said. In any event, imposing an arbitrary deadline has its own costs — moral, economic, political, and scientific.

Paradoxically, getting to sixty-four actually required the administration to loosen ethical constraints recommended by the National Bioethics Advisory Commission and the National Institutes of Health. Rather than limiting researchers to frozen embryos left over from in vitro fertilization after a couple had had ample time to reflect on their decision to give them up, the president's policy would simply permit federal funding of all previously created stem cell lines from embryos created in excess of clinical need, whether or not they were frozen. The requirements for the embryo donors' "informed consent" were loosened in two ways: Rather than listing the specific information that had to be given to prospective donors, the new policy simply required "informed consent." Nor does the retroactive policy require researchers to have waited until after the embryos had been created to approach the donors; they could be asked before. (Without these more relaxed ethical standards, the University of Wisconsin's pre-existing stem cell lines, among others, would not be eligible for federal research funds.) Finally, the new policy does away with an ethics review panel for stem cell research, replacing it with a more generic Council on Bioethics that will not have oversight powers.

Said Richard Doerflinger of the U.S. Conference of Catholic Bishops: "It's very troubling to find that this policy may actually grandfather in cell lines that were ineligible on ethical grounds, even under the Clinton guidelines." Nor is there any guarantee that the committees reviewing the ethics of research with human subjects will accept the informed-consent statements accompanying each cell line, especially from countries whose cultural practices of informed consent may differ from the United States's.

Another irony of the Bush policy, coming from an administration fervent about the virtues of competition, is that by limiting federal funding to the sixty-four lines in existence by August 9, 2001, it locks in an oligopoly. Those few sources that hold stem cell lines and can defend their intellectual-property claims in court are assured of no new competition. NIH is the engine that drives biomedical research in the United States; researchers vie for federal funding, which has three great virtues: prestige, reasonable coverage of the actual costs of research, and enormous intellectual freedom. Other embryonic stem cell lines will be created with private money, but researchers likely will prefer to use lines approved for federal funding. Some subset of the sixty-four lines will probably become the dominant models for basic research in embryonic stem cells for the near future, bolstering the oligopoly that this policy reinforces.

Scientists have complained about barriers to research, too few cell lines, and the uncertainty about how many of the sixty-four lines will be scientifically useful and practically available without unacceptable conditions. Scientists, it should be noted, hold a wide range of political views. But when it comes to research, a bipartisan community of scientists rallies reliably in favor of more funding with an absolute minimum of strings. Both Republicans and Democrats have supported — and funded — an ever-growing National Institutes of Health.

If there are many scientists opposed to funding embryonic stem cell research, they have been fairly quiet — with one exception: David Prentice, from Indiana State University, was plucked from obscurity to became a regular at hearings, on television, and in print reports, insisting that stem cells from adults were every bit as promising as those from embryos. One of the researchers cited in support of this claim is Baylor College of Medicine professor Margaret Goodell, who reported in 1999 that stem cells derived from muscle were able to produce blood cells. This study and similar ones suggested that adult stem cells, rather than being committed to a particular tissue type, might be more versatile. Subsequent research by Goodell, however, has demonstrated that she had discovered an unanticipated type of blood stem cells that happen to reside within muscle. In June she said, "The science doesn't justify . . . saying 'adult stem cells can do anything.'"

MISREPRESENTING SCIENCE

There is an interesting lesson here about science and public policy. Taking a cue from the tobacco industry, pro-life operatives learned that you do not need masses of scientists on your side. For decades tobacco lobbyists trotted out a handful of scientists who were willing to express their doubts about one or another facet of the scientific evidence linking smoking with illness and death. The industry could then say, see, even scientists disagree. They did not bother to inform policy makers and the public that the overwhelming consensus among scientists was that the connection was long since proven. For any given hearing or public forum, they had only to produce a scientist to say what they wanted the audience to hear, even if the opinion was far off the mainstream scientific map. Opponents of embryonic stem cell research hoped to impress policy makers and influence reporting by having even one scientist to provide "balance," much the way the tobacco industry salted hearings and occasionally the scientific literature with their smattering of scientist allies.

The bottom line on adult stem cells is that they are promising, and research on them should be funded as well. But they are more difficult to gather in large numbers, more difficult to grow in the laboratory, and — so far at least — less versatile. Adult stem cells may turn out to be clinically important. But knowledgeable scientists observe that research on embryonic stem cells is necessary to learn how to grow, channel, and perhaps ultimately use adult stem cells.

Will sixty-four embryonic stem cell lines be enough? Will these lines be safe and function correctly? We will begin to know in the next few years, once studies on human subjects get under way. It will not be sufficient merely to have "good enough" stem cell lines: Scientists and the people into whose bodies these cells are placed will want to know that they are the very best we can design.

Imagine a government edict that prohibits drug companies from creating or testing any new compounds and limits them to the ones they've already created. Even if research shows that tweaking the chemical structure a bit would likely yield a better drug — fewer side effects, better therapeutic value — the government's response is, "That's tough." The pressure to lift such a ban would be nearly irresistible. The Bush administration must be hoping that progress is slow enough to avoid such pressures — at least until the next presidential election.

BEHIND THE LINES

While there is no reason to doubt the existence of the sixty-four stem cell lines reported by NIH, nothing guarantees that all the lines will be suitable for research or that those who control the lines will be able and willing to provide them to U.S. researchers. An embryonic stem cell line can lack some of the properties researchers require. The NIH list of eligible cell lines, released on August 27, shows Sweden with the most — twenty-four — and the United States with twenty. It is now clear that the scientific barriers set to declare a particular line as a genuine embryonic stem cell line were very low. This confirms concerns expressed by scientists that not all of the sixty-four eligible lines may be stable and useful for research.

Cell lines can also come with too many strings attached. Late last year, it was reported that Doug Melton, who works at Harvard and is supported by the prestigious Howard Hughes Medical Institute, was unable to use stem cells from the WiCell Research Institute, a subsidiary of WARF, the Wisconsin Alumni Research Foundation, because of two conditions rejected by both Harvard and Hughes. One gives Geron Corporation the rights to certain discoveries that arise from Melton's research using these cells. The other — even more unpalatable, I suspect — gives WiCell the authority to order Melton to destroy the cells and any experiments using them within ninety days. Harvard, with the support of the Howard Hughes Medical Institute, has since struck a deal for embryos with Boston IVF, a fertility clinic.

Geron funded the work at Wisconsin and at Johns Hopkins University that opened the door to human stem cell research. Wisconsin holds the key patent on human embryonic stem cells and has granted exclusive rights to Geron for commercialization of six cell types: blood, bone, liver, muscle, nerve, and pancreas. Nerve cells will be of great interest to people suffering with Parkinson's disease or from a spinal cord injury; islet cells in the pancreas fail in people with diabetes. The Wisconsin Alumni Research Foundation filed a lawsuit against Geron in August. Geron wants exclusive rights to an additional twelve cell types; WARF argues that Geron was obligated to make substantial progress on the six types for which it already holds the rights and has not done so. Geron, by the way, has doubters in other corners as well. A recent column posted on the Motley Fool, a popular finance Web site, was less interested in the ethics of stem cell research than in Geron's balance sheet, which showed the company burning through its remaining cash at a fair clip with little evidence of a breakthrough product in the near future. Scientists are understandably concerned that disputes such as this will make it more difficult to gain access to embryonic stem cells.

Another legal morass also looms. The Wisconsin patent is very broad; it covers both embryonic stem cells and the process for deriving them. The legal status of stem cell lines from other countries will need to be clarified. WARF will want to protect its patent rights from infringement, and the holders of lines outside the United States may not want to risk costly legal battles.

At least one notable U.S. researcher, Roger Pedersen of the University of California San Francisco, has announced his plan to leave for Cambridge University and the more politically hospitable environment of the United Kingdom. If additional scientifically valuable lines are created, or if researchers find ways to create lines without infringing Wisconsin's patent, then scientists working in the United Kingdom and other nations will have an edge over their American counterparts. Other U.S. scientists may follow Pedersen's lead.

There are two additional reasons to worry whether the sixty-four cell lines are adequate. Pedersen points out that mouse "feeder" cells and bovine serum have been used in developing current cell lines, thus creating the possibility that animal viruses or proteins may have contaminated those lines and made them unfit for transplantation into humans. It will be difficult to prove that cell lines created in this manner are free of contaminants.

At this moment, no one knows how the problem of immune rejection will be handled when embryonic stem cells are placed into the human body. Each of our cells carries a set of markers — flags, if you like — on its outside. Our immune system uses these flags to tell friend from possible foe. Preventing such recognition and the subsequent attack on tissue identified as foreign is a lifelong problem for people who receive transplanted organs. Researchers will have to find ways to tame or eliminate immune responses to transplanted stem cells if they are ever to become useful treatments. One of the most likely ways to accomplish this is to create a catalog of stem cell lines representing all the sets of flags (or, if you want to be scientifically precise, the major histocompatibility complex alleles) likely to be found. This might require hundreds or even thousands of lines.

We do not yet know how broad an array of flags is represented in those sixty-four existing lines, but there is no guarantee that they cover a broad spectrum. With the current limited set, some Americans might be fortunate enough to find good matches; many others might not. And because particular flag combinations show up with predictable frequency in different populations, it could be that the out-of-luck folks are disproportionately from specific ethnic groups. Imagine the outcry, the deep feeling of injustice, if Americans whose ancestors came from southern Europe, or Africa, or Asia found that there were no good matches for them in the available pool. Depending on the extent of the mismatch, they might nonetheless be offered stem cell transplants, but they might have to take higher doses of drugs to ward off immune rejection and endure all of the side effects such higher doses bring. In this scenario, entire groups of Americans would be condemned to inferior therapies, solely as a consequence of the president's policy dictum. Any or all of these factors may challenge the stability of the White House policy on stem cell research.

AN EMBRYONIC SPLIT

The most significant and lasting political effect of the debate over embryonic stem cells may be its role as a wedge dividing usually reliable allies in the antiabortion camp. Conservative commentator George F. Will hailed the address as one that "changes American politics profoundly." Will may be more correct than he realizes. In lofty language more suited to a college commencement address than a political column, he applauded Bush's "measured and principled" position as far better than any compromise. Rather, he wrote, it is nothing less than a "solution . . . in strict fidelity to his campaign promise" not to fund research "that involves destroying living human embryos." He further asserted that the president's critics are "in danger of embracing extremism." In his applause for Bush's statement, Will has plenty of company on the right, including Pat Robertson, Jerry Falwell, and James Dobson of Focus on the Family.

But there is serious grumbling in the right-to-life camp. Columnist Cal Thomas composed a screed condemning the Bush policy as "fruit of the poisoned tree" — a door opened on a culture headed to perdition ever since *Roe v. Wade*. Thomas compared Europe's exterminated Jews to the "millions of unborn babies" who "had the bad luck to be conceived in the antilife era that began in 1973 . . . but had its roots in an anti-God culture which began decades earlier." Why not, Thomas wonders, kill the elderly and the infirm, or the relative whose estate you are tired of waiting to inherit? The logic, he writes, starts with using embryos for research and carries us relentlessly onward to euthanasia and beyond. The Roman Catholic bishops have been consistent in their criticism, and the editor of a Catholic magazine laments the decision to fund embryonic stem cell research as a "descent into chaos, barbarism, anarchy, tyranny, and death." So much for unity within the pro-life movement.

It was no accident that one of the earliest important voices among abortion opponents to support embryonic stem cell research was a Mormon, Republican Senator Orrin Hatch. Mormon theology holds that all of us begin as spirit children of God; our earthly lives begin when our spirit is united with our physical body, and that may not coincide with conception. (It is misleading to refer to the "moment" of conception, as the actual process is complex, involving multiple steps over a period of time.)

Doerflinger, of the U.S. Conference of Catholic Bishops, derided as "amateur theology" the efforts of another Mormon senator, Gordon Smith of Oregon, to distinguish between the flesh and the spirit in the creation of life. In a similar vein, he ridiculed Senator Hatch as claiming that there is "something magical about the mother's womb," alluding to the Utah senator's argument that an embryo frozen in liquid nitrogen is different from one implanted in a woman. Doerflinger said one more thing worth noting. Acknowledging that he cannot persuade Senator Hatch to abandon the tenets of his faith, he concluded nonetheless, "I don't think he should make the rest of us fund this research based on them." Or refuse to fund it?

It isn't only Mormons within the nominally pro-life camp who support embryonic stem cell research. Just as defenders of a woman's right to abortion found that not all who shared their general view were equally ardent in their defense of late-term abortion, not all abortion opponents are equally convinced that the (relatively) clear and bright line of fertilization marks the indisputable beginning of a human person. Whatever your stance on abortion, you can believe that human embryos, even in their first few days of development, are much more than mere pinpoints of human tissue, though not identical physically or morally with children or even fetuses. Indeed, that statement, vague as it is, probably describes roughly what most Americans believe.

The antiabortion movement has been able to escape confronting latent disagreements over the moral standing of frozen in vitro human embryos — until now. The debate over embryonic stem cells has brought the fate of excess in vitro fertilization (IVF) embryos before the public as people are increasingly aware that embryos are routinely created through IVF, frozen, and discarded. Some are flushed down the drain, some taken out as medical waste, others thawed and permitted to expire on their own. The precise number of embryos destroyed in the United States is not known, in part owing to the astonishingly minimal regulation of IVF and related reproductive technologies. Britain has recorded some 50,000 IVF births since 1991, with nearly 300,000 embryos discarded. The American Society for Reproductive Medicine estimates that roughly 100,000 babies have been born through IVF in the United States. If the same ratio holds here as in Britain, approximately 600,000 embryos would have been destroyed in the last decade.

Where, you might ask, is the outcry over the mass murder taking place in infertility clinics? The moral logic seems inescapable: If you believe that human embryos are persons, then their intentional destruction is a grievous moral offense. Disposing of an embryo after five years in the deep freeze is morally indistinguishable from aborting a mid-trimester fetus or killing a child or an adult. Yet, there is no broad social movement to condemn in vitro fertilization, to close the clinics performing it, or to harass or intimidate the physicians who work there. Nor are there crowds of demonstrators accusing couples who enter such clinics of being murderers.

The Catholic Church has been consistent in its disapproval of IVF but has not chosen to highlight its position to the American public or to expend political resources to try to stop the practice. The National Right to Life Committee has gone lately from saying that IVF "is outside our purview" to refusing to comment in a recent *Christian Science Monitor* story on the increasing calls for regulation of fertility clinics.

The truth is that most Americans probably do not agree with the founder of the Snowflakes Embryo Adoption Program that frozen embryos are "preborn children," nor with his employee who asserted, "We believe life begins at conception, so every one of these frozen embryos is a baby waiting for a home." In his August 9 address, the president borrowed the snowflake metaphor to describe embryos. According to the Snowflakes Program, eight children have been born thus far from its "adopted" embryos, with seven more on the way (being carried by four women). We can take delight when people have a wanted child, rejoicing for them and for their baby. But that does not oblige us to believe that every single one of the 150,000 or 200,000 — no one knows the actual number — frozen embryos in the United States must be placed in a womb, or that choosing to thaw an embryo without implanting it is murder.

ETHICAL THREADS

Thinking responsibly and sensitively about human embryos is not easy. Some years ago, when I was writing *The Worth of a Child*, I tried a thought experiment: Imagine some new fact or argument so utterly persuasive that it caused virtually all persons on one side of the moral-status-of-the-embryo divide to acknowledge that they had been wrong all this time and that, yes, the other side was correct.

Maybe my imagination is defective, but I don't see that happening. For one thing, there seems little or nothing new to be said. For another, there is faint prospect that great masses of people would turn 180 degrees on a metaphysical dime.

Note that I did not say which side was changing its mind. A philosophical conversion is equally unlikely for both. You can recruit a variety of scientific evidence, moral arguments, or metaphysical claims to support whichever position you hold. Treating folks who disagree with you as mental (and moral) midgets accomplishes nothing worthwhile. It would be far better to reflect on the central threads of the tapestries formed by our images of good lives for women, children, and men; the reasons we value families; and the losses we most fear. I believe that we would find important differences between the threads of those who assert that embryos, even those immersed in liquid nitrogen, are morally identical with born children and adults and the threads of those who discern a distinction. These differences likely will have to do with whether good lives for women and for men are fundamentally similar or distinct; whether men are capable of nurturing and women of competing; whether women are meant to raise children while men, in Newt Gingrich's unforgettable description, are meant to hunt giraffes.

If the dispute over funding research on human embryonic stem cells brings to light some of the implications of the view that embryos are full and complete moral persons and holds those implications out for public inspection, that will be useful. If it leads to closer scrutiny of the infertility industry, that will be good. If it prompts us to look deeply into the tapestries that inform and order our lives and examine their relationship to public debates over abortion, affirmative action, and family policy, that will be an extraordinarily valuable outcome.

20. The Wisdom of Repugnance

LEON R. KASS

The notion of cloning human beings has been a staple of science fiction at least since Aldous Huxley's Brave New World *(1932). It moved a large step closer to reality in 1997 when Ian Wilmut, a Scottish scientist, succeeded in cloning a sheep from an adult cell. While some scientists expressed skepticism about whether Wilmut had really accomplished what he claimed, a number of other experimenters have since reported success in cloning large mammals. Cloning sheep is still far removed from cloning humans, but the threshold has been crossed. Geneticists and reproductive scientists generally agree that cloning humans is possible, although they differ on how soon it could actually be accomplished. Consequently, the ethical, religious, and policy dimensions of this new technology have exploded into public discussion.*

There are profound risks in going down the road that is opened by the prospect of human cloning, believes Leon Kass. "Cloning personifies our desire fully to control the future," he writes. We are so enchanted by technology that we have lost sight of the mysteries of nature and of life. At the same time, however, many people intuitively recoil from the idea of cloning human beings, finding it repugnant. There is good reason for this, Kass argues, for it violates very basic notions of human dignity. In a concise and clearly argued essay, Kass explains the reasons for his beliefs and suggests what the government and we, as individuals, should do.

Leon Kass is a highly respected scholar of biomedical ethics. He is the Addie Clark Harding Professor in the Committee on Social Thought and the College of the University of Chicago and the author of Toward a More Natural Science: Biology and Human Affairs *(1988) and* The Hungry Soul: Eating and the Perfecting of Our Nature *(1994). Kass is a graduate of the University of Chicago School of Medicine and also holds a Ph.D. in biochemistry from Harvard University. He has served as a surgeon for the U.S. Public Health Service and has held positions in the field of medical ethics at the National Academy of Science, St. John's College, and the Kennedy Institute of Ethics at Georgetown University. In August 2001, he was named chair of the new Council on Biomedical Ethics by President Bush. (See Chapter 18.)*

THE STATE OF THE ART

If we should not underestimate the significance of human cloning, neither should we exaggerate its imminence or misunderstand just what is involved. The procedure is conceptually simple. The nucleus of a mature but unfertilized egg is removed and replaced with a nucleus obtained from a specialized cell of an adult

From *The Ethics of Human Cloning* by Leon R. Kass and James Q. Wilson (Washington, DC: AEI Press, 1998), pp. 3–59.

(or fetal) organism (in Dolly's case, the donor nucleus came from mammary epithelium). Since almost all the hereditary material of a cell is contained within its nucleus, the renucleated egg and the individual into which that egg develops are genetically identical to the organism that was the source of the transferred nucleus. An unlimited number of genetically identical individuals — clones — could be produced by nuclear transfer. In principle, any person, male or female, newborn or adult, could be cloned, and in any quantity. With laboratory cultivation and storage of tissues, cells outliving their sources make it possible even to clone the dead.

The technical stumbling block, overcome by Wilmut and his colleagues, was to find a means of reprogramming the state of the DNA in the donor cells, reversing its differentiated expression and restoring its full totipotency, so that it could again direct the entire process of producing a mature organism. Now that the problem has been solved, we should expect a rush to develop cloning for other animals, especially livestock, to propagate in perpetuity the champion meat or milk producers. Though exactly how soon someone will succeed in cloning a human being is anybody's guess, Wilmut's technique, almost certainly applicable to humans, makes attempting the feat an imminent possibility.

Yet, some cautions are in order, and some possible misconceptions need correcting. For a start, cloning is not Xeroxing. As has been reassuringly reiterated, the clone of Mel Gibson, though his genetic double, would enter the world hairless, toothless, and peeing in his diapers, just like any other human infant. Moreover, the success rate, at least at first, will probably not be very high: The British transferred 277 adult nuclei into enucleated sheep eggs and implanted twenty-nine clonal embryos, but they achieved the birth of only one live lamb clone. For that reason, among others, it is unlikely that, at least for now, the practice would be very popular, and there is no immediate worry of mass-scale production of multicopies. The need of repeated surgery to obtain eggs and, more crucially, of numerous borrowed wombs for implantation will surely limit use, as will the expense; besides, almost everyone who is able will doubtless prefer nature's sexier way of conceiving.

Still, for the tens of thousands of people already sustaining over 200 assisted-reproduction clinics in the United States and already availing themselves of in vitro fertilization, intracytoplasmic sperm injection, and other techniques of assisted reproduction, cloning would be an option with virtually no added fuss (especially when the success rate improves). Should commercial interests develop in "nucleus banking," as they have in sperm banking; should famous athletes or other celebrities decide to market their DNA the way they now market their autographs and just about everything else; should techniques of embryo and germline genetic testing and manipulation arrive as anticipated, increasing the use of laboratory assistance to obtain "better" babies — should all this come to pass, then cloning, if it is permitted, could become more than a marginal practice simply on the basis of free reproductive choice, even without any social encouragement to upgrade the gene pool or to replicate superior types. Moreover, if laboratory research on human cloning proceeds, even without any intention to produce cloned humans, the existence of cloned human embryos in the laboratory, created to begin with only for research purposes, would surely pave the way for later baby-making implantations.

In anticipation of human cloning, apologists and proponents have already made clear possible uses of the perfected technology, ranging from the sentimental and compassionate to the grandiose. They include providing a child for an infertile couple; "replacing" a beloved spouse or child who is dying or has died; avoiding the risk of genetic disease; permitting reproduction for homosexual men and lesbians who want nothing sexual to do with the opposite sex; securing a genetically identical source of organs or tissues perfectly suitable for transplantation; getting a child with a genotype of one's own choosing, not excluding oneself; replicating individuals of great genius, talent, or beauty — having a child who really could "be like Mike"; and creating large sets of genetically identical humans suitable for research on, for instance, the question of nature versus nurture, or for special missions in peace and war (not excluding espionage), in which using identical humans would be an advantage. Most people who envision the cloning of human beings, of course, want none of those scenarios. That they cannot say why is not surprising. What is surprising, and welcome, is that, in our cynical age, they are saying anything at all.

THE WISDOM OF REPUGNANCE

Offensive, grotesque, revolting, repugnant, and repulsive — those are the words most commonly heard regarding the prospect of human cloning. Such reactions come both from the man or woman in the street and from the intellectuals, from believers and atheists, from humanists and scientists. Even Dolly's creator has said he "would find it offensive" to clone a human being.

People are repelled by many aspects of human cloning. They recoil from the prospect of mass production of human beings, with large clones of look-alikes, compromised in their individuality; the idea of father–son or mother–daughter twins; the bizarre prospects of a woman's giving birth to and rearing a genetic copy of herself, her spouse, or even her deceased father or mother; the grotesqueness of conceiving a child as an exact replacement for another who has died; the utilitarian creation of embryonic genetic duplicates of oneself, to be frozen away or created when necessary, in case of need for homologous tissues or organs for transplantation; the narcissism of those who would clone themselves and the arrogance of others who think they know who deserves to be cloned or which genotype any child-to-be should be thrilled to receive; the Frankensteinian hubris to create human life and increasingly to control its destiny; man playing God. Almost no one finds any of the suggested reasons for human cloning compelling; almost everyone anticipates its possible misuses and abuses. Moreover, many people feel oppressed by the sense that there is probably nothing we can do to prevent it from happening. That makes the prospect all the more revolting.

Revulsion is not an argument, and some of yesterday's repugnances are today calmly accepted — though, one must add, not always for the better. In crucial cases, however, repugnance is the emotional expression of deep wisdom, beyond reason's power fully to articulate it. Can anyone really give an argument fully ade-quate to the horror that is father–daughter incest (even with consent), or having sex with animals, or mutilating a corpse, or eating human flesh, or raping or mur-dering another human being? Would anybody's failure to give full rational justifi-cation for his revulsion at those practices make that revulsion ethically suspect? Not at all. On the contrary, we are suspicious of those who think that they can rationalize away our horror, say, by trying to explain the enormity of incest with arguments only about the genetic risks of inbreeding.

The repugnance at human cloning belongs in that category. We are repelled by the prospect of cloning human beings not because of the strangeness or novelty of the undertaking, but because we intuit and feel, immediately and without argu-ment, the violation of things that we rightfully hold dear. Repugnance, here as elsewhere, revolts against the excesses of human willfulness, warning us not to transgress what is unspeakably profound. Indeed, in this age in which everything is held to be permissible so long as it is freely done, in which our given human nature no longer commands respect, in which our bodies are regarded as mere instruments of our autonomous rational wills, repugnance may be the only voice left that speaks up to defend the central core of our humanity. Shallow are the souls that have forgotten how to shudder.

The goods protected by repugnance are generally overlooked by our customary ways of approaching all new biomedical technologies. The way we evaluate cloning ethically will in fact be shaped by how we characterize it descriptively, by the context into which we place it, and by the perspective from which we view it. The first task for ethics is proper description. And here is where our failure begins.

Typically, cloning is discussed in one or more of three familiar contexts, which one might call the technological, the liberal, and the meliorist. Under the first, cloning will be seen as an extension of existing techniques for assisting reproduc-tion and determining the genetic makeup of children. Like them, cloning is to be regarded as a neutral technique, with no inherent meaning or goodness, but sub-ject to multiple uses, some good, some bad. The morality of cloning thus depends absolutely on the goodness or badness of the motives and intentions of the clon-ers. As one bioethicist defender of cloning puts it, "The ethics must be judged [only] by the way the parents nurture and rear their resulting child and whether they bestow the same love and affection on a child brought into existence by a technique of assisted reproduction as they would on a child born in the usual way."

The liberal (or libertarian or liberationist) perspective sets cloning in the con-text of rights, freedoms, and personal empowerment. Cloning is just a new option for exercising an individual's right to reproduce or to have the kind of child that he wants. Alternatively, cloning enhances our liberation (especially women's lib-eration) from the confines of nature, the vagaries of chance, or the necessity for sexual mating. Indeed, it liberates women from the need for men altogether, for the process requires only eggs, nuclei, and (for the time being) uteri — plus, of course, a healthy dose of our (allegedly "masculine") manipulative science that likes to do all those things to Mother Nature and nature's mothers. For those who hold this outlook, the only moral restraints on cloning are adequately informed consent and the avoidance of bodily harm. If no one is cloned without her consent, and if the clonant is not physically damaged, then the liberal conditions for licit, hence moral, conduct are met. Worries that go beyond violating the will or maiming the body are dismissed as "symbolic" — which is to say, unreal.

The meliorist perspective embraces valetudinarians and also eugenicists. The latter were formerly more vocal in those discussions, but they are now generally happy to see their goals advanced under the less threatening banners of freedom and technological growth. These people see in cloning a new prospect for improving human beings — minimally, by ensuring the perpetuation of healthy individuals by avoiding the risks of genetic disease inherent in the lottery of sex, and, maximally, by producing "optimum babies," preserving outstanding genetic material, and (with the help of soon-to-come techniques for precise genetic engineering) enhancing inborn human capacities on many fronts. Here the morality of cloning as a means is justified solely by the excellence of the end, that is, by the outstanding traits of individuals cloned — beauty, or brawn, or brains.

These three approaches, all quintessentially American and all perfectly fine in their places, are sorely wanting as approaches to human procreation. It is, to say the least, grossly distorting to view the wondrous mysteries of birth, renewal, and individuality, and the deep meaning of parent–child relations, largely through the lens of our reductive science and its potent technologies. Similarly, considering reproduction (and the intimate relations of family life) primarily under the political-legal, adversarial, and individualistic notion of rights can only undermine the private yet fundamentally social, cooperative, and duty-laden character of child bearing, child rearing, and their bond to the covenant of marriage. Seeking to escape entirely from nature (to satisfy a natural desire or a natural right to reproduce) is self-contradictory in theory and self-alienating in practice. For we are erotic beings only because we are embodied beings and not merely intellects and wills unfortunately imprisoned in our bodies. And, though health and fitness are clearly great goods, there is something deeply disquieting in looking on our prospective children as artful products perfectible by genetic engineering, increasingly held to our willfully imposed designs, specifications, and margins of tolerable error.

The technical, liberal, and meliorist approaches all ignore the deeper anthropological, social, and, indeed, ontological meanings of bringing forth a new life. To this more fitting and profound point of view cloning shows itself to be a major violation of our given nature as embodied, gendered, and engendering beings — and of the social relations built on this natural ground. Once this perspective is recognized, the ethical judgment on cloning can no longer be reduced to a matter of motives and intentions, rights and freedoms, benefits and harms, or even means and ends. It must be regarded primarily as a matter of meaning: Is cloning a fulfillment of human begetting and belonging? Or is cloning rather, as I contend, their pollution and perversion? To pollution and perversion the fitting response can only be horror and revulsion, and, conversely, generalized horror and revulsion are prima facie evidence of foulness and violation. The burden of moral argument must fall entirely on those who want to declare the widespread repugnances of humankind to be mere timidity or superstition.

Yet, repugnance need not stand naked before the bar of reason. The wisdom of our horror at human cloning can be partially articulated, even if this is finally one of those instances about which the heart has its reasons that reason cannot entirely know.

THE PROFUNDITY OF SEX

To see cloning in its proper context, we must begin not, as I did before, with laboratory technique, but with the anthropology — natural and social — of sexual reproduction.

Sexual reproduction — by which I mean the generation of new life from (exactly) two complementary elements, one female, one male, (usually) through coitus — is established (if that is the right term) not by human decision, culture, or tradition, but by nature; it is the natural way of all mammalian reproduction. By nature, each child has two complementary biological progenitors. Each child thus stems from and unites exactly two lineages. In natural generation, moreover, the precise genetic constitution of the resulting offspring is determined by a combination of nature and chance, not by human design: Each human child shares the common natural human species genotype, each child is genetically (equally) kin to each (both) parent(s), yet each child is also genetically unique.

Those biological truths about our origins foretell deep truths about our identity and about our human condition altogether. Every one of us is at once equally human, equally enmeshed in a particular familial nexus of origin, and equally individuated in our trajectory from birth to death — and, if all goes well, equally capable (despite our mortality) of participating, with a complementary other, in the very same renewal of such human possibility through procreation. Though less momentous than our common humanity, our genetic individuality is not humanly trivial. It shows itself forth in our distinctive appearance, through which we are everywhere recognized; it is revealed in our "signature" marks of fingerprints and our self-recognizing immune system; it symbolizes and foreshadows exactly the unique, never-to-be-repeated character of each human life.

Human societies virtually everywhere have structured child-rearing responsibilities and systems of identity and relationship on the bases of those deep, natural facts of begetting. The mysterious yet ubiquitous "love of one's own" is everywhere culturally exploited, to make sure that children are not just produced but well cared for and to create for everyone clear ties of meaning, belonging, and obligation. But it is wrong to treat such naturally rooted social practices as mere cultural constructs (like left- or right-driving, or like burying or cremating the dead) that we can alter with little human cost. What would kinship be without its clear, natural grounding? And what would identity be without kinship? We must resist those who have begun to refer to sexual reproduction as the "traditional method of reproduction," who would have us regard as merely traditional, and by implication arbitrary, what is in truth not only natural but most certainly profound.

Asexual reproduction, which produces "single-parent" offspring, is a radical departure from the natural human way, confounding all normal understandings of father, mother, sibling, and grandparent and all moral relations tied thereto. It becomes even more of a radical departure when the resulting offspring is a clone derived not from an embryo, but from a mature adult to whom the clone would be an identical twin; and when the process occurs not by natural accident (as in natural twinning), but by deliberate human design and manipulation; and when the child's (or children's) genetic constitution is preselected by the parent(s) (or scientists). Accordingly, as we shall see, cloning is vulnerable to three kinds of concerns and objections, related to these three points: Cloning threatens confusion of identity and individuality, even in small-scale cloning; cloning represents a giant step (though not the first one) toward transforming procreation into manufacture, that is, toward the increasing depersonalization of the process of generation and, increasingly, toward the "production" of human children as artifacts, products of human will and design (what others have called the problem of "commodification" of new life); and cloning — like other forms of eugenic engineering of the next generation — represents a form of despotism of the cloners over the cloned and thus (even in benevolent cases) represents a blatant violation of the inner meaning of parent–child relations, of what it means to have a child, of what it means to say yes to our own demise and "replacement."

Before turning to those specific ethical objections, let me test my claim of the profundity of the natural way by taking up a challenge recently posed by a friend. What if the given natural human way of reproduction were asexual, and we now had to deal with a new technological innovation — artificially induced sexual dimorphism and the fusing of complementary gametes — whose inventors argued that sexual reproduction promised all sorts of advantages, including hybrid vigor and the creation of greatly increased individuality? Would one then be forced to defend natural asexuality because it was natural? Could one claim that it carried deep human meaning?

The response to that challenge broaches the ontological meaning of sexual reproduction. For it is impossible, I submit, for there to have been human life — or even higher forms of animal life — in the absence of sexuality and sexual reproduction. We find asexual reproduction only in the lowest forms of life: bacteria, algae, fungi, some lower invertebrates. Sexuality brings with it a new and enriched relationship to the world. Only sexual animals can seek and find complementary others with whom to pursue a goal that transcends their own existence. For a sexual being, the world is no longer an indifferent and largely homogeneous otherness, in part edible, in part dangerous. It also contains some very special and related and complementary beings, of the same kind but of opposite sex, toward whom one reaches out with special interest and intensity. In higher birds and mammals, the outward gaze keeps a lookout not only for food and predators, but also for prospective mates; the beholding of the many-splendored world is suffused with desire for union — the animal antecedent of human eros and the germ of sociality. Not by accident is the human animal both the sexiest animal — whose females do not go into heat but are receptive throughout the estrous cycle and whose males must therefore have greater sexual appetite and energy to reproduce successfully — and also the most aspiring, the most social, the most open, and the most intelligent animal.

The soul-elevating power of sexuality is, at bottom, rooted in its strange connection to mortality, which it simultaneously accepts and tries to overcome. Asexual reproduction may be seen as a continuation of the activity of self-preservation.

When one organism buds or divides to become two, the original being is (doubly) preserved, and nothing dies. Sexuality, by contrast, means perishability and serves replacement; the two that come together to generate one soon will die. Sexual desire, in human beings as in animals, thus serves an end that is partly hidden from, and finally at odds with, the self-serving individual. Whether we know it or not, when we are sexually active we are voting with our genitalia for our own demise. The salmon swimming upstream to spawn and die tell the universal story: Sex is bound up with death, to which it holds a partial answer in procreation.

The salmon and the other animals evince that truth blindly. Only the human being can understand what it means. As we learn so powerfully from the story of the Garden of Eden, our humanization is coincident with sexual self-consciousness, with the recognition of our sexual nakedness and all that it implies: shame at our needy incompleteness, unruly self-division, and finitude; awe before the eternal; hope in the self-transcending possibilities of children and a relationship to the divine. In the sexually self-conscious animal, sexual desire can become eros, lust can become love. Sexual desire humanly regarded is thus sublimated into erotic longing for wholeness, completion, and immortality, which drives us knowingly into the embrace and its generative fruit — as well as into all the higher human possibilities of deed, speech, and song.

Through children, a good common to both husband and wife, male and female achieve some genuine unification (beyond the mere sexual "union," which fails to do so). The two become one through sharing generous (not needy) love for that third being as good. Flesh of their flesh, the child is the parents' own commingled being externalized and given a separate and persisting existence. Unification is enhanced also by their commingled work of rearing. Providing an opening to the future beyond the grave, carrying not only our seed but also our names, our ways, and our hopes that they will surpass us in goodness and happiness, children are a testament to the possibility of transcendence. Gender duality and sexual desire, which first draw our love upward and outside of ourselves, finally provide for the partial overcoming of the confinement and limitation of perishable embodiment altogether.

Human procreation, in sum, is not simply an activity of our rational wills. It is a more complete activity precisely because it engages us bodily, erotically, and spiritually as well as rationally. There is wisdom in the mystery of nature that has joined the pleasure of sex, the inarticulate longing for union, the communication of the loving embrace, and the deep-seated and only partly articulate desire for children in the very activity by which we continue the chain of human existence and participate in the renewal of human possibility. Whether or not we know it, the severing of procreation from sex, love, and intimacy is inherently dehumanizing, no matter how good the product.

We are now ready for the more specific objections to cloning.

THE PERVERSITIES OF CLONING

First, an important if formal objection: Any attempt to clone a human being would constitute an unethical experiment upon the resulting child-to-be. As the animal experiments (frog and sheep) indicate, there are grave risks of mishaps and deformities. Moreover, because of what cloning means, one cannot presume a future cloned child's consent to be a clone, even a healthy one. Thus, ethically speaking, we cannot even get to know whether or not human cloning is feasible.

I understand, of course, the philosophical difficulty of trying to compare a life with defects against nonexistence. Several bioethicists, proud of their philosophical cleverness, use that conundrum to embarrass claims that one can injure a child in its conception, precisely because it is only thanks to that complained-of conception that the child is alive to complain. But common sense tells us that we have no reason to fear such philosophisms. For we surely know that people can harm and even maim children in the very act of conceiving them, say, by paternal transmission of the AIDS virus, maternal transmission of heroin dependence, or, arguably, even by bringing them into being as bastards or with no capacity or willingness to look after them properly. And we believe that to do that intentionally, or even negligently, is inexcusable and clearly unethical.

The objection about the impossibility of presuming consent may even go beyond the obvious and sufficient point that a clonant, were he subsequently to be asked, could rightly resent having been made a clone. At issue are not just benefits and harms, but doubts about the very independence needed to give proper (even retroactive) consent, that is, not just the capacity to choose but the disposition and ability to choose freely and well. It is not at all clear to what extent a clone will fully be a moral agent. For, as we shall see, in the very fact of cloning, and especially of rearing him as a clone, his makers subvert the cloned child's independence, beginning with that aspect that comes from knowing that one was an unbidden surprise, a gift to the world, rather than the designed result of someone's artful project.

Cloning creates serious issues of identity and individuality. The cloned person may experience concerns about his distinctive identity not only because he will be in genotype and appearance identical to another human being, but, in this case, because he may also be twin to the person who is his "father" or "mother" — if one can still call them that. What would be the psychic burdens of being the "child" or "parent" of your twin? The cloned individual, moreover, will be saddled with a genotype that has already lived. He will not be fully a surprise to the world. People are likely always to compare his performances in life with that of his alter ego. True, his nurture and his circumstance in life will be different; genotype is not exactly destiny. Still, one must also expect parental and other efforts to shape that new life after the original — or at least to view the child with the original version always firmly in mind. Why else did they clone from the star basketball player, mathematician, and beauty queen — or even dear old dad — in the first place?

Since the birth of Dolly, there has been a fair amount of doublespeak on the matter of genetic identity. Experts have rushed in to reassure the public that the clone would in no way be the same person or have any confusions about his identity: As previously noted, they are pleased to point out that the clone of Mel Gibson would not be Mel Gibson. Fair enough. But one is shortchanging the truth by emphasizing the additional importance of the intrauterine environment, rearing, and social setting: Genotype obviously matters plenty. That, after all, is the only reason to clone, whether human beings or sheep. The odds that clones of Wilt Chamberlain will play in the NBA are, I submit, infinitely greater than they are for clones of [five-foot-tall former Secretary of Labor] Robert Reich.

Curiously, this conclusion is supported, inadvertently, by the one ethical sticking point insisted on by friends of cloning: no cloning without the donor's consent. Though an orthodox liberal objection, it is in fact quite puzzling when it comes from people (such as Ruth Macklin) who also insist that genotype is not identity or individuality and who deny that a child could reasonably complain about being made a genetic copy. If the clone of Mel Gibson would not be Mel Gibson, why should Mel Gibson have grounds to object that someone had been made his clone? We already allow researchers to use blood and tissue samples for research purposes of no benefit to their sources: My falling hair, my expectorations, my urine, and even my biopsied tissues are "not me" and not mine. Courts have held that the profit gained from uses to which scientists put my discarded tissues do not legally belong to me. Why, then, no cloning without consent — including, I assume, no cloning from the body of someone who just died? What harm is done the donor, if genotype is "not me"? Truth to tell, the only powerful justification for objecting is that genotype really does have something to do with identity, and everybody knows it. If not, on what basis could Michael Jordan object that someone cloned "him," say, from cells taken from a "lost," scraped-off piece of his skin? The insistence on donor consent unwittingly reveals the problem of identity in all cloning.

Genetic distinctiveness not only symbolizes the uniqueness of each human life and the independence of its parents that each human child rightfully attains. It can also be an important support for living a worthy and dignified life. Such arguments apply with great force to any large-scale replication of human individuals. But they are sufficient, in my view, to rebut even the first attempts to clone a human being. One must never forget that these are human beings upon whom our eugenic or merely playful fantasies are to be enacted.

Troubled psychic identity (distinctiveness), based on all-too-evident genetic identity (sameness), will be made much worse by the utter confusion of social identity and kinship ties. For, as already noted, cloning radically confounds lineage and social relations, for "offspring" as for "parents." As bioethicist James Nelson has pointed out, a female child cloned from her "mother" might develop a desire for a relationship to her "father" and might understandably seek out the father of her "mother," who is after all also her biological twin sister. Would "grandpa," who thought his paternal duties concluded, be pleased to discover that the clonant looked to him for paternal attention and support?

Social identity and social ties of relationship and responsibility are widely connected to, and supported by, biological kinship. Social taboos on incest (and adultery) everywhere serve to keep clear who is related to whom (and especially which child belongs to which parents), as well as to avoid confounding the social identity of parent and child (or brother and sister) with the social identity of lovers, spouses, and coparents. True, social identity is altered by adoption (but as a matter of the best interest of already living children: We do not deliberately produce children for adoption). True, artificial insemination and in vitro fertilization with donor sperm, or whole embryo donation, are in some way forms of "prenatal adoption" — a not altogether unproblematic practice. Even here, though, there is in each case (as in all sexual reproduction) a known male source of sperm and a known single female source of egg — a genetic father and a genetic mother — should anyone care to know (as adopted children often do) who is genetically related to whom.

In the case of cloning, however, there is but one "parent." The usually sad situation of the "single-parent child" is here deliberately planned, and with a vengeance. In the case of self-cloning, the "offspring" is, in addition, one's twin, and so the dreaded result of incest — to be parent to one's sibling — is here brought about deliberately, albeit without any act of coitus. Moreover, all other relationships will be confounded. What will "father," "grandfather," "aunt," "cousin," and "sister" mean? Who will bear what ties and what burdens? What sort of social identity will someone have with one whole side "father's" or "mother's" — necessarily excluded? It is no answer to say that our society, high incidence of divorce, remarriage, adoption, extramarital childbearing, and the rest, already confounds lineage and confuses kinship and responsibility for children (and everyone else), unless one also wants to argue that this is, for children, a preferable state of affairs.

Human cloning would also represent a giant step toward turning begetting into making, procreation into manufacture (literally, something "handmade"), a process already begun with in vitro fertilization and genetic testing of embryos. With cloning, not only is the process in hand, but the total genetic blueprint of the cloned individual is selected and determined by the human artisans. To be sure, subsequent development will take place according to natural processes, and the resulting children will still be recognizably human. But we here would be taking a major step into making man himself simply another one of the man-made things. Human nature becomes merely the last part of nature to succumb to the technological project, which turns all of nature into raw material at human disposal, to be homogenized by our rationalized technique according to the subjective prejudices of the day.

How does begetting differ from making? In natural procreation, human beings come together, complementarily male and female, to give existence to another being who is formed, exactly as we were, by what we are: living, hence perishable, hence aspiringly erotic, human beings. In clonal reproduction, by contrast, and in the more advanced forms of manufacture to which it leads, we give existence to a being not by what we are but by what we intend and design. As with any product of our making, no matter how excellent, the artificer stands above it, not as an equal but as a superior, transcending it by his will and creative prowess. Scientists who clone animals make it perfectly clear that they are engaged in instrumental making; the animals are, from the start, designed as means to serve rational human purposes. In human cloning, scientists and prospective "parents" would be adopting the same technocratic mentality to human children: Human children would be their artifacts.

Such an arrangement is profoundly dehumanizing, no matter how good the product. Mass-scale cloning of the same individual makes the point vividly, but the violation of human equality, freedom, and dignity is present even in a single planned clone. And procreation dehumanized into manufacture is further degraded by commodification, a virtually inescapable result of allowing baby making to proceed under the banner of commerce. Genetic and reproductive biotechnology companies are already growth industries, but they will go into commercial orbit once the [federal government's] Human Genome Project nears completion. Supply will create enormous demand. Even before the capacity for human cloning arrives, established companies will have invested in the harvesting of eggs from ovaries obtained at autopsy or through ovarian surgery, practiced embryonic genetic alteration, and initiated the stockpiling of prospective donor tissues. Through the rental of surrogate-womb services and through the buying and selling of tissues and embryos, priced according to the merit of the donor, the commodification of nascent human life will be unstoppable.

Finally, and perhaps most important, the practice of human cloning by nuclear transfer — like other anticipated forms of genetic engineering of the next generation — would enshrine and aggravate a profound and mischievous misunderstanding of the meaning of having children and of the parent–child relationship. When a couple now chooses to procreate, the partners are saying yes to the emergence of new life in its novelty, saying yes not only to having a child but also, tacitly, to having whatever child the child turns out to be. In accepting our finitude and opening ourselves to our replacement, we are tacitly confessing the limits of our control. In this ubiquitous way of nature, embracing the future by procreating means precisely that we are relinquishing our grip, in the very activity of taking up our own share in what we hope will be the immortality of human life and the human species. This means that our children are not our children: They are not our property, not our possessions. Neither are they supposed to live our lives for us, or anyone else's life but their own. To be sure, we seek to guide them on their way, imparting to them not just life but nurturing, love, and a way of life; to be sure, they bear our hopes that they will live fine and flourishing lives, enabling us in small measure to transcend our own limitations. Still, their genetic distinctiveness and independence are the natural foreshadowing of the deep truth that they have their own and never-before-enacted life to live. They are sprung from a past, but they take an uncharted course into the future.

Much harm is already done by parents who try to live vicariously through their children. Children are sometimes compelled to fulfill the broken dreams of unhappy parents; John Doe, Jr., or John Doe III is under the burden of having to live up to his forebear's name. Still, if most parents have hopes for their children, cloning parents will have expectations. In cloning, such overbearing parents take at the start a decisive step that contradicts the entire meaning of the open and forward-looking nature of parent–child relations. The child is given a genotype that has already lived, with full expectation that the blueprint of a past life ought to be controlling of the life that is to come. Cloning is inherently despotic, for it seeks to make one's children (or someone else's children) after one's own image (or an image of one's choosing) and their future according to one's will. In some cases, the despotism may be mild and benevolent. In other cases, it will be mischievous and downright tyrannical. But despotism — the control of another through one's will — it inevitably will be.

MEETING SOME OBJECTIONS

The defenders of cloning, of course, are not wittingly friends of despotism. Indeed, they regard themselves mainly as friends of freedom: the freedom of individuals to reproduce, the freedom of scientists and inventors to discover and devise and to foster "progress" in genetic knowledge and technique. They want large-scale cloning only for animals, but they wish to preserve cloning as a human option for exercising our "right to reproduce" — our right to have children, and children with "desirable genes." As law professor John Robertson points out, under our "right to reproduce" we already practice early forms of unnatural, artificial, and extramarital reproduction, and we already practice early forms of eugenic choice. For that reason, he argues, cloning is no big deal.

We have here a perfect example of the logic of the slippery slope, and the slippery way in which it already works in that area. Only a few years ago, slippery-slope arguments were advanced to oppose artificial insemination and in vitro fertilization using unrelated sperm donors. Principles used to justify those practices, it was said, will be used to justify more artificial and more eugenic practices, including cloning. Not so, the defenders retorted, since we can make the necessary distinctions. And now, without even a gesture at making the necessary distinctions, the continuity of practice is held by itself to be justificatory.

The principle of reproductive freedom as currently enunciated by the proponents of cloning logically embraces the ethical acceptability of sliding down the entire rest of the slope — to producing children ectogenetically from sperm to term (should it become feasible) and to producing children whose entire genetic makeup will be the product of parental eugenic planning and choice. If reproductive freedom means the right to have a child of one's own choosing, by whatever means, it knows and accepts no limits.

But, far from being legitimated by a "right to reproduce," the emergence of techniques of assisted reproduction and genetic engineering should compel us to reconsider the meaning and limits of such a putative right. In truth, a "right to reproduce" has always been a peculiar and problematic notion. Rights generally belong to individuals, but this is a right that (before cloning) no one can exercise alone. Does the right then inhere only in couples? Only in married couples? Is it a (woman's) right to carry or deliver or a right (of one or more parents) to nurture and rear? Is it a right to have your own biological child? Is it a right only to attempt reproduction or a right also to succeed? Is it a right to acquire the baby of one's choice?

The assertion of a negative "right to reproduce" certainly makes sense when it claims protection against state interference with procreative liberty, say, through a program of compulsory sterilization. But surely it cannot be the basis of a tort claim against nature, to be made good by technology, should free efforts at natural procreation fail. Some insist that the right to reproduce embraces also the right against state interference with the free use of all technological means to obtain a child. Yet, such a position cannot be sustained: For reasons having to do with the means employed, any community may rightfully prohibit surrogate pregnancy, polygamy, or the sale of babies to infertile couples without violating anyone's basic human "right to reproduce." When the exercise of a previously innocuous freedom now involves or impinges on troublesome practices that the original freedom never was intended to reach, the general presumption of liberty needs to be reconsidered.

We do indeed already practice negative eugenic selection, through genetic screening and prenatal diagnosis. Yet, our practices are governed by a norm of health. We seek to prevent the birth of children who suffer from known (serious) genetic diseases. When and if gene therapy becomes possible, such diseases could then be treated, in utero or even before implantation. I have no ethical objection in principle to such a practice (though I have some practical worries), precisely because it serves the medical goal of healing existing individuals. But therapy, to be therapy, implies not only an existing "patient." It also implies a norm of health. In this respect, even germline gene "therapy," though practiced not on a human being but on egg and sperm, is less radical than cloning, which is in no way therapeutic. But once one blurs the distinction between health promotion and genetic enhancement, between so-called negative and positive eugenics, one opens the door to all future eugenic designs. "To make sure that a child will be healthy and have good chances in life": that is Robertson's principle, and, owing to its latter clause, it is an utterly elastic principle, with no boundaries. Being over eight feet tall will likely produce some very good chances in life, and so will having the looks of Marilyn Monroe, and so will genius-level intelligence.

Proponents want us to believe that there are legitimate uses of cloning that can be distinguished from illegitimate uses, but by their own principles no such limits can be found. (Nor could any such limits be enforced in practice.) Reproductive freedom, as they understand it, is governed solely by the subjective wishes of the parents-to-be (plus the avoidance of bodily harm to the child). The sentimentally appealing case of the childless married couple is, on those grounds, indistinguishable from the case of an individual (married or not) who would like to clone someone famous or talented, living or dead. Further, the principle here endorsed justifies not only cloning but, indeed, all future artificial attempts to create (manufacture) "perfect" babies.

A concrete example will show how, in practice no less than in principle, the so-called innocent case will merge with, or even turn into, the more troubling ones. In practice, the eager parent-to-be will necessarily be subject to the tyranny of expertise. Consider an infertile married couple, she lacking eggs or he lacking sperm, that wants a child of their (genetic) own and proposes to clone either husband or wife. The scientist-physician (who is also coowner of the cloning company) points out the likely difficulties: A cloned child is not really their (genetic) child, but the child of only one of them; that imbalance may produce strains on the marriage; the child might suffer identity confusion; there is a risk of perpetuating the cause of sterility. The scientist-physician also points out the advantages of choosing a donor nucleus. Far better than a child of their own would be a child of their own choosing. Touting his own expertise in selecting healthy and talented donors, the doctor presents the couple with his latest catalog containing the pictures, the health records, and the accomplishments of his stable of cloning donors, samples of whose tissues are in his deep freeze. Why not, dearly beloved, a more perfect baby?

The "perfect baby," of course, is the project not of the infertility doctors, but of the eugenic scientists and their supporters. For them, the paramount right is not the so-called right to reproduce but what biologist Bentley Glass called, a quarter of a century ago, "the right of every child to be born with a sound physical and mental constitution, based on a sound genotype . . . the inalienable right to a sound heritage." But to secure that right and to achieve the requisite quality control over new human life, human conception and gestation will need to be brought fully into the bright light of the laboratory, beneath which the child-to-be can be fertilized, nourished, pruned, weeded, watched, inspected, prodded, pinched, cajoled, injected, tested, rated, graded, approved, stamped, wrapped, sealed, and delivered. There is no other way to produce the perfect baby.

Yet we are urged by proponents of cloning to forget about the science-fiction scenarios of laboratory manufacture and multiple-copied clones and to focus only on the homely cases of infertile couples exercising their reproductive rights. But why, if the single cases are so innocent, should multiplying their performance be so off-putting? (Similarly, why do others object to people's making money from that practice if the practice itself is perfectly acceptable?) When we follow the sound ethical principle of universalizing our choice — Would it be right if everyone cloned a Wilt Chamberlain (with his consent, of course)? Would it be right if everyone decided to practice asexual reproduction? — we discover what is wrong with such seemingly innocent cases. The so-called science fiction cases make vivid the meaning of what looks to us, mistakenly, to be benign.

Though I recognize certain continuities between cloning and, say, in vitro fertilization, I believe that cloning differs in essential and important ways. Yet those who disagree should be reminded that the "continuity" argument cuts both ways. Sometimes we establish bad precedents and discover that they were bad only when we follow their inexorable logic to places we never meant to go. Can the defenders of cloning show us today how, on their principles, we shall be able to see producing babies ("perfect babies") entirely in the laboratory or exercising full control over their genotypes (including so-called enhancement) as ethically different, in any essential way, from present forms of assisted reproduction? Or are they willing to admit, despite their attachment to the principle of continuity, that the complete obliteration of "mother" or "father," the complete depersonalization of procreation, the complete manufacture of human beings, and the complete genetic control of one generation over the next would be ethically problematic and essentially different from current forms of assisted reproduction? If so, where and how will they draw the line, and why? I draw it at cloning, for all the reasons given.

BAN THE CLONING OF HUMANS

What, then, should we do? We should declare that human cloning is unethical in itself and dangerous in its likely consequences. In so doing, we shall have the backing of the overwhelming majority of our fellow Americans, of the human race, and (I believe) of most practicing scientists. Next, we should do all that we can to prevent the cloning of human beings. We should do that by means of an international legal ban, if possible, and by a unilateral national ban at a minimum. Scientists may secretly undertake to violate such a law, but they will be deterred by not being able to stand up proudly to claim the credit for their technological bravado and success. Such a ban on clonal baby making, moreover, will not harm the progress of basic genetic science and technology. On the contrary, it will reassure the public that scientists are happy to proceed without violating the deep ethical norms and institutions of the human community.

* * *

The president's call for a moratorium on human cloning has given us an important opportunity. In a truly unprecedented way, we can strike a blow for the human control of the technological project, for wisdom, prudence, and human dignity. The prospect of human cloning, so repulsive to contemplate, is the occasion for deciding whether we shall be slaves of unregulated progress and ultimately its artifacts, or whether we shall remain free human beings who guide our technique toward the enhancement of human dignity.

21. Science Fiction: A Comment on Leon Kass's Bioethics

JEROME GROOPMAN

Jerome Groopman holds the Dina and Raphael Recanati Chair of Medicine at the Harvard Medical School and is Chief of Experimental Medicine at the Beth Israel Deaconess Medical Center. He received his B.A. from Columbia College summa cum laude and his M.D. from Columbia College of Physicians and Surgeons in New York. He is a member of the Institute of Medicine of the National Academy of Sciences. He is author of The Measure of Our Days *(1997) and* Second Opinions: Stories of Intuition and Choice in the Changing World of Medicine *(2000). A television series, "Gideon's Crossing," based on the* Second Opinions, *ran on ABC from October 2001 through April 2001. This article, in which Groopman comments on Leon Kass and his stewardship of the National Bioethics Council, originally appeared in* The New Yorker, *for which he writes regularly.*

The future of the life sciences in America may depend, in some small part, on the opinions of a bioethicist named Dr. Leon R. Kass. Kass, who was trained as a physician, is now a scholar at the American Enterprise Institute, on leave from the University of Chicago's Committee on Social Thought. He has devoted a book to "eating and the perfecting of our nature" and has contributed to books with titles like *The Neoconservative Imagination.* In August, President Bush appointed him chairman of the new National Bioethics Commission [the official name seems to be the President's Council on Bioethics — ED.], which the President has asked to be "the conscience of our country" and be his guide on all ethical matters relating to biomedical advances.

At the commission's first meeting the other week in Washington, Kass opened a discussion not with facts but with fiction. He talked about Nathaniel Hawthorne's tale "The Birthmark," in which a brilliant scientist marries a woman whose extraordinary beauty is marred only by a blemish on her cheek and becomes obsessed with eliminating the imperfection. The story has all the gothic conventions: bubbling beakers; arcane tomes; elixirs of immortality; a stunted, apelike assistant. In the end, the scientist's treatment cures the blemish but kills the wife.

Using literature to warn against the scientific search for perfection is a hallmark of Kass's approach to bioethics. (Hawthorne, Homer, and Huxley are among his touchstones.) So is a reflexive suspicion toward the enterprise of biotechnology. In a series of essays published in the 1970s, Kass opposed what is now the commonplace practice of in vitro fertilization. He worried that it could erode traditional marriage and create a baby market and that children conceived

From "Science Fiction" by Jerome Groopman, from *The New Yorker* (February 4, 2002). Reprinted with permission of Condé Nast.

by the process would be stigmatized. (He has since dropped the subject.) Last summer, Kass came to public notice when he advised President Bush on his decision to prohibit the creation of any new stem cell lines derived from human embryos. Now Kass's commission is deliberating stem cell research as the Senate begins debate on several bills on human cloning.

There are two types of human cloning, popularly called reproductive and therapeutic. In both types, a nucleus from a cell is inserted into an unfertilized egg, and the egg takes on that cell's genetic characteristics. In reproductive cloning, the manipulated egg would grow to be a baby that is a genetic copy of the donor. In therapeutic cloning, the manipulated egg grows into a microscopic clump, which provides primitive stem cells, and the process is terminated. Cloned stem cells may one day provide treatments for scores of currently incurable diseases, including juvenile diabetes, Parkinson's, Alzheimer's, and spinal-cord paralysis. As the Kass commission met, the National Academy of Sciences, the most august research organization in American science — and one that was also created to advise the federal government — issued a report that called for a ban on reproductive cloning but reaffirmed its support for research on therapeutic cloning.

Unfortunately, the scientific consensus isn't accompanied by a political one. The President opposes all cloning — he told the bioethics commission, "I just don't think it's right" — and Kass has taken a similar position. In a 1998 book, *The Ethics of Human Cloning* [the book from which the previous chapter was taken], he warns that even therapeutic cloning may lead us into a world where science is used for "replicating individuals of great genius, talent, or beauty" or creating "genetically identical humans suitable for research" or for "special missions in peace and war (not excluding espionage)."

Kass's vision is dismally remote from what actually goes on in the nation's laboratories. There are no wild-eyed wizards with perfection potions. Instead, medical scientists stare at diseases against which frustratingly little progress has been made, despite years of dedicated research. While Kass conjures a world of lab-bred James Bonds, 200,000 Americans live with spinal-cord injuries, a million and a half have Parkinson's, and four million have Alzheimer's.

How does Kass defend his hostility toward stem-cell research and cloning? With a doctrine that he calls "the wisdom of repugnance," and which states, basically, that if you find something repugnant — if you just don't think it's right — then it must be wrong. The problem with this argument is that it is impervious to reason and severely constrained by time and place. Whether repugnance really offers wisdom depends, of course, on what you find repugnant. The practice of autopsy, which made modern medicine possible, was for centuries widely considered repugnant. More recently, in 1976, the city of Cambridge, Massachusetts, decided that recombinant-DNA technology was repugnant, and it called for a moratorium on the cloning of genes at institutions such as Harvard and MIT. This research became the basis of modern biotechnology. If Cambridge's distaste had been sustained, or shared, by San Francisco, we would have been denied many of our most important treatments for cancer, rheumatoid arthritis, and heart disease.

There is, however, a tactical advantage in applying the wisdom of repugnance to the stem cell debate, in that it skirts the familiar theological argument that a manipulated egg is a human life. It therefore enables the Bush Administration to accommodate the religious right without openly embracing its fundamentalism.

The commission is due to meet a few more times and to publish its proposals by the summer. Its critics have noted that most of the eighteen members are conservatives like Kass who are unlikely to recommend anything that the President would not want to hear. One has to hope that the few working scientists on the commission, such as Dr. Janet D. Rowley, a leukemia expert who is also a member of the National Academy of Sciences, can help shape a medical guideline that is based on fact, not on literature or aesthetics — one that distinguishes real science from science fiction.

PART VI
DILEMMAS OF NEW TECHNOLOGY:
COMPUTERS AND INFORMATION

While many of the social impacts of the new genetics and other biomedical advances are speculative and in the future, the impacts of computers and information technology are being felt right now. Computers, especially personal computers, are a part of most people's lives in the United States in the early twenty-first century. Increasingly, moreover, having a PC means being connected to the Internet. Computers began to have substantial effects on human work, on power and control in society, and on social and economic equity decades ago. But the Internet, which, in the space of a decade, has exploded into an entirely new medium of communication, has intensified these effects, added new ones, and accelerated the pace at which they are being felt.

Little of this was foreseen or planned. For starters, the engineers and scientists responsible for developing computers, and even the heads of the companies that made the early ones, completely failed to see the extent to which computers would permeate society. In the first chapter in Part VI, historian Paul Ceruzzi conducts a kind of retrospective technology assessment, looking at early expectations of the usefulness and impact of computers and finding them remarkably myopic.

Following Ceruzzi, Tom Forester and Perry Morrison survey the social problems and the range of ethical issues raised by developments in information technology — issues that face computer users as well as computer professionals. Although their analysis is several years old (which can be an eternity in the fast-moving world of information technology), the issues it covers still provide a solid introduction to information age dilemmas. Picking up where Forester and Morrison leave off, Stanford University law professor Lawrence Lessig examines how the potential of the Internet to foster innovation, democracy, and economic growth worldwide is being eroded by new laws and large corporations that are seeking to protect their own interests.

Next, Shoshana Zuboff, professor at Harvard Business School, reports on a major study of how information technology (the "smart machine" in her title) is shaping the working lives of men and women and the nature of work itself. Zuboff's influential writings are helping workers and managers alike to understand both the challenges and the opportunities created by computers in the workplace. Finally, Gene Rochlin, professor of energy and resources at the University of California, Berkeley, examines the impacts of computers on warfare, impacts that are creating interdependencies among military units that may not be fully appreciated by those who are affected by them.

22.   An Unforeseen Revolution: Computers and Expectations, 1935–1985

PAUL CERUZZI

Paul Ceruzzi's fine essay, "An Unforeseen Revolution: Computers and Expectations, 1935–1985," looks back at the early forecasts of the societal impact of computers. Ceruzzi writes that the computer pioneers of the 1940s assumed that perhaps half a dozen of the new machines would serve the world's needs for the foreseeable future. As Joseph Corn notes in the introduction to his book, Imagining Tomorrow, *where this reading was first published, this "dazzling failure of prophecy" is explained by the fact that most of the computer pioneers were physicists who viewed the new devices as equipment for their experiments and found it hard to imagine that their inventions might be applied to entirely different fields, such as payroll processing, trading recorded music, publishing books, and making animated films. The impact of computers on society has been staggering, and it is sobering to realize how little of this impact was anticipated by those most responsible for developing and introducing this new technology.*

Paul Ceruzzi is Curator of Aerospace Electronics and Computing at the National Air and Space Museum in Washington, D.C. He is the author of A History of Modern Computing *(Cambridge, MA: MIT Press, 1998).*

The "computer revolution" is here. Computers seem to be everywhere: at work, at play, and in all sorts of places in between. There are perhaps half a million large computers in use in America today [in 1986], seven or eight million personal computers, five million programmable calculators, and millions of dedicated microprocessors built into other machines of every description.

The changes these machines are bringing to society are profound, if not revolutionary. And, like many previous revolutions, the computer revolution is happening very quickly. The computer as defined today did not exist in 1950. Before World War II, the word *computer* meant a human being who worked at a desk with a calculating machine, or something built by a physics professor to solve a particular problem, used once or twice, and then retired to a basement storeroom. Modern computers — machines that do a wide variety of things, many having little to do with mathematics or physics — emerged after World War II from the work of a dozen or so individuals in England, Germany, and the United States. The "revolution," however one may define it, began only when their work became better known and appreciated.

From *Imagining Tomorrow: History, Technology and the American Future,* edited by Joseph J. Corn (Cambridge, MA: MIT Press, 1986). Reprinted by permission of MIT Press.

The computer age dawned in the United States in the summer of 1944, when a Harvard physics instructor named Howard Aiken publicly unveiled a giant electromechanical machine called the Mark I. At the same time, in Philadelphia, J. Presper Eckert, Jr., a young electrical engineer, and John Mauchly, a physicist, were building the ENIAC, which, when completed in 1945, was the world's first machine to do numerical computing with electronic rather than mechanical switches.

Computing also got under way in Europe during the war. In 1943, the British built an electronic machine that allowed them to decode intercepted German radio messages. They built several copies of this so-called Colossus, and by the late 1940s general-purpose computers were being built at a number of British institutions. In Germany, Konrad Zuse, an engineer, was building computers out of used telephone equipment. One of them, the Z4, survived the war and had a long and productive life at the Federal Technical Institute in Zurich.

These machines were the ancestors of today's computers. They were among the first machines to have the ability to carry out any sequence of arithmetic operations, keep track of what they had just done, and adjust their actions accordingly. But machines that only solve esoteric physics problems or replace a few human workers, as those computers did, do not a revolution make. The computer pioneers did not foresee their creations as doing much more than that. They had no glimmering of how thoroughly the computer would permeate modern life. The computer's inventors saw a market restricted to few scientific, military, or large-scale business applications. For them, a computer was akin to a wind tunnel: a vital and necessary piece of apparatus, but one whose expense and size limited it to a few installations.

For example, when Howard Aiken heard of the plans of Eckert and Mauchly to produce and market a more elegant version of the ENIAC, he was skeptical. He felt they would never sell more than a few of them, and he stated that four or five electronic digital computers would satisfy all the country's computing needs.[1] In Britain in 1951, the physicist Douglas Hartree remarked, "We have a computer here in Cambridge; there is one in Manchester and one at the [National Physical Laboratory]. I suppose there ought to be one in Scotland, but that's about all."[2] Similar statements appear again and again in the folklore of computing.[3] This perception clearly dominated early discussions about the future of the new technology.[4] At least two other American computer pioneers, Edmund Berkeley and John V. Atanasoff, also recall hearing estimates that fewer than ten computers would satisfy all of America's computing needs.[5]

By 1951, about half a dozen electronic computers were running, and in May of that year companies in the United States and England began producing them for commercial customers. Eckert and Mauchly's dream became the UNIVAC — a commercial electronic machine that for a while was a synonym for *computer*, as *Scotch Tape* is for cellophane tape or *Thermos* is for vacuum bottles. It was the star of CBS's television coverage of the 1952 presidential election when it predicted, with only a few percent of the vote gathered, Eisenhower's landslide victory over Adlai Stevenson. With this election, Americans in large numbers suddenly became aware of this new and marvelous device. Projects got under way at universities and government agencies across the United States and Europe to build computers. Clearly, there was a demand for more than just a few of the large-scale machines.

But not many more. The UNIVAC was large and expensive, and its market was limited to places like the U.S. Census Bureau, military installations, and a few large industries. (Only the fledgling aerospace industry seemed to have an insatiable appetite for those costly machines in the early years.) Nonetheless, UNIVAC and its peers set the stage for computing's next giant leap, from one-of-a-kind special projects built at universities to mass-produced products designed for the world of commercial and business data processing, banking, sales, routine accounting, and inventory control.

Yet, despite the publicity accorded the UNIVAC, skepticism prevailed. The manufacturers were by no means sure of how many computers they could sell. Like the inventors before them, the manufacturers felt that only a few commercial computers would saturate the market. For example, an internal IBM study regarding the potential market for a computer called the Tape Processing Machine (a prototype of which had been completed by 1951) estimated that there was a market for no more than twenty-five machines of its size.[6] Two years later, IBM developed a smaller computer for business use, the Model 650, which was designed to rent for $3,000 a month — far less than the going price for large computers like the UNIVAC, but nonetheless a lot more than IBM charged for its other office equipment. When it was announced in 1953, those who were backing the project optimistically foresaw a market for 250 machines. They had to convince others in the IBM organization that this figure was not inflated.[7]

As it turned out, businesses snapped up the 650 by the thousands. It became the Model T of computers, and its success helped establish IBM as the dominant computer manufacturer it is today. The idea finally caught on that a private company could manufacture and sell computers — of modest power, and at lower prices than the first monsters — in large quantities. The 650 established the notion of the computer as a machine for business as well as for science, and its success showed that the low estimates of how many computers the world needed were wrong.

Why the inventors and the first commercial manufacturers underestimated the computer's potential market by a wide margin is an interesting question for followers of the computer industry and for historians of modern technology. There is no single cause that accounts for the misperception. Rather, three factors contributed to the erroneous picture of the computer's future: a mistaken feeling that computers were fragile and unreliable; the institutional biases of those who shaped policies toward computer use in the early days; and an almost universal failure, even among the computer pioneers themselves, to understand the very nature of computing (how one got a computer to do work, and just how much work it could do).

It was widely believed that computers were unreliable because their vacuum-tube circuits were so prone to failure. Large numbers of computers would not be built and sold, it was believed, because their unreliability made them totally unsuitable for routine use in a small business or factory. (Tubes failed so frequently they were plugged into sockets to make it easy to replace them. Other electronic components were more reliable and so were soldered in place.) Eckert and

Mauchly's ENIAC had 18,000 vacuum tubes. Other electronic computers got by with fewer, but they all had many more than most other electronic equipment of the day. The ENIAC was a room-sized Leviathan whose tubes generated a lot of heat and used great quantities of Philadelphia's electric power. Tube failures were indeed a serious problem, for if even one tube blew out during a computation it might render the whole machine inoperative. Since tubes are most likely to blow out within a few minutes after being switched on, the ENIAC's power was left on all the time, whether it was performing a computation or not.

Howard Aiken was especially wary of computers that used thousands of vacuum tubes as their switching elements. His Mark I, an electromechanical machine using parts taken from standard IBM accounting equipment of the day, was much slower but more rugged than computers that used vacuum tubes. Aiken felt that the higher speeds vacuum tubes offered did not offset their tendency to burn out. He reluctantly designed computers that used vacuum tubes, but he always kept the numbers of tubes to a minimum and used electromechanical relays wherever he could.[8] Not everyone shared Aiken's wariness, but his arguments against using vacuum-tube circuits were taken seriously by many other computer designers, especially those whose own computer projects were shaped by the policies of Aiken's Harvard laboratory.

That leads to the next reason for the low estimates: Scientists controlled the early development of the computer, and they steered postwar computing projects away from machines and applications that might have a mass market. Howard Aiken, John von Neumann, and Douglas Hartree were physicists or mathematicians, members of a scientific elite. For the most part, they were little concerned with the mundane payroll and accounting problems that business faced every day. Such problems involved little in the way of higher mathematics, and their solutions contributed little to the advancement of scientific knowledge. Scientists perceived their own place in society as an important one but did not imagine that the world would need many more men like themselves. Because their own needs were satisfied by a few powerful computers, they could not imagine a need for many more such machines. Even at IBM, where commercial applications took precedence, scientists shaped the perceptions of the new invention. In the early 1950s, the mathematician John von Neumann was a part-time consultant to the company, where he played no little role in shaping expectations for the new technology.

The perception of a modest and limited future for electronic computing came, most of all, from misunderstandings of its very nature. The pioneers did not really understand how humans would interact with machines that worked at the speed of light, and they were far too modest in their assessments of what their inventions could really do. They felt they had made a breakthrough in numerical calculating, but they missed seeing that the breakthrough was in fact a much bigger one. Computing turned out to encompass far more than just doing complicated sequences of arithmetic. But just how much more was not apparent until much later, when other people gained familiarity with computers. A few examples of objections raised to computer projects in the early days will make this clear.

When Howard Aiken first proposed building an automatic computer, in 1937, his colleagues at Harvard objected. Such a machine, they said, would lie idle most of the time, because it would soon do all the work required of it. They were clearly thinking of his proposed machine in terms of a piece of experimental apparatus constructed by a physicist; after the experiment is performed and the results gathered, such an apparatus has no further use and is then either stored or dismantled so that the parts can be reused for new experiments. Aiken's proposed "automatic calculating machine," as he called it in 1937, was perceived that way. After he had used it to perform the calculations he wanted it to perform, would the machine be good for anything else? Probably not. No one had built computers before. One could not propose building one just to see what it would look like; a researcher had to demonstrate the need for a machine with which he could solve a specific problem that was otherwise insoluble. Even if he could show that only with the aid of a computer could he solve the problem, that did not necessarily justify its cost.[9]

Later on, when the much faster electronic computers appeared, this argument surfaced again. Mechanical computers had proved their worth, but some felt that electronic computers worked so fast that they would spew out results much faster than human beings could assimilate them. Once again, the expensive computer would lie idle, while its human operators pondered over the results of a few minutes of its activity. Even if enough work was found to keep an electronic computer busy, some felt that the work could not be fed into the machine rapidly enough to keep its internal circuits busy.[10]

Finally, it was noted that humans had to program a computer before it could do any work. Those programs took the form of long lists of arcane symbols punched into strips of paper tape. For the first electronic computers, it was mostly mathematicians who prepared those tapes. If someone wanted to use the computer to solve a problem, he was allotted some time during which he had complete control over the machine; he wrote the program, fed it into the computer, ran it, and took out the results. By the early 1950s, computing installations saw the need for a staff of mathematicians and programmers to assist the person who wanted a problem solved, since few users would be expected to know the details of programming each specific machine. That meant that every computer installation would require the services of skilled mathematicians, and there would never be enough of them to keep more than a few machines busy. R. F. Clippinger discussed this problem at a meeting of the American Mathematical Society in 1950, stating, "In order to operate the modern computing machine for maximum output, a staff of perhaps twenty mathematicians of varying degrees of training are required. There is currently such a shortage of persons trained for this work that machines are not working full time."[11] Clippinger forecast a need for 2,000 such persons by 1960, implying that there would be a mere 100 computers in operation by then.

These perceptions, which lay behind the widely held belief that computers would never find more than a limited (though important) market in the industrialized world, came mainly from looking at the new invention strictly in the context of what it was replacing: calculating machines and their human operators. That context was what limited the pioneers' vision.

Whenever a new technology is born, few see its ultimate place in society. The inventors of radio did not foresee its use for broadcasting entertainment, sports, and news; they saw it as a telegraph without wires. The early builders of automobiles did not see an age of "automobility"; they saw a "horseless carriage."

Likewise, the computer's inventors perceived its role in future society in terms of the functions it was specifically replacing in contemporary society. The predictions that they made about potential applications for the new invention had to come from the context of "computing" that they knew. Though they recognized the electronic computer's novelty, they did not see how it would permit operations fundamentally different from those performed by human computers.

Before there were digital computers, a mathematician solved a complex computational problem by first recasting it into a set of simpler problems, usually involving only the four ordinary operations of arithmetic — addition, subtraction, multiplication, and division. Then he would take this set of more elementary problems to human computers who would do the arithmetic with the aid of mechanical desktop calculators. He would supply these persons with the initial input data, books of logarithmic and trigonometric tables, paper on which to record intermediate results, and instructions on how to proceed. Depending on the computer's mathematical skill, the instructions would be more or less detailed. An unskilled computer had to be told, for example, that the product of two negative numbers is a positive number; someone with more mathematical training might need only a general outline of the computation.[12]

The inventors of the first digital computers saw their machines as direct replacements for this system of humans, calculators, tables, pencils and paper, and instructions. We know this because many early experts on automatic computing used the human computing process as the standard against which the new electronic computers were compared. Writers of early textbooks on "automatic computing" started with the time a calculator took to multiply two ten-digit numbers. To that time they added the times for the other operations: writing and copying intermediate results, consulting tables, and keying in input values. Although a skilled operator could multiply two numbers in ten or twelve seconds, in an eight-hour day he or she could be expected to perform only 400 such operations, each of which required about seventy-two seconds.[13] The first electronic computers could multiply two ten-digit decimal numbers in about 0.003 second; they could copy and read internally stored numbers even faster. Not only that, they never had to take a coffee break, stop for a meal, or sleep; they could compute as long as their circuits were working.

Right away, these speeds radically altered the context of the arguments that electronic components were too unreliable to be used in more than a few computers. It was true that tubes were unreliable and that the failure of even one during a calculation might vitiate the results. But the measure of reliability was the number of operations between failures, not the absolute number of hours the machine was in service. In terms of the number of elementary operations it could do before a tube failed, a machine such as ENIAC turned out to be quite reliable after all. If it could be kept running for even one hour without a tube failure, during that hour it could do more arithmetic than the supposedly more reliable mechanical calculators could do in weeks. Eventually the ENIAC's operators were able to keep it running for more than twenty hours a day, seven days a week. Computers were reliable enough long before the introduction of the transistor provided a smaller and more rugged alternative to the vacuum tube.

So an electronic computer like the ENIAC could do the equivalent of about thirty million elementary operations in a day — the equivalent of the work of 75,000 humans. By that standard, five or six computers of the ENIAC's speed and size could do the work of 400,000 humans. However, measuring electronic computing power by comparing it with that of humans makes no sense. It is like measuring the output of a steam engine in "horsepower." For a one- or two-horsepower engine, the comparison is appropriate, but it would be impossible to replace a locomotive with an equivalent number of horses. So it is with computing power. But the human measure was the only one the pioneers knew. Recall that between 1945 and 1950 the ENIAC was the only working electronic computer in the United States. At its public dedication in February 1946, Arthur Burks demonstrated the machine's powers to the press by having it add a number to itself over and over again — an operation that reporters could easily visualize in terms of human abilities. Cables were plugged in, switches set, and a few numbers keyed in. Burks then said to the audience, "I am now going to add 5,000 numbers together," and pushed a button on the machine. The ENIAC took about a second to add the numbers.[14]

Almost from the day the first digital computers began working, they seldom lay idle. As long as they were in working order, they were busy, even long after they had done the computations for which they were built.

As electronic computers were fundamentally different from the human computers they replaced, they were also different from special-purpose pieces of experimental apparatus. The reason was that the computer, unlike other experimental apparatus, was programmable. That is, the computer itself was not just "a machine," but at any moment it was one of an almost infinite number of machines, depending on what its program told it to do. The ENIAC's users programmed it by plugging in cables from one part of the machine to another (an idea borrowed from telephone switchboards). This rewiring essentially changed it into a new machine for each new problem it solved. Other early computers got their instructions from punched strips of paper tape; the holes in the tape set switches in the machine, which amounted to the same kind of rewiring effected by the ENIAC's plugboards. Feeding the computer a new strip of paper tape transformed it into a completely different device that could do something entirely different from what its designers had intended it to do. Howard Aiken designed his Automatic Sequence Controlled Calculator to compute tables of mathematical functions, and that it did reliably for many years. But in between that work it also solved problems in hydrodynamics, nuclear physics, and even economics.[15]

The computer, by virtue of its programmability, is not a machine like a printing press or a player piano — devices that are configured to perform a specific function.[16] By the classical definition, a machine is a set of devices configured to perform a specific function: One employs motors, levers, gears, and wire to print newspapers; another uses motors, levers, gears, and wire to play a prerecorded song. A computer is also made by configuring a set of devices, but its function is not implied by that configuration. It acquires its function only when someone programs it. Before that time it is an abstract machine, one that can do "anything." (It can even be made to print a newspaper or play a tune.) To many people accustomed to the machines of the Industrial Revolution, a machine having such general capabilities seemed absurd, like a toaster that could sew buttons on a shirt. But the computer was just such a device; it could do many things its design-ers never anticipated.

The computer pioneers understood the concept of the computer as a general-purpose machine, but only in the narrow sense of its ability to solve a wide range of mathematical problems. Largely because of their institutional backgrounds, they did not anticipate that many of the applications computers would find would require the sorting and retrieval of nonnumeric data. Yet, outside the scientific and university milieu, especially after 1950, it was just such work in industry and business that underlay the early expansion of the computer industry. Owing to the fact that the first computers did not do business work, the misunderstanding persisted that anything done by a computer was somehow more "mathematical" or precise than that same work, done by other means. Howard Aiken probably never fully understood that a computer could not only be programmed to do dif-ferent mathematical problems but could also do problems having little to do with mathematics. In 1956, he made the following statement, ". . . if it should ever turn out that the basic logics of a machine designed for the numerical solution of differential equations coincide with the logics of a machine intended to make bills for a department store, I would regard this as the most amazing coincidence that I have ever encountered."[17] But the logical design of modern computers for scientific work in fact coincides with the logical design of computers for business purposes. It is a "coincidence," all right, but one fully intended by today's computer designers.

The question remained whether electronic computers worked too fast for humans to feed work into them. Engineers and computer designers met the prob-lem of imbalance of speeds head-on, by technical advances at both the input and output stages of computing. To feed in programs and data, they developed mag-netic tapes and disks instead of tedious plugboard wiring or slow paper tape. For displaying the results of a computation, high-speed line printers, plotters, and video terminals replaced the slow and cumbersome electric typewriters and card punches used by the first machines.

Still, the sheer bulk of the computer's output threatened to inundate the humans who ultimately wanted to use it. But that was not a fatal fault, owing (again) to the computer's programmability. Even if in the course of a computa-tion a machine handles millions of numbers, it need not present them all as its output. The humans who use the computer need only a few numbers, which the computer's program itself can select and deliver. The program may not only direct the machine to solve a problem, it also may tell the machine to select only the "important" part of the answer and suppress the rest.

Ultimately, the spread of the computer beyond physics labs and large govern-ment agencies depended on whether people could write programs that would solve different types of problems and that would make efficient use of the high internal speed of electronic circuits. That challenge was not met by simply train-ing and hiring armies of programmers (although sometimes it must have seemed that way). It was met by taking advantage of the computer's ability to store its programs internally. By transforming the programming into an activity that did not require mathematical training, computer designers exploited a property of the machine itself to sidestep the shortage of mathematically trained programmers.

Although the computer pioneers recognized the need for internal program storage, they did not at first see that such a feature would have such a significant effect on the nature of programming. The idea of storing both the program and data in the same internal memory grew from the realization that the high speed at which a computer could do arithmetic made sense only if it got its instructions at an equally high speed. The plugboard method used with the ENIAC got instructions to the machine quickly but made programming awkward and slow for humans. In 1944, Eckert proposed a successor to the ENIAC (eventually called the EDVAC), whose program would be supplied not by plugboards but by instructions stored on a high-speed magnetic disk or drum.

In the summer of 1944, John von Neumann first learned (by chance) of the ENIAC project, and within a few months he had grasped that giant machine's fundamentals — and its deficiencies, which Eckert and Mauchly hoped to remedy with their next computer. Von Neumann then began to develop a general theory of computing that would influence computer design to the present day.[18] In a 1945 report on the progress of the EDVAC, he stated clearly the concept of the stored program and how a computer might be organized around it.[19] Von Neumann was not the only one to do that, but it was mainly from his report and others following it that many modern notions of how best to design a computer originated.

For von Neumann, programming a digital computer never seemed to be much of an intellectual challenge; once a problem was stated in mathematical terms, the "programming" was done. The actual writing of the binary codes that got a computer to carry out that program was an activity he called coding, and from his writings it is clear that he regarded the relationship of coding to programming as similar to that of typing to writing. That "coding" would be as difficult as it turned out to be, and that there could emerge a profession devoted to that task, seems not to have occurred to him. That was due in part to von Neumann's tremendous mental abilities and in part to the fact that the problems that interested him (such as long-range weather forecasting and complicated aspects of fluid dynamics)[20] required programs that were short relative to the time the computer took to digest the numbers. Von Neumann and Herman Goldstine developed a method (still used today) of representing programs by flow charts. However, such charts could not be fed directly into a machine. Humans still had to do that, and for those who lacked von Neumann's mental abilities, the job remained as difficult as ever.

The intermediate step of casting a problem in the form of a flow chart, whatever its benefits, did not meet the challenge of making it easy for nonspecialists to program a computer. A more enduring method came from reconsidering, once again, the fact that the computer stored its program internally.

In his reports on the EDVAC, von Neumann had noted the fact that the computer could perform arithmetic on (and thus modify) its instructions as if they were data, since both were stored in the same physical device.[21] Therefore, the computer could give itself new orders. Von Neumann saw this as a way of getting a computer with a modest memory capacity to generate the longer sequences of instructions needed to solve complex problems. For von Neumann, that was a way of condensing the code and saving space.

However, von Neumann did not see that the output of a computer program could be, rather than numerical information, another program. That idea seemed preposterous at first, but once implemented it meant that users could write computer programs without having to be skilled mathematicians. Programs could take on forms resembling English and other natural languages. Computers then would translate these programs into long complex sequences of ones and zeroes, which would set their internal switches. One even could program a computer by simply selecting from a "menu" of commands (as at an automated bank teller) or by paddles and buttons (as on a computerized video game). A person need not even be literate to program.

That innovation, the development of computer programs that translated commands simple for humans to learn into commands the computer needs to know, broke through the last barrier to the spread of the new invention.[22] Of course, the widespread use of computers today owes a lot to the technical revolution that has made the circuits so much smaller and cheaper. But today's computers-on-a-chip, like the "giant brains" before them, would never have found a large market had a way not been found to program them. When the low-cost, mass-produced integrated circuits are combined with programming languages and applications packages (such as those for word processing) that are fairly easy for the novice to grasp, all limits to the spread of computing seem to drop away. Predictions of the numbers of computers that will be in operation in the future become meaningless.

What of the computer pioneers' early predictions? They could not foresee the programming developments that would spread computer technology beyond anything imaginable in the 1940s. Today, students with pocket calculators solve the mathematical problems that prompted the pioneers of that era to build the first computers. Furthermore, general-purpose machines are now doing things, such as word processing and game playing, that no one then would have thought appropriate for a computer. The pioneers did recognize that they were creating a new type of machine, a device that could do more than one thing depending on its programming. It was this understanding that prompted their notion that a computer could do "anything." Paradoxically, the claim was more prophetic than they could ever have known. Its implications have given us the unforeseen computer revolution amid which we are living.

NOTES

1. Harold Bergstein, "An Interview with Eckert and Mauchly," *Datamation* 8, no. 4 (1962), pp. 25–30.
2. Simon Lavington, *Early British Computers* (Bedford, MA: Digital Press, 1980), p. 104.
3. See, for example, John Wells, "The Origins of the Computer Industry: A Case Study in Radial Technological Change," Ph.D. Diss., Yale University, 1978, pp. 93, 96, 119; Robert N. Noyce, "Microelectronics," *Scientific American* 237 (September 1977), p. 674; Edmund C. Berkeley, "Sense and Nonsense about Computers and Their Applications," in *Proceedings of World Computer Pioneer Conference*, Llandudno, Wales, 1970, also in Phillip J. Davis and Reuben Hersh (eds.), *The Mathematical Experience* (New York: Houghton Mifflin, 1981).

4. See, for example, the proceedings of two early conferences: *Symposium on Large-Scale Digital Calculation Machinery, Annals of Harvard University Computation Laboratory,* vol. 16, 1949; *The Moore School Lecturers: Theory and Techniques for Design of Electronic Digital Computers,* lectures given at Moore School of Electrical Engineering, University of Pennsylvania, 1946 (Cambridge, MA: MIT Press, 1986).

5. Georgia G. Mollenhoff, "John V. Atanasoff, DP Pioneer," *Computerworld* 8, no. 11 (1974), pp. 1, 13.

6. Byron E. Phelps, *The Beginnings of Electronic Computation,* IBM Corporation Technical Report TR-00.2259, Poughkeepsie, NY, 1971, p. 19.

7. Cuthbert C. Hurd, "Early IBM Computers: Edited Testimony," *Annals of the History of Computing* 3 (1981), pp. 162–82.

8. Anthony Oettinger, "Howard Aiken," *Communications* ACM 5 (1962), pp. 298–9, 352.

9. Henry Tropp, "The Effervescent Years: A Retrospective," *IEEE Spectrum* 11 (February 1974), pp. 70–81.

10. For an example of this argument, and a refutation of it, see John von Neumann, *Collected Works,* vol. 5 (Oxford: Pergamon, 1961), pp. 182, 365.

11. R. F. Clippinger, "Mathematical Requirements of the Personnel of a Computing Laboratory," *American Mathematical Monthly* 57 (1950), p. 439; Edmund Berkeley, *Giant Brains, or Machines That Think* (New York: Wiley, 1949), pp. 108–9.

12. Ralph J. Slutz, "Memories of the Bureau of Standards SEAC," in N. Metropolis, J. Howlett, and G. Rota (eds.), *A History of Computing in the Twentieth Century* (New York: Academic, 1980), pp. 471–7.

13. In a typical computing installation of the 1930s, humans worked, with mechanical calculators that could perform the four elementary operations of arithmetic, on decimal numbers having up to ten digits, taking a few seconds per operation. Although the machines were powered by electric motors, the arithmetic itself was always done by mechanical parts — gears, wheels, racks, and levers. The machines were sophisticated and complex, and they were not cheap; good ones cost hundreds of dollars. For a survey of early mechanical calculators and early computers, see Francis J. Murray, *Mathematical Machines,* vol. 1: *Digital Computers* (New York: Columbia University Press, 1961); see also Engineering Research Associates, *High-Speed Computing Devices* (New York: McGraw-Hill, 1950; Cambridge, MA: MIT Press, 1984).

14. Quoted in Nancy Stern, *From ENIAC to UNIVAC* (Bedford, MA: Digital Press, 1981), p. 87.

15. Oettinger, "Howard Aiken."

16. Abbott Payson Usher, *A History of Mechanical Inventions,* second edition (Cambridge, MA: Harvard University Press, 1966), p. 117.

17. Howard Aiken, "The Future of Automatic Computing Machinery," in *Elektronische Rechenmaschinen und Informationsverabeitung,* proceedings of a symposium, published in *Nachrichtentechnische Fachberichte,* no. 4 (Braunschweig: Vieweg, 1956), pp. 32–34.

18. Herman H. Goldstine, *The Computer from Pascal to von Neumann* (Princeton, NJ: Princeton University Press, 1972), p. 182.

19. Von Neumann's "First Draft of a Report on the EDVAC" was circulated in typescript for many years. It was not meant to be published, but it nonetheless had an influence on nearly every subsequent computer design. The complete text has been published for the first time as an appendix to Nancy Stern's *From ENIAC to UNIVAC.*

20. Von Neumann, *Collected Works,* vol. 5, pp. 182, 236.

21. Martin Campbell-Kelley, "Programming the EDVAC," *Annals of the History of Computing* 2 (1980), p. 15.

22. For a discussion of the concept of high-level programming languages and how they evolved, see H. Wexelblatt (ed.), *History of Programming Languages* (New York: Academic, 1981), especially the papers on FORTRAN, BASIC, and ALGOL.

23. Computer Ethics

TOM FORESTER AND PERRY MORRISON

The technologies of computers, computer networks, and information processing figure in numerous readings throughout this book. As Forester and Morrison put it, "Computers are the core technology of our times." During the past forty-five years (and especially in the past two decades), they have become central to the functioning of our society. As we have become increasingly dependent on computers and networks, we have become more vulnerable to their malfunctions and their misuse. Examples abound. Forester and Morrison cite case after case, including hacker break-ins to military computers, software bugs causing aircraft accidents, software and hardware sabotage, disruptions of telephone service, and the shutdown of four major U.S. air traffic control centers caused by a farmer cutting a fiber optic cable while burying a dead cow.

The pervasiveness of computer technology and its susceptibility to misuse and malfunction raise a great many ethical, social, and legal issues. How can the intellectual property rights of software developers be protected when copying software is easy and widely practiced? Are hackers criminals or just pranksters? Is electronic mail private, or do employers have the right to monitor their employees' communications? Are computer professionals legally or ethically responsible for the consequences of flaws in the systems they have created? These and other questions are the subject of Forester and Morrison's highly readable and provocative introduction to the increasingly important subject of computer ethics.

Until his death in late 1993, Tom Forester was a senior lecturer in the School of Computer and Information Technology at Griffith University in Queensland, Australia. He was the editor or author of seven books on the social aspects of computing. Perry Morrison is director of Morrison Associates Pty, Ltd, a management and information technology consulting firm in Darwin, Australia, where he works to assist in the development of communications infrastructure and IT in remote Aboriginal communities.

Computers are the core technology of our times. They are the new paradigm, the new "common sense." In the comparatively short space of forty years, computers have become central to the operations of industrial societies. Without computers and computer networks, much of manufacturing industry, commerce, transport and distribution, government, the military, health services, education, and research would simply grind to a halt.

Computers are certainly the most important technology to have come along this century, and the current Information Technology Revolution may in time equal or even exceed the Industrial Revolution in terms of social significance. We are still trying to understand the full implications of the computerization that has

From *Computer Ethics: Cautionary Tales and Ethical Dilemmas in Computing*, 2/e (Cambridge, MA: MIT Press, 1993). Reprinted by permission of MIT Press.

already taken place in key areas of society, such as the workplace. The impact of computers and computer-based information and communication systems on our way of life will continue to grow in the coming years.

Yet as society becomes more dependent on computers and computer networks, we also become more and more vulnerable to computer malfunctions (usually caused by unreliable software) and to computer misuse — that is, to the misuse of computers and computer networks by human beings. Malfunctioning computers and the misuse of computers have created a whole new range of social problems, such as computer crime, software theft, hacking, the creation of viruses, invasions of privacy, overreliance on intelligent machines, and workplace stress. In turn, each of these problems creates ethical dilemmas for computer professionals and users. Ethical theory and professional codes of ethics can help us resolve these ethical dilemmas to some extent, while computing educators have a special responsibility to try to ensure more ethical behavior among future generations of computer users.

OUR COMPUTERIZED SOCIETY

When computers hit the headlines, it usually results in bad publicity for them. When power supplies fail, phone systems go down, air traffic control systems seize up, or traffic lights go on the blink, there is nearly always a spokesperson ready to blame the problem on a luckless computer. When public utilities, credit-checking agencies, the police, tax departments, or motor vehicle license centers make hideous mistakes, they invariably blame it on computer error. When the bank or the airline cannot process our transaction, we're told that "the computer is down" or that "we're having problems with our computer." The poor old computer gets the blame on these and many other occasions, although frequently something else is at fault. Even when the problem is computer related, the ultimate cause of failure is human error rather than machine error, because humans design the computers and write the software that tells computers what to do.

Computers have been associated with some major blunders in recent times. For instance, the infamous hole in the ozone layer remained undetected for seven years because of a program design error. No less than twenty-two U.S. servicemen died in the early 1980s in five separate crashes of the U.S. Air Force's Blackhawk helicopter as a result of radio interference with its novel, computer-based, fly-by-wire system. At least four people died in North America because of computer glitches in the Therac-25 cancer radiotherapy machine, while similar disasters have been reported recently in England and Spain. During the 1991 Gulf War, software failure in the Patriot missile defense system enabled an Iraqi Scud missile to penetrate the U.S. military barracks in Dhahran, killing twenty-eight people, while the notorious trouble with the Hubble space telescope in the same year was exacerbated by a programming error that shut down the onboard computer.[1]

In fact, computers have figured one way or another in almost every famous system failure, from Three Mile Island, Chernobyl, and the Challenger space shuttle disaster, to the Air New Zealand Antarctic crash and the downing of the Korean Air Lines flight 007 over Sakhalin Island, not to mention the sinking of HMS

Sheffield in the Falklands war and the shooting down of an Iranian Airbus by the USS *Vincennes* over the Persian Gulf. A software bug lay behind the massive New York phone failure of January 1990, which shut down AT&T's phone network and New York's airports for nine hours, while a system design error helped shut down New York's phones for another four hours in September 1991 (key AT&T engineers were away at a seminar on how to cope with emergencies). A whole series of aerospace accidents, such as the French, Indian, and Nepalese A320 Airbus disasters; the Bell V-22 Osprey and Northrop YF-23 crashes; and the downing of the Lauda Air Boeing 767 in Thailand, has been attributed to unreliable software in computerized fly-by-wire systems. Undeterred, engineers are now developing sail-by-wire navigation systems for ships and drive-by-wire systems for our cars.[2]

Computers and computer networks are vulnerable to physical breaches, such as fires, floods, earthquakes, and power cuts — including very short power spikes or voltage sags ("dirty power") that can be enough to knock out a sensitive system. A good example was the fire in the Setagaya telephone office in Tokyo in 1984 that instantly cut 3,000 data and 89,000 telephone lines and resulted in huge losses for Japanese businesses. Communication networks are also vulnerable to inadvertent human or animal intervention. For instance, increasingly popular fiber optic cables, containing thousands of phone circuits, have been devoured by hungry beavers in Missouri, foxes in outback Australia, and sharks and beam-trawling fishermen in the Pacific Ocean. In January 1991, a clumsy New Jersey repair crew sliced through a major optical fiber artery, shutting down New York's phones for a further six hours, while similar breaks have been reported from Chicago, Los Angeles, and Washington, D.C. The Federal Aviation Administration recently recorded the shutdown of four major U.S. air traffic control centers. The cause? "Fiber cable cut by farmer burying dead cow," said the official report.[3]

Computers and communication systems are also vulnerable to physical attacks by humans and to software sabotage by outside hackers and inside employees. For example, a saboteur entered telecommunications tunnels in Sydney, Australia, one day in 1987 and carefully severed twenty-four cables, knocking out 35,000 telephone lines in forty Sydney suburbs and bringing down hundreds of computers, automated teller machines (ATMs), and point of sale (POS), telex, and fax terminals with it. Some businesses were put out of action for forty-eight hours as engineers battled to restore services. Had the saboteur not been working with an out-of-date plan, the whole of Australia's telecommunications system might have been blacked out. In Chicago in 1986, a disgruntled employee at Encyclopaedia Brittanica, angry at having been laid off, merely tapped into the encyclopedia's database and made a few alterations to the text being prepared for a new edition of the renowned work — like changing references to Jesus Christ to Allah and inserting the names of company executives in odd positions. As one executive commented, "In the computer age, this is exactly what we have nightmares about."[4]

Our growing dependency on computers has been highlighted further in recent years by such incidents as the theft in the former Soviet Union in 1990 of computer disks containing medical information on some 670,000 people exposed to radiation in the Chernobyl nuclear disaster. The disks were simply wiped and then resold by the teenaged thieves. In 1989, vital information about the infamous Alaskan oil spill was "inadvertently" destroyed at a stroke by an Exxon computer operator. In the same year, U.S. retailer Montgomery Ward allegedly discovered one of its warehouses in California that had been lost for three years because of an error in its master inventory program. Apparently, one day the trucks stopped arriving at the warehouse: Nothing came in or went out. But the paychecks were issued on a different system, so for three whole years (so the story goes) the employees went to work every day, moved boxes around, and submitted timecards — without ever telling company headquarters. "It was a bit like a job with the government," said one worker after the blunder had been discovered.[5]

In Amsterdam, Holland, in 1991, the body of an old man who had died six months earlier was found in an apartment by a caretaker who had been concerned about a large pile of mail for him. The man had been something of a recluse, but because his rent, gas, and electricity bills were paid automatically by computer, he wasn't missed. His pension also had been transferred into his bank account every month, so all the relevant authorities assumed that he was still alive. Another particularly disturbing example of computer dependency came from London during the Gulf War, when computer disks containing the Allies' plans for Desert Storm disappeared, along with a laptop computer, from a parked car belonging to Wing Commander David Farquhar of the Royal Air Force Strike Command. Luckily for the Allies, the thieves did not recognize the value of the unencrypted data, which did not fall into Iraqi hands. But a court-martial for negligence and breach of security awaited Farquhar.[6]

Computers are changing our way of life in all sorts of ways. At work, we may have our performance monitored by computer and our electronic mail read by the boss. It's no good trying to delete embarrassing e-mail statements, because someone probably will have a backup copy of what you wrote. This is what happened to White House adviser Colonel Oliver North and to John Poindexter, the former national security adviser to President Ronald Reagan, when they tried to cover up evidence of the Iran-Contra scandal. Poindexter allegedly sat up all night deleting 5,012 e-mail messages, while North destroyed a further 736, but, unknown to Poindexter and North, the messages were all preserved on backup tapes that were subsequently read by congressional investigators. And if you use a spell-checker or language-corrector in your word-processing program, be sure that it doesn't land you in trouble. For example, the *Fresno Bee* newspaper in California recently had to run a correction that read, "An item in Thursday's Nation Digest about the Massachusetts budget crisis made reference to new taxes that will help 'put Massachusetts back in the African-American.' This item should have read 'put Massachusetts back in the black.'"[7]

Recent government reports have confirmed that our growing dependence on computers leaves society increasingly vulnerable to software bugs, physical accidents, and attacks on critical systems. In 1989, a report to the U.S. Congress from one of its subcommittees, written by James H. Paul and Gregory C. Simon, found that the U.S. government was wasting millions of dollars a year on software that was overdue, inadequate, unsafe, and riddled with bugs. In 1990, the Canadian auditor-general, Ken Dye, warned that most of the Canadian government's computer systems were vulnerable to physical or logical attack: "That's like running a railroad without signals or a busy airport without traffic controls," he said. In

1991, a major report by the System Security Study Committee of the U.S. National Academy of Sciences, published as *Computers at Risk,* called for improved security, safety, and reliability in computer systems. The report declared that society was becoming more vulnerable to "poor system design, accidents that disable systems, and attacks on computer systems."[8]

SOME NEW SOCIAL PROBLEMS CREATED BY COMPUTERS

Although society as a whole derives benefit from the use of computers and computer networks, computerization has created some serious problems for society that were largely unforeseen.

We classify the new social problems created by computers into seven main categories: computer crime and the problem of computer security, software theft and the question of intellectual property rights, the new phenomena of hacking and the creation of viruses, computer unreliability and the key question of software quality, data storage and the invasion of privacy, the social implications of artificial intelligence and expert systems, and the many problems associated with workplace computerization.

These new problems have proved to be costly: computer crime costs companies millions of dollars a year, while software producers lose staggering sums as a result of widespread software theft. In recent years, huge amounts of time and money have had to be devoted to repairing the damage to systems caused by the activities of malicious hackers and virus creators. Unreliable hardware and software costs society untold billions every year in terms of downtime, cost overruns, and abandoned systems, while invasions of privacy and database mix-ups have resulted in expensive lawsuits and much individual stress. Sophisticated expert systems lie unused for fear of attracting lawsuits, and workplace stress caused by inappropriate computerization costs society millions in absenteeism, sickness benefits, and reduced productivity.

Computer crime is a growing problem for companies, according to recent reports. Every new technology introduced into society creates new opportunities for crime, and information technology is no exception. A new generation of high-tech criminals is busy stealing data, doctoring data, and threatening to destroy data for monetary gain. New types of fraud made possible by computers include ATM fraud, EFT (electronic funds transfer) fraud, EDI (electronic data interchange) fraud, mobile phone fraud, cable TV fraud, and telemarketing fraud. Desktop printing (DTP) has even made desktop forgery possible. Perhaps the biggest new crime is phone fraud, which may be costing American companies as much as $2 billion a year. Most analysts think that reported computer crime is just the tip of an iceberg of underground digital deviance that sees criminals and the crime authorities competing to stay one jump ahead of each other.

Software theft or the illegal copying of software is a major problem that is costing software producers an estimated $12 billion a year. Recent cases of software piracy highlight the prevalence of software copying and the worldwide threat posed by organized software pirates. Computer users and software developers tend to have very different ethical positions on the question of copying software, while the law in most countries is confusing and out of date. There is an ongoing debate about whether copyright law or patent law provides the most appropriate protection for software. Meanwhile, the legal position in the United States, for example, has been confused further by the widely varying judgments handed down by U.S. courts in recent years. The recent rash of look-and-feel suits launched by companies such as Lotus and Apple have muddied the waters still further. The central question facing the information technology (IT) industry is how to reward innovation without stifling creativity, but there is no obvious answer to this conundrum and no consensus as to what constitutes ethical practice.

Attacks by hackers and virus creators on computer systems have proved enormously costly to computer operators. In recent cases, hackers have broken into university computers in order to alter exam results, downloaded software worth millions, disrupted the 911 emergency phone system in the United States, stolen credit card numbers, hacked into U.S. military computers and sold the stolen data to the KGB, and blackmailed London banks into employing them as security advisers. Hackers also have planted viruses that have caused computer users untold misery in recent years. Viruses have erased files, damaged disks, and completely shut down systems. For example, the famous Internet worm, let loose by Cornell student Robert Morris in 1988, badly damaged 6,000 systems across the United States. There is ongoing debate about whether hackers can sometimes function as guardians of our civil liberties, but in most countries the response to the hacking craze has been new security measures, new laws such as Britain's Computer Misuse Act (1990), and new calls for improved network ethics. Peter J. Denning, editor-in-chief of *Communications of the ACM*, says that we must expect increasing attacks on computers by hackers and virus creators in the years ahead. Professor Lance J. Hoffman has called for all new computers to be fitted with antiviral protection as standard equipment, rather like seat belts on cars.[9]

Unreliable computers are proving to be a major headache for modern society. Computer crashes or downtime — usually caused by buggy software — are estimated to cost the United States as much as $4 billion a year, according to a recent report. When bug-ridden software has been used to control fly-by-wire aircraft, railroad signals, and ambulance dispatch systems, the cost of unreliable computers sometimes has had to be measured in terms of human lives. Computers tend to be unreliable because they are digital devices prone to total failure and because their complexity ensures that they cannot be tested thoroughly before use. Massive complexity can make computer systems completely unmanageable and can result in huge cost overruns or budget runaways. For example, in 1988 the Bank of America had to abandon an $80 million computer system that failed to work, while in 1992 American Airlines announced a loss of over $100 million on a runaway computer project. The Wessex Regional Health Authority in England scrapped a system in 1990 that had cost $60 million, and Blue Cross & Blue Shield of Massachusetts pulled the plug in 1992 on a project that had cost a staggering $120 million. U.S. Department of Defense runaways are rumored to have easily exceeded these sums. Computer scientists are exploring a variety of ways to improve software quality, but progress with this key problem is slow.[10]

The problem of safeguarding privacy in a society where computers can store, manipulate, and transmit at a stroke vast quantities of information about individuals is proving to be intractable. In recent years, a whole series of database disasters involving mistaken identities, data mix-ups, and doctored data have indicated that we probably place too much faith in information stored on computers. People have had their driver's licenses and credit records altered or stolen and their lives generally made a misery by inaccurate computer records. There is growing concern about the volume and the quality of the data stored by the FBI's National Crime Information Center (NCIC), the United Kingdom's Police National Computer (PNC), and other national security agencies. (Such concerns even led to a public riot in Switzerland in 1990.) Moreover, new controversies have erupted over the privacy aspects of such practices as calling number identification (CNID) on phone networks, the monitoring of e-mail (by employers such as Nissan and Epson and, it seems, the mayor of Colorado Springs), and the phenomenon of database marketing, which involves the sale of mailing lists and other personal information to junk mailers (in 1990, Lotus and Equifax were forced to drop their Lotus Marketplace: Households, which put on disk personal information about 120 million Americans). Governments around the world are now being pushed into tightening privacy laws.[11]

The arrival of expert systems and primitive forms of artificial intelligence (AI) have generated a number of technical, legal, and ethical problems that have yet to be resolved. Technical problems have seriously slowed progress toward the Holy Grail of AI, while many are now asking whether computers could ever be trusted to make medical, legal, judicial, political, and administrative judgments. Given what we know about bugs in software, some are saying that it will never be safe to let computers run, for instance, air traffic control systems and nuclear power stations without human expert backup. Legal difficulties associated with product liability laws have meant that nobody dares use many of the expert systems that have been developed. In addition, AI critics are asking serious ethical questions, such as, Is AI a proper goal for humanity? Do we really need to replace humans in so many tasks when there is so much unemployment?[12]

Because paid employment is still central to the lives of most people and, according to the U.S. Bureau of Labor Statistics, about forty-six million Americans now work with computers, workplace computerization is clearly an important issue. Indeed, it has proved to be fertile ground for controversies, debates, and choices about the quantity of work available and the quality of working life. While the 1980s did not see massive technological unemployment precisely because of the slow and messy nature of IT implementation, there is now renewed concern that computers are steadily eroding job opportunities in manufacturing and services. Moreover, concern about the impact of computers on the quality of working life has increased with the realization that managers can go in very different directions with the design and implementation of new work systems. Computers have the ability to enhance or degrade the quality of working life, depending upon the route chosen. Computer monitoring of employees has become a controversial issue, as have the alleged health hazards of computer keyboard usage, which has resulted recently in some celebrated RSI (repetitive strain injury) legal suits against employers and computer vendors.[13]

ETHICAL DILEMMAS FOR COMPUTER USERS

Each of the new social problems just outlined generates all sorts of ethical dilemmas for computer users. Some of these dilemmas — such as whether or not to copy software — are entirely new, while others are new versions of old moral issues, such as right and wrong, honesty, loyalty, responsibility, confidentiality, trust, accountability, and fairness. Some of these ethical dilemmas are faced by all computer users; others are faced only by computer professionals. But many of these dilemmas constitute new gray areas for which there are few accepted rules or social conventions, let alone established legal case law.

Another way of saying that computers create new versions of old moral issues is to say that information technology transforms the context in which old ethical issues arise and adds interesting new twists to old problems.[14] These issues arise from the fact that computers are machines that control other machines and from the specific, revolutionary characteristics of IT. Thus, new storage devices allow us to store massive amounts of information, but they also generate new ethical choices about access to that information and about the use or misuse of that information. Ethical issues concerning privacy, confidentiality, and security thus come to the fore. The arrival of new media, such as e-mail, bulletin boards, faxes, mobile phones, and EDI, has generated new ethical and legal issues concerning user identity, authenticity, the legal status of such communications, and whether or not free speech protection and/or defamation law applies to them.

IT provides powerful new capabilities, such as monitoring, surveillance, data linking, and database searching. These capabilities can be utilized wisely and ethically, or they can be used to create mischief, to spy on people, and to profit from new scams. IT transforms relationships between people, depersonalizing human contact and replacing it with instant, paperless communication. This phenomenon can sometimes lead people into temptation by creating a false sense of reality and by disguising the true nature of their actions, such as breaking into a computer system. IT transforms relationships between individuals and organizations, raising new versions of issues, such as accountability and responsibility. Finally, IT unreliability creates new uncertainties and a whole series of ethical choices for those who operate complex systems and those who design and build them. Computer producers and vendors too often neglect to adequately consider the eventual users of their systems, yet they should not escape responsibility for the consequences of their system design.[15]

Under the heading of computer crime and security, a number of ethical issues have been raised — despite the fact that the choice of whether or not to commit a crime should not present a moral dilemma for most people. For example, some have sought to make a distinction between crimes against other persons and so-called victimless crimes against, for example, banks, phone companies, and computer companies. While not wishing to excuse victimless crimes, some have suggested that they somehow be placed in a less serious category, especially when it comes to sentencing. Yet it is hard to accept that a company is any less a victim than an individual when it is deprived of its wealth. Because so many computer criminals appear to be first-time offenders who have fallen victim to temptation, do employers bear any responsibility for misdeeds that have occurred on their premises? And how far should employers or security agencies be allowed to go in their attempts to prevent or detect crime? (Should they be allowed to monitor e-mail or spy on people in toilets, for example?)

The ease with which computer software can be copied presents ethical dilemmas to computer users and professionals almost every day of the year. Some justify the widespread copying of software because everybody else does it or because the cost of well-known software packages is seen as too high. But copying software is a form of stealing and a blatant infringement of the developer's intellectual property rights. In the past, intellectual property such as literary works and mechanical inventions was protected by copyright and patents, but software is a new and unique hybrid. How do we protect the rights of software developers so as to ensure that innovation in the industry continues? What does the responsible computer professional do? Is all copying of software wrong, or are some kinds worse than others? How should the individual user behave when the law is unclear and when people in the industry disagree as to what constitutes ethical practice?

The new phenomena of computer hacking and the creation of computer viruses have raised many unresolved ethical questions. Is hacking merely harmless fun, or is it the computer equivalent of burglary, fraud, and theft? When do high-tech high jinks become seriously criminal behavior? Because hacking almost always involves unauthorized access to other people's systems, should all hacking activity be considered unethical? What are we to make of hackers themselves? Are they well-intentioned guardians of our civil liberties and useful amateur security advisers, or are they mixed-up adolescents whose stock in trade is malicious damage and theft? Can the creation of viruses ever be justified in any circumstances? If not, what punishment should be meted out to virus creators? Finally, what should responsible individuals do if they hear of people who are hacking?

The reality of computer unreliability creates many ethical dilemmas, mainly for the computer professionals who are charged with creating and installing systems. Who is responsible when things go wrong? When a system malfunctions or completely crashes because of an error in a computer program, who is to blame — the original programmers, the system designer, the software supplier, or someone else? More to the point, should system suppliers warn users that computer systems are prone to failure, are often too complex to be fully understood, have not been thoroughly tested before sale, and are likely to contain buggy software? Should software producers be made to provide a warranty on software? And to whom should individual computer professionals ultimately be responsible — the companies they work for, their colleagues, the customers, or the wider society?

The recurring issue of privacy confronts computer professionals and users in all sorts of contexts. First, there are general questions, such as, "What is privacy, and how much of it are individuals entitled to, even in today's society?" "Does individual information stored on databases pose a threat to privacy?" "What right do governments and commercial organizations have to store personal information on individuals?" "What steps should be taken to ensure the accuracy of such information?" Then there are the dilemmas faced by computer professionals and users over whether or not to use information collected for another purpose, whether to purchase personal information illicitly obtained, whether to link information in disparate databases, and so on. Practically every attempt to improve security (and sometimes even productivity) in organizations involves choices about the degree of privacy to which employees are entitled, while new controversies have arisen over the privacy aspects of e-mail and caller ID.

In a sense, the quest for artificial intelligence is one big ethical problem for the computing world, because we have yet to determine whether AI is a proper goal — let alone a realistic goal — for humanity. Should computer professionals work on systems and devices that they know will make yet more humans redundant? Should we really be aiming to replace humans in more tasks? Isn't it somehow demeaning to human intelligence to put so much emphasis on making a machine version of it? Perhaps even more to the point, given what we know about computer unreliability, can we afford to trust our lives to artificially intelligent expert systems? What should be the attitude of responsible computer professionals: Should they warn users of the risks involved or refuse to work on life-critical applications? Should they refuse to work on the many AI projects funded by the military? Moreover, should institutional users trust computers to make judicial, administrative, and medical judgments when human judgment has often proved to be superior?

Some might think that the workplace does not provide an obviously rich source of ethical dilemmas for computer professionals and users. Yet, workplace computerization involves numerous choices for management about the type of system to be implemented, and different systems have radically different impacts on both the quantity and the quality of work. Generally speaking, computers in factories can be used to enhance the quality of working life, to improve job satisfaction, to provide more responsibility, and to upgrade or reskill the workforce, or they can be used to get rid of as many people as possible and to turn those remaining into deskilled, degraded machine-minders, pressing buttons in a soulless, depersonalized environment. Office computerization can increase stress levels and thus health hazards if the new work process is badly designed or even if the new office furniture and equipment are badly designed. Employee monitoring often makes matters worse, while speedups and the creation of excessively repetitive tasks like keying in data for hours can result in cases of repetitive strain injury. Computer professionals and managers have a responsibility to ensure that these outcomes are avoided.

HOW ETHICAL THEORY CAN HELP

"Ethics" has been defined as the code or set of principles by which people live. Ethics is about what is considered to be right and what is considered to be wrong. When people make ethical judgments, they are making prescriptive or normative statements about what ought to be done, not descriptive statements about what is being done.

But when people face ethical dilemmas in their everyday lives, they tend to make very different judgments about what is the right and what is the wrong thing to do. Ensuing discussions between the parties often remain unresolved, because individuals find it hard to explain the reasoning behind their subjective, moral judgments. It is virtually impossible to conclude what ought to be the most appropriate behavior. Ethical theory — sometimes referred to as moral philosophy — is the study of the rules or principles that lie behind moral decisions. This theory helps provide us with a rational basis for moral judgments, enables us to classify and compare different ethical positions, and enables people to defend a particular position on a given issue. Thus, the use of ethical theory can help us throw some light on the moral dilemmas faced by computer professionals and users and may even go some way toward determining how people ought to behave when using computers.[16]

Classical ethical theories are worth knowing, because they provide useful background in some of the terminology, but they have limited relevance to everyday behavior in the IT industry. For example, Plato (429–347 B.C.) talked about the "good life," and much of his life was spent searching for the one good life. He also believed that an action was right or wrong in itself — a so-called objectivist (later, deontological) position. Aristotle (384–322 B.C.), on the other hand, adopted a more relativist and empiricist approach, arguing that there were many good and bad lives and that good lives were happy lives created by practicing "moderation in all things." Epicurus (341–270 B.C.) was the exact opposite, promoting hedonism, or the pursuit of pleasure, as the sole goal of life (although modern hedonists tend to forget that he also warned that too much pleasure was harmful and that the highest form of pleasure was practicing virtue and improving one's mind).

Diogenes (413–323 B.C.) was leader of the cynics, who believed that the world was fundamentally evil. The cynics were antisocial; they shunned public life and led an ascetic, privatized life — rising early, eating frugally, working hard, sleeping rough, and so on. Individual cynics found salvation in themselves and their honest life-style, not in worldly possessions. Modern cynics don't necessarily do this, but they are very distrustful of what they see as a thoroughly corrupt world. Finally, the stoics, such as Zeno (ca. 335–263 B.C.) and Epictetus (ca. 55–135 A.D.), were the essential fatalists, arguing that people should learn to accept whatever happened to them and that everything in the world occurs according to a plan that we do not understand. A true stoic believes that there is no such thing as good or evil and seeks to rise above the circumstances of everyday life, rejecting temptations, controlling emotions, and eschewing ambitions.

But probably the three most influential ethical theories of recent times — and the three of most likely relevance for our purposes — are ethical relativism (associated with Spinoza, 1632–1677), utilitarianism (J. S. Mill, 1806–1873) or consequentialism, and Kantianism (Kant, 1724–1804) or deontologism. Ethical relativism, which says that there are no universal moral norms, need not detain us for long, for it offers no guidance as to what is correct behavior. Ethical relativists merely point to the variety of behaviors in different cultures and conclude that the issue of right and wrong is all relative. Ethical relativism is a descriptive account of what is being done rather than a normative theory of what should be done. While it is true that people in different societies have different moralities, this does not prove that one morality might not be the correct one or that one might not constitute the universal moral code. Ethical relativism is not much use when trying to decide what is the right thing to do in today's world of computing.

Consequentialism and deontologism are much more relevant for our purposes. Consequentialism says simply that an action is right or wrong depending upon its consequences, such as its effects on society. Utilitarianism, as outlined by J. S. Mill and Jeremy Bentham, is one form of consequentialism. Its basic principle is that everyone should behave in such a way as to bring about the greatest happiness of the greatest number of people. Utilitarians arrive at this cardinal principle by arguing that happiness is the ultimate good, because everything else in life is desired as a means of achieving happiness. Happiness is the ultimate goal of humans, and thus all actions must be evaluated on the basis of whether they increase or decrease human happiness. An action is therefore right or wrong depending upon whether it contributes to the sum total of human happiness.

By contrast, deontologism says that an action is right or wrong in itself. Deontologists stress the intrinsic character of an act and disregard motives or consequences. Thus, a deontologist might say that the act of copying software is always wrong, regardless of other considerations, while a utilitarian might say that it was justified if it had a beneficial effect on society as a whole. Deontologists appear to be on particularly strong ground when they state, for example, that killing is wrong no matter what the circumstances, but they are on weaker ground when they say that lying is always wrong. Utilitarians would say that lying can be justified in certain circumstances, as in the case of white lies. On the other hand, utilitarians can find themselves in the position of defending actions that are morally wrong (like lying) or condoning actions that penalize the few in order to benefit the many (such as exploiting labor in a third-world manufacturing plant). Consequentialists tend to look at the overall impact on society, whereas deontologists tend to focus on individuals and their rights. Kantians, in particular, argue strongly that people should always be treated as ends and never merely as means.

The distinction between consequentialists and deontologists is quite useful when we consider the ethical issues confronting computer professionals and users.

ETHICS AND THE COMPUTER PROFESSIONAL

Because computing is a relatively new field, the emerging computer profession has had neither the time nor the organizational capability to establish a binding set of moral rules or ethics. Older professions, like medicine and the law, have had centuries to formulate their codes of ethics and professional conduct. And there is another problem, too: The practice of computing, unlike the practice of medicine or the law, goes on outside the profession — This is an open field, with unfenced boundaries.

Computing, with its subdisciplines, like software engineering, has not yet emerged as a full-fledged profession. Classic professions involve mental work, a high level of skill, and a lengthy period of training, and they perform some vital service to society — just like computing. But more than that, the classic profession is highly organized, with a central body that admits members only when they have achieved a certain level of skill. Although members have a considerable degree of autonomy, they are expected to exercise their professional judgment within the framework of a set of ethical principles laid down by the profession's central organization. Transgressors can be disciplined or even thrown out of the profession altogether. Some see the development of professions as a sign of a well-ordered, mature society, whereas critics have seen them as little more than self-serving protection rackets (the British author and playwright George Bernard Shaw once described all professions as "a conspiracy against the people").

So what sort of profession is computing? Members of the fledgling computer profession do not yet have the social status of doctors or lawyers. Instead, their status has been likened to that of engineers, who work mostly as employees rather than in their own right, who have esoteric knowledge but quite limited autonomy, and who often work in teams or on small segments of large projects rather than alone. Worryingly, they are often distant from the effects of their work. Yet, despite the lower social status of computer professionals, the widespread use of information technology for storing all sorts of vital information puts considerable power into their hands, from the humble operator to the top systems developer. This power has not been sought specifically but arises from the nature of the technology. Computer professionals often find themselves in positions of power over employers, clients, coprofessionals, and the wider public, and this power can be abused easily by those without scruples or those who easily fall victim to temptation.[17]

Computer professionals face all sorts of ethical dilemmas in their everyday work life. First, although they have obligations to their employers, to the customers, to their coprofessionals, and to the general public, these obligations often come into conflict and need to be resolved one way or another. For example, what should be the response of a systems analyst whose employer insists on selling an overengineered, expensive system to gullible customers? Go along with the scam, or tell the customers that they are being duped? Second, almost every day the computer professional is confronted with issues of responsibility, intellectual property, and privacy. Who should take the blame when a system malfunctions or crashes? What attitude should professionals take when someone's intellectual property rights are clearly being infringed? How should they balance the need for greater system security with the right of individuals to privacy?

In an effort to help computer professionals cope with these kinds of conflicts, professional organizations such as the ACM (Association for Computing Machinery), the IEEE (Institute of Electrical and Electronics Engineers), the British Computer Society (BCS), and IFIP (International Federation for Information Processing) have been formulating and revising codes of ethics and professional conduct applicable to the IT industry. One problem with these codes is that they often have consisted mainly of motherhood statements like, "I will avoid harm to others," and "I will always be honest and trustworthy." These proclamations could just as easily apply to any profession or walk of life and say nothing of specific relevance to computing. However, the new ACM code is much improved in this respect in that it talks about specific IT industry responsibilities. A more serious criticism is that these codes contain little in the way of sanctions by which their laudable aims could be enforced. A number of critics have pointed out that these codes have never been used and their language never interpreted. Furthermore, the codes usually have talked purely in terms of individuals being at fault and not whole organizations (although this, too, is addressed to some extent in the new IFIP and ACM codes).[18]

An even more fundamental difficulty with all such codes of ethics is that they don't necessarily do much to make people behave more ethically. The pressure, financial or otherwise, to conform with unethical industry practices is often too great. Thus, in a classic critique of professional ethics, John Ladd argued that attempts to develop professional codes of ethics are not only marked by intellectual and moral confusion (such as describing a code of conduct as ethics), they are also likely to fail. Codes of conduct, he says, are widely disregarded by members of professions. Worthy and inspirational though such codes may be, he says that their existence leads to complacency and to self-congratulation — and maybe even to the cover-up of unethical conduct. "Look, we have a code of ethics," professionals might say, "so everything we do must be ethical." The real objectives of such codes, Ladd says, are to enhance the image of the profession in the outside world and to protect the monopoly of the profession. In other words, they are a bit of window dressing designed to improve the status and the income of members.[19]

Another debate has arisen over suggestions that computer professionals be licensed or certified. Under this proposal, a programmer would have to obtain a certificate of competence before being allowed to work on major projects — especially those involving life-critical systems — and perhaps every computer user would have to obtain a kind of driver's license before being allowed onto the computer networks. Certification of software developers might help reduce the number of software project runaways. But there would be endless difficulties involved in measuring programming competence, and these problems could perhaps lead to religious wars in the profession![20] Moreover, there is a danger that certification could create a closed shop or craft guild that might exclude talented and innovative newcomers. On the other hand, it seems likely that some sort of certification safeguards will have to be introduced in the future to cover high-risk systems.

THE RESPONSIBILITY OF COMPUTING EDUCATORS

Recent well-publicized incidents of hacking, virus creation, computer-based fraud, and invasions of privacy have increased the pressure on computing educators to help instill a greater sense of responsibility in today's students. The world of computing has been portrayed in the media as a kind of electronic frontier society where a "shoot from the hip" mentality prevails. It is widely believed that there is far too much computerized anarchy and mayhem.

We believe that computing educators need to do three things. They must encourage tomorrow's computer professionals to behave in a more ethical, responsible manner for the long-term good of the IT industry. They also need to help make students aware of the social problems caused by computers and the social context in which computerization occurs. And they need to sensitize students to the kinds of moral dilemmas they will face in their everyday lives as computer professionals. Many of today's computer science undergraduates will go on to create systems that will have major impacts on people, organizations, and society in general. If those systems are to be successful economically and socially, graduates will need to know the lessons from the computerization story so far, the ethical and social issues involved, and the range of choices available to computer professionals.

NOTES

1. Sources for the ozone hole: *The New York Times*, Science section, 29 July 1986, page C1; the Blackhawk crashed: B. Cooper and D. Newkirk, *Risks to the Public in Computers and Related Systems*, on the Internet, compiled by Peter G. Neumann, November 1987; Therac-25 and other radiation therapy cases: Jonathan Jacky, "Programmed for Disaster — Software Errors Imperil Lives," in *The Sciences*, September–October 1989; Jonathan Jacky, "Risks in Medical Electronics," *Communications of the ACM*, vol. 33, no. 12, December 1990, p. 138; "Patients Die after Radiation Mix-Up," *The Guardian*, London, 23 February 1991; John Arlidge, "Hospital Admits Errors in Treating Cancer Patients," *The Independent*, London, 7 February 1992; Patriot missile: *New York Times*, 21 May 1991, and *Patriot Missile Defense: Software Problem Led to System Failure at Dhahran, Saudi Arabia*, U.S. General Accounting Office, February 1992; Hubble trouble: *Software Engineering Notes*, vol. 17, no. 1, January 1992, p. 3.

2. AT&T phone outages, January 1990 and September 1991: *Software Engineering Notes*, vol. 15, no. 2, April 1990, and vol. 16, no. 4, October 1991, pp. 6–7; *Time*, 30 September 1991; *Fortune*, 13 January 1992; A320 crashes: "Airbus Safety Claim 'Cannot Be Proved,'" *New Scientist*, 7 September 1991, p. 16, and successive reports in *Software Engineering Notes*, esp. vol. 13, 14, and 15; Osprey crashes: *Flight International*, 18–24 September 1991; *New Scientist*, 15 August 1792; YF-23 and other fly-by-wire glitches: *Software Engineering Notes*, vol. 16, no. 3, July 1991, pp. 21–22; Lauda crash: various reports in *Software Engineering Notes*, vols. 16 and 17.

3. "The 'Dirty Power' Clogging Industry's Pipeline," *Business Week*, 8 April 1991; Naruko Taknashi et al., "The Achilles Heel of the Information Society: Socioeconomic Impacts of the Telecommunications Cable Fire in the Setagaya Telephone Office, Tokyo," *Technological Forecasting and Social Change*, vol. 34, no. 1, 1988, pp. 27–52; Beavers and dead cows: AP report in *Software Engineering Notes*, vol. 17, no. 1, January 1992; Foxes: *The Riverine Grazier*, Hay, New South Wales, Australia, 10 April 1991; Trawlers: *The Australian*, 16 April 1991; New Jersey and others: *Software Engineering Notes*, vol. 16, no. 2, April 1991, p. 4, and vol. 16, no. 3, July 1991, pp. 16–17.

4. "Saboteur Tries to Blank Out Oz," *The Australian*, 23 November 1987, p. 1; "Laid-Off Worker Sabotages Encyclopaedia," *San Jose Mercury News*, 5 September 1986.

5. "Thieves Destroy Data on Chernobyl Victims," *New Scientist*, 22 September 1990; "Exxon Man Destroys Oil Spill Documents," UPI report in *The Australian*, 4 July 1989; "'Losing' a Warehouse," *Software Engineering Notes*, vol. 16, no. 3, July 1991, p. 7.

6. "Inhabitant of Amsterdam Lies Dead in Apartment for Half a Year," *Software Engineering Notes*, vol. 16, no. 2, April 1991, p. 11; "Defence of the Data," *New Scientist*, 19 January

1991, and "Theft of Computer Puts Allies' Plan at Risk," report from *The Times* (London) in *The Australian*, 14 March 1991.

7. "Poindexter Deleted 5,000 Computer Notes," Reuters and AP reports in *The Weekend Australian*, 17–18 March 1990; "Terminally Dumb Substitutions," *Software Engineering Notes*, vol. 15, no. 5, October 1990, p. 4.

8. James H. Paul and Gregory C. Simon, *Bugs in the Program: Problems in Federal Government Computer Software Development and Regulation* (Subcommittee on Investigations and Oversight of the House Committee on Science, Space and Technology, U.S. Government Printing Office, Washington, DC, September 1989); Shawn McCarthy, "Dye Fears Computer Sabotage," *Toronto Star*, 31 October 1990; *Computers at Risk: Safe Computing in the Information Age* (National Academy Press 1991).

9. Peter J. Denning (ed.), *Computers under Attack: Intruders, Worms, and Viruses* (Reading, MA: ACM Press/Addison-Wesley, 1990), p. iii; Lance J. Hoffman (ed.), *Rogue Programs: Viruses, Worms, and Trojan Horses* (New York: Van Nostrand Reinhold, 1990), p. 1.

10. Reports in *Business Week*, 7 November 1988, 3 April 1989, 15 June 1992, and 27 July 1992; *The Australian*, 4 August 1992.

11. Peter G. Neumann, "What's in a Name?" *Communications of the ACM*, vol. 35, no. 1, January 1992, p. 186; *Software Engineering Notes*, vol. 14, no. 5, July 1989, p. 11; vol. 16, no. 3, July 1991, pp. 3–4; and vol. 17, no. 1, January 1992, pp. 12–13; *Business Week*, 18 June 1990, 18 May 1991, and 8 June 1992; Marc Rotenberg, "Protecting Privacy," *Communications of the ACM*, vol. 35, no. 4, p. 164; *The New York Times*, 4 May 1990, p. A12; *The Los Angeles Times*, 8 January 1991; *Computing Australia*, 20 August 1990; Langdon Winner, "A Victory for Computer Populism," *Technology Review*, May–June 1991, p. 66.

12. "Expert Systems Fail to Flourish," *The Australian*, 22 May 1990; Harvey P. Newquist III, "Experts at Retail," *Datamation* 1 April 1990, pp. 53–56; Dianne Berry and Anna Hart (ed.), *Expert Systems: Human Issues* (Cambridge, MA: MIT Press, 1990); Roger Penrose, *The Emperor's New Mind* (New York: Oxford University Press, 1989).

13. Reports in *Business Week*, 19 August 1991, 15 June 1992, 13 July 1992; *Fortune*, 4 November 1991, 24 February 1992, 24 August 1992; Barbara Goldoftas, "Hands That Hurt: Repetitive Motion Injuries on the Job," *Technology Review*, January 1991, pp. 43–50.

14. Deborah C. Johnson, *Computer Ethics* (Englewood Cliffs, NJ: Prentice-Hall, 1985), p. 3; John Ladd, "Computers and Moral Responsibility: A Framework for an Ethical Analysis," in Carol C. Gould (ed.), *The Information Web: Ethical and Social Implications of Computer Networking* (Boulder, CO: Westview Press, 1989), pp. 218–20.

15. Peter G. Neumann, "Computers, Ethics and Values," *Communications of the ACM*, vol. 34, no. 7, July 1991, p. 106; Leslie S. Chalmers, "A Question of Ethics," *Journal of Accounting and EDP*, vol. 5, no. 2, Summer 1989, pp. 50–53.

16. See Deborah C. Johnson, op. cit., 1985, chapter 1; and M. David Ermann, Mary B. Williams, and Claudio Gutierrez (eds.) *Computers, Ethics and Society* (Oxford University Press, New York, 1990), part 1.

17. Deborah C. Johnson, op. cit., 1985, chapter 2; Deborah C. Johnson and John W. Snapper (eds.), *Ethical Issues in the Use of Computers* (Belmont, CA: Wadsworth, 1985), part 1; Donn B. Parker, Susan Swope, and Bruce N. Baker (eds.), *Ethical Conflicts in Information and Computer Science, Technology, and Business* (Wellesley, MA: QED, 1990), parts 2, 4, 5, and 6.

18. Donn B. Parker et al., op. cit., 1990, p. 5; Charles Dunlop and Rob Kling (eds.), *Computerization and Controversy: Value Conflicts and Social Choices* (San Diego, CA: Academic Press, 1991), pp. 656–7; D. Dianne Martin and David H. Martin, "Professional Codes of Conduct and Computer Ethics Education," *Social Science Computer Review*, vol. 8, no. 1, Spring 1990, pp. 96–108.

19. John Ladd, "The Quest for a Code of Professional Ethics: An Intellectual and Moral Confusion," in Deborah C. Johnson and John W. Snapper (eds.), op. cit., 1985, p. 813.

20. Peter G. Neumann, "Certifying Professionals," *Communications of the ACM*, vol. 34, no. 2, February 1991, p. 130.

24.   The Internet Under Siege

LAWRENCE LESSIG

In the early and mid-1990s, when the Internet was just beginning to grow into the vast network it is today, it was a huge laboratory for experimentation with new technologies and new ideas. Its capabilities, Lawrence Lessig writes, engendered "an explosion of creativity." But that era has passed as quickly as it arose. Today, says Lessig, "Under the guise of protecting private property, a series of new laws and regulations are dismantling the very architecture that made the Internet a framework for global innovation." The owners of old media (for example, the firms that control the production and distribution of popular music) are reining in the potential of the Internet to make fundamental changes in the way media are distributed (e.g., through Napster and other on-line music trading technologies). Worst of all, Lessig believes, the U.S. Congress and governments throughout the industrialized world are collaborating in the actions of these reactionary forces through such regulations and laws as the Digital Millennium Copyright Act, which bans technologies intended to circumvent copyright protections.

Lawrence Lessig is one of the most articulate and thoughtful spokesmen for openness in information and telecommunications technology. He is professor of law at Stanford University and author of The Future of Ideas: The Fate of the Commons in the Connected World *(New York: Random House, 2001) and* Code and Other Laws of Cyberspace *(New York: Basic Books, 2000). Lessig is a prolific writer and a much sought after speaker and has been a witness in many court proceedings and congressional hearings relating to such topics as* The U.S. v. Microsoft, The Computer Decency Act, *and Napster.*

The Internet revolution has ended just as surprisingly as it began. None expected the explosion of creativity that the network produced; few expected that explosion to collapse as quickly and profoundly as it has. The phenomenon has the feel of a shooting star, flaring unannounced across the night sky, then disappearing just as unexpectedly. Under the guise of protecting private property, a series of new laws and regulations are dismantling the very architecture that made the Internet a framework for global innovation.

Neither the appearance nor disappearance of this revolution is difficult to understand. The difficulty is in accepting the lessons of the Internet's evolution. The Internet was born in the United States, but its success grew out of notions that seem far from the modern American ideals of property and the market. Americans are captivated by the idea, as explained by Yale Law School professor Carol Rose, that the world is best managed "when divided among private owners" and when the market perfectly regulates those divided resources. But the Internet took off precisely because core resources were not "divided among pri-

From *Foreign Policy*, Issue #127, Nov. - Dec. 2001. Reprinted by permission of International Creative Management, Inc.

vate owners." Instead, the core resources of the Internet were left in a "commons." It was this commons that engendered the extraordinary innovation that the Internet has seen. It is the enclosure of this commons that will bring about the Internet's demise.

This commons was built into the very architecture of the original network. Its design secured a right of decentralized innovation. It was this "innovation commons" that produced the diversity of creativity that the network has seen within the United States and, even more dramatically, abroad. Many of the Internet innovations we now take for granted (not the least of which is the World Wide Web) were the creations of "outsiders" — foreign inventors who freely roamed the commons. Policymakers need to understand the importance of this architectural design to the innovation and creativity of the original network. The potential of the Internet has just begun to be realized, especially in the developing world, where many "real space" alternatives for commerce and innovation are neither free nor open.

Yet, old ways of thinking are reasserting themselves within the United States to modify this design. Changes to the Internet's original core will in turn threaten the network's potential everywhere — staunching the opportunity for innovation and creativity. Thus, at the moment this transformation could have a meaningful effect, a counterrevolution is succeeding in undermining the potential of this network.

The motivation for this counterrevolution is as old as revolutions themselves. As Niccolò Machiavelli described long before the Internet, "Innovation makes enemies of all those who prospered under the old regime, and only lukewarm support is forthcoming from those who would prosper under the new." And so it is today with us. Those who prospered under the old regime are threatened by the Internet. Those who would prosper under the new regime have not risen to defend it against the old; whether they will is still a question. So far, it appears they will not.

THE NEUTRAL ZONE

A "commons" is a resource to which everyone within a relevant community has equal access. It is a resource that is not, in an important sense, "controlled." Private or state-owned property is a controlled resource; only as the owner specifies may that property be used. But a commons is not subject to this sort of control. Neutral or equal restrictions may apply to it (an entrance fee to a park, for example), but not the restrictions of an owner. A commons, in this sense, leaves its resources "free."

Commons are features of all cultures. They have been especially important to cultures outside the United States — from communal tenure systems in Switzerland and Japan to irrigation communities within the Philippines. But within American intellectual culture, commons are treated as imperfect resources. They are the object of "tragedy," as ecologist Garrett Hardin famously described. Wherever a commons exists, the aim is to enclose it. In the American psyche, commons are unnecessary vestiges from times past and best removed, if possible.

For most resources, for most of the time, the bias against commons makes good sense. When resources are left in common, individuals may be driven to overconsume, and therefore deplete, them. But for some resources, the bias against commons is blinding. Some resources are not subject to the "tragedy of the commons" because some resources cannot be "depleted." (No matter how much we use Einstein's theories of relativity or copy Robert Frost's poem "New Hampshire," those resources will survive.) For these resources, the challenge is to induce provision, not to avoid depletion. The problems of provision are very different from the problems of depletion — confusing the two only leads to misguided policies.

This confusion is particularly acute when considering the Internet. At the core of the Internet is a design (chosen without a clear sense of its consequences) that was new among large-scale computer and communications networks. Named the "end-to-end argument" by network theorists Jerome Saltzer, David Clark, and David Reed in 1984, this design influences where "intelligence" in the network is placed. Traditional computer-communications systems located intelligence, and hence control, within the network itself. Networks were "smart"; they were designed by people who believed they knew exactly what the network would be used for.

But the Internet was born at a time when a different philosophy was taking shape within computer science. This philosophy ranked humility above omniscience and anticipated that network designers would have no clear idea about all the ways the network could be used. It therefore counseled a design that built little into the network itself, leaving the network free to develop as the ends (the applications) wanted.

The motivation for this new design was flexibility. The consequence was innovation. Because innovators needed no permission from the network owner before different applications or content got served across the network, innovators were freer to develop new modes of connection. Technically, the network achieved this design simply by focusing on the delivery of packets of data, oblivious to either the contents of the packets or their owners. Nor does the network concern itself that all the packets make their way to the other side. The network is "best efforts"; anything more is provided by the applications at both ends. Like an efficient post office (imagine!), the system simply forwards the data along.

Since the network was not optimized for any single application or service, the Internet remained open to new innovation. The World Wide Web is perhaps the best example. The Web was the creation of computer scientist Tim Berners-Lee at the European Organization for Nuclear Research (CERN) laboratory in Geneva in late 1990. Berners-Lee wanted to enable users on a network to have easy access to documents located elsewhere on the network. He therefore developed a set of protocols to enable hypertext links among documents located across the network. Because of end-to-end, these protocols could be layered on top of the initial protocols of the Internet. This meant the Internet could grow to embrace the Web. Had the network compromised its commitment to end-to-end — had its design been optimized to favor telephony, for example, as many in the 1980s wanted — then the Web would not have been possible.

This end-to-end design is the "core" of the Internet. If we can think of the network as built in layers, then the end-to-end design was created by a set of protocols implemented at the middle layer — what we might call the logical, or code, layer of the Internet. Below the code layer is a physical layer (computers and the wires that link them). Above the code layer is a content layer (material that gets served across the network). Not all these layers were organized as commons. The computers at the physical layer are private property, not "free" in the sense of a commons. Much of the content served across the network is protected by copyright. It, too, is not "free."

At the code layer, however, the Internet is a commons. By design, no one controls the resources for innovation that get served across this layer. Individuals control the physical layer, deciding whether a machine or network gets connected to the Internet. But once connected, at least under the Internet's original design, the innovation resources for the network remained free.

No other large-scale network left the code layer free in this way. For most of the history of telephone monopolies worldwide, permission to innovate on the telephone platform was vigorously controlled. In the United States in 1956, AT&T successfully persuaded the U.S. Federal Communications Commission to block the use of a plastic cup on a telephone receiver, designed to block noise from the telephone microphone, on the theory that AT&T alone had the right to innovation on the telephone network.

The Internet might have remained an obscure tool of government-backed researchers if the telephone company had maintained this control. The Internet would never have taken off if ordinary individuals had been unable to connect to the network by way of Internet service providers (ISPs) through already existing telephone lines. Yet this right to connect was not preordained. It is here that an accident in regulatory history played an important role. Just at the moment the Internet was emerging, the telephone monopoly was being moved to a different regulatory paradigm. Previously, the telephone monopoly was essentially free to control its wires as it wished. Beginning in the late 1960s, and then more vigorously throughout the 1980s, the government began to require that the telephone industry behave neutrally — first by insisting that telephone companies permit customer premises equipment (such as modems) to be connected to the network and then by requiring that telephone companies allow others to have access to their wires.

This kind of regulation was rare among telecommunications monopolies worldwide. In Europe and throughout the world, telecommunications monopolies were permitted to control the uses of their networks. No requirement of access operated to enable competition. Thus, no system of competition grew up around these other monopolies. But when the United States broke up AT&T in 1984, the resulting companies no longer had the freedom to discriminate against other uses of their lines. And ISPs sought access to the local Bell lines to enable customers to connect to the Internet, the local Bells were required to grant access equally. This enabled a vigorous competition in Internet access, and this competition meant that the network could not behave strategically against this new technology. In effect, through a competitive market, an end-to-end design was created at the physical layer of the telephone network, which meant that an end-to-end design could be layered on top of that.

This innovation commons was thus layered onto a physical infrastructure that, through regulation, had important commons-like features. Common-carrier regulation of the telephone system assured that the system could not discriminate against an emerging competitor, the Internet. And the Internet itself was created, through its end-to-end design, to assure that no particular application or use could discriminate against any other innovations. Neutrality existed at the physical and code layer of the Internet.

An important neutrality also existed at the content layer of the Internet. This layer includes all the content streamed across the network — Web pages, MP3s, e-mail, streaming video — as well as application programs that run on, or feed, the network. These programs are distinct from the protocols at the code layer, collectively referred to as TCP/IP (including the protocols of the World Wide Web). TCP/IP is dedicated to the public domain.

But the code above these protocols is not in the public domain. It is, instead, of two sorts: proprietary and nonproprietary. The proprietary includes the familiar Microsoft operating systems and Web servers, as well as programs from other software companies. The nonproprietary includes open source and free software, especially the Linux (or GNU/Linux) operating system, the Apache server, as well as a host of other plumbing-oriented code that makes the Net run.

Nonproprietary code creates a commons at the content layer. The commons here is not just the resource that a particular program might provide — for example, the functionality of an operating system or Web server. The commons also includes the source code of software that can be drawn upon and modified by others. Open source and free software ("open code" for short) must be distributed with the source code. The source code must be free for others to take and modify. This commons at the content layer means that others can take and build upon open source and free software. It also means that open code can't be captured and tilted against any particular competitor. Open code can always be modified by subsequent adopters. It, therefore, is licensed to remain neutral among subsequent uses. There is no "owner" of an open code project.

In this way, and again, parallel to the end-to-end principle at the code layer, open code decentralizes innovation. It keeps a platform neutral. This neutrality in turn inspires innovators to build for that platform, because they need not fear the platform will turn against them. Open code builds a commons for innovation at the content layer. Like the commons at the code layer, open code preserves the opportunity for innovation and protects innovation against the strategic behavior of competitors. Free resources induce innovation.

AN ENGINE OF INNOVATION

The original Internet, as it was extended to society generally, mixed controlled and free resources at each layer of the network. At the core code layer, the network was free. The end-to-end design assured that no network owner could exercise control over the network. At the physical layer, the resources were essentially controlled, but even here, important aspects were free. One had the right to connect a machine to the network or not, but telephone companies didn't have the right to discriminate against this particular use of their network. And, finally, at the content layer, many of the resources served across the Internet were controlled. But a crucial range of software building essential services on the Internet remained free. Whether through an open source or free software license, these resources could not be controlled.

This balance of control and freedom produced an unprecedented explosion in innovation. The power, and hence the right, to innovate was essentially decentralized. The Internet might have been an American invention, but creators from around the world could build upon this network platform. Significantly, some of the most important innovations for the Internet came from these "outsiders." As noted, the most important technology for accessing and browsing the Internet (the World Wide Web) was not invented by companies specializing in network access. It wasn't America Online (AOL) or Compuserve. The Web was developed by a researcher in a Swiss laboratory who first saw its potential and then fought to bring it to fruition. Likewise, it wasn't existing e-mail providers who came up with the idea of Web-based e-mail. That was cocreated by an immigrant to the United States from India, Sabeer Bhatia, and it gave birth to one of the fastest growing communities in history — Hotmail. And it wasn't traditional network providers or telephone companies that invented the applications that enabled online chatting to take off. The original community-based chatting service (ICQ) was the invention of an Israeli, far from the trenches of network design. His service could explode (and then be purchased by AOL for $400 million) only because the network was left open for this type of innovation.

Similarly, the revolution in bookselling initiated by Amazon.com (through the use of technologies that "match preferences" of customers) was invented far from the traditional organs of publishers. By gathering a broad range of data about purchases by customers, Amazon — drawing upon technology first developed at MIT and the University of Minnesota to filter Usenet news — can predict what a customer is likely to want. These recommendations drive sales, but without the high cost of advertising or promotion. Consequently, booksellers such as Amazon can outcompete traditional marketers of books, which may account for the rapid expansion of Amazon into Asia and Europe.

These innovations are at the level of Internet services. Far more profound have been innovations at the level of content. The Internet has not only inspired invention, it has also inspired publication in a way that would never have been produced by the world of existing publishers. The creation of online archives of lyrics and chord sequences and of collaborative databases collecting information about compact discs and movies demonstrates the kind of creativity that was possible because the right to create was not controlled.

Again, the innovations have not been limited to the United States. OpenDemocracy.org, for example, is a London-based, Web-centered forum for debate and exchange about democracy and governance throughout the world. Such a forum is possible only because no coordination among international actors is needed. And it thrives because it can engender debate at a low cost.

This history should be a lesson. Every significant innovation on the Internet has emerged outside of traditional providers. The new grows away from the old. This trend teaches the value of leaving the platform open for innovation. Unfortunately, that platform is now under siege. Every technological disruption creates winners and losers. The losers have an interest in avoiding that disruption if they can. This was the lesson Machiavelli taught, and it is the experience with every important technological change over time. It is also what we are now seeing with the Internet. The innovation commons of the Internet threatens important and powerful pre-Internet interests. During the past five years, those interests have mobilized to launch a counterrevolution that is now having a global impact.

This movement is fueled by pressure at both the physical and content layers of the network. These changes, in turn, put pressure on the freedom of the code layer. These changes will have an effect on the opportunity for growth and innovation that the Internet presents. Policymakers keen to protect that growth should be skeptical of changes that will threaten it. Broad-based innovation may threaten the profits of some existing interests, but the social gains from this unpredictable growth will far outstrip the private losses, especially in nations just beginning to connect.

FENCING OFF THE COMMONS

The Internet took off on telephone lines. Narrowband service across acoustic modems enabled millions of computers to connect through thousands of ISPs. Local telephone service providers had to provide ISPs with access to local wires; they were not permitted to discriminate against Internet service. Thus, the physical platform on which the Internet was born was regulated to remain neutral. This regulation had an important effect. A nascent industry could be born on the telephone wires, regardless of the desires of telephone companies.

But as the Internet moves from narrowband to broadband, the regulatory environment is changing. The dominant broadband technology in the United States is currently cable. Cable lives under a different regulatory regime. Cable providers in general have no obligation to grant access to their facilities. And cable has asserted the right to discriminate in the Internet service it provides.

Consequently, cable has begun to push for a different set of principles at the code layer of the network. Cable companies have deployed technologies to enable them to engage in a form of discrimination in the service they provide. Cisco, for example, developed "policy-based routers" that enable cable companies to choose which content flows quickly and which flows slowly. With these, and other technologies, cable companies will be in a position to exercise power over the content and applications that operate on their networks.

This control has already begun in the United States. ISPs running cable services have exercised their power to ban certain kinds of applications (specifically, those that enable peer-to-peer service). They have blocked particular content (advertising from competitors, for example) when that content was not consistent with their business model. The model for these providers is the model of cable television generally — controlling access and content to the cable providers' end.

The environment of innovation on the original network will change according to the extent that cable becomes the primary mode of access to the Internet.

Rather than a network that vests intelligence in the ends, the cable-dominated network will vest an increasing degree of intelligence within the network itself. And to the extent it does this, the network will increase the opportunity for strategic behavior in favor of some technologies and against others. An essential feature of neutrality at the code layer will have been compromised, reducing the opportunity for innovation worldwide.

Far more dramatic, however, has been the pressure from the content layer on the code layer. This pressure has come in two forms. First, and most directly related to the content described above, there has been an explosion of patent regulation in the context of software. Second, copyright holders have exercised increasing control over new technologies for distribution.

The changes in patent regulation are more difficult to explain, though the consequence is not hard to track. Two decades ago, the U.S. Patent Office began granting patents for software-like inventions. In the late 1990s, the court overseeing these patents finally approved the practice and approved their extension to "business methods." The European Union (EU), meanwhile, initially adopted a more skeptical attitude toward software patents. But pressure from the United States will eventually bring the EU into alignment with American policy.

In principle, these patents are designed to spur innovation. But with sequential and complementary innovation, little evidence exists that suggests such patents will do any good, and there is increasing evidence that they will do harm. Like any regulation, patents tax the innovative process generally. As with any tax, some firms — large rather than small, U.S. rather than foreign — are better able to bear that tax than others. Open code projects, in particular, are threatened by this trend, as they are least able to negotiate appropriate patent licenses.

The most dramatic restrictions on innovation, however, have come at the hands of copyright holders. Copyright is designed to ensure that artists control their "writings" for a limited time. The aim is to secure to copyright holders a sufficient interest to produce new work. But copyright laws were crafted in an era long before the Internet. And their effect on the Internet has been to transfer control over innovation in distribution from many innovators to a concentrated few.

The clearest example of this effect is online music. Before the Internet, the production and distribution of music had become extraordinarily concentrated. In 2000, for example, five companies controlled 84 percent of music distribution in the world. The reasons for this concentration are many — including the high costs of promotion — but the effect of concentration on artist development is profound. Very few artists make any money from their work, and the few that do are able to do so because of mass marketing from record labels. The Internet had the potential to change this reality. Both because the costs of distribution were so low, and because the network also had the potential to significantly lower the costs of promotion, the cost of music could fall, and revenues to artists could rise.

Five years ago, this market took off. A large number of online music providers began competing for new ways to distribute music. Some distributed MP3s for money (eMusic.com). Some built technology for giving owners of music easier access to their music (mp3.com). And some made it much easier for ordinary users to "share" their music with other users (Napster). But as quickly as these companies took off, lawyers representing old media succeeded in shutting them down. These lawyers argued that copyright law gave the holders (some say hoarders) of these copyrights the exclusive right to control how they get used. American courts agreed.

To keep this dispute in context, we should think about the last example of a technological change that facilitated a much different model for distributing content: cable TV, which has been accurately hailed as the first great Napster. Owners of cable television systems essentially set up antenna and "stole" over-the-air broadcasts and then sold that "stolen property" to their customers. But when U.S. courts were asked to stop this "theft," they refused. Twice the U.S. Supreme Court held that this use of someone else's copyrighted material was not inconsistent with copyright law.

When the U.S. Congress finally got around to changing the law, it struck an importantly illustrative balance. Congress granted copyright owners the right to compensation from the use of their material on cable broadcasts, but cable companies were given the right to broadcast the copyrighted material. The reason for this balance is not hard to see. Copyright owners certainly are entitled to compensation for their work. But the right to compensation shouldn't translate into the power to control innovation. Rather than giving copyright holders the right to veto a particular new use of their work (in this case, because it would compete with over-the-air broadcasting), Congress assured copyright owners would get paid without having the power to control — compensation without control.

The same deal could have been struck by Congress in the context of online music. But this time, the courts did not hesitate to extend control to the copyright holders. So the concentrated holders of these copyrights were able to stop the deployment of competing distributors. And Congress was not motivated to respond by granting an equivalent compulsory right. The aim of the recording company's strategy was plain enough: shut down these new and competing models of distribution and replace them with a model for distributing music online more consistent with the traditional model.

This trend has been supported by the actions of Congress. In 1998, Congress passed the Digital Millennium Copyright Act (DMCA), which (in)famously banned technologies designed to circumvent copyright protection technologies and also created strong incentives for ISPs to remove from their sites any material claimed to be a violation of copyright.

On the surface, both changes seem sensible enough. Copyright protection technologies are analogous to locks. What right does anyone have to pick a lock? And ISPs are in the best position to assure that copyright violations don't occur on their Web sites. Why not create incentives for them to remove infringing copyrighted material?

But intuitions here mislead. A copyright protection technology is just code that controls access to copyrighted material. But that code can restrict access more effectively (and certainly less subtly) than copyright law does. Often, the desire to crack protection systems is nothing more than a desire to exercise what is sometimes called a fair-use right over the copyrighted material. Yet the DMCA bans that technology, regardless of its ultimate effect.

More troubling, however, is that the DMCA effectively bans this technology on a worldwide basis. Russian programmer Dimitry Sklyarov, for example, wrote code to crack Adobe's eBook technology in order to enable users to move eBooks from one machine to another and to give blind consumers the ability to "read" out loud the books they purchased. The code Sklyarov wrote was legal where it was written, but when it was sold by his company in the United States, it became illegal. When he came to the United States in July 2001 to talk about that code, the FBI arrested him. Today, Sklyarov faces a sentence of 25 years for writing code that could be used for fair-use purposes, as well as to violate copyright laws.

Similar trouble has arisen with the provision that gives ISPs the incentive to take down infringing copyrighted material. When an ISP is notified that material on its site violates copyright, it can avoid liability if it removes the material. As it doesn't have any incentive to expose itself to liability, the ordinary result of such notification is for the ISP to remove the material. Increasingly, companies trying to protect themselves from criticism have used this provision to silence critics. In August 2001, for example, a British pharmaceutical company invoked the DMCA in order to force an ISP to shut down an animal-rights site that criticized the British company. Said the ISP, "It's very clear [the British company] just wants to shut them up," but ISPs have no incentive to resist the claims.

In all these cases, there is a common pattern. In the push to give copyright owners control over their content, copyright holders also receive the ability to protect themselves against innovations that might threaten existing business models. The law becomes a tool to assure that new innovations don't displace old ones — when, instead, the aim of copyright and patent law should be, as the U.S. Constitution requires, to "promote the progress of science and useful arts."

These regulations will not only affect Americans. The expanding jurisdiction that American courts claim, combined with the push by the World Intellectual Property Organization to enact similar legislation elsewhere, means that the impact of this sort of control will be felt worldwide. There is no "local" when it comes to corruption of the Internet's basic principles. As these changes weaken the open source and free software movements, countries with the most to gain from a free and open platform lose. Those affected will include nations in the developing world and nations that do not want to cede control to a single private corporation. And as content becomes more controlled, nations that could otherwise benefit from vigorous competition in the delivery and production of content will also lose. An explosion of innovation to deliver MP3s would directly translate into innovation to deliver telephone calls and video content. Lowering the cost of this medium would dramatically benefit nations that still suffer from weak technical infrastructures.

Policymakers around the world must recognize that the interests most strongly protected by the Internet counterrevolution are not their own. They should be skeptical of legal mechanisms that enable those most threatened by the innovation commons to resist it. The Internet promised the world — particularly the weakest in the world — the fastest and most dramatic change to existing barriers to growth. That promise depends on the network remaining open to innovation. That openness depends upon policy that better understands the Internet's past.

25. In the Age of the Smart Machine

SHOSHANA ZUBOFF

As other readings in this section and elsewhere make clear, developments in computers and information technology are a driving force in virtually all areas of technological advance. Nowhere are the impacts likely to be more profound than in the nature of work, its organization, and its management. In her widely discussed and influential book In the Age of the Smart Machine: The Future of Work and Power, *Shoshana Zuboff argues that the computerized workplace is qualitatively different from its predecessors. Traditional approaches to organizing and managing work will not work in the new, "informated" environment. An alternative vision is needed for the organization of the twenty-first century.*

Changes in the workplace will affect the fundamental nature of society, as authority relationships, class structure, individuals' control over their own fates, and opportunities for self-fulfillment all take new shapes. The new information technology "offers a historical opportunity to more fully develop the economic and human potential of our work organizations," according to Zuboff. If we fail to seize this opportunity, we run the risk of seeing the future become nothing but a "stale reproduction of the past." Like many of the other works represented in this anthology, In the Age of the Smart Machine *is rich and complex, and the brief excerpt that follows can do little but give the reader an idea of its flavor and introduce a few of its basic ideas.*

Shoshana Zuboff is Charles Edward Wilson Professor of Business Administration at Harvard University's Graduate School of Business Administration, where she joined the faculty in 1981. She holds a Ph.D. in social psychology from Harvard and an undergraduate degree from the University of Chicago. She has published numerous articles and cases on information technology in the workplace and lectures and consults widely on this subject.

Piney Wood, one of the nation's largest pulp mills, was in the throes of a mass modernization effort that would place every aspect of the production process under computer control. Six workers were crowded around a table in the snack area outside what they called the Star Trek Suite, one of the first control rooms to have been completely converted to microprocessor-based instrumentation. It looked enough like a NASA control room to have earned its name.

It was almost midnight, but despite the late hour and the approach of the shift change, each of the six workers was at once animated and thoughtful. "Knowledge and technology are changing so fast," they said, "What will happen to us?" Their visions of the future foresaw wrenching change. They feared that today's working assumptions could not be relied upon to carry them through, that the future would not resemble the past or the present. More frightening still was the sense of a future moving out of reach so rapidly that there was little opportunity to plan or make choices. The speed of dissolution and renovation seemed to leave no time for assurances that we were not heading toward calamity — and it would be all the more regrettable for having been something of an accident.

The discussion around the table betrayed a grudging admiration for the new technology — its power, its intelligence, and the aura of progress surrounding it. That admiration, however, bore a sense of grief. Each expression of gee-whiz-Buck-Rogers breathless wonder brought with it an aching dread conveyed in images of a future that rendered their authors obsolete. In what ways would computer technology transform their work lives? Did it promise the Big Rock Candy Mountain or a silent graveyard?

> In fifteen years, there will be nothing for the worker to do. The technology will be so good it will operate itself. You will just sit there behind a desk running two or three areas of the mill yourself and get bored.

The group concluded that the worker of the future would need "an extremely flexible personality" so that he or she would not be "mentally affected" by the velocity of change. They anticipated that workers would need a great deal of education and training in order to "breed flexibility." "We find it all to be a great stress," they said, "but it won't be that way for the new, flexible people." Nor did they perceive any real choice, for most agreed that without an investment in the new technology, the company could not remain competitive. They also knew that without their additional flexibility, the technology would not fly right. "We are in a bind," one man groaned, "and there is no way out." The most they could do, it was agreed, was to avoid thinking too hard about the loss of overtime pay; the diminished probability of jobs for their sons and daughters; the fears of seeming incompetent in a strange, new milieu; or the possibility that the company might welsh on its promise not to lay off workers.

During the conversation, a woman in stained overalls had remained silent with her head bowed, apparently lost in thought. Suddenly, she raised her face to us. It was lined with decades of hard work, her brow drawn together. Her hands lay quietly on the table. They were calloused and swollen, but her deep brown eyes were luminous, youthful, and kind. She seemed frozen, chilled by her own insight, as she solemnly delivered her conclusion:

> I think the country has a problem. The managers want everything to be run by computers. But if no one has a job, no one will know how to do anything anymore. Who will pay the taxes? What kind of society will it be when people have lost their knowledge and depend on computers for everything?

Her voice trailed off as the men stared at her in dazzled silence. They slowly turned their heads to look at one another and nodded in agreement. The forecast seemed true enough. Yes, there was a problem. They looked as though they had just run a hard race, only to stop short at the edge of a cliff. As their heels skidded in the dirt, they could see nothing ahead but a steep drop downward.

Must it be so? Should the advent of the smart machine be taken as an invitation to relax the demands upon human comprehension and critical judgment? Does the massive diffusion of computer technology throughout our workplaces necessarily entail an equally dramatic loss of meaningful employment opportunities? Must the new electronic milieu engender a world in which individuals have lost control over their daily work lives? Do these visions of the future represent the price of economic success, or might they signal an industrial legacy that must be overcome if intelligent technology is to yield its full value? Will the new information technology represent an opportunity for the rejuvenation of competitiveness, productive vitality, and organizational ingenuity? Which aspects of the future of working life can we predict, and which will depend upon the choices we make today?

The workers outside the Star Trek Suite knew that the so-called technological choices we face are really much more than that. Their consternation puts us on alert. There is a world to be lost and a world to be gained. Choices that appear to be merely technical will redefine our lives together at work. This means more than simply contemplating the implications or consequences of a new technology. It means that a powerful new technology, such as that represented by the computer, fundamentally reorganizes the infrastructure of our material world. It eliminates former alternatives. It creates new possibilities. It necessitates fresh choices.

The choices that we face concern the conception and distribution of knowledge in the workplace. Imagine the following scenario: Intelligence is lodged in the smart machine at the expense of the human capacity for critical judgment. Organizational members become ever more dependent, docile, and secretly cynical. As more tasks must be accomplished through the medium of information technology (I call this "computer-mediated work"), the sentient body loses its salience as a source of knowledge, resulting in profound disorientation and loss of meaning. People intensify their search for avenues of escape through drugs, apathy, or adversarial conflict, as the majority of jobs in our offices and factories become increasingly isolated, remote, routine, and perfunctory. Alternatively, imagine this scenario: Organizational leaders recognize the new forms of skill and knowledge needed to truly exploit the potential of an intelligent technology. They direct their resources toward creating a work force that can exercise critical judgment as it manages the surrounding machine systems. Work becomes more abstract as it depends upon understanding and manipulating information. This marks the beginning of new forms of mastery and provides an opportunity to imbue jobs with more comprehensive meaning. A new array of work tasks offer unprecedented opportunities for a wide range of employees to add value to products and services.

The choices that we make will shape relations of authority in the workplace. Once more, imagine: Managers struggle to retain their traditional sources of authority, which have depended in an important way upon their exclusive control of the organization's knowledge base. They use the new technology to structure organizational experience in ways that help reproduce the legitimacy of their traditional roles. Managers insist on the prerogatives of command and seek methods that protect the hierarchical distance that distinguishes them from their subordinates. Employees barred from the new forms of mastery relinquish their sense of responsibility for the organization's work and use obedience to authority as a means of expressing their resentment. Imagine an alternative: This technological transformation engenders a new approach to organizational behavior, one in which relationships are more intricate, collaborative, and bound by the mutual responsibilities of colleagues. As the new technology integrates information across time and space, managers and workers each overcome their narrow functional perspectives and create new roles that are better suited to enhancing value-adding activities in a data-rich environment. As the quality of skills at each organizational level becomes similar, hierarchical distinctions begin to blur. Authority comes to depend more upon an appropriate fit between knowledge and responsibility than upon the ranking rules of the traditional organizational pyramid.

The choices that we make will determine the techniques of administration that color the psychological ambiences and shape communicative behavior in the emerging workplace. Imagine this scenario: The new technology becomes the source of surveillance techniques that are used to ensnare organizational members or to subtly bully them into conformity. Managers employ the technology to circumvent the demanding work of face-to-face engagement, substituting instead techniques of remote management and automated administration. The new technological infrastructure becomes a battlefield of techniques, with managers inventing novel ways to enhance certainty and control while employees discover new methods of self-protection and even sabotage. Imagine the alternative: The new technological milieu becomes a resource from which are fashioned innovative methods of information sharing and social exchange. These methods in turn produce a deepened sense of collective responsibility and joint ownership, as access to ever-broader domains of information lend new objectivity to data and preempt the dictates of hierarchical authority.

[The book from which this selection is drawn] is about these alternative futures. Computer-based technologies are not neutral; they embody essential characteristics that are bound to alter the nature of work within our factories and offices and among workers, professionals, and managers. New choices are laid open by these technologies, and these choices are being confronted in the daily lives of men and women across the landscape of modern organizations. [The] book is an effort to understand the deep structure of these choices — the historical, psychological, and organizational forces that imbue our conduct and sensibility. It is also a vision of a fruitful future, a call for action that can lead us beyond the stale reproduction of the past into an era that offers a historical opportunity to more fully develop the economic and human potential of our work organizations.

THE TWO FACES OF INTELLIGENT TECHNOLOGY

The past twenty years have seen their share of soothsayers ready to predict with conviction one extreme or another of the alternative futures I have presented. From the unmanned factory to the automated cockpit, visions of the future hail information technology as the final answer to "the labor question," the ultimate opportunity to rid ourselves of the thorny problems associated with training and managing a competent and committed work force. These very same technologies have been applauded as the hallmark of a second industrial revolution in which the classic conflicts of knowledge and power associated with an earlier age will be synthesized in an array of organizational innovations and new procedures for the production of goods and services, all characterized by an unprecedented degree of labor harmony and widespread participation in management process.[1] Why the paradox? How can the very same technologies be interpreted in these different ways? Is this evidence that the technology is indeed neutral, a blank screen upon which managers project their biases and encounter only their own limitations? Alternatively, might it tell us something else about the interior structure of information technology?

Throughout history, humans have designed mechanisms to reproduce and extend the capacity of the human body as an instrument of work. The industrial age has carried this principle to a dramatic new level of sophistication with machines that can substitute for and amplify the abilities of the human body. Because machines are mute, and because they are precise and repetitive, they can be controlled according to a set of rational principles in a way that human bodies cannot.

There is no doubt that information technology can provide substitutes for the human body that reach an even greater degree of certainty and precision. When a task is automated by a computer, it must first be broken down to its smallest components. Whether the activity involves spraying paint on an automobile or performing in a clerical transaction, it is the information contained in this analysis that translates human agency into a computer program. The resulting software can be used to automatically guide equipment, as in the case of a robot, or to execute an information transaction, as in the case of an automated teller machine.

A computer program makes it possible to rationalize activities more comprehensively than if they had been undertaken by a human being. Programmability means, for example, that a robot will respond with unwavering precision because the instructions that guide it are themselves unvarying, or that office transactions will be uniform because the instructions that guide them have been standardized. Events and processes can be rationalized to the extent that human agency can be analyzed and translated into a computer program.

What is it, then, that distinguishes information technology from earlier generations of machine technology? As information technology is used to reproduce, extend, and improve upon the process of substituting machines for human agency, it simultaneously accomplishes something quite different. The devices that automate by translating information into action also register data about those automated activities, thus generating new streams of information. For example, computer-based, numerically controlled machine tools or microprocessor-based sensing devices not only apply programmed instructions to equipment but also convert the current state of equipment, product, or process into data. Scanner devices in supermarkets automate the checkout process and simultaneously generate data that can be used for inventory control, warehousing, scheduling of deliveries, and market analysis. The same systems that make it possible to automate office trans-actions also create a vast overview of an organization's operations, with many lev-els of data coordinated and accessible for a variety of analytical efforts.

Thus, information technology, even when it is applied to automatically repro-duce a finite activity, is not mute. It not only imposes information (in the form of programmed instructions) but also produces information. The action of a machine is entirely invested in its object, the product. Information technology, on the other hand, introduces an additional dimension of reflexivity: It makes its contribution to the product, but it also reflects back on its activities and on the system of activities to which it is related. Information technology not only pro-duces action but also produces a voice that symbolically renders events, objects, and processes so that they become visible, knowable, and shareable in a new way.

Viewed from this interior perspective, information technology is characterized by a fundamental duality that has not yet been fully appreciated. On the one hand, the technology can be applied to automating operations according to a logic that hardly differs from that of the nineteenth-century machine system — replace the human body with a technology that enables the same processes to be performed with more continuity and control. On the other, the same technology simultaneously generates information about the underlying productive and administrative processes through which an organization accomplishes its work. It provides a deeper level of transparency to activities that had been either partially or completely opaque. In this way, information technology supersedes the tradi-tional logic of automation. The word that I have coined to describe this unique capacity is informate. Activities, events, and objects are translated into and made visible by information when a technology informates as well as automates.

The information power of intelligent technology can be seen in the manufac-turing environment when microprocessor-based devices such as robots, program-mable logic controllers, or sensors are used to translate the three-dimensional production process into digitized data. These data are then made available within a two-dimensional space, typically on the screen of a video display terminal or on a computer printout, in the form of electronic symbols, numbers, letters, and graphics. These data constitute a quality of information that did not exist before. The programmable controller not only tells the machine what to do — imposing information that guides operating equipment — but also tells what the machine has done — translating the production process and making it visible.

In the office environment, the combination of on-line transaction systems, information systems, and communications systems creates a vast information presence that now includes data formerly stored in people's heads, in face-to-face conversations, in metal file drawers, and on widely dispersed pieces of paper. The same technology that processes documents more rapidly, and with less interven-tion, than a mechanical typewriter or pen and ink can be used to display those documents in a communications network. As more of the underlying transac-tional and communicative processes of an organization become automated, they, too, become available as items in a growing organizational data base.

In its capacity as an automating technology, information technology has a vast potential to displace the human presence. Its implications as an informating technology, on the other hand, are not well understood. The distinction between automate and informate provides one way to understand how this technology represents both continuities and discontinuities with the traditions of industrial history. As long as the technology is treated narrowly in its automating function, it perpetuates the logic of the industrial machine, which, over the course of this century, has made it possible to rationalize work while decreasing the dependence on human skills. However, when the technology also informates the processes to which it is applied, it increases the explicit information content of tasks and sets into motion a series of dynamics that will ultimately reconfigure the nature of work and the social relationships that organize productive activity.

Because this duality of intelligent technology has not been clearly recognized, the consequences of the technology's informating capacity are often regarded as unintended. Its effects are not planned, and the potential that it lays open remains relatively unexploited. Because the informating process is poorly defined, it often evades the conventional categories of description that are used to gauge the effects of industrial technology.

These dual capacities of information technology are not opposites; they are hierarchically integrated. Informating derives from and builds upon automation. Automation is a necessary but not sufficient condition for informating. It is quite possible to proceed with automation without reference to how it will contribute to the technology's informating potential. When this occurs, informating is experienced as an unintended consequence of automation. This is one point at which choices are laid open. Managers can choose to exploit the emergent informating capacity and explore the organizational innovations required to sustain and develop it. Alternatively, they can choose to ignore or suppress the informating process. In contrast, it is possible to consider informating objectives at the start of an automation process. When this occurs, the choices that are made with respect to how and what to automate are guided by criteria that reflect developmental goals associated with using the technology's unique informating power.

Information technology is frequently hailed as "revolutionary." What are the implications of this term? *Revolution* means a pervasive, marked, radical change, but revolution also refers to a movement around a fixed course that returns to the starting point. Each sense of the word has relevance for the central problem of this [study]. The informating capacity of the new computer-based technologies brings about radical change as it alters the intrinsic character of work — the way millions of people experience daily life on the job. It also poses fundamentally new choices for our organizational futures, and the ways in which labor and management respond to these new choices will finally determine whether our era becomes a time for radical change or a return to the familiar patterns and pitfalls of the traditional workplace. An emphasis on the informating capacity of intelligent technology can provide a point of origin for new conceptions of work and power. A more restricted emphasis on its automating capacity can provide the occasion for that second kind of revolution — a return to the familiar grounds of industrial society with divergent interests battling for control, augmented by an array of new material resources with which to attack and defend.

The questions that we face today are finally about leadership. Will there be leaders who are able to recognize the historical moment and the choices it presents? Will they find ways to create the organizational conditions in which new visions, new concepts, and a new language of workplace relations can emerge? Will they be able to create organizational innovations that can exploit the unique capacities of the new technology and thus mobilize their organization's productive potential to meet the heightened rigors of global competition? Will there be leaders who understand the crucial role that human beings from each organizational stratum can play in adding value to the production of goods and services? If not, we will be stranded in a new world with old solutions. We will suffer through the unintended consequences of change, because we have failed to understand this technology and how it differs from what came before. By neglecting the unique informating capacity of advanced computer-based technology and ignoring the need for a new vision of work and organization, we will have forfeited the dramatic business benefits it can provide. Instead, we will find ways to absorb the dysfunctions, putting out brush fires and patching wounds in a slow-burning bewilderment.

NOTE

1. See, for example, Michael Piore and Charles F. Sabel, *The Second Industrial Divide: Possibilities for Prosperity* (New York: Basic Books, 1984).

26.   The Logistics of Techno-War

GENE I. ROCHLIN

"Warfare is being transformed by the combination of computerized systems: high-technology weapons; communications; command-and-control." So writes Gene Rochlin in "The Logistics of Techno-War." Rochlin analyzes the experience of the 1991 Gulf War to show the dramatic changes in warfare that new technologies have produced, as well as the limitations of these technologies. Rochlin is professor in the Energy and Resources Group at the University of California, Berkeley. Originally a physicist, he has taught and conducted research in science, technology, and society for many years. Trapped in the Net, the book from which this selection was taken, received the Don K. Price award from the American Political Science Association in 1999 as the best book on science, technology, and politics published in the previous two years.

[The Gulf War] was the first space war . . . it was the first war of the space age.

General Merrill McPeak

INTRODUCTION

Despite its hyperbole, the preceding statement by General McPeak, then chief of staff of the U.S. Air Force, represented the dominant politico-military view of the U.S. performance in the 1991 Gulf War that drove the Iraqi military out of Kuwait[1] The minority view that it was logistics and preparation rather than technology that was responsible for the quick victory was perhaps best expressed at the time by Lawrence Korb: "If you've got enough time, American logistics will always overwhelm you. . . . You would not be writing the same story if the war had come in August or September."[2]

This pair of quotes beautifully represents the two ideal positions in the long-standing argument about quality versus quantity in military weapons systems, exposing in the process the generational differences that underlie the two positions.[3] Korb speaks from the conservative historical tradition, in which wars are won on logistics and organization, on fundamentals and mass, providing both robustness and resilience against the expected surprises of armed conflict. McPeak belongs to the new generation of technicians, whose military thinking is based on the introduction of high technology and computers everywhere possible, in "smart" weapons and smart systems, under computerized command and control, with com-

From *Trapped in the Nest* by Gene I. Rochlin, p. 169–187, 255–259. © 1997 Princeton University Press.

plete computer-mediated connectivity and integration both horizontally across the battlefield and vertically from the smallest fighting unit to central command.

The defeat of the traditionalists was probably inevitable even in the case of the U.S. Army, long dominated by conservatism and tradition. Military officers, particularly senior ones, have careers that are intertwined with the civilian economy, and, in particular, with those sectors most closely connected with the military. The shift in the civilian economy from mass-production industry to high-tech industry, with its focus on technology and change as the basis for competitiveness and success, caused a marked shift in the balance of power in the military from warriors to technocrats.[4]

The traditional warriors might nevertheless have won more often in the political struggle if it were not for the persistent social and political denial in U.S. history and politics of the difference between U.S. conduct in warfare and its stated politico-military doctrine. From the Civil War through Vietnam, the United States has always emphasized the quality and performance of the individual, and, by extension, the quality and superiority of his weapons. But when war has come, be it the Civil War, the two world wars, the Korean War, or Vietnam, the United States relied for victory far more on quantity than quality, depending more on its huge industrial base and manpower pool than on technology or training to wear down its opponents.[5]

The "U.S." side (i.e., the Union) in the Civil War was infamous for pouring men into slaughterhouse battlefields to overwhelm the Confederates by sheer numbers.[6] The United States behaved no differently from any of the Western powers in the equally horrible trench battles of the First World War. And victory in the Second World War was clearly based more on logistics and industrial might than on technical innovation.[7] Victories in both wars resulted from the ability and willingness of the United States (and its allies) to maximize effectiveness even at the expense of quality, to absorb losses in attrition warfare with a view to wearing the enemy down rather than outfighting him.[8]

Unable to make use of nuclear weapons, or to fully exploit its slim margin of superiority in radar or other electronics, the U.S. experience in Korea was little different. Only the long and painful experience of fighting a nontraditional conflict in Vietnam was to expose the cost of the traditional American way of war and led to increasing pressure to substitute money, equipment, or technical sophistication for the loss of American lives.

The United States was not the first great power to be faced with the dilemma of seeking to preserve hegemonic control in the face of political protest against the costs, nor will it be the last.[9] During Britain's long reign, it vacillated between exporting the costs (e.g., by using colonial troops) and mobilizing public opinion (e.g., the War of Jenkin's Ear).[10] But in the U.S. case, there was already a putative resolution on the table. The long-term investments made by ARPA and other government agencies in computer technology were just beginning to turn into real products,[11] and the resulting transformation of American society and industry was already under way. Advanced technology, and, in particular, advanced computer technology, in which Americans held an enormous and unchallenged lead, was to allow the United States to continue to project power overseas without at the same time putting American lives unduly at risk.

The first real test of the newly designed, newly integrated military was to come not on the battlefields of central Europe for which the expenditures had been justified, nor in the jungles of Asia, which remain the most problematic arena for technological warfare, but in the flat sands of the Middle East, on a ground more closely resembling American weapons test ranges than even the most optimistic of the new weaponeers could have hoped for.

THE GULF WAR

When Iraqi forces invaded Kuwait in August 1990, they did so at least partially under the delusion that the United States would have neither the will nor the capability to fight the supposedly experienced Iraqi forces in the desert.[12] Following the amazing success of the United States and its coalition allies in the hundred-hour ground war in February 1991, neither the will nor the capability of the United States and its coalition allies could be questioned. And neither, apparently, could the decision to modernize and computerize American and NATO military forces.

The verdict in the quality-quantity debate seemed clear.[13] Promoters of the high-technology strategy proclaimed that the new weapons systems were the key to victory, that their performance discredited critics of high-technology military postures and that the war further demonstrated the ability of "smart" weapons and other sophisticated technical systems to fight effectively while minimizing U.S. casualties.[14] Building on globally televised images of smart bombs flying down air shafts, Tomahawk missiles cruising the skies of Baghdad looking for their targets, and Patriot missiles rushing skyward in a great plume of fire and smoke to hunt incoming Scuds, promoters of sophisticated military technologies boldly announced that technological innovation was now proven to be the best and most reliable guide to the future of American military forces.[15]

The official Department of Defense assessment of the Gulf War therefore took a more sober and balanced approach than that of the technology promoters inside and outside the military.[16] The war demonstrated dramatically the possibilities of the still-ongoing technological revolution in weapons and warfare. Many of the platforms, weapons, and systems were used in combat for the first time, and most performed superbly. Coordinated air power in particular was used with extraordinary effectiveness. But this technological euphoria overlooked the special conditions under which the war was fought, including not only the availability of a neighboring country as a base and lack of Iraqi opposition during the buildup, but also the desert climate, the clear weather, the political isolation of Iraq, and the lack of any other disturbance abroad to divide our attention and assets.[17] The war also exposed serious vulnerabilities in the network of intelligence, logistics, communications, and other infrastructure required to support the sophisticated and complex military technologies.

The high costs of the advanced weapons had been justified as necessary to counter a sudden Soviet attack in Europe, to offset NATO's numerical inferiority and choice of defensive posture. Instead, they were deployed in the Gulf with abundant time and adequate buildup and launched in a time and place of our own choosing, against an enemy with numerical inferiority and poor morale, in combat that turned out to be of no more than moderate intensity. Moreover, the decline of the Soviet threat allowed the United States to divert resources, manpower, and equipment from all over the world. Weapons and systems that had been developed to fight a high-technology war on the central front in Europe while coping with a second, regional conflict were brought to the Gulf to forge and sustain General Schwartzkopf's buildup in Saudi Arabia.

Despite minimal Iraqi opposition, and six long months to prepare and position forces without significant interference, the logistics chain was stretched to the utmost. By the time the ground war started in February, the United States alone had transported more than 500,000 troops, 3,500 aircraft, 4,200 armored vehicles, and seven million tons of cargo to the Gulf — a buildup that gave Desert Storm more ground and support forces to dispose of than had been available at the peak of the war in Vietnam. The U.S. Air Force deployed to the Gulf almost half of its total available combat force, including more than ninety percent of all aircraft capable of designating targets for precision-guided weapons, two-thirds of its total stock of laser-guided bombs, more than half of its electronic warfare and command-and-control aircraft, and ninety percent of all of its mobile fueling equipment.[18] Almost all its airlift capacity was pressed into use on an overtime basis, just to meet the demand for operations-critical items. The U.S. Army moved sixty percent of its total inventory of modern M1 Abrams tanks and M2 and M3 Bradley fighting vehicles to Saudi Arabian bases, along with almost three-quarters of its truck companies (and 100 percent of its heavy trucks), to support only one-quarter of its combat divisions. And although the U.S. Navy deployed almost all of its own combat logistics force, inadequate capacity led to extensive chartering of commercial carriers — over half of which flew a foreign flag.[19]

It was known even before hostilities began that there would be little capacity to surge production of major weapons or systems — one of the known problems with advanced, high-technology, low-production rate goods, whether military or not. The need for manufactured goods was greatest for secondary parts for maintenance and repair, such as transmissions and engines. But production capacity was marginal even for peacetime attrition rates, which could have had serious consequences had the ground war begun earlier, lasted longer, or been more costly. The estimated surge time was six to nine months minimum, even for such low-technology items as barbed wire.[20] By some estimates, there was not even enough ammunition for the Army and Marines to have fought for another week and no capacity to surge production to make up the shortfall.[21]

Fortunately for the coalition, the attrition rate during the air war was much lower than expected, and the ground war swift and relatively low cost in equipment as well as personnel losses. Given the other factors, such as Iraqi incapabilities in electronic warfare and poor morale, it is by now generally agreed that neither the air war nor the actual ground fighting provided a real test of U.S. military strength or overall performance.

Caring Enough to Send the Very Best

The ambiguity in the use of the term "high technology" in both military and popular reporting of the war also tended to confuse the issues. It was rarely clear in any instance whether the term was being applied to individual pieces of hardware, integrated technical fighting components, technical infrastructure, or the integration of the force by the web of communication, surveillance, intelligence, and command-and-control required. Equally praised for their performance, for example, were laser-guided bombs (ordnance); the F-117A stealth aircraft (platform); the Tomahawk cruise missile (weapons system); satellite photography and communications (infrastructure); "AirLand Battle" (doctrine); JSTARS, the experimental Joint Surveillance Target Attack Radar System (combat intelligence); and the actual management of the complex, multinational force (integration).

In the absence of reliable battle damage assessment (BDA), early reporting from the front tended to exaggerate the effectiveness of some of the weapons used.[22] The most glaring example was the performance of the Patriot missile. Hardly a week went by without some dramatic footage of a Patriot blazing off into the sky to intercept a Scud heading for our bases in Saudi Arabia, or for Israel. Even before realistic assessments could be made, the performance of the Patriot was being used to justify further expenditures on ballistic missile defenses and other advanced, highly computerized, high-tech "Star Wars" systems. Later assessments were more sober.[23] Many reported Patriot intercepts were hits on discarded missile bodies or other parts as the Iraqi-modified Scuds broke up in flight. The warheads were usually not destroyed; they were just very inaccurate. Indeed, many in Israel now believe that more damage was done with Patriot in place than would have occurred without it.[24]

There was hardly any system that did not experience some operational surprise. F-16s, for example, had problems with their electronic countermeasure pods because their onboard computers were so packed with information that they could not accommodate the programming to update them for new weapons systems.[25] When friendly-fire incidents started to occur, an emergency order was put through for special infrared emitting attachments to provide better identification.[26] Perhaps more relevant to the future of electronics in warfare, the many laptop and desktop computers shipped out to the Gulf began to collapse under the heat, sand, and strain of operations in the theater — to the point where the United States was seriously considering treating them as disposable items.[27] Ruggedized models were eventually shipped out as replacements, but that took time. Even the invulnerability of the F-117 has been called into question: "It is also debatable whether the F-117s emerged unscathed because of superior stealth technology, the effectiveness of allied air defense suppression aircraft, the incompetence of Iraqi air defense operators, or some combination of all three."[28]

The tactical problems of sending high-tech systems against low-tech armies were prominent in the "traditionalist" position in the quality-quantity debate. The disruption of large, complex, tightly integrated, highly specialized, high-technology militaries can at times be accomplished even with relatively simple weapons. The classic examples come from the Vietnam and Afghanistan wars, in which relatively primitive opponents were able to bring down expensive, highly capable helicopters with small arms and man-carried surface-to-air missiles, because low-level attacks were necessary to find the enemy amidst the ground cover.

Small-arms fire and other portable small weapons were still a very real threat to the expensive, high-technology aircraft providing close air support in Iraq. Fighter and helicopter pilots had to be retrained to fly their attack missions at higher altitudes, or to loiter behind sand dunes and "pop up" for attack to avoid antiaircraft fire; the long-standing assumption in European war-gaming had been a requirement for low-level attack to avoid the presumably more serious threat from Soviet high-altitude air defenses.[29] Had there been a real air war more evenly matched in electronic as well as airframe capabilities, even one not involving continual or heavy combat, the struggle for air superiority would not have allowed such free choice of gaining height or loitering whenever desired.

Even without serious enemy challenge, deadly surprises and close calls occurred. Tactical aircraft and tanks working in daylight hours produced an unprecedentedly high rate of casualties from "friendly fire."[30] Satellites passing overhead mistakenly identified a flight of B-52 bombers as a barrage of Scud missiles. Airborne Warning and Control Systems aircraft (AWACS) had to intervene to prevent allied fighters from attacking their own returning bombers.[31] And, in the few cases when tanks did become entangled in more traditional battles, close air support often had to be foregone to avoid indiscriminate attacks on friend and foe alike.

The success of military technology is measured by the performance of those systems for which electronics, and in particular computerized electronics, is central to performance as well as missions: intelligence and surveillance; navigation; air-to-air and air-to-surface missiles; and, above all, the ability to create, supply, inform, coordinate, and integrate the forces in the field. Although these capabilities were tested in the Gulf War, the inability of Iraq to interfere or intervene, particularly with electronic countermeasures, made it more of a field exercise than a real combat situation.

But separate assessments of individual weapons or systems are not really to the point. Because modern militaries are increasingly designed to operate in a computer-integrated environment when the level and intensity of conflict is high, an *overall* assessment of system performance is required. Given the nature and duration of the battle in Iraq, all that has been proven is that the forces we have are very successful given open skies, a preponderance of force, and minimal effective opposition.

Iraq had no meaningful capability at all in the critical area of electronic warfare, enabling coalition forces to move freely while keeping close tabs on Iraqi forces, particularly at night. Furthermore, the conditions of desert warfare — flat and open land free of the dense jungle cover of Vietnam or the mountainous and craggy terrain of Afghanistan — also provided little or no natural interference with surveillance, intelligence, and communications and no place for Iraq to hide, disperse, or mask their combat forces effectively.

The Logistics of Cyberspace

With six months to establish the command-and-control network and accumulate supplies without interference, combat experience provided few surprises. In contrast, the more general lessons about the organization, management, and integration of forces were numerous, and potentially disturbing. The organization behind the weapons did work, but only at tremendous cost, even under uniquely favorable conditions. The United States was able to mobilize, on its own schedule, whatever pieces were required out of a force structure intended to fight one and a half wars simultaneously, and then to use it to fight a half-war under maximally favorable conditions, at the cost of almost totally stripping Europe and the United States of systems, spares, and maintenance.[32]

Up and down the line of logistics and supply, the United States and its allies had time to train, to tighten up, to identify problems, and to reflect upon the battle terrain in ways that would not otherwise have been possible. There is every reason to question whether the coalition would have been able to act as well, and with such small losses, if it had been denied the time to mobilize and prepare its forces, the logistics to bring them to the battle and keep them resupplied, and the freedom to use its advanced intelligence and communication technologies without hindrance. Although U.S. forces arrived in Saudi Arabia quickly after the first Iraqi move to Kuwait in August 1990, there was a lengthy period thereafter when the coalition could not have defended its bases or its position from a follow-on Iraqi invasion.[33]

Considerable resources had to be diverted, even in the relatively one-sided conditions. High-technology weapons systems using black boxes operated smoothly, but only at enormous expense, and at the cost of moving almost all of the U.S. reserve repair capacity into sprawling Saudi bases that would have been quite vulnerable to a serious Iraqi attack. As many as eight scarce and expensive electronic warfare aircraft were used to cover a dozen F-16s on a raid; the high ratio of support to combat aircraft was not untypical for air operations, and, in some cases, was a limiting factor. Satellites intended to cover the Soviet Union and other areas of the world had to be moved into position to provide surveillance and intelligence. Command-and-control resources intended to fight a major, global war were diverted to the Gulf to manage the intricacies of the battle.

The high level of redundancy in resources and ample preparation time made possible by the six-month buildup preceding hostilities were not as apparent to the press, or as widely publicized, as fancy weapons, but they were unquestionably the most important factors in the smoothness and effectiveness of military operations, particularly in the four-day ground war. That time was needed to test, adjust, maintain, and make fully operational a large number of the high-tech platforms and systems. It was also needed to collect data and develop intelligence and information. At the beginning of the buildup there were almost no up-to-date photos of the combat area. In fact, it took almost all of the six months to acquire, analyze, digitize, and program the key terrain and target information needed for programming the Tomahawk cruise missile's guidance computers.[34]

As materiél and logistical support accumulated in the theater by stripping units in Germany and the United States, maintenance bases in Saudi Arabia had virtually unprecedented access to parts and to diagnostic and other critical skills in a U.S. military establishment designed and sized to fight not one, but two global wars. National Guard and other reserve units were mined for resources. Missing personnel for critical slots, always in short supply even in peacetime, were sought out and brought to the theater. Even active duty personnel for whom there was no immediate use were nevertheless alerted and retained.[35]

Military skills were further augmented by an extraordinary amount of on-site contractor expertise, in the form of special teams of civilian experts who helped diagnose problems and supplied needed parts.[36] In many cases, this involved direct communication with or transport to and from the United States. Computerized electronic warfare aboard aircraft, for example, needed to be updated constantly to adjust to changing evaluation of threats. At first, this involved the awkward and time-consuming shuttling of tapes between the U.S. and the Saudi bases. Given the time to adjust, the United States was able to establish direct, secure communication links, allowing the direct updating and reprogramming from the United States of aircraft computer systems located in the Gulf.[37] And many of the black-box electronic packages aboard tanks and naval vessels, as well as aircraft, were shuttled back and forth for maintenance, updating, and servicing.

The amount of expert support needed to achieve high levels of availability was never given much prominence in military or press accounts, even though they foreshadow the demands new weapons systems will impose upon even a smaller high-technology military. Many support roles have been transferred to civilian employees or contractors to conserve military manpower; many more are being so designated because the specialized skills are not and will not be available. As the DoD report concludes, "It seems clear that future contingencies also will require the presence and involvement of civilians in active theaters of operations."[38] But "active theaters" generally mean within zones of combat. Given that civilians are, after all, civilians, and receive no hazard pay and few awards for being in a combat zone, it is an open question whether maintenance bases will be able to draw as easily on civilian personnel if U.S. forces are required to construct and use their forward bases under the threat of serious enemy attack.

Some of the war's success stories become more problematic when examined in this light. Although such adaptations are normal for battlefield conditions, these conditions eliminate many of the supposed advantages of advanced over-the-horizon and fire-and-forget weapons. Rather than adding flexibility, these advanced systems must be closely constrained in their application by integrated command networks that guarantee that they are allocated efficiently and that the right targets are being destroyed. The resulting military organization needs relatively predictable conditions to assure that these networks perform successfully and is less likely to be effective in a disruptive, hard-fought conflict.

This vivid demonstration of the depth and breadth of support necessary to support a large, complex military organization equipped with advanced, complex, and often fragile technologies and machines is perhaps the single greatest lesson of the war in the Gulf, however long it took to sink in. It is not clear if even six months would have been adequate if Iraq had been willing (or able) to actively disrupt organizational growth, training, and integration.

The Electronic Web

The DoD noted that, "The services put more electronics communications connectivity into the Gulf in ninety days than we put in Europe in forty years."[39] The largest complete C³I (command, control, communications, and intelligence) system ever assembled was put into place to connect not only the U.S. forces in the Gulf, but to sustain bases in the United States, the national command authority in Washington, and other coalition forces. The achievement was so stunning that the mere existence and reliable functioning of the network was one of the great successes of the war. But later analysis has also shown that the performance of the electronic warfare and command-and-control systems left much to be desired.

Shortfalls in operations caused by lack of equipment hampered many operations, particularly of the more advanced weapons and systems. "The greatest limitation on the U.S. ability to apply combat power . . . was our own lack of systems to support combat aircraft in theater. At any given time we were only able to use twenty-five percent of the combat air assets we had in theater simply because it took . . . 100 percent of the electronic war assets to support that limited effort."[40] Aircraft IFF equipment reliability and maintenance was a constant problem, both at the individual aircraft level and to the airborne war-fighting command posts. This was further exacerbated by the lack of interoperability or standardization among the several coalition air forces. Some analysts even suggested that the United States would be better off investing in more electronic warfare equipment instead of buying more combat aircraft.

The demand for intelligence data, particularly satellite and reconnaissance imagery, for targeting precision-guided munitions was insatiable and simply could not be met even by the commitment of as many U.S. resources as could be made available.[41] Nor were the services able to organize, process, and coordinate it efficiently. The volume of data simply swamped the tactical intelligence system and came near to paralyzing other systems for electronic integration and command-and-control.[42] And it is likely to continue to do so in the future, no matter what steps are taken, since data-gathering technology tends to stay ahead of data-processing capabilities and perhaps always will.

Maintaining the volume of communication also turned out to be an incredible problem, even in the absence of effective Iraqi capabilities for jamming or other countercommunications measures expected in a major combat theater. At the peak, 286 separate communications centers were interacting with each other and with out-of-theater command centers. A hybrid telephone system made up of several generations of different communications equipment from different services, and from different countries, handled more than 700,000 telephone calls and 150,000 important messages a day. Daily management and monitoring of more than 35,000 frequencies was required to assure that channels were clear and free of interference.[43]

Communications links included SHF military satellite channels, UHF tactical channels, the military's automatic digital network (AUTODIN) and worldwide military command-and-control system, and even channels made available over more secure defense satellite systems intended for other purposes. Even that was not enough. The Navy's UHF satellite communications links were so overtaxed that at one point in late November, Naval Space Command announced that no more coverage was available. Commercial terminals and leased commercial channels were used to augment the capacity, including INTELSAT and even the Saudi national telephone service. Some commercial equipment was even installed on Navy ships.[44] The serious weakness of the resulting system, its vulnerability to both electronic and physical interference, was never exposed because Iraq never put it to the test.

Other command-and-control problems were worked out during the six months of buildup to the point where little friction occurred during the operational ground war phase. This was no small task considering the number of allied as well as U.S. units that had to be integrated into a single, coordinated structure and the breadth and complexity of the frontal attack that had to be synchronized. Even so, the postwar evaluation was that combined forces command and control is still rudimentary and might have proved inflexible and unwieldy if there had been any setback or surprises during execution of planned joint maneuvers. As it was, technological improvisation was called into play many times to develop innovations or other workarounds. Once again, the amount of time available to test systems and practice using them proved crucial.

The greatest success of C³I was in the critical task of integrating and coordinating the air war, both before the ground attack and during it. When data and targeting information were available, mission planning was frequently accomplished in hours rather than the days that had characterized combat in Vietnam. Also highly praised was the NAVSTAR Global Positioning System (GPS), a network of satellites whose transmitted data allow accurate determination of the receiver's position to within a few meters. Indeed, some units used comparison of GPS position readings as a method of IFF [identify friend or foe] verification during the ground war. In addition to terrestrial navigation, GPS was also used to improve aircraft navigation accuracy and provide midcourse guidance for cruise missiles.

On the other hand, there was often some confusion and delay in getting ground targets identified and targeted, owing to the long and complex chain of command involved. The shortage of military GPS receivers also forced mass purchases of commercial units, which in turn meant that the United States had to disable the security provisions of GPS that normally deny such accurate positioning to nonsecurity–cleared receivers.[45]

Fortunately for the coalition, the rapid Iraqi collapse eased the strain as the war went on instead of increasing it. Such rudimentary electronic warfare capabilities as Iraq had were targeted early on and quickly rendered inoperable or unusable, and other, more devious strategies for interfering with the web of coalition communication and information nets were apparently not tried. But at no time did the Gulf War test whether the required electronic infrastructure was really robust or resilient against a systematic, capable, and determined effort to disrupt it at either the tactical or command level.

REDEFINING EFFECTIVENESS

Military technologies, like civil ones, are subject to the familiar drive of the "product displacement cycle."[46] The United States can attempt to maintain dominance by continuing to generate ever more advanced and complex weapons systems, even as the last generation is sold to or coproduced by our allies. If the historical cycle holds, European powers will then buy or codevelop the equivalent of today's high-tech systems, while the United States continues its search for newer, more advanced, and far more expensive ones. In turn, the Europeans will seek to keep their costs down by marketing their technology, or their skills, to the richer of the developing countries. This, at least, would replicate the history of the arms race in the Middle East.

Under such circumstances, the future U.S. force would still be capable of inflicting greater and greater damage, but at ever-increasing costs and risks. It could be used with assured success only against opponents who lack the countering technical capabilities. Given the vigor of the arms markets, especially after the Gulf War, the number of such convenient countries will continue to decline. The United States would then be unable credibly to protect its interests, or project force, against less accommodating opponents who are too large or too technically knowledgeable for the intricately integrated U.S. systems to defeat with the required minimal casualties.

Until recently, U.S. armed forces justified their "inefficiently" duplicative resources in terms of slack — unused reserves to be drawn upon and orchestrated when these inevitable disruptions occur. The move to greater efficiency by reducing organizational slack, to cut personnel and compensate with computers and electronic networks, to substitute "just-in-time" resupply for stockpiles, is familiar enough to students of modern industrial policies. But civilian firms that rely on electronic systems, and, in particular, on computerized equipment for integration, coordination, and control generally do not face the same consequences if systems fail and are almost never expected to perform under armed attack.

Able to purchase fewer and fewer of the new systems in times of budgetary restraint, the U.S. might increasingly shift to forces shaped primarily for high-tech intervention without a full appreciation for the risks that might be entailed. Claiming to have learned the double lesson of high-technology and low-cost intervention from its success in the Gulf, the military might well move toward a high-technology "surgical" force directed primarily at smaller and less capable powers. But to do so without providing a proportionately larger support system will produce a military that lacks robustness and resilience against errors, against surprises, and against clever, if unsophisticated, countermeasures.

The modern U.S. military is increasingly becoming a complex, highly interconnected, integrated sociotechnical system with high interdependence between and among units.[47] As such, it requires intensive, timely logistics and information support. The high-technology weapons were effective because their support systems were allowed to train and operate without hindrance and almost without time or resource constraint. Because the conflict did not test the combat robustness of U.S. forces adequately, there is reason for caution about potential vulnerabilities if the United States is pressured by time or circumstance to deploy against a similar opponent at less than full strength or against a more powerful opponent even if its full strength can be brought to bear.

The Gulf War victory crystallized the emerging redefinition of military effectiveness through advanced technology as a substitute for American lives discussed at the beginning of this chapter. This emphasis may be more sensible in peacetime than in war. Peacetime militaries are not threatened with a sudden loss of staff as a matter of daily routine. They do not face a malicious enemy trying to physically cause as much trouble as possible to critical communication or information links.

The underlying arguments of the quantity-quality debate concerning robustness, reliability, and the ability to cope with fundamental surprise have not been resolved. What is more, the subsequent political and bureaucratic reinforcement of those who have based their careers and their futures on advanced, computerized military technologies almost certainly guarantees that they will hardly be addressed.

COMPUTERS AND THE TRANSFORMATION OF WAR

Because of the many special conditions, the coalition's invasion of Iraq bore more resemblance to an elaborate simulation, or perhaps video game, than the hypercomplex, high-attrition, electronic scramble that is usually envisioned when analysts talk about the coming technological transition in warfare. This goes beyond the question of what success the United States would have had if the Iraqis had fought back effectively. Given the positions, the isolation of Iraq, and the military asymmetries, the coalition would have won regardless. But the costs might have been far, far higher.

The most lasting lessons of the Gulf War were the indirect ones learned by the troops in their day-to-day operations; the real transition that is taking place is more a transition in the perception of combat than in the nature and structure of warfare. In the future, survival in combat may come to depend almost entirely on getting off the first accurate shot.

Even without a major war, the battlefield environment has been transformed by technical innovation in the past fifty years. It is a long way from the desperate and closely fought tank meleés of the Ukraine or North Africa to an M1A1 commander blowing up Iraqi tanks with precise single shots while moving across rough terrain. Fighter pilots operating under the control of AWACS with an umbrella of electronic warfare support, firing missiles at signals seen only on their radar, are even farther technically from the Battle of Britain. And the pilot of an F-117, flying to Baghdad in a cloak of stealth with television-guided precision weapons, may not even have been born when James Michener immortalized the dangers of flying into the teeth of air defenses in Korea to attack the bridges at Toko-ri.[48]

When the rain of arrows fell on the French knights at Agincourt, the archers knew that they were no longer fodder to be fed into the periphery of battles between armored nobles, even if the kings and princes were slow to catch up. The U.S. Marines cheering the Gatling guns at San Juan Hill, the British Maxim gunners mowing down rank after rank of Dervishes at Omdurman and Zulus at Mome Gorge, and even the Tibetans, Furani, or Ashanti who simply dropped their weapons and walked away once they realized what was happening, knew that the day of infantry advancing in formation across open ground was over, even if the generals refused to listen.[49] At some future date, the single-shot kills of the M1A1 tanks in Iraq may rank with these as a turning point in the understanding by soldiers of the nature and risks of a new battlefield.

Warfare is being transformed by the combination of computerized systems: high-technology weapons; communications; command-and-control. The Gulf War demonstrated clearly how much military analysts believe that it has already transformed military operations.[50] Massive attacks, front lines, indeed the whole apparatus of attrition warfare are now claimed to be obsolete. Instead, it is argued, the new mode of war will be "nonlinear"; an assemblage of small units, moving quickly and independently, striking at will and at night, coordinating with each other flexibly as the situation demands.[51] This new "maneuver warfare" would seem very postmodern indeed were it not for the massive requirements for central control and coordination built in to AirLand Battle and the other new force structure designs and doctrines.[52]

Having overcome what they regarded as the traditionalist school of linear, attrition warfare, the new cadre of senior officers is now trying to lead rather than follow, to promote rather than resist. The smart-weapon, smart-system revolution has penetrated the military establishment from top to bottom, from the grunt on the ground confirming his squad's position with GPS or using satellite communications to call in a precision air or artillery strike to the general or admiral monitoring or being briefed on the progress of the fighting almost in real time. At every level, and in every service, the introduction of weapons based on or incorporating computers and the rapid and elaborate communications and data processing they make possible has transformed not only the nature and definition of combat, but the linkage among and between commanders and soldiers, the front line of battle and the zones behind it where the smart weapons are mustered, launched, and directed.

It is this complex web of interactions and relationships and the degree of control they make possible that makes the new weapons systems usable and effective. It is force structure and doctrine that determines their role. Yet, arguments about the modernization of military forces almost always focus on the cost and performance of the weapons, neglecting both the costs and the vulnerabilities of the increasingly complex organization needed to support them. This inevitably leads to the conclusion that small numbers of new systems with greater individual capabilities should replace larger numbers of older, "dumber" ones, reinforcing and building on the judgments and evaluations of the personnel who use them.

But wars are won in the large, not in the small; cost-effectiveness is properly measured in terms of the goals of war and not the protection of individual lives. What is not generally realized is how the cost and scarcity of the new systems lock them into networks of mutual dependency, reducing unit autonomy by forcing integration into large-scale tactics and doctrines. Units now fight more effectively, but far less independently. These tendencies were most apparent in the coordination of air power; however, the tendencies were already apparent in other, more traditional areas, such as artillery coordination and tank movements.

Unwilling, and perhaps unable, to fight another high-loss war of attrition, the United States and other NATO powers claim that the new high-technology weapons increase both the power and the autonomy of smaller units. But . . . the future battlefield is being designed as an electronic "battlespace" and the need to maintain tightly integrated command-and-control will overwhelm the presumptive discretion given to individual soldiers or units with supposedly smart weapons, even if those weapons are independently targetable and programmable.

NOTES

1. Craig Covault, "Desert Storm Reinforces Military Space Directions," *Aviation Week and Space Technology* 134 (April 8, 1991): 42–47. The epigraph to this chapter is a direct quote made while General McPeak was still chief of staff of the U.S. Air Force.
2. Secretary of Defense for Manpower, Logistics, and Reserve Affairs from 1981 to 1985, as quoted by David C. Morrison, "Logistic War's Long, Long Lines," *National Journal* 23 (March 2, 1991): 514–5.
3. The fundamental question of the quantity-quality debate was whether the United States should spend, for example, a $400 million procurement budget by buying ten advanced fighter aircraft at $40 million each or forty at $10 million each. The "quantity" side emphasized survival of the force in the face of possible surprises or unexpected vulnerabilities; the "quality" side emphasized survival of the individual and the need, therefore, to maintain an edge over opponents. The substance of the debate is much too long to summarize here. Some useful readings are Stephen Peter Rosen, *Winning the Next War: Innovation and the Modern Military* (Ithaca, NY: Cornell University Press, 1991); Arthur T. Hadley, *Straw Giant: A Report from the Field* (New York: Random House, 1986); David Bellin and Gary Chapman, *Computers in Battle: Will They Work?* (New York: Harcourt Brace Jovanovich, 1987); James Fallows, *National Defense* (New York: Random House, 1981); Edward N. Luttwak, *The Pentagon and the Art of War* (New York: Simon & Schuster, 1984); Franklin C. Spinney, *Defense Facts of Life: the Plans/Reality Mismatch* (Boulder, CO: Westview Press, 1985); Asa A. Clark IV, et al., (eds.) *The Defense Reform Debate* (Baltimore, MD: Johns Hopkins University Press, 1984); Martin Binkin, *Military Technology and Defense Manpower* (Washington, DC: Brookings Institution, 1986); and Frank Barnaby and Marlies ter Borg (eds.), *Emerging Technologies and Military Doctrine: A Political Assessment* (New York: St. Martin's Press, 1986). What is most interesting is that the recognition by the United States in the 1970s that it had to choose at all was caused not so much by the economic constraints that surfaced in the 1990s as by the exponentially rising cost of state-of-the-art technology in military systems once technology, rather than use, became the driving force in weapons acquisition.
4. Seymour J. Deitchman, *Military Power and the Advance of Technology* (Boulder, CO: Westview Press, 1985), 246ff. Also see Martin van Creveld *Technology and War: From 2000 B.C. to the Present* (New York: Free Press, 1989); Luttwak, *Art of War*; Spinney, *Defense Facts of Life*; Binkin, *Defense Manpower*; Gary Chapman, "The New Generation of High-Technology Weapons," in Bellin and Chapman, *Computers in Battle* (pp. 61–100); and Jacques S. Gansler, *The Defense Industry* (Cambridge, MA: MIT Press, 1980).

5. See, for example, the extended discussions in Russell Weigley, *The American Way of War* (New York: Macmillan, 1973).

6. Ibid., 128ff.

7. This is the main thrust of *The American Way of War*. There were certainly a number of technical triumphs on the Allied side in the Second World War, many of which, including cryptography and systems analysis as well as nuclear weapons, contributed greatly to the outcome. But few of these affected the actual fighting, particularly on the ground. Only when the tide of war had turned and there was spare production capacity was the possibility of seeking new weapons for the individual soldier, sailor, or airman given serious consideration.

8. Many comparative evaluations of Allied and German performance in both World Wars have come to the conclusion that man-for-man and unit-for-unit the German forces fought more effectively — unless they were similarly constrained. See, for example, Allan R. Millett and Williamson Murray, *The Second World War: Military Effectiveness* (Boston: Allen & Unwin, 1988); Trevor Dupuy, *A Genius for War: The German Army and the General Staff, 1087–1945* (Englewood Cliffs, NJ: Prentice-Hall, 1977); and Sam Sarkesian (ed.), *Combat Effectiveness: Cohesion, Stress, and the Volunteer Military* (Beverly Hills: Sage Publications, 1980). The Germans, for example, had better and more innovative weapons, and, surprisingly to many, were more practiced in nurturing cohesion in combat, even at the end of the war. The American rhetorical posture of precision shooting and bombing, technical superiority, and troop nurture did not match the reality of mass bombing, sketchy training, and the freezing of many design and training innovations to encourage mass production at maximum volume.

9. See, for example, Paul Kennedy, *The Rise and Fall of the Great Powers* (New York: Random House, 1987).

10. An excellent summary of Britain's dilemma following the Second World War is given by Correlli Barnett in *Audit of War: The Illusion and Reality of Britain as a Great Nation* (London: Macmillan, 1986).

11. For a concise history of military-funded support of strategic and other forms of computing, see Paul N. Edwards, *The Closed World: Computers and the Politics of Discourse in Cold War America* (Cambridge, MA: MIT Press, 1980); and Bellin and Chapman, *Computers in Battle*.

12. This section draws heavily on Gene I. Rochlin and Chris C. Demchak, *Lessons of the Gulf War: Policy Papers in International Affairs* (Berkeley: Institute of International Studies, University of California, 1991). Since that time, several other major reviews of the Gulf War have come to similar conclusions. See especially, U.S. Department of Defense, *Conduct of the Persian Gulf War: Final Report to Congress* (Washington, DC: U.S. Government Printing Office, 1992); Lawrence Freedman and Efraim Karsh, *The Gulf Conflict 1990–1991: Diplomacy and War in the New World Order* (Princeton, NJ: Princeton University Press, 1993); and Michael J. Mazarr, Don M. Snider, and James A. Blackwell, Jr., *Desert Storm: The Gulf War and What We Learned* (Boulder, CO: Westview Press, 1993).

13. For a brief review, see Gene I. Rochlin and Chris C. Demchak, "The Gulf War: Technological and Organizational Implications," *Survival* 33 (May/June 1991): 260–73.

14. That this was a popular theme may be seen by glancing at "America at War," *Newsweek*, Spring/Summer 1991.

15. For example, Air Force General Merrill McPeak, as quoted in the *Washington Post*, March 15, 1991; and John D. Morrocco, "Gulf War Boosts Prospects for High Technology Weapons," *Aviation Week and Space Technology* 134 (March 18, 1991): 45–47. Even long after the Gulf War, the argument for moving to more reliance on air forces and sophisticated weapons systems as a fundamental element of U.S. military forces for all theaters of war persists. See, for example, "Air Dominance Called Key to U.S. Defense." One of the things that got forgotten in this rush to technology was that those emphasizing quantity had called for less expensive technology, not less altogether; the cruise missile was one of the favored systems.

16. Department of Defense, *Persian Gulf War*.

17. Mazarr et al., *Desert Storm*, 4ff. See, also, Freedman and Karsh, *Gulf Conflict*, who argue that the victory was due more to "traditional" failings on the Iraqi side than to the coalition's technological superiority.

18. Eliot A. Cohen, "Air War in the Persian Gulf," *Armed Forces Journal International* (June 1993): 10–14.
19. Department of Defense, *Persian Gulf War*, 416ff.
20. Ibid., 444ff.
21. James Blackwell, *Thunder in the Desert: The Strategy and Tactics of the Persian Gulf War* (New York: Bantam, 1991), 229. Other estimates range up to three or four weeks' supply, arguing that the intensity of the first four days could not have continued. Indeed, it probably could not have. In a situation reminiscent of Patton in France in 1944, the speed of the armored attack during the four days of the ground war far exceeded the ability of the logistics system to supply it. In addition, the ground war was being fought almost twenty-four hours a day; simple exhaustion would soon have forced a slower tempo.
22. The lack of effective BDA was pointed out as one of the critical shortcomings of U.S. technology during the entire period. See, for example, Department of Defense, *Persian Gulf War*, where it is mentioned in several places as one of the more pressing future needs.
23. Theodore A. Postol, "Lessons of the Gulf War Experience with Patriot," *International Security* 16 (Winter 1991/1992): 119–71.
24. Eric Schmitt, "Israel Plays Down Effectiveness of Patriot Missile," *New York Times*, October 31, 1991, A5.
25. Mazarr et al., *Desert Storm*, 107. They also cite one reference as having likened the F-16 to a big computer game that needed more disk space.
26. David Hughes, "Small Firm Acted Quickly to Design, Field Infrared Beacons for Vehicles," *Aviation Week and Space Technology* 134 (May 20, 1991): 54–56. In only twenty-four days, a small Texas firm produced 3,000 infrared beacons for $3.2 million as AFID (Antifratricide Identification Devices). They worked in Kuwait and Iraq primarily because suppression of Iraqi air prevented using the beacons to target coalition forces.
27. "Word Perfect Called to Action for Desert Storm," *Word Perfect Report*, May 1991, 9.
28. "Let's Clear the Air on Stealth," *Aviation Week and Space Technology* 134 (May 20, 1991): 9.
29. Jeffrey M. Lenorovitz, "Air National Guard Unit's F-16 Pilots Say Small Arms Fire Is the Primary Threat," *Aviation Week and Space Technology* 134 (February 25, 1991): 42–44. As many as fifteen coalition aircraft were lost to small arms of man-carried infrared missiles, including several British Tornados (*Newsweek*, "America at War," 76–77). Note that these were the mission profiles for which the Tornados were designed.
30. Although friendly fire casualties averaged five percent for previous American wars, nine of seventeen British soldiers killed in action in Iraq were victims of friendly fire. Of the American deaths, 35 of the 146 soldiers killed (twenty-five percent), and 72 of the 467 wounded (fifteen percent) were friendly-fire casualties (Department of Defense, *Persian Gulf War*, 589ff.). All of the damaging hits on M1A1 tanks turned out to be from friendlies. Despite efforts to seek new identification technologies, the report also states that the combination of longer-range weapons, low-visibility and night fighting, high-kill-probability weapons and ammunition, and the necessity to engage rapidly and (almost) automatically to survive on the modern battlefield will greatly complicate efforts to devise better methods for battlefield identification.
31. Schmitt, "Unforeseen Problems." Friendly fire losses were common even in the Second World War. However, the costs and scarcity of the new technology aircraft, and the amount of time and training their pilots receive, makes them far more valuable assets, on a comparative basis, than individual aircraft of earlier wars — perhaps one might use the analogy of losing a whole flight or wing (which is quite different in terms of effectiveness from losing a number of individual aircraft). The point is that even with the best of modern technology, such incidents *still* occur. The difference is that in the modern era of very expensive and sophisticated weapons and very highly trained crews, the cost of even a single incident is very high.
32. Department of Defense, *Persian Gulf War*; Rochlin and Demchak, "Lessons of the Gulf War"; Rochlin and Demchak, "Gulf War"; U.S. General Accounting Office, *Operation Desert Storm: The Services' Efforts to Provide Logistics Support for Selected Weapons Systems*, Report GAO/NSIAD-91-321 (Washington, DC: Author, September 1991).
33. Department of Defense, *Persian Gulf War*, 389.

34. "As You Were?" *The Economist*, March 9, 1991, 26–27. According to *Newsweek*, "America at War": "Schwartzkopf had to improvise a credible defense from whatever he could scratch up. At one point, he phoned the Navy to ask what Iraqi targets the USS *Wisconsin* could hit with its sea-launched Tomahawk cruise missiles. The answer came back: zero. The Tomahawks must be programmed with electronic terrain maps to home in on their targets. The CIA and DIA, preoccupied with monitoring the Soviet Union's withdrawal of conventional forces in Eastern Europe, hadn't programmed their satellites to make such maps for Iraq. The maps didn't arrive until the end of August."

35. Rochlin and Demchak, "Gulf War."

36. See, for example, David F. Bond, "Troop and Materiel Deployment Missions," *Aviation Week and Space Technology* 134 (April 22, 1991): 94–95. Bond, "Army Speeds Helicopter Enhancements," *Aviation Week and Space Technology* 134 (April 1, 1991): 24–25. "The Army beefed up Apache maintenance at unit and higher levels with personnel from the AH-64 manufacturer, McDonnel Douglas Helicopter Co. Army personnel levels were below those authorized and were insufficient to support a wartime tempo of operations. The AH-64 maintenance training base was geared simply to support the continued fielding of Apache units. AH-64 readiness had been low during much of the aircraft's lifetime in the field, *and the Army brought in contractor support rather than take chances in wartime*" [Emphasis supplied].

37. Department of Defense, *Persian Gulf War*, 439.

38. Ibid., App. N, especially at 599–600.

39. Lt. General James S. Cassity, as quoted in Department of Defense, *Persian Gulf War*, 559.

40. Philip J. Klass, "Gulf War Highlights Benefits, Future Needs of EW Systems," *Aviation Week and Space Technology* 135 (October 21, 1991): 34–37.

41. Department of Defense, *Persian Gulf War*, especially 337ff.

42. Jeffrey T. Richelson, "Volume of Data Cripples Tactical Intelligence System," *Armed Forces Journal International* (June 1992): 35–37.

43. Department of Defense, *Persian Gulf War*, 560.

44. Most of the preceding was digested from *Persian Gulf War*, App. K, "Command, Control, Communications, and Space."

45. The inability of the Iraqis to appreciate the situation they were in is dramatically apparent from the lack of any attempt to exploit the open availability of GPS data, or to interfere with the signals, even though most analysts credit them with the capability in principle.

46. The "product displacement cycle" represents the gradual transfer of technology down the hierarchy of industrialized nations. Because labor costs also decline as one moves down the chain, the country at the top must continue to innovate technologically to maintain its markets. And, because the dominant power almost always also favors a liberal (open) trading system, it cannot otherwise protect itself without incurring serious costs. Thus, the "technological imperative" of product innovation can be seen to be a political-economic as well as sociotechnical consequence of the structure of the international system.

47. See, for example, Chris C. Demchak, *Military Organizations, Complex Machines: Modernization in the U.S. Armed Services* (Ithaca, NY: Cornell University Press, 1991); Gene I. Rochlin, "Informal Organizational Networking as a Crisis Avoidance Strategy," *Industrial Crisis Quarterly* 3 (1989): 159–76; Rochlin and Demchak, "Gulf War"; Demchak, "Fully Networked Battlespace," Euro XIV Operations Research Conference (Jerusalem, Israel, July 1995).

48. James A. Michener, *Bridges at Toko-ri* (New York: Random House, 1953).

49. John Ellis, *Social History of the Machine Gun* (New York: Arno Press, 1981).

50. Mazarr and others, *Desert Storm*.

51. Ibid., 97.

52. See, for example, U.S. Department of the Army, *Force XXI . . . America's Army of the 21st Century* (Fort Monroe, VA: DACS-LM, U.S. Army 1995).

PART VII
DEBATING TECHNOLOGY:
21ST CENTURY STYLE

The comparison between the 1960s-style debate on technology between Emmanuel Mesthene and John McDermott in Part II of this book and the twenty-first-century debate between Bill Joy and his critics in the next two chapters is a remarkable illustration both of how much and how little has changed during the past thirty-plus years (which coincide, more or less, with the period that *Technology and the Future* has been in print).

The Mesthene–McDermott dispute is strongly ideological. McDermott represents the "New Left" of the 1960s and 70s and its attendant counterculture. Although Mesthene would have disagreed strongly with the characterization, McDermott places him squarely in the camp of the reactionary "establishment" seeking to preserve the status quo and all the inequities and injustices it implies. Mesthene would probably have regarded McDermott as a Luddite, heir to the antitechnology tradition of those British activists who went about destroying machines in the early days of the Industrial Revolution nearly 200 years ago. The Bill Joy–John Seely Brown/ Paul Duguid argument lacks the ideological edge and the bitterness of the 1960s debate. Their arguments are largely devoid of politics and ideology. Both sides in the dispute are technophiles, although Joy is a technophile who believes he has seen the future and is very frightened by it. Nonetheless, the opposite sides in both of these debates (Mesthene vs. McDermott and Joy vs. Brown/Duguid) reflect sharply different perspectives on the balance between the benefits and the harmful impacts of technology.

The shift back to debating this balance between harm and benefits represents something of a departure during the past few years. In the previous edition of *Technology and the Future,* the counterpart to this section ("Debating Technology: Turn of the Millennium Style") featured Nicholas Negroponte and Donald Norman in a friendly disagreement over whether the future is going to be "digital" (i.e., shaped by our ability to digitize any kind of information — Negroponte's view) or analog (i.e., whether the headlong rush to digitization is causing us to lose sight of the fact that we are analog creatures and need to design technologies to suit ourselves rather than designing technologies and expecting that we will adapt — Norman's perspective).

The technologies about which Bill Joy and John Seely Brown and Paul Duguid are arguing — genetic engineering, robotics, and nanotechnology —

were barely imagined in the 1960s Yet, whether we fear them or look to them as the potential sources of enormous economic, health, and societal benefits, we need to be thinking carefully and constantly about the ways in which society is affected by them and can shape their development in positive ways. The articles in this part can help us do this.

27.   Why the Future Doesn't Need Us

BILL JOY

The publication of Bill Joy's article, "Why the Future Doesn't Need Us," in Wired *in April 2000 caused quite a stir among the so-called digerati (the elite of the Internet and information technology world). Joy sees the convergence of genetic engineering, robotics, and nanotechnology (GNR) as posing a grave threat to the future of humanity. He argues that these new technologies are qualitatively different from those with which we are familiar. "Accustomed to living with almost routine scientific breakthroughs, we have yet to come to terms with the fact that the most compelling twenty-first-century technologies — robotics, genetic engineering, and nanotechnology — pose a different threat than the technologies that have come before. Specifically, robots, engineered organisms, and nanobots share a dangerous amplifying factor: They can self-replicate. A bomb is blown up only once — but one bot can become many, and quickly get out of control."*

Joy develops his argument in detail, drawing on his knowledge of these technologies, conversations with, and writings of many contemporary leaders in technology, as well as a number of well-known science-fiction writers. His scenario is pessimistic in the extreme. If these technologies are allowed to develop unchecked, Joy fears, they could lead to the extinction of the human species. In response, he calls for the voluntary relinquishment of certain of these technologies by scientists, technologists, and the firms and nations that sponsor their work. Had such a polemic been published by one of the many well-known technological critics (several of whom are represented in this book), it might not have attracted much attention. Bill Joy, however, is one of the leading figures of the high-tech world. He is cofounder, chief scientist, and corporate executive officer of Sun Microsystems, the principal designer of the Berkeley version of UNIX, and one of the developers of the Java Programming Language that is now ubiquitous on the Web. In 1997, he was appointed cochairman of the President's Information Technology Advisory Committee. His essay, and the rebuttal by two other technologists that follows it, is well worth reading.

From the moment I became involved in the creation of new technologies, their ethical dimensions have concerned me, but it was only in the autumn of 1998 that I became anxiously aware of how great are the dangers facing us in the twenty-first century. I can date the onset of my unease to the day I met Ray Kurzweil, the deservedly famous inventor of the first reading machine for the blind and many other amazing things.

Ray and I were both speakers at George Gilder's Telecosm conference, and I encountered him by chance in the bar of the hotel after both our sessions were over. I was sitting with John Searle, a Berkeley philosopher who studies consciousness. While we were talking, Ray approached and a conversation began, the subject of which haunts me to this day.

I had missed Ray's talk and the subsequent panel that Ray and John had been on, and they now picked right up where they'd left off, with Ray saying that the rate of improvement of technology was going to accelerate and that we were going to become robots or fuse with robots or something like that, and John countering that this couldn't happen, because the robots couldn't be conscious.

While I had heard such talk before, I had always felt sentient robots were in the realm of science fiction. But now, from someone I respected, I was hearing a strong argument that they were a near-term possibility. I was taken aback, especially given Ray's proven ability to imagine and create the future. I already knew that new technologies like genetic engineering and nanotechnology were giving us the power to remake the world, but a realistic and imminent scenario for intelligent robots surprised me.

It's easy to get jaded about such breakthroughs. We hear in the news almost every day of some kind of technological or scientific advance. Yet this was no ordinary prediction. In the hotel bar, Ray gave me a partial preprint of his then-forthcoming book, *The Age of Spiritual Machines*, which outlined a utopia he foresaw — one in which humans gained near immortality by becoming one with robotic technology. On reading it, my sense of unease only intensified; I felt sure he had to be understating the dangers, understating the probability of a bad outcome along this path.

I found myself most troubled by a passage detailing a dystopian scenario:

The New Luddite Challenge

First, let us postulate that the computer scientists succeed in developing intelligent machines that can do all things better than human beings can do them. In that case, presumably all work will be done by vast, highly organized systems of machines and no human effort will be necessary. Either of two cases might occur. The machines might be permitted to make all of their own decisions without human oversight, or else human control over the machines might be retained.

If the machines are permitted to make all their own decisions, we can't make any conjectures as to the results, because it is impossible to guess how such machines might behave. We only point out that the fate of the human race would be at the mercy of the machines. It might be argued that the human race would never be foolish enough to hand over all the power to the machines. But we are suggesting neither that the human race would voluntarily turn power over to the machines, nor that the machines would willfully seize power. What we do suggest is that the human race might easily permit itself to drift into a position of such dependence on the machines that it would have no practical choice but to accept all of the machines' decisions. As society and the problems that face it become more and more complex and machines become more and more intelligent, people will let machines make more of their decisions for them, simply because machine-made decisions will bring better results than man-made ones. Eventually, a stage may be reached at which the decisions necessary to keep the system running will be so complex that human beings will be incapable of making them intelligently. At that stage the machines will be in effective control. People won't be able to just turn the machines off, because they will be so dependent on them that turning them off would amount to suicide.

On the other hand, it is possible that human control over the machines may be retained. In that case, the average man may have control over certain private machines of his own, such as his car or his personal computer, but control over large systems of machines will be in the hands of a tiny elite — just as it is today, but with two differences. Due to improved techniques the elite will have greater control over the masses, and, because human work will no longer be necessary, the masses will be superfluous, a useless burden on the system. If the elite is ruthless, they may simply decide to exterminate the mass of humanity. If they are humane, they may use propaganda or other psychological or biological techniques to reduce the birth rate until the mass of humanity becomes extinct, leaving the world to the elite. Or, if the elite consists of soft-hearted liberals, they may decide to play the role of good shepherds to the rest of the human race. They will see to it that everyone's physical needs are satisfied, that all children are raised under psychologically hygienic conditions, that everyone has a wholesome hobby to keep him busy, and that anyone who may become dissatisfied undergoes "treatment" to cure his "problem." Of course, life will be so purposeless that people will have to be biologically or psychologically engineered either to remove their need for the power process or make them "sublimate" their drive for power into some harmless hobby. These engineered human beings may be happy in such a society, but they will most certainly not be free. They will have been reduced to the status of domestic animals.[1]

In the book, you don't discover until you turn the page that the author of this passage is Theodore Kaczynski — the Unabomber. I am no apologist for Kaczynski. His bombs killed three people during a seventeen-year terror campaign and wounded many others. One of his bombs gravely injured my friend David Gelernter, one of the most brilliant and visionary computer scientists of our time. Like many of my colleagues, I felt that I could easily have been the Unabomber's next target.

Kaczynski's actions were murderous and, in my view, criminally insane. He is clearly a Luddite, but simply saying this does not dismiss his argument; as difficult as it is for me to acknowledge, I saw some merit in the reasoning in this single passage. I felt compelled to confront it.

Kaczynski's dystopian vision describes unintended consequences, a well-known problem with the design and use of technology and one that is clearly related to Murphy's law — "Anything that can go wrong, will." (Actually, this is Finagle's law, which in itself shows that Finagle was right.) Our overuse of antibiotics has led to what may be the biggest such problem so far: the emergence of antibiotic-resistant and much more dangerous bacteria. Similar things happened when attempts to eliminate malarial mosquitoes using DDT caused them to acquire DDT resistance; malarial parasites likewise acquired multidrug-resistant genes.[2]

The cause of many such surprises seems clear: The systems involved are complex, involving interaction among and feedback between many parts. Any changes to such a system will cascade in ways that are difficult to predict; this is especially true when human actions are involved.

I started showing friends the Kaczynski quote from *The Age of Spiritual Machines;* I would hand them Kurzweil's book, let them read the quote, and then watch their reaction as they discovered who had written it. At around the same time, I found Hans Moravec's book *Robot: Mere Machine to Transcendent Mind.* Moravec is one of the leaders in robotics research and was a founder of the world's largest robotics research program, at Carnegie Mellon University. *Robot* gave me more material to try out on my friends — material surprisingly supportive of Kaczynski's argument. For example:

The Short Run (Early 2000s)

Biological species almost never survive encounters with superior competitors. Ten million years ago, South and North America were separated by a sunken Panama isthmus. South America, like Australia today, was populated by marsupial mammals, including pouched equivalents of rats, deer, and tigers. When the isthmus connecting North and South America rose, it took only a few thousand years for the northern placental species, with slightly more effective metabolisms and reproductive and nervous systems, to displace and eliminate almost all the southern marsupials.

In a completely free marketplace, superior robots would surely affect humans as North American placentals affected South American marsupials (and as humans have affected countless species). Robotic industries would compete vigorously among themselves for matter, energy, and space, incidentally driving their price beyond human reach. Unable to afford the necessities of life, biological humans would be squeezed out of existence.

There is probably some breathing room, because we do not live in a completely free marketplace. Government coerces nonmarket behavior, especially by collecting taxes. Judiciously applied, governmental coercion could support human populations in high style on the fruits of robot labor, perhaps for a long while.

A textbook dystopia — and Moravec is just getting wound up. He goes on to discuss how our main job in the twenty-first century will be "ensuring continued cooperation from the robot industries" by passing laws decreeing that they be "nice"[3] and to describe how seriously dangerous a human can be "once transformed into an unbounded superintelligent robot." Moravec's view is that the robots will eventually succeed us — that humans clearly face extinction.

I decided it was time to talk to my friend Danny Hillis. Danny became famous as the cofounder of Thinking Machines Corporation, which built a very powerful parallel supercomputer. Despite my current job title of Chief Scientist at Sun

Microsystems, I am more a computer architect than a scientist, and I respect Danny's knowledge of the information and physical sciences more than that of any other single person I know. Danny is also a highly regarded futurist who thinks long-term: Four years ago he started the Long Now Foundation, which is building a clock designed to last 10,000 years, in an attempt to draw attention to the pitifully short attention span of our society. (See "Test of Time," *Wired* 8.03, page 78.)

So I flew to Los Angeles for the express purpose of having dinner with Danny and his wife, Pati. I went through my now-familiar routine, trotting out the ideas and passages that I found so disturbing. Danny's answer — directed specifically at Kurzweil's scenario of humans merging with robots — came swiftly and quite surprised me. He said, simply, that the changes would come gradually and that we would get used to them.

But I guess I wasn't totally surprised. I had seen a quote from Danny in Kurzweil's book in which he said, "I'm as fond of my body as anyone, but if I can be 200 with a body of silicon, I'll take it." It seemed that he was at peace with this process and its attendant risks, while I was not.

While talking and thinking about Kurzweil, Kaczynski, and Moravec, I suddenly remembered a novel I had read almost 20 years ago — *The White Plague*, by Frank Herbert — in which a molecular biologist is driven insane by the senseless murder of his family. To seek revenge, he constructs and disseminates a new and highly contagious plague that kills widely but selectively. (We're lucky Kaczynski was a mathematician, not a molecular biologist.) I was also reminded of the Borg of Star Trek, a hive of partly biological, partly robotic creatures with a strong destructive streak. Borg-like disasters are a staple of science fiction, so why hadn't I been more concerned about such robotic dystopias earlier? Why weren't other people more concerned about these nightmarish scenarios?

Part of the answer certainly lies in our attitude toward the new — in our bias toward instant familiarity and unquestioning acceptance. Accustomed to living with almost routine scientific breakthroughs, we have yet to come to terms with the fact that the most compelling twenty-first-century technologies — robotics, genetic engineering, and nanotechnology — pose a different threat than the technologies that have come before. Specifically, robots, engineered organisms, and nanobots share a dangerous amplifying factor: They can self-replicate. A bomb is blown up only once — but one 'bot can become many and quickly get out of control.

Much of my work over the past twenty-five years has been on computer networking, where the sending and receiving of messages creates the opportunity for out-of-control replication. But while replication in a computer or a computer network can be a nuisance, at worst it disables a machine or takes down a network or network service. Uncontrolled self-replication in these newer technologies runs a much greater risk: a risk of substantial damage in the physical world.

Each of these technologies also offers untold promise: The vision of near immortality that Kurzweil sees in his robot dreams drives us forward; genetic engineering may soon provide treatments, if not outright cures, for most diseases, and nanotechnology and nanomedicine can address yet more ills. Together they could significantly extend our average life span and improve the quality of our lives. Yet, with each of these technologies, a sequence of small, individually sensible advances leads to an accumulation of great power and, concomitantly, great danger.

What was different in the twentieth century? Certainly, the technologies underlying the weapons of mass destruction (WMD) — nuclear, biological, and chemical (NBC) — were powerful and the weapons an enormous threat. But building nuclear weapons required, at least for a time, access to both rare — indeed, effectively unavailable — raw materials and highly protected information; biological and chemical weapons programs also tended to require large-scale activities.

The twenty-first-century technologies — genetics, nanotechnology, and robotics (GNR) — are so powerful that they can spawn whole new classes of accidents and abuses. Most dangerously, for the first time, these accidents and abuses are widely within the reach of individuals or small groups. They will not require large facilities or rare raw materials. Knowledge alone will enable the use of them.

Thus, we have the possibility not just of weapons of mass destruction but of knowledge-enabled mass destruction (KMD), this destructiveness hugely amplified by the power of self-replication.

I think it is no exaggeration to say we are on the cusp of the further perfection of extreme evil, an evil whose possibility spreads well beyond that which weapons of mass destruction bequeathed to the nation-states, on to a surprising and terrible empowerment of extreme individuals.

Nothing about the way I got involved with computers suggested to me that I was going to be facing these kinds of issues.

My life has been driven by a deep need to ask questions and find answers. When I was three, I was already reading, so my father took me to the elementary school, where I sat on the principal's lap and read him a story. I started school early, later skipped a grade, and escaped into books — I was incredibly motivated to learn. I asked lots of questions, often driving adults to distraction.

As a teenager, I was very interested in science and technology. I wanted to be a ham radio operator but didn't have the money to buy the equipment. Ham radio was the Internet of its time: very addictive and quite solitary. Money issues aside, my mother put her foot down — I was not to be a ham; I was antisocial enough already.

I may not have had many close friends, but I was awash in ideas. By high school, I had discovered the great science-fiction writers. I remember especially Heinlein's *Have Spacesuit Will Travel* and Asimov's *I, Robot*, with its Three Laws of Robotics. I was enchanted by the descriptions of space travel and wanted to have a telescope to look at the stars; since I had no money to buy or make one, I checked books on telescope making out of the library and read about making them instead. I soared in my imagination.

Thursday nights my parents went bowling, and we kids stayed home alone. It was the night of Gene Roddenberry's original Star Trek, and the program made a big impression on me. I came to accept its notion that humans had a future in space, Western-style, with big heroes and adventures. Roddenberry's vision of the centuries to come was one with strong moral values, embodied in codes like the Prime Directive: to not interfere in the development of less technologically advanced civilizations. This had an incredible appeal to me; ethical humans, not robots, dominated this future, and I took Roddenberry's dream as part of my own.

I excelled in mathematics in high school, and when I went to the University of Michigan as an undergraduate engineering student I took the advanced curriculum of the mathematics majors. Solving math problems was an exciting challenge, but when I discovered computers I found something much more interesting: a machine into which you could put a program that attempted to solve a problem, after which the machine quickly checked the solution. The computer had a clear notion of correct and incorrect, true and false. Were my ideas correct? The machine could tell me. This was very seductive. I was lucky enough to get a job programming early supercomputers and discovered the amazing power of large machines to numerically simulate advanced designs. When I went to graduate school at UC Berkeley in the mid-1970s, I started staying up late, often all night, inventing new worlds inside the machines. Solving problems. Writing the code that argued so strongly to be written.

In *The Agony and the Ecstasy,* Irving Stone's biographical novel of Michelangelo, Stone described vividly how Michelangelo released the statues from the stone, "breaking the marble spell," carving from the images in his mind.[4] In my most ecstatic moments, the software in the computer emerged in the same way. Once I had imagined it in my mind, I felt that it was already there in the machine, waiting to be released. Staying up all night seemed a small price to pay to free it — to give the ideas concrete form.

After a few years at Berkeley, I started to send out some of the software I had written — an instructional Pascal system, Unix utilities, and a text editor called vi (which is still, to my surprise, widely used more than twenty years later) — to others who had similar small PDP-11 and VAX minicomputers. These adventures in software eventually turned into the Berkeley version of the Unix operating system, which became a personal "success disaster" — So many people wanted it that I never finished my Ph.D. Instead, I got a job working for DARPA [Defense Advanced Research Projects Agency] putting Berkeley Unix on the Internet and fixing it to be reliable and to run large research applications well. This was all great fun and very rewarding. And, frankly, I saw no robots here, or anywhere near.

Still, by the early 1980s, I was drowning. The Unix releases were very successful, and my little project of one soon had money and some staff, but the problem at Berkeley was always office space rather than money. There wasn't room for the help the project needed, so when the other founders of Sun Microsystems showed up, I jumped at the chance to join them. At Sun, the long hours continued into the early days of workstations and personal computers, and I have enjoyed participating in the creation of advanced microprocessor technologies and Internet technologies such as Java and Jini.

From all this, I trust it is clear that I am not a Luddite. I have always, rather, had a strong belief in the value of the scientific search for truth and in the ability of great engineering to bring material progress. The Industrial Revolution has immeasurably improved everyone's life over the last couple hundred years, and I always expected my career to involve the building of worthwhile solutions to real problems, one problem at a time.

I have not been disappointed. My work has had more impact than I had ever hoped for and has been more widely used than I could have reasonably expected. I have spent the last twenty years still trying to figure out how to make computers as reliable as I want them to be (they are not nearly there yet) and how to make them simple to use (a goal that has met with even less relative success). Despite some progress, the problems that remain seem even more daunting.

But while I was aware of the moral dilemmas surrounding technology's consequences in fields like weapons research, I did not expect that I would confront such issues in my own field, or at least not so soon.

Perhaps it is always hard to see the bigger impact while you are in the vortex of a change. Failing to understand the consequences of our inventions while we are in the rapture of discovery and innovation seems to be a common fault of scientists and technologists; we have long been driven by the overarching desire to know that is the nature of science's quest, not stopping to notice that the progress to newer and more powerful technologies can take on a life of its own.

I have long realized that the big advances in information technology come not from the work of computer scientists, computer architects, or electrical engineers, but from that of physical scientists. The physicists Stephen Wolfram and Brosl Hasslacher introduced me, in the early 1980s, to chaos theory and nonlinear systems. In the 1990s, I learned about complex systems from conversations with Danny Hillis, the biologist Stuart Kauffman, the Nobel-laureate physicist Murray Gell-Mann, and others. Most recently, Hasslacher and the electrical engineer and device physicist Mark Reed have been giving me insight into the incredible possibilities of molecular electronics.

In my own work, as codesigner of three microprocessor architectures — SPARC, picoJava, and MAJC — and as the designer of several implementations thereof, I've been afforded a deep and firsthand acquaintance with Moore's law. For decades, Moore's law has correctly predicted the exponential rate of improvement of semiconductor technology. Until last year, I believed that the rate of advances predicted by Moore's law might continue only until roughly 2010, when some physical limits would begin to be reached. It was not obvious to me that a new technology would arrive in time to keep performance advancing smoothly.

But because of the recent rapid and radical progress in molecular electronics — where individual atoms and molecules replace lithographically drawn transistors — and related nanoscale technologies, we should be able to meet or exceed the Moore's law rate of progress for another thirty years. By 2030, we are likely to be able to build machines, in quantity, a million times as powerful as the personal computers of today — sufficient to implement the dreams of Kurzweil and Moravec.

As this enormous computing power is combined with the manipulative advances of the physical sciences and the new, deep understandings in genetics, enormous transformative power is being unleashed. These combinations open up the opportunity to completely redesign the world, for better or worse: The replicating and evolving processes that have been confined to the natural world are about to become realms of human endeavor.

In designing software and microprocessors, I have never had the feeling that I was designing an intelligent machine. The software and hardware is so fragile and the capabilities of the machine to "think" so clearly absent that, even as a possibility, this has always seemed very far in the future.

But now, with the prospect of human-level computing power in about thirty years, a new idea suggests itself: that I may be working to create tools which will enable the construction of the technology that may replace our species. How do I feel about this? Very uncomfortable. Having struggled my entire career to build reliable software systems, it seems to me more than likely that this future will not work out as well as some people may imagine. My personal experience suggests we tend to overestimate our design abilities.

Given the incredible power of these new technologies, shouldn't we be asking how we can best coexist with them? And if our own extinction is a likely, or even possible, outcome of our technological development, shouldn't we proceed with great caution?

The dream of robotics is, first, that intelligent machines can do our work for us, allowing us lives of leisure, restoring us to Eden. Yet in his history of such ideas, *Darwin Among the Machines,* George Dyson warns, "In the game of life and evolution there are three players at the table: human beings, nature, and machines. I am firmly on the side of nature. But nature, I suspect, is on the side of the machines." As we have seen, Moravec agrees, believing we may well not survive the encounter with the superior robot species.

How soon could such an intelligent robot be built? The coming advances in computing power seem to make it possible by 2030. And once an intelligent robot exists, it is only a small step to a robot species — to an intelligent robot that can make evolved copies of itself.

A second dream of robotics is that we will gradually replace ourselves with our robotic technology, achieving near immortality by downloading our consciousnesses; it is this process that Danny Hillis thinks we will gradually get used to and that Ray Kurzweil elegantly details in *The Age of Spiritual Machines.* (We are beginning to see intimations of this in the implantation of computer devices into the human body, as illustrated on the cover of *Wired* 8.02.)

But if we are downloaded into our technology, what are the chances that we will thereafter be ourselves or even human? It seems to me far more likely that a robotic existence would not be like a human one in any sense that we understand, that the robots would in no sense be our children, that on this path our humanity may well be lost.

Genetic engineering promises to revolutionize agriculture by increasing crop yields while reducing the use of pesticides; to create tens of thousands of novel species of bacteria, plants, viruses, and animals; to replace reproduction, or supplement it, with cloning; to create cures for many diseases, increasing our life span and our quality of life; and much, much more. We now know with certainty that these profound changes in the biological sciences are imminent and will challenge all our notions of what life is.

Technologies such as human cloning have in particular raised our awareness of the profound ethical and moral issues we face. If, for example, we were to reengineer ourselves into several separate and unequal species using the power of genetic engineering, then we would threaten the notion of equality that is the very cornerstone of our democracy.

Given the incredible power of genetic engineering, it's no surprise that there are significant safety issues in its use. My friend Amory Lovins recently cowrote, along with Hunter Lovins, an editorial that provides an ecological view of some of these dangers. Among their concerns: that "the new botany aligns the development of plants with their economic, not evolutionary, success." Amory's long career has been focused on energy and resource efficiency by taking a whole-system view of human-made systems; such a whole-system view often finds simple, smart solutions to otherwise seemingly difficult problems and is usefully applied here as well.

After reading the Lovins' editorial, I saw an op-ed by Gregg Easterbrook in *The New York Times* (November 19, 1999) about genetically engineered crops, under the headline: "Food for the Future: Someday, rice will have built-in vitamin A. Unless the Luddites win."

Are Amory and Hunter Lovins Luddites? Certainly not. I believe we all would agree that golden rice, with its built-in vitamin A, is probably a good thing, if developed with proper care and respect for the likely dangers in moving genes across species boundaries.

Awareness of the dangers inherent in genetic engineering is beginning to grow, as reflected in the Lovins' editorial. The general public is aware of, and uneasy about, genetically modified foods and seems to be rejecting the notion that such foods should be permitted to be unlabeled.

But genetic engineering technology is already very far along. As the Lovins note, the USDA has already approved about fifty genetically engineered crops for unlimited release; more than half of the world's soybeans and a third of its corn now contain genes spliced in from other forms of life.

While there are many important issues here, my own major concern with genetic engineering is narrower: that it gives the power — whether militarily, accidentally, or in a deliberate terrorist act — to create a White Plague.

The many wonders of nanotechnology were first imagined by the Nobel-laureate physicist Richard Feynman in a speech he gave in 1959, subsequently published under the title "There's Plenty of Room at the Bottom." The book that made a big impression on me, in the mid-'80s, was Eric Drexler's *Engines of Creation,* in which he described beautifully how manipulation of matter at the atomic level could create a utopian future of abundance, where just about everything could be made cheaply, and almost any imaginable disease or physical problem could be solved using nanotechnology and artificial intelligences.

A subsequent book, *Unbounding the Future: The Nanotechnology Revolution,* which Drexler cowrote, imagines some of the changes that might take place in a world where we had molecular-level "assemblers." Assemblers could make possible incredibly low-cost solar power, cures for cancer and the common cold by augmentation of the human immune system, essentially complete cleanup of the environment, incredibly inexpensive pocket supercomputers — in fact, any product would be manufactured by assemblers at a cost no greater than that of wood — spaceflight more accessible than transoceanic travel today, and restoration of extinct species.

I remember feeling good about nanotechnology after reading *Engines of Creation.* As a technologist, it gave me a sense of calm — that is, nanotechnology showed us that incredible progress was possible, and indeed perhaps inevitable. If nanotechnology was our future, then I didn't feel pressed to solve so many problems in the present. I would get to Drexler's utopian future in due time; I might as well enjoy life more in the here and now. It didn't make sense, given his vision, to stay up all night, all the time.

Drexler's vision also led to a lot of good fun. I would occasionally get to describe the wonders of nanotechnology to others who had not heard of it. After teasing them with all the things Drexler described, I would give a homework assignment of my own: "Use nanotechnology to create a vampire; for extra credit create an antidote."

With these wonders came clear dangers, of which I was acutely aware. As I said at a nanotechnology conference in 1989, "We can't simply do our science and not worry about these ethical issues."[5] But my subsequent conversations with physicists convinced me that nanotechnology might not even work — or, at least, it wouldn't work anytime soon. Shortly thereafter I moved to Colorado, to a skunk works I had set up, and the focus of my work shifted to software for the Internet, specifically on ideas that became Java and Jini.

Then, last summer, Brosl Hasslacher told me that nanoscale molecular electronics was now practical. This was new news, at least to me, and I think to many people — and it radically changed my opinion about nanotechnology. It sent me back to *Engines of Creation*. Rereading Drexler's work after more than ten years, I was dismayed to realize how little I had remembered of its lengthy section called "Dangers and Hopes," including a discussion of how nanotechnologies can become "engines of destruction." Indeed, in my rereading of this cautionary material today, I am struck by how naive some of Drexler's safeguard proposals seem and how much greater I judge the dangers to be now than even he seemed to then. (Having anticipated and described many technical and political problems with nanotechnology, Drexler started the Foresight Institute in the late 1980s "to help prepare society for anticipated advanced technologies" — most important, nanotechnology.)

The enabling breakthrough to assemblers seems quite likely within the next twenty years. Molecular electronics — the new subfield of nanotechnology where individual molecules are circuit elements — should mature quickly and become enormously lucrative within this decade, causing a large incremental investment in all nanotechnologies.

Unfortunately, as with nuclear technology, it is far easier to create destructive uses for nanotechnology than constructive ones. Nanotechnology has clear military and terrorist uses, and you need not be suicidal to release a massively destructive nanotechnological device. Such devices can be built to be selectively destructive, affecting, for example, only a certain geographical area or a group of people who are genetically distinct.

An immediate consequence of the Faustian bargain in obtaining the great power of nanotechnology is that we run a grave risk — the risk that we might destroy the biosphere on which all life depends.

As Drexler explained:

"Plants" with "leaves" no more efficient than today's solar cells could outcompete real plants, crowding the biosphere with an inedible foliage. Tough omnivorous "bacteria" could out-compete real bacteria: They could spread like blowing pollen, replicate swiftly, and reduce the biosphere to dust in a matter of days. Dangerous replicators could easily be too tough, small, and rapidly spreading to stop — at least if we make no preparation. We have trouble enough controlling viruses and fruit flies.

Among the cognoscenti of nanotechnology, this threat has become known as the "gray goo problem." Though masses of uncontrolled replicators need not be gray or gooey, the term "gray goo" emphasizes that replicators able to obliterate life might be less inspiring than a single species of crabgrass. They might be superior in an evolutionary sense, but this need not make them valuable.

The gray goo threat makes one thing perfectly clear: We cannot afford certain kinds of accidents with replicating assemblers.

Gray goo would surely be a depressing ending to our human adventure on Earth, far worse than mere fire or ice, and one that could stem from a simple laboratory accident.[6] Oops.

It is most of all the power of destructive self-replication in genetics, nanotechnology, and robotics (GNR) that should give us pause. Self-replication is the modus operandi of genetic engineering, which uses the machinery of the cell to replicate its designs, and the prime danger underlying gray goo in nanotechnology. Stories of run-amok robots like the Borg, replicating or mutating to escape from the ethical constraints imposed on them by their creators, are well established in our science fiction books and movies. It is even possible that self-replication may be more fundamental than we thought, and hence harder — or even impossible — to control. A recent article by Stuart Kauffman in *Nature* titled "Self-Replication: Even Peptides Do It" discusses the discovery that a thirty-two-amino-acid peptide can "autocatalyse its own synthesis." We don't know how widespread this ability is, but Kauffman notes that it may hint at "a route to self-reproducing molecular systems on a basis far wider than Watson-Crick base-pairing."[7]

In truth, we have had in hand for years clear warnings of the dangers inherent in widespread knowledge of GNR technologies — of the possibility of knowledge alone enabling mass destruction. But these warnings haven't been widely publicized; the public discussions have been clearly inadequate. There is no profit in publicizing the dangers.

The nuclear, biological, and chemical (NBC) technologies used in twentieth-century weapons of mass destruction were and are largely military, developed in government laboratories. In sharp contrast, the twenty-first-century GNR technologies have clear commercial uses and are being developed almost exclusively by corporate enterprises. In this age of triumphant commercialism, technology — with science as its handmaiden — is delivering a series of almost magical inventions that are the most phenomenally lucrative ever seen. We are aggressively pursuing the promises of these new technologies within the now-unchallenged system of global capitalism and its manifold financial incentives and competitive pressures.

This is the first moment in the history of our planet when any species, by its own voluntary actions, has become a danger to itself — as well as to vast numbers of others.

It might be a familiar progression, transpiring on many worlds — a planet, newly formed, placidly revolves around its star; life slowly forms; a kaleidoscopic procession of creatures evolves; intelligence emerges which, at least up to a point, confers enormous survival value; and then technology is invented. It dawns on them that there are such things as laws of Nature, that these laws can be revealed by experiment, and that knowledge of these laws can be made both to save and to take lives, both on unprecedented scales. Science, they recognize, grants immense powers. In a flash, they create world-altering contrivances. Some planetary civilizations see their way through, place limits on what may and what must not be done, and safely pass through the time of perils. Others, not so lucky or so prudent, perish.

That is Carl Sagan, writing in 1994, in *Pale Blue Dot,* a book describing his vision of the human future in space. I am only now realizing how deep his insight was, and how sorely I miss, and will miss, his voice. For all its eloquence, Sagan's contribution was not least that of simple common sense — an attribute that, along with humility, many of the leading advocates of the twenty-first-century technologies seem to lack.

I remember from my childhood that my grandmother was strongly against the overuse of antibiotics. She had worked since before the first World War as a nurse and had a commonsense attitude that taking antibiotics, unless they were absolutely necessary, was bad for you.

It is not that she was an enemy of progress. She saw much progress in an almost seventy-year nursing career; my grandfather, a diabetic, benefited greatly from the improved treatments that became available in his lifetime. But she, like many levelheaded people, would probably think it greatly arrogant for us, now, to be designing a robotic "replacement species" when we obviously have so much trouble making relatively simple things work and so much trouble managing — or even understanding — ourselves.

I realize now that she had an awareness of the nature of the order of life and of the necessity of living with and respecting that order. With this respect comes a necessary humility that we, with our early-twenty-first-century chutzpah, lack at our peril. The commonsense view, grounded in this respect, is often right, in advance of the scientific evidence. The clear fragility and inefficiencies of the human-made systems we have built should give us all pause; the fragility of the systems I have worked on certainly humbles me.

We should have learned a lesson from the making of the first atomic bomb and the resulting arms race. We didn't do well then, and the parallels to our current situation are troubling.

The effort to build the first atomic bomb was led by the brilliant physicist J. Robert Oppenheimer. Oppenheimer was not naturally interested in politics but became painfully aware of what he perceived as the grave threat to Western civilization from the Third Reich, a threat surely grave because of the possibility that Hitler might obtain nuclear weapons. Energized by this concern, he brought his strong intellect, passion for physics, and charismatic leadership skills to Los Alamos and led a rapid and successful effort by an incredible collection of great minds to quickly invent the bomb.

What is striking is how this effort continued so naturally after the initial impetus was removed. In a meeting shortly after V-E Day with some physicists who felt that perhaps the effort should stop, Oppenheimer argued to continue. His stated reason seems a bit strange: not because of the fear of large casualties from an invasion of Japan, but because the United Nations, which was soon to be formed, should have foreknowledge of atomic weapons. A more likely reason the project continued is the momentum that had built up — the first atomic test, Trinity, was nearly at hand.

We know that in preparing this first atomic test the physicists proceeded despite a large number of possible dangers. They were initially worried, based on a calculation by Edward Teller, that an atomic explosion might set fire to the atmosphere. A revised calculation reduced the danger of destroying the world to a three-in-a-million chance. (Teller says he was later able to dismiss the prospect of atmospheric ignition entirely.) Oppenheimer, though, was sufficiently concerned about the result of Trinity that he arranged for a possible evacuation of the southwest part of the state of New Mexico. And, of course, there was the clear danger of starting a nuclear arms race.

Within a month of that first, successful test, two atomic bombs destroyed Hiroshima and Nagasaki. Some scientists had suggested that the bomb simply be demonstrated, rather than dropped on Japanese cities — saying that this would greatly improve the chances for arms control after the war — but to no avail. With the tragedy of Pearl Harbor still fresh in Americans' minds, it would have been very difficult for President Truman to order a demonstration of the weapons rather than use them as he did — the desire to quickly end the war and save the lives that would have been lost in any invasion of Japan was very strong. Yet the overriding truth was probably very simple: As the physicist Freeman Dyson later said, "The reason that it was dropped was just that nobody had the courage or the foresight to say no."

It's important to realize how shocked the physicists were in the aftermath of the bombing of Hiroshima, on August 6, 1945. They describe a series of waves of emotion: first, a sense of fulfillment that the bomb worked, then horror at all the people that had been killed, and then a convincing feeling that on no account should another bomb be dropped. Yet of course another bomb was dropped, on Nagasaki, only three days after the bombing of Hiroshima.

In November 1945, three months after the atomic bombings, Oppenheimer stood firmly behind the scientific attitude, saying, "It is not possible to be a scientist unless you believe that the knowledge of the world, and the power which this gives, is a thing which is of intrinsic value to humanity, and that you are using it to help in the spread of knowledge and are willing to take the consequences."

Oppenheimer went on to work, with others, on the Acheson-Lilienthal report, which, as Richard Rhodes says in his recent book *Visions of Technology*, "found a way to prevent a clandestine nuclear arms race without resorting to armed world government"; their suggestion was a form of relinquishment of nuclear weapons work by nation-states to an international agency.

This proposal led to the Baruch Plan, which was submitted to the United Nations in June 1946 but never adopted (perhaps because, as Rhodes suggests,

Bernard Baruch had "insisted on burdening the plan with conventional sanctions," thereby inevitably dooming it, even though it would "almost certainly have been rejected by Stalinist Russia anyway"). Other efforts to promote sensible steps toward internationalizing nuclear power to prevent an arms race ran afoul either of U.S. politics and internal distrust, or distrust by the Soviets. The opportunity to avoid the arms race was lost and very quickly.

Two years later, in 1948, Oppenheimer seemed to have reached another stage in his thinking, saying, "In some sort of crude sense which no vulgarity, no humor, no overstatement can quite extinguish, the physicists have known sin; and this is a knowledge they cannot lose."

In 1949, the Soviets exploded an atom bomb. By 1955, both the U.S. and the Soviet Union had tested hydrogen bombs suitable for delivery by aircraft. And so the nuclear arms race began.

Nearly twenty years ago, in the documentary *The Day After Trinity*, Freeman Dyson summarized the scientific attitudes that brought us to the nuclear precipice:

> I have felt it myself. The glitter of nuclear weapons. It is irresistible if you come to them as a scientist. To feel it's there in your hands, to release this energy that fuels the stars, to let it do your bidding. To perform these miracles, to lift a million tons of rock into the sky. It is something that gives people an illusion of illimitable power, and it is, in some ways, responsible for all our troubles — this, what you might call technical arrogance, that overcomes people when they see what they can do with their minds.[8]

Now, as then, we are creators of new technologies and stars of the imagined future, driven — this time by great financial rewards and global competition — despite the clear dangers, hardly evaluating what it may be like to try to live in a world that is the realistic outcome of what we are creating and imagining.

In 1947, *The Bulletin of the Atomic Scientists* began putting a Doomsday Clock on its cover. For more than fifty years, it has shown an estimate of the relative nuclear danger we have faced, reflecting the changing international conditions. The hands on the clock have moved fifteen times and today, standing at nine minutes to midnight, reflect continuing and real danger from nuclear weapons. The recent addition of India and Pakistan to the list of nuclear powers has increased the threat of failure of the nonproliferation goal, and this danger was reflected by moving the hands closer to midnight in 1998.

In our time, how much danger do we face, not just from nuclear weapons, but from all of these technologies? How high are the extinction risks?

The philosopher John Leslie has studied this question and concluded that the risk of human extinction is at least 30 percent,[9] while Ray Kurzweil believes we have "a better than even chance of making it through," with the caveat that he has "always been accused of being an optimist." Not only are these estimates not encouraging, but they do not include the probability of many horrid outcomes that lie short of extinction.

Faced with such assessments, some serious people are already suggesting that we simply move beyond Earth as quickly as possible. We would colonize the galaxy using von Neumann probes, which hop from star system to star system, replicating as they go. This step will almost certainly be necessary five billion years from now (or sooner if our solar system is disastrously impacted by the impending collision of our galaxy with the Andromeda galaxy within the next three billion years), but if we take Kurzweil and Moravec at their word, it might be necessary by the middle of this century.

What are the moral implications here? If we must move beyond Earth this quickly in order for the species to survive, who accepts the responsibility for the fate of those (most of us, after all) who are left behind? And even if we scatter to the stars, isn't it likely that we may take our problems with us or find, later, that they have followed us? The fate of our species on Earth and our fate in the galaxy seem inextricably linked.

Another idea is to erect a series of shields to defend against each of the dangerous technologies. The Strategic Defense Initiative, proposed by the Reagan administration, was an attempt to design such a shield against the threat of a nuclear attack from the Soviet Union. But as Arthur C. Clarke, who was privy to discussions about the project, observed:

> Though it might be possible, at vast expense, to construct local defense systems that would 'only' let through a few percent of ballistic missiles, the much touted idea of a national umbrella was nonsense. Luis Alvarez, perhaps the greatest experimental physicist of this century, remarked to me that the advocates of such schemes were 'very bright guys with no common sense.'

Clarke continued:

> Looking into my often cloudy crystal ball, I suspect that a total defense might indeed be possible in a century or so. But the technology involved would produce, as a by-product, weapons so terrible that no one would bother with anything as primitive as ballistic missiles."[10]

In *Engines of Creation*, Eric Drexler proposed that we build an active nanotechnological shield — a form of immune system for the biosphere — to defend against dangerous replicators of all kinds that might escape from laboratories or otherwise be maliciously created. But the shield he proposed would itself be extremely dangerous — nothing could prevent it from developing autoimmune problems and attacking the biosphere itself.[11]

Similar difficulties apply to the construction of shields against robotics and genetic engineering. These technologies are too powerful to be shielded against in the time frame of interest; even if it were possible to implement defensive shields, the side effects of their development would be at least as dangerous as the technologies we are trying to protect against.

These possibilities are all thus either undesirable or unachievable or both. The only realistic alternative I see is relinquishment: to limit development of the technologies that are too dangerous, by limiting our pursuit of certain kinds of knowledge.

Yes, I know, knowledge is good, as is the search for new truths. We have been seeking knowledge since ancient times. Aristotle opened his *Metaphysics* with the simple statement, "All men by nature desire to know." We have, as a bedrock value in our society, long agreed on the value of open access to information, and recognize the problems that arise with attempts to restrict access to and development of knowledge. In recent times, we have come to revere scientific knowledge.

But despite the strong historical precedents, if open access to and unlimited development of knowledge henceforth puts us all in clear danger of extinction, then common sense demands that we reexamine even these basic, long-held beliefs.

It was Nietzsche who warned us, at the end of the nineteenth century, not only that God is dead but that "faith in science, which after all exists undeniably, cannot owe its origin to a calculus of utility; it must have originated in spite of the fact that the disutility and dangerousness of the 'will to truth,' of 'truth at any price' is proved to it constantly." It is this further danger that we now fully face — the consequences of our truth seeking. The truth that science seeks can certainly be considered a dangerous substitute for God if it is likely to lead to our extinction.

If we could agree, as a species, what we wanted, where we were headed, and why, then we would make our future much less dangerous — then we might understand what we can and should relinquish. Otherwise, we can easily imagine an arms race developing over GNR technologies, as it did with the NBC technologies in the twentieth century. This is perhaps the greatest risk, for once such a race begins, it's very hard to end it. This time — unlike during the Manhattan Project — we aren't in a war, facing an implacable enemy that is threatening our civilization; we are driven, instead, by our habits, our desires, our economic system, and our competitive need to know.

I believe that we all wish our course could be determined by our collective values, ethics, and morals. If we had gained more collective wisdom over the past few thousand years, then a dialogue to this end would be more practical, and the incredible powers we are about to unleash would not be nearly so troubling.

One would think we might be driven to such a dialogue by our instinct for self-preservation. Individuals clearly have this desire, yet as a species our behavior seems to be not in our favor. In dealing with the nuclear threat, we often spoke dishonestly to ourselves and to each other, thereby greatly increasing the risks. Whether this was politically motivated, or because we chose not to think ahead, or because when faced with such grave threats we acted irrationally out of fear, I do not know, but it does not bode well.

The new Pandora's boxes of genetics, nanotechnology, and robotics are almost open, yet we seem hardly to have noticed. Ideas can't be put back in a box; unlike uranium or plutonium, they don't need to be mined and refined, and they can be freely copied. Once they are out, they are out. Churchill remarked, in a famous left-handed compliment, that the American people and their leaders "invariably do the right thing, after they have examined every other alternative." In this case, however, we must act more presciently, as to do the right thing only at last may be to lose the chance to do it at all.

As Thoreau said, "We do not ride on the railroad; it rides upon us"; and this is what we must fight, in our time. The question is, indeed, Which is to be master? Will we survive our technologies?

We are being propelled into this new century with no plan, no control, no brakes. Have we already gone too far down the path to alter course? I don't believe so, but we aren't trying yet, and the last chance to assert control — the fail-safe point — is rapidly approaching. We have our first pet robots, as well as commercially available genetic engineering techniques, and our nanoscale techniques are advancing rapidly. While the development of these technologies proceeds through a number of steps, it isn't necessarily the case — as happened in the Manhattan Project and the Trinity test — that the last step in proving a technology is large and hard. The breakthrough to wild self-replication in robotics, genetic engineering, or nanotechnology could come suddenly, reprising the surprise we felt when we learned of the cloning of a mammal.

And yet I believe we do have a strong and solid basis for hope. Our attempts to deal with weapons of mass destruction in the last century provide a shining example of relinquishment for us to consider: the unilateral U.S. abandonment, without preconditions, of the development of biological weapons. This relinquishment stemmed from the realization that while it would take an enormous effort to create these terrible weapons, they could from then on easily be duplicated and fall into the hands of rogue nations or terrorist groups.

The clear conclusion was that we would create additional threats to ourselves by pursuing these weapons and that we would be more secure if we did not pursue them. We have embodied our relinquishment of biological and chemical weapons in the 1972 Biological Weapons Convention (BWC) and the 1993 Chemical Weapons Convention (CWC).[12]

As for the continuing sizable threat from nuclear weapons, which we have lived with now for more than fifty years, the U.S. Senate's recent rejection of the Comprehensive Test Ban Treaty makes it clear relinquishing nuclear weapons will not be politically easy. But we have a unique opportunity, with the end of the Cold War, to avert a multipolar arms race. Building on the BWC and CWC relinquishments, successful abolition of nuclear weapons could help us build toward a habit of relinquishing dangerous technologies. (Actually, by getting rid of all but 100 nuclear weapons worldwide — roughly the total destructive power of World War II and a considerably easier task — we could eliminate this extinction threat.[13])

Verifying relinquishment will be a difficult problem, but not an unsolvable one. We are fortunate to have already done a lot of relevant work in the context of the BWC and other treaties. Our major task will be to apply this to technologies that are naturally much more commercial than military. The substantial need here is for transparency, as difficulty of verification is directly proportional to the difficulty of distinguishing relinquished from legitimate activities.

I frankly believe that the situation in 1945 was simpler than the one we now face: The nuclear technologies were reasonably separable into commercial and military uses and monitoring was aided by the nature of atomic tests and the ease with which radioactivity could be measured. Research on military applications could be performed at national laboratories such as Los Alamos, with the results kept secret as long as possible.

The GNR technologies do not divide clearly into commercial and military uses; given their potential in the market, it's hard to imagine pursuing them only in national laboratories. With their widespread commercial pursuit, enforcing relinquishment will require a verification regime similar to that for biological weapons, but on an unprecedented scale. This, inevitably, will raise tensions between our individual privacy and desire for proprietary information and the need for verification to protect us all. We will undoubtedly encounter strong resistance to this loss of privacy and freedom of action.

Verifying the relinquishment of certain GNR technologies will have to occur in cyberspace as well as at physical facilities. The critical issue will be to make the necessary transparency acceptable in a world of proprietary information, presumably by providing new forms of protection for intellectual property.

Verifying compliance will also require that scientists and engineers adopt a strong code of ethical conduct, resembling the Hippocratic oath, and that they have the courage to whistleblow as necessary, even at high personal cost. This would answer the call — fifty years after Hiroshima — by the Nobel laureate Hans Bethe, one of the most senior of the surviving members of the Manhattan Project, that all scientists "cease and desist from work creating, developing, improving, and manufacturing nuclear weapons and other weapons of potential mass destruction."[14] In the twenty-first century, this requires vigilance and personal responsibility by those who would work on both NBC and GNR technologies to avoid implementing weapons of mass destruction and knowledge-enabled mass destruction.

Thoreau also said that we will be "rich in proportion to the number of things which we can afford to let alone." We each seek to be happy, but it would seem worthwhile to question whether we need to take such a high risk of total destruction to gain yet more knowledge and yet more things; common sense says that there is a limit to our material needs — and that certain knowledge is too dangerous and is best forgone.

Neither should we pursue near immortality without considering the costs, without considering the commensurate increase in the risk of extinction. Immortality, while perhaps the original, is certainly not the only possible utopian dream.

I recently had the good fortune to meet the distinguished author and scholar Jacques Attali, whose book *Lignes d'horizons* (*Millennium*, in the English translation) helped inspire the Java and Jini approach to the coming age of pervasive computing, as previously described in [*Wired*]. In his new book *Fraternités*, Attali describes how our dreams of utopia have changed over time:

> At the dawn of societies, men saw their passage on Earth as nothing more than a labyrinth of pain, at the end of which stood a door leading, via their death, to the company of gods and to *Eternity*. With the Hebrews and then the Greeks, some men dared free themselves from theological demands and dream of an ideal City where *Liberty* would flourish. Others, noting the evolution of the market society, understood that the liberty of some would entail the alienation of others, and they sought *Equality*.

Jacques helped me understand how these three different utopian goals exist in tension in our society today. He goes on to describe a fourth utopia, Fraternity, whose foundation is altruism. Fraternity alone associates individual happiness with the happiness of others, affording the promise of self-sustainment.

This crystallized for me my problem with Kurzweil's dream. A technological approach to Eternity — near immortality through robotics — may not be the most desirable utopia, and its pursuit brings clear dangers. Maybe we should rethink our utopian choices.

Where can we look for a new ethical basis to set our course? I have found the ideas in the book *Ethics for the New Millennium,* by the Dalai Lama, to be very helpful. As is perhaps well known but little heeded, the Dalai Lama argues that the most important thing is for us to conduct our lives with love and compassion for others and that our societies need to develop a stronger notion of universal responsibility and of our interdependency; he proposes a standard of positive ethical conduct for individuals and societies that seems consonant with Attali's Fraternity utopia.

The Dalai Lama further argues that we must understand what it is that makes people happy and acknowledge the strong evidence that neither material progress nor the pursuit of the power of knowledge is the key — that there are limits to what science and the scientific pursuit alone can do.

Our Western notion of happiness seems to come from the Greeks, who defined it as "the exercise of vital powers along lines of excellence in a life affording them scope."[15]

Clearly, we need to find meaningful challenges and sufficient scope in our lives if we are to be happy in whatever is to come. But I believe we must find alternative outlets for our creative forces, beyond the culture of perpetual economic growth; this growth has largely been a blessing for several hundred years, but it has not brought us unalloyed happiness, and we must now choose between the pursuit of unrestricted and undirected growth through science and technology and the clear accompanying dangers.

It is now more than a year since my first encounter with Ray Kurzweil and John Searle. I see around me cause for hope in the voices for caution and relinquishment and in those people I have discovered who are as concerned as I am about our current predicament. I feel, too, a deepened sense of personal responsibility — not for the work I have already done, but for the work that I might yet do, at the confluence of the sciences.

But many other people who know about the dangers still seem strangely silent. When pressed, they trot out the "this is nothing new" riposte — as if awareness of what could happen is response enough. They tell me, There are universities filled with bioethicists who study this stuff all day long. They say, All this has been written about before, and by experts. They complain, Your worries and your arguments are already old hat.

I don't know where these people hide their fear. As an architect of complex systems I enter this arena as a generalist. But should this diminish my concerns? I am aware of how much has been written about, talked about, and lectured about so authoritatively. But does this mean it has reached people? Does this mean we can discount the dangers before us?

Knowing is not a rationale for not acting. Can we doubt that knowledge has become a weapon we wield against ourselves?

The experiences of the atomic scientists clearly show the need to take personal responsibility, the danger that things will move too fast, and the way in which a process can take on a life of its own. We can, as they did, create insurmountable problems in almost no time flat. We must do more thinking up front if we are not to be similarly surprised and shocked by the consequences of our inventions.

My continuing professional work is on improving the reliability of software. Software is a tool, and as a toolbuilder I must struggle with the uses to which the tools I make are put. I have always believed that making software more reliable, given its many uses, will make the world a safer and better place; if I were to come to believe the opposite, then I would be morally obligated to stop this work. I can now imagine such a day may come.

This all leaves me not angry but at least a bit melancholic. Henceforth, for me, progress will be somewhat bittersweet.

Do you remember the beautiful penultimate scene in *Manhattan* where Woody Allen is lying on his couch and talking into a tape recorder? He is writing a short story about people who are creating unnecessary, neurotic problems for themselves, because it keeps them from dealing with more unsolvable, terrifying problems about the universe.

He leads himself to the question, "Why is life worth living?" and to consider what makes it worthwhile for him: Groucho Marx, Willie Mays, the second movement of the Jupiter Symphony, Louis Armstrong's recording of "Potato Head Blues," Swedish movies, Flaubert's *Sentimental Education*, Marlon Brando, Frank Sinatra, the apples and pears by Cézanne, the crabs at Sam Wo's, and, finally, the showstopper: his love Tracy's face.

Each of us has our precious things, and as we care for them we locate the essence of our humanity. In the end, it is because of our great capacity for caring that I remain optimistic we will confront the dangerous issues now before us.

My immediate hope is to participate in a much larger discussion of the issues raised here, with people from many different backgrounds, in settings not predisposed to fear or favor technology for its own sake.

As a start, I have twice raised many of these issues at events sponsored by the Aspen Institute and have separately proposed that the American Academy of Arts and Sciences take them up as an extension of its work with the Pugwash Conferences. (These have been held since 1957 to discuss arms control, especially of nuclear weapons, and to formulate workable policies.)

It's unfortunate that the Pugwash meetings started only well after the nuclear genie was out of the bottle — roughly fifteen years too late. We are also getting a belated start on seriously addressing the issues around twenty-first-century technologies — the prevention of knowledge-enabled mass destruction — and further delay seems unacceptable.

So I'm still searching; there are many more things to learn. Whether we are to succeed or fail, to survive or fall victim to these technologies, is not yet decided. I'm up late again — it's almost 6 A.M. I'm trying to imagine some better answers, to break the spell and free them from the stone.

NOTES

1. The passage Kurzweil quotes is from Kaczynski's "Unabomber Manifesto," which was published jointly, under duress, by *The New York Times* and *The Washington Post* to attempt

to bring his campaign of terror to an end. I agree with David Gelernter, who said about their decision:

> "It was a tough call for the newspapers. To say yes would be giving in to terrorism, and for all they knew he was lying anyway. On the other hand, to say yes might stop the killing. There was also a chance that someone would read the tract and get a hunch about the author; and that is exactly what happened. The suspect's brother read it, and it rang a bell.
>
> "I would have told them not to publish. I'm glad they didn't ask me. I guess." (*Drawing Life: Surviving the Unabomber*. Free Press, 1997:120.)

2. Garrett, Laurie. *The Coming Plague: Newly Emerging Diseases in a World Out of Balance.* Penguin, 1994: 47–52, 414, 419, 452.
3. Isaac Asimov described what became the most famous view of ethical rules for robot behavior in his book *I, Robot* in 1950, in his Three Laws of Robotics: 1. A robot may not injure a human being, or, through inaction, allow a human being to come to harm. 2. A robot must obey the orders given it by human beings, except where such orders would conflict with the First Law. 3. A robot must protect its own existence, as long as such protection does not conflict with the First or Second Law.
4. Michelangelo wrote a sonnet that begins:

Non ha l' ottimo artista alcun concetto
Ch' un marmo solo in sè non circonscriva
Col suo soverchio; e solo a quello arriva
La man che ubbidisce all' intelleto.

Stone translates this as:

The best of artists hath no thought to show
which the rough stone in its superfluous shell
doth not include; to break the marble spell
is all the hand that serves the brain can do.

Stone describes the process: "He was not working from his drawings or clay models; they had all been put away. He was carving from the images in his mind. His eyes and hands knew where every line, curve, mass must emerge, and at what depth in the heart of the stone to create the low relief." (*The Agony and the Ecstasy*. Doubleday, 1961: 6, 144.)

5. First Foresight Conference on Nanotechnology in October 1989, a talk titled "The Future of Computation." Published in Crandall, B. C. and James Lewis (eds.) *Nanotechnology: Research and Perspectives*. MIT Press, 1992: 269. See also <www.foresight.org/Conferences/MNT01/Nano1.html>.
6. In his 1963 novel *Cat's Cradle*, Kurt Vonnegut imagined a gray-goo-like accident where a form of ice called ice-nine, which becomes solid at a much higher temperature, freezes the oceans.
7. Kauffman, Stuart. "Self-replication: Even Peptides Do It." *Nature*, 382, August 8, 1996: 496. See <www.santafe.edu/sfi/People/kauffman/sak-peptides.html>.
8. Else, Jon. *The Day After Trinity: J. Robert Oppenheimer and The Atomic Bomb* (available at <www.pyramiddirect.com>).
9. This estimate is in Leslie's book *The End of the World: The Science and Ethics of Human Extinction,* where he notes that the probability of extinction is substantially higher if we accept Brandon Carter's Doomsday Argument, which is, briefly, that "we ought to have some reluctance to believe that we are very exceptionally early, for instance in the earliest 0.001 percent, among all humans who will ever have lived. This would be some reason for thinking that humankind will not survive for many more centuries, let alone colonize the galaxy. Carter's doomsday argument doesn't generate any risk estimates just by itself. It is an argument for revising the estimates which we generate when we consider various possible dangers." (Routledge, 1996: 1, 3, 145.)

10. Clarke, Arthur C. "Presidents, Experts, and Asteroids." *Science,* June 5, 1998. Reprinted as "Science and Society" in *Greetings, Carbon-Based Bipeds! Collected Essays, 1934–1998.* St. Martin's Press, 1999: 526.
11. And, as David Forrest suggests in his paper "Regulating Nanotechnology Development," available at <www.foresight.org/NanoRev/Forrest1989.html>, "If we used strict liability as an alternative to regulation it would be impossible for any developer to internalize the cost of the risk (destruction of the biosphere), so theoretically the activity of developing nanotechnology should never be undertaken." Forrest's analysis leaves us with only government regulation to protect us — not a comforting thought.
12. Meselson, Matthew. "The Problem of Biological Weapons." Presentation to the 1,818th Stated Meeting of the American Academy of Arts and Sciences, January 13, 1999. (<minerva.amacad.org/archive/bulletin4.htm>)
13. Doty, Paul. "The Forgotten Menace: Nuclear Weapons Stockpiles Still Represent the Biggest Threat to Civilization." *Nature,* 402, December 9, 1999: 583.
14. See also Hans Bethe's 1997 letter to President Clinton, at <www.fas.org/bethecr.htm>.
15. Hamilton, Edith. *The Greek Way.* (New York: W. W. Norton & Co., 1942): 35.

28.   A Response to Bill Joy and the Doom-and-Gloom Technofuturists

JOHN SEELY BROWN AND PAUL DUGUID

Bill Joy's article drew many responses, some concurring with Joy's argument, most not. Among the more interesting and articulate rebuttals of the Joy thesis was one published not long after Joy's in The Industry Standard, *a magazine of e-commerce, technology, media, and politics that was launched in early 1998 and became an unfortunate casualty of the dot.com crash in September 2001. The authors of that piece, colleagues of Joy in high-tech industry, take him to task for basing his pessimistic vision on an overly simplistic way of viewing the influence of technology on society. "Technology and society are constantly forming and reforming new dynamic equilibriums with far-reaching implications," they write. "The challenge for futurology (and for all of us) is to see beyond the hype and past the oversimplifications to the full import of these new sociotechnical formations." In essence, they are restating the outlook articulated by Robert Pool in Part I of this book.*

John Seely Brown is chief scientist of the Xerox Corporation, and director of the Xerox Palo Alto Research Center (PARC). He is also a cofounder of the Institute for Research on Learning, a non-profit institute for addressing the problems of lifelong learning. Paul Duguid is a historian and social theorist affiliated with the University of California, Berkeley, and Xerox PARC. He was formerly a member of the Institute for Research on Learning, and is coauthor, with John Seely Brown, of The Social Life of Information *(Harvard Business School Press, 2000).*

If you lived through the 1950s, you might remember President Eisenhower, orderly suburban housing tracts, backyard bomb shelters — and dreams of a nuclear power plant in every home. Plans for industrial nuclear generators had barely left the drawing board before futurists predicted that every house would have a miniature version. From there, technoenthusiasts predicted the end of power monopolies, the emergence of the "electronic cottage," the death of the city and the decline of the corporation.

. . . Pessimists and Luddites, of course, envisioned nuclear apocalypse. Each side waited for nirvana, or Armageddon, so it could triumphantly tell the other, "I told you so."

. . . With "Why the Future Doesn't Need Us" in the April issue of *Wired*, Bill Joy invokes those years gone by. No Luddite, Joy is an awe-inspiring technologist — as cofounder and chief scientist of Sun Microsystems, he coauthored, among other things, the Java programming language. So when his article describes a technological juggernaut thundering toward society — bringing with

From *The Industry Standard* (April 13, 2000).

it mutant genes, molecular-level nanotechnology machines, and superintelligent robots — all need to listen. Like the nuclear prognosticators, Joy can see the juggernaut clearly. What he can't see — which is precisely what makes his vision so scary — are any controls.

But it doesn't follow that the juggernaut is uncontrollable. To understand why not, readers should note the publication in which this article appeared. For the better part of a decade, *Wired* has been a cheerleader for the digital age. Until now, *Wired* has rarely been a venue to which people have looked for a way to put a brake on innovation. Therefore, its shift with Joy's article from cheering to warning marks an important and surprising moment in the digital zeitgeist.

In an effort to locate some controls, let's go back to the nuclear age. Innovation, the argument went back in the 1950s, would make nuclear power plants smaller and cheaper. They would enter mass production and quickly become available to all.

Even today, the argument might appear inescapable until you notice what's missing: The tight focus of this vision makes it almost impossible to see forces other than technology at work. In the case of nuclear development, a host of forces worked to dismantle the dream of a peaceful atom, including the environmental movement, antinuclear protests, concerned scientists, worried neighbors of Chernobyl and Three Mile Island, government regulators and antiproliferation treaties. Cumulatively, these forces slowed the nuclear juggernaut to a crawl.

Similar social forces are at work on technologies today. But because the digerati, like technoenthusiasts before them, look to the future with technological tunnel vision, they too have trouble bringing other forces into view.

THE TUNNEL AHEAD

In Joy's vision, as in the nuclear one, there's a recognizable tunnel vision that leaves people out of the picture and focuses on technology in splendid isolation. This vision leads not only to doom-and-gloom scenarios, but also to tunnel design: the design of "simple" technologies that are actually difficult to use.

To escape both trite scenarios and bad design, we have to widen our horizons and bring into view not only technological systems, but also social systems. Good designs look beyond the dazzling potential of the technology to social factors, such as the limited patience of most users.

Paying attention to the latter has, for example, allowed the Palm Pilot and Nintendo Game Boy to sweep aside more complex rivals. Their elegant simplicity has made them readily usable. And their usability has in turn created an important social support system. The devices are so widely used that anyone having trouble with a Pilot or Game Boy rarely has to look far for advice from a more experienced user.

As this small example suggests, technological and social systems shape each other. The same is true on a larger scale. Technologies — such as gunpowder, the printing press, the railroad, the telegraph, and the Internet — can shape society in profound ways. But, on the other hand, social systems — in the form of governments, the courts, formal and informal organizations, social movements, professional networks, local communities, market institutions, and so forth — shape, moderate, and redirect the raw power of technologies.

Given the crisp edges of technology and the fuzzy outlines of society, it certainly isn't easy to use these two worldviews simultaneously. But if you want to see where we are going, or design the means to get there, you need to grasp both.

This perspective allows a more sanguine look at Joy's central concerns: genetic engineering, nanotechnology, and robotics. Undoubtedly, each deserves serious thought. But each should be viewed in the context of the social system in which it is inevitably embedded.

Genetic engineering presents the clearest example. Barely a year ago, the technology seemed to be an unstoppable force. Major chemical and agricultural interests were barreling down an open highway. In the past year, however, road conditions changed dramatically for the worse: Cargill faced Third World protests against its patents; Monsanto suspended research on sterile seeds; and champions of genetically modified foods, who once saw an unproblematic and lucrative future, are scurrying to counter consumer boycotts of their products.

Almost certainly, those who support genetic modification will have to look beyond the technology if they want to advance it. They need to address society directly — not just by putting labels on modified foods, but by educating people about the costs and the benefits of these new agricultural products. Having ignored social concerns, however, proponents have made the people they need to educate profoundly suspicious and hostile.

Nanotechnology offers a rather different example of how the future can frighten us. Because the technology involves engineering at a molecular level, both the promise and the threat seem immeasurable. But they are immeasurable for a good reason: The technology is still almost wholly on the drawing board.

Two of nanotechnology's main proponents, Ralph Merkle and Eric Drexler, worked with us at the Xerox Palo Alto Research Center in Palo Alto, California. The two built powerful nano-CAD tools and then ran simulations of the resulting molecular-level designs. These experiments showed definitively that nano devices are theoretically feasible. No one, however, has laid out a route from lab-based simulation to practical systems in any detail.

In the absence of a plan, it's important to ask the right questions: Can nanotechnology fulfill its great potential in tasks ranging from data storage to pollution control, all without spiraling out of control? If the lesson of genetic engineering is any guide, planners would do well to consult and educate the public early on, even though useful nano systems are probably decades away.

Worries about robotics appear premature, as well. Internet "bots" that search, communicate, and negotiate for their human masters may appear to behave like Homo sapiens, but, in fact, bots are often quite inept at functions that humans do well — functions that call for judgment, discretion, initiative, or tacit understanding. They are good (and useful) for those tasks that humans do poorly. So they are better thought of as complementary systems, not rivals to humanity. Although bots will undoubtedly get better at what they do, such development will not necessarily make them more human.

Are more conventional clanking robots — the villains of science fiction — any great threat to society? We doubt it. Xerox PARC research on self-aware, reconfigurable "polybots" has pushed the boundaries of what robots can do, pointing the way to "morphing robots" that are able to move and change shape.

Nonetheless, for all their cutting-edge agility, these robots are a long way from making good dance partners. The chattiness of *Star Wars'* C-3PO still lies well beyond real-world machines. Indeed, what talk robots or computers achieve, though it may appear similar, is quite different from human talk. Talking machines travel routes designed specifically to avoid the full complexities of human language.

Robots may seem intelligent, but such intelligence is profoundly hampered by their inability to learn in any significant way. (This failing has apparently led Toyota, after heavy investment in robotics, to consider replacing robots with humans on many production lines.) And, without learning, simple common sense will lie beyond robots for a long time to come.

Indeed, despite years of startling advances and innumerable successes like the chess-playing Big Blue, computer science is still about as far as it ever was from building a machine with the learning abilities, linguistic competence, common sense or social skills of a five-year-old child.

As with Internet bots, real-world robots will no doubt become increasingly useful. But they will probably also become increasingly frustrating to use as a result of tunnel design. In that regard, they may indeed seem antisocial, but not in the way of *Terminator*-like fantasies of robot armies that lay waste to human society.

Indeed, the thing that handicaps robots most is their lack of a social existence. For it is our social existence as humans that shapes how we speak, learn, think, and develop common sense. All forms of artificial life (whether bugs or bots) will remain primarily a metaphor for — rather than a threat to — society, at least until they manage to enter a debate, sing in a choir, take a class, survive a committee meeting, join a union, pass a law, engineer a cartel, or summon a constitutional convention.

These critical social mechanisms allow society to shape its future. It is through planned, collective action that society forestalls expected consequences (such as Y2K) and responds to unexpected events (such as epidemics).

THE FAILURE OF A "6-D" VISION

Why does the threat of a cunning, replicating robot society look so close from one perspective, yet so distant from another? The difference lies in the well-known tendency of futurologists to count "1, 2, 3 . . . a million." That is, once the first step on a path is taken, it's very easy to assume that all subsequent steps are trivial.

Several of the steps Joy asks us to take — the leap from genetic engineering to a "white plague," from simulations to out-of-control nanotechnology, from replicating peptides to a "robot species" — are extremely large. And they are certainly not steps that will be taken without diversions, regulations, or controls.

One of the lessons of Joy's article, then, is that the path to the future can look simple (and sometimes downright terrifying) if you look at it through what we call "6-D lenses." We coined this phrase having so often in our research hit up against upon such "de-" or "di-" words as demassification, decentralization, disintermediation, despacialization, disaggregation, and demarketization in the canon of futurology.

If you take any one of these words in isolation, it's easy to follow their relentless logic to its evident conclusion. Because firms are getting smaller, for example, it's easy to assume that companies and other intermediaries are simply disintegrating into markets. And because communication is growing cheaper and more powerful, it's easy to believe in the "death of distance."

But things rarely work in such linear fashion. Other forces are often at work, such as those driving firms into larger and larger mergers to take advantage of social, rather than merely technological, networks. Similarly, even though communications technology has killed distance, people curiously can't stay away from the social hotbed of modern communications technology, Silicon Valley.

Importantly, these d-words indicate that the old ties that once bound communities, organizations, and institutions are being picked apart by technologies. A simple, linear reading, then, suggests that these communities, organizations, and institutions will now simply fall apart. A more complex reading, taking into account the multiple forces at work, offers another picture.

While many powerful national corporations have grown insignificant, some have transformed into more powerful transnational firms. While some forms of community may be dying, others, bolstered by technology, are growing stronger.

Technology and society are constantly forming and reforming new dynamic equilibriums with far-reaching implications. The challenge for futurology (and for all of us) is to see beyond the hype and past the oversimplifications to the full import of these new sociotechnical formations.

Two hundred years ago, Thomas Malthus, assuming that human society and agricultural technology developed on separate paths, predicted that society was growing so fast that it would starve itself to death, the so-called Malthusian trap.

A hundred years later, H. G. Wells similarly assumed that society and technology were developing independently. Like many people today, Wells saw the advance of technology outstripping the evolution of society, leading him to predict that technology's relentless juggernaut would unfeelingly crush society. Like Joy, both Malthus and Wells issued important warnings, alerting society to the dangers it faced. But by their actions, Malthus and Wells helped prevent the very future they were so certain would come about.

These self-*un*fulfilling prophecies failed to see that, once warned, society could galvanize itself into action. Of course, this social action in the face of threats showed that Malthus and Wells were most at fault in their initial assumption. Social and technological systems do not develop independently; the two evolve together in complex feedback loops, wherein each drives, restrains, and accelerates change in the other. Malthus and Wells — and now Joy — are, indeed, critical parts of these complex loops. Each knew when and how to sound the alarm. But each thought little about how to respond to that alarm.

Once the social system is factored back into the equation like this, the road ahead becomes harder to navigate. Ultimately we should be grateful to Joy for saying, at the least, that there could be trouble ahead when so many of his fellow digerati will only tell us complacently that the road is clear.

PART VIII
CODA

Following a tradition begun in the seventh edition of *Technology and the Future,* the last article is a bit different from those that precede it. First of all, although it is written to appear like a first-person account of a scientific discovery, it is fiction. In addition, it is written in a more casual, lighter style and is a far easier read than some of what comes before. It is included here partly for fun and partly for a serious reason. You could call it a reward for making your way through the rest of the book, or (if you are one of those people who likes to look at the end of a book first) it could serve as a teaser to engage your interest in thinking about technology and the future.

Author Seth Shostak, an astronomer with the SETI Institute, which is engaged in the search for intelligent life in the universe beyond Earth, considers the possibility that his institute's quest might someday succeed. His short story is entertaining, but it is also thought provoking. Consider for yourself, as you read it, what the discovery of intelligence outside of Earth might mean for human civilization — not an invasion by aliens bent on conquest, but simply evidence that other civilizations exist. How would that change our view of ourselves, our religious beliefs, our ethical and philosophical perspectives, your own way of looking at the world? There's a great deal to think about and discuss in these notions. And, if, by the way, you want to participate in the search for extraterrestrial intelligence, you can sign up for SETI at home. See "Searching for Aliens from Your Home Computer," on *Al Teich's Technology and the Future Toolkit* Web site: <http://www.alteich.com/tidbits/t083099.htm>.

29.　In Touch at Last

SETH SHOSTAK

In the early 1960s, radio astronomers realized that microwave radio signals might provide a means of communicating with civilizations outside our solar system. With support from NASA, they began scanning the airwaves for signs of extraterrestrial intelligence. There were skeptics, of course, but supporters of the programs only had to point to the fact that the Soviet Union was very active in this area and U.S. government funding was forthcoming. In 1992, however, with the Soviet Union gone, Congress terminated funding for the program. Since that time, the search, now called "Project Phoenix," has continued with private funding, spearheaded by the SETI (Search for Extraterrestrial Intelligence) Institute in Mountain View, California.

What if Project Phoenix should succeed? How might an alien civilization make its presence in the universe known in a way that we might recognize as indicative of intelligent life? Seth Shostak, an astronomer with a Ph.D. from Caltech, who is responsible for public outreach activities at the SETI Institute, has an answer, one that is both entertaining and thought provoking. His essay, "In Touch at Last," was published in Science *magazine in 1999, as part of a series on what life might be like for scientists in the year 2050.*

It may be the biggest science discovery of the millennium, but somehow that's hard for me to swallow.

Sure, I've got a closet stuffed with awards and offers from two dozen publishers to write the whole thing up. But the awards don't mean much (although my wife enjoyed the trip to Stockholm), and as for the book — well, I'll leave that to the science historians. They'll be better at injecting drama even when there wasn't any. As it is, most of the Web sites already embellish my little result with florid hyperbole such as "the triumph of one man's vision" or describe it with metaphorical chutzpah as "how a lone science prospector hit the mother lode."

I didn't hit the mother lode. Sure, I found something that was important and reactivated a moribund field of research. But mother lode? I just stumbled on a loose nugget.

There is one thing the Web texts get right, though. I managed this discovery on my own. And that's unusual these days. Two centuries ago, an individual researcher could do something significant. Isaac Newton didn't need a lot of pals to puzzle out mechanics. Maxwell wasn't juggling a small coterie of coworkers as he wrote his four equations. But times change. If I log onto the Astrophysical News, I'm hard pressed to find a single submission involving fewer people than signed the Constitution. The physics journals are worse: They've resorted to an "authors" link, rather than crowd the first two pages of each paper with the

From "In Touch at Last" by Seth Shostak, in *Science*, Vol. 286 (Dec. 3, 1999), p. 1872–1874. © 1999 American Association for the Advancement of Science. Reprinted with permission.

names of academics in eight-point type. Modern science may have begun in the fifteenth century, but a half-millennium later, it's running out of steam. New results, at least in the physical sciences, are harder to come by, and one brain is not enough.

Personally, I figure the decline and fall began when Bernstein's Theory of Everything deprived theoreticians of something to live for. Astronomy has been on the skids for years. Sure, researchers try to keep themselves busy populating odd nooks and crannies of the cosmic bestiary, but there's a limit to Nature's inventiveness. Most astronomers go through the motions, collecting more parallaxes, mapping pulsars in nearby galaxies, or making interminable N-body simulations to understand how everything from solar systems to galaxies eventually evaporates, thereby ensuring a thoroughly dull universe.

I had never been keen to join this lackluster crowd, so I opted for SETI, the search for extraterrestrial intelligence. SETI is a niche area, and the niche seemed to be shrinking — a fact I found comforting, probably thinking it meant more for me. A back-burner project that had moved up to the front of the stove when arthropods were found on Europa, SETI was now stalled thanks to its failure to find any intelligent aliens. It's not that people doubted the existence of the extraterrestrials. After the news from Europa and the discovery of a fecund Mars deep under the polar caps, it was clear to anyone with a warm cerebellum that biology was universal. As for smart biology — intelligence — it might not be common, but let's face it: The galaxy's a mighty poor place if Homo sapiens is its smartest inhabitant.

Sadly, the conventional scheme for finding the aliens wasn't working, and maybe it never would. Traditional SETI, now nearly four-score years old, hoped to detect cosmic company in situ, by eavesdropping on radio-wave or light broadcasts. Aliens might not come here, but they would presumably spit the evidence of their presence into space as a hail of photons. But the sobering truth was that no radio whine, no faint infrared pulse, had ever been found.

The pundits explained this disappointing result with tautological simplicity: The aliens were not broadcasting. After all, why should they? We don't. Our planet signed off the air less than two centuries after Heinrich Hertz concocted radio. Communications on this planet are now effected by optical fibers and tightly focused infrared and microwave links. The spindly red-and-white towers on the hills at the outskirts of town are history. So are the energy-wasting broadcasts they would spew over the landscape and over the horizon, to leak into space and inadvertently mark our position. We aren't broadcasting, so why would the extraterrestrials?

Sure, the aliens could invest in deliberate, interstellar beacons to get our attention, but SETI hadn't found them. Perhaps beacons were too altruistic, or too dangerous, for E.T. Despite nearly a century of thinking about this problem, no one had figured out how to beat this transmission rap. No one had fashioned an alternative scheme for tracking down celestial beings whose communications were either highly directional or in pipes. Consequently, many of the large radio and optical arrays built in the first two decades of the century were abandoned and donated to amateur astronomy groups who, while grateful, inevitably groused about the cost of maintenance.

But there was one SETI instrument that was still collecting bits: the GRAV craft. GRAV, the General Relativity Amplification Viewer, had been launched in 2028 and reached its orbit, 520 astronomical units from the Sun, a decade later. The idea behind GRAV was simple: It would aim its 500-meter, thin-film antenna at the Sun, which, at this distance, would act as an enormous gravitational lens, amplifying signals from distant stars by thousands of times. It was a simple scheme for building the most sensitive receiving system ever conceived. In the early decades of the twenty-first century, it had been the Holy Grail of SETI research.

Now the Grail was largely uncoveted. For ten years, the small GRAV team had assiduously sifted through the ceaseless stream of data beamed back to Earth from the craft, looking for signals. In 2044, there was even a bit of excitement when a signal and success seemed at hand. But euphoria yielded to embarrassment when someone realized that the putative extraterrestrial transmission was from the forgotten Pioneer 6 spacecraft, still mindlessly belching worthless telemetry as it continued to orbit the Sun seven decades after launch. I think the false alarm dulled a lot of the excitement for the search team. In 2048, when GRAV's beam passed over the galactic center without finding any alien beacons, the money ran out. I saw my chance and took it. I pitched a small grant for a five-year, one-man operation to do rudimentary analysis on the GRAV data. My proposal was modest, and it slipped through without waking a single referee. The International Science Foundation views small science as quaint. It's like tiny spiders in the kitchen corners: not important enough to bother.

My setup was pretty simple, just a couple of computers and some off-the-shelf software. Most of the work was in getting it all lashed together. Then I just let it run. For the first year, I must have checked the outputs a dozen times each day. Then I got jaded and relied on the automatic detection algorithms. My wife wondered if I still had a day job. I don't know whether I really expected to find anything or not; one gets so engrossed in the technical details, it's easy to forget what the original idea was.

July 20 was the big day, of course. I remember, because the kids were watching a syrupy documentary on the first moon landing. When I got to the office, I saw that the display on the data logger had gone bonkers. GRAV had found a signal — a steady carrier, remarkably strong. I thought it was a practical joke.

The rest is history, in every sense. Verification is always tricky for SETI, and for GRAV, which is seventy light-hours from Earth and can't be pointed, it's even trickier. So GRAV had an outrigger, a trailing craft with its own antenna — even larger than GRAV itself — following 200 hours behind the main instrument. The sibling could be activated to collect a second scan of any interesting signals at high temporal resolution and to relay them to Earth via the main craft, but not in real time. Of course, for a confirmation, that didn't matter. Needless to say, I gave the outrigger a nudge. You wouldn't be reading this otherwise.

The modulation, now so obvious to everyone, was a bit puzzling at first. I guess that's because experts expected that the aliens would be sending us pictures, or maybe simple mathematics. I always found the idea amusing: The aliens will send us the value of π, as if we didn't already know! Well, what was coming in was clearly a raster: There was a lone "on" bit every 10,330 bits, an obvious retrace signal, making a never-ending scroll. And it was all just binary. There was no compression, no color, no gray scale; it was the lowest common denominator of imagery possible.

But the rows were empty, or nearly so. Typically, there would be 10,330 "offs," and then an "on." It seemed to be just a blank picture, one that no self-respecting alien would bother to transmit. For a while, I considered the possibility that the alien transmitter was on the fritz. Maybe this was a crippled machine, a relic from a civilization that had built a transmitter and then died, leaving it without maintenance. The carrier was still operational, but the modulator was toast. Frankly, though, I didn't consider this theory for very long. Within hours, I made a startling observation: Not all the rows were empty. Every seventy-fourth row had some bits that were set. The bits came in groups of four. They were simple characters, for sure, sixteen in total. Many people have said this proves that the aliens who built this machine have eight fingers on each hand. Sure, if they have two hands. But maybe they have four hands each with four fingers, or perhaps just a single, sixteen-fingered hand. It's all speculation if you ask me, probably prompted by the glove industry.

But the simplicity of the message was staggering. Empty strings of bits, marching down the screen in regular formation, like a huge military parade. Everyone wore a white hat, except a few in every seventy-fourth row. On July 22, just for the heck of it, I connected the bit stream to the audio channel of my porta-computer. The result was no surprise: regular clicks every 10,330 bits, and then a bit of a "buzz" every seventy-fourth row. That's when my wife walked in. "What are you listening to?" she asked. "Sounds like WWV."

Indeed, it did. It sounded very much like WWV, the Bureau of Standards' time-keeping service. I had found an alien signal, and it was, well . . . a clock. A clock! My first thought was, "Who needs a clock?" But of course, societies with fast rockets could use some sort of universal, or at least galactic, time. Special relativity guarantees that the timepieces aboard their ships will lose synch with one another. This alien transmitter supplied the equivalent of the "star date" of old science fiction: a calendar that everyone could use. Sure, not everyone would agree on the length of the ticks — it would depend on their speed — but none of that matters. This clock would serve to log events. At least it would help the historians.

There's been a lot of uproar since those early days. SETI is back in business, and in a big way. The philosophical impact of knowing that we're not alone has still not been felt, but that's coming. For myself, I guess I'm both elated and disappointed. For decades, researchers had speculated on E.T.'s message: how the extraterrestrials would impart to us the wisdom of the ages, and perhaps offer us a free copy of the *Encyclopaedia Galactica*. I was a bit more cynical, figuring that we wouldn't be very important to the aliens. I didn't expect them to give us the time of day.

But they did.

This essay is a work of fiction. Names, characters, places, and incidents either are the product of the author's imagination or are used fictitiously. Any resemblance to actual persons, living or dead, events, or locales is entirely coincidental.

Credits

This page constitutes an extension of the copyright page. We have made every effort to trace the ownership of all copyrighted material and to secure permission from copyright holders. In the event of any question arising as to the use of any material, we will be pleased to make the necessary corrections in future printings. Thanks are due to the following authors, publishers, and agents for permission to use the material indicated.

Chapter 15. 167: From "Brittle Times, RMI's Response," in *RMI Solutions*, Vol. XVII, No. 3 (Fall 2000), p. 1–3.

Chapter 16. 172: From "Technology Vulnerability" in *Technology in Society*, Vol. 18, No. 4, 1996. Reprinted with permission of Elsevier Science.

Chapter 17. 187: From *Technology Review* (April 1991). © 1991 *Technology Review*. Reprinted with permission.

Chapter 19. 200: Reprinted with permission from *The American Prospect* Vol. 12, No. 17 (September 24–October 8, 2001. *The American Prospect*, 5 Broad Street, Boston, MA 02109. All rights reserved.

Chapter 20. 209: From *The Ethics of Human Cloning* by Leon R. Kass and James Q. Wilson (Washington, DC: AEI Press, 1998), p. 3–59. Copyright © 1998 The American Enterprise Institute for Public Policy Research.

Chapter 21. 225: From "Science Fiction" by Jerome Groopman, from *The New Yorker* (February 4, 2002). Reprinted with permission of Condé Nast.

Chapter 22. 231: From *Imagining Tomorrow: History, Technology and the American Future*, edited by Joseph J. Corn (Cambridge, MA: MIT Press, 1986). Reprinted by permission of MIT Press.

Chapter 23. 242: From *Computer Ethics: Cautionary Tales and Ethical Dilemmas in Computing*, 2/e (Cambridge, MA: MIT Press, 1993). Reprinted by permission of MIT Press.

Chapter 24. 258: From *Foreign Policy*, Issue #127, Nov.–Dec. 2001. Reprinted by permission of International Creative Management, Inc. Copyright © 2001 by Lawrence Lessig.

Chapter 25. 268: From *In the Age of the Smart Machine: The Future of Work and Power* by Shoshona Zuboff. Copyright © 1988 by Basic Books, Inc. Reprinted by permission of Basic Books, a member of Perseus Books, L.L.C.

Chapter 26. 276: From *Trapped in the Nest* by Gene I. Rochlin, p. 169–187, 255–259. © 1997 Princeton University Press.

Chapter 27. 295: From "Why the Future Doesn't Need Us" © August 4, 2000 by Bill Joy. This article originally appeared in *Wired Magazine*. Reprinted by permission of the author.

Chapter 28. 318: From *The Industry Standard* (April 13, 2000).

Chapter 29. 325: From "In Touch at Last" by Seth Shostak, in *Science*, Vol. 286 (Dec. 3, 1999), p. 1872–1874. © 1999 American Association for the Advancement of Science. Reprinted with permission.